Japan at Play

Play may seem such a simple activity, but it is actually far more complex and elusive than first glance might suggest. It is fundamental rather than superficial: all humans play – at any age. It can be both a carefree, joyful activity, but can equally sometimes disclose a fierce, secret violence. This book combines careful consideration of age-old questions about the nature of play, alongside delightful detail about the playful world of contemporary Japan. Drawing on the work of theorists such as Huizinga, Caillois, Turner and Wittgenstein, *Japan at Play* raises key questions about the relationship between play and culture. The chapters demonstrate how the power of play can express deep social divisions, burning political antagonism, and eternal religious dilemmas.

They show how laughter may upset the perception of reality, and free the mind for a path to deeper wisdom. From the playful work of creating cartoon characters to hunting and fishing for relaxation (and the problems tourists cause for local industry); from drinking with workmates to *karaoke* training for leisure; with pop fans and gangsters, in gay bars, and at the heart of a country festival, the authors of this book lead the reader through Japanese worlds little known even to many Japanese.

Way beyond the conventional idea of play as trivia, *Japan at Play* illuminates the historical relationship between Japan and Europe; it offers playful attitudes to technological invention; it re-examines the Disney phenomenon in a global context, and explores the role of football in contemporary Japan, co-host of the 2002 World Cup. This book touches the very dynamic of culture itself: the game that plays us all.

Joy Hendry is Professor of Social Anthropology at Oxford Brookes University. Her many publications include, *Wrapping Culture: Politeness, Presentation and Power in Japan and Other Societies; An Anthropologist in Japan; Other People's Worlds: an Introduction to Social Anthropology;* and *The Orient Strikes Back: Cultural Display in a Global Perspective.*

Massimo Raveri is Professor of East Asian Religions at the University Ca' Foscari in Venice. His books include *Il Corpo e il Paradiso* (The Body and Paradise) and *Del Bene e del Male* (On Good and Evil).

Japan: beyond the end of history
David Williams

Ceremony and Ritual in Japan:
religious practices in an
industrialized society
Edited by Jan van Bremen and D.P. Martinez

Understanding Japanese Society:
second edition
Joy Hendry

The Fantastic in Modern Japanese
Literature: the subversion of
modernity
Susan J. Napier

Militarization and Demilitarization
in Contemporary Japan
Glenn D. Hook

Growing a Japanese Science City:
communication in scientific
research
James W. Dearing

Architecture and Authority in Japan
William H. Coaldrake

Women's Gidayū and the Japanese
Theatre Tradition
A. Kimi Coaldrake

Democracy in Post-war Japan:
Maruyama Masao and the search
for autonomy
Rikki Kersten

Treacherous Women of Imperial
Japan: patriarchal fictions,
patricidal fantasies
Hélène Bowen Raddeker

Japanese–German Business
Relations: competition and rivalry
in the inter-war period
Akira Kudō

Japan, Race and Equality: the Racial
Equality Proposal of 1919
Naoko Shimazu

Japan, Internationalism and the UN
Ronald Dore

Life in a Japanese Women's College:
learning to be ladylike
Brian J. McVeigh

On The Margins of Japanese
Society: volunteers and the welfare
of the urban underclass
Carolyn S. Stevens

The Dynamics of Japan's Relations
with Africa: South Africa, Tanzania
and Nigeria
Kweku Ampiah

The Right to Life in Japan
Noel Williams

The Nature of the Japanese State:
rationality and rituality
Brian J. McVeigh

Society and the State in Inter-war
Japan
Edited by Elise K. Tipton

Japanese–Soviet/Russian Relations
since 1945: a difficult peace
Kimie Hara

Interpreting History in Sino-
Japanese Relations: a case study in
political decision making
Caroline Rose

Endō Shûsaku: a literature of
reconciliation
Mark B. Williams

Green Politics in Japan
Lam Peng-Er

The Japanese High School: silence
and resistance
Shoko Yoneyama

Engineers in Japan and Britain:
education, training and employment
Kevin McCormick

The Politics of Agriculture in Japan
Aurelia George Mulgan

Opposition Politics in Japan:
strategies under a one-party
dominant regime
Stephen Johnson

The Changing Face of Japanese
Retail: working in a chain store
Louella Matsunaga

Japan and East Asian Regionalism
Edited by S. Javed Maswood

Globalizing Japan: ethnography of
the Japanese presence in America,
Asia and Europe
Edited by Harumi Befu and Sylvie Guichard-
Anguis

Japan at Play: the ludic and the logic
of power
Edited by Joy Hendry and Massimo Raveri

Japan at Play

The ludic and the logic of power

**Edited by Joy Hendry and
Massimo Raveri**

London and New York

First published 2002 by Routledge
2 Park Square, Milton Park, Abingdon, Oxon, OX14 4RN
Simultaneously published in the USA and Canada
by Routledge
270 Madison Ave, New York NY 10016

Routledge is an imprint of the Taylor & Francis Group

Transferred to Digital Printing 2005

© 2002 Selection and editorial material, Joy Hendry and Massimo Raveri;
individual chapters the contributors

Typeset in Baskerville by Keystroke, Jacaranda Lodge, Wolverhampton

British Library Cataloguing in Publication Data
A catalogue record for this book is available from the British Library

Library of Congress Cataloging in Publication Data
Japan at play : the ludic and logic of power / edited by Joy Hendry and
Massimo Raveri.
    p. cm. – (Nissan Institute/Routledge Japanese studies series)
    Includes bibliographical references and index.
    1. Recreation – Japan. 2. Leisure – Japan. 3. Play – Japan. I. Hendry,
    Joy. II. Raveri, Massimo. III. Series.

GV125 .J365 2001
306.4'8'0952 – dc21   2001052013

ISBN 0–415–21501–3
ISBN 0–415–37937–7

Contents

Illustrations

Figures

Tables

Contributors

Michael Ashkenazi is Deputy Academic Dean at Regents College, where he also teaches anthropology. He has carried out fieldwork in Tokyo, Akita-ken, Hokkaido, Israel, Korea and China on festivals, food, tourism, and business organizations. His most recent publications include *The Essence of Japanese Cuisine* (London: Curzon Press) and *Consumption and Material Culture in Japan* (co-edited with J. Clammer, Kegan Paul International). His current interests are in food culture and in the social effects of technology.

Eyal Ben-Ari is professor in the Department of Sociology and Anthropology of the Hebrew University of Jerusalem. He has carried out fieldwork in Japan (suburbs and daycare centres), Singapore (the Japanese expatriate community) and Israel (Jewish saint-worship and the Israeli Defence Forces). His recent publications include *Body Projects in Japanese Childcare* (London: Curzon Press) and *Mastering Soldiers: Conflict, Emotions and the Enemy in an Israeli Military Unit* (Oxford: Berghahn Books). He has recently carried out field research among Japan's Self-Defence Forces.

Rupert Cox is currently undertaking an ESRC research project on 'Culture and copying in Japan' at Oxford Brookes University. As a postgraduate student at Edinburgh University and a research fellow at the Royal Asiatic Society he conducted extensive investigations into the Japanese Arts and their connections with Zen, and his book *Zen Arts in Japan* will be published by Curzon Press in 2001.

Simone Dalla Chiesa is contract professor of Japanese language at the University of Venice and at the University of Pavia (Faculty of Political Sciences). He carried out his fieldwork in Japan during the 1980s in Ibaraki-ken, studying the daily life of children. During his student years in Japan he played football and table tennis in Tsukuba University's teams. He is author of anthropological articles in the Italian language about Japanese sports such as football, hiking (English title: *Human and 'Natural' Space in Japanese National Parks*) and *dō* (*Beyond the Mystique of Gesture: A Psychological Analysis of Motor Behaviour in dō*), and of various Japanese language teaching aids.

Sylvie Guichard-Anguis as a geographer is a researcher for the French National Centre of Scientific Research (CNRS) and a member of the research group

'Space and Culture' of the Geography Department of the University of Paris IV Sorbonne. Her main interests lie in protection, traditions, tea culture, tourism and illustrated books in Japan. She has carried out fieldwork mainly in Ishikawa prefecture, Kansai and Mie prefecture. She is currently co-editing two books *Globalizing Japan* and *Crossed Gazes at International Cultural Heritage* with the collaboration of UNESCO.

Joy Hendry is professor of social anthropology at Oxford Brookes University, where she is also Director of the Europe Japan Research Centre. She has carried out fieldwork in various parts of Japan, notably Kyushu and Chiba-ken. Her recent publications include *The Orient Strikes Back: A Global View of Cultural Display* (Oxford: Berg), and *An Anthropologist in Japan* (London: Routledge).

John Horne lectures in the sociology of sport and leisure at the Scottish Centre of Physical Education, Sport and Leisure Studies, University of Edinburgh. He has visited Japan four times since the start of the J League. His publications include 'The contemporary politics of sport and leisure in Japan: global power and local resistance', *International Review for the Sociology of Sport* 33 (2) and 'Understanding sport and body culture in Japan', *Body and Society* 6 (2). His current substantive research interests are sport, leisure and body culture in Japan, consumer culture and consumption, cultural and social diversity, and social theory and sport.

William H. Kelly is a postdoctoral research fellow at the Manchester Business School, University of Manchester. He is currently involved in collaborative research focusing on Japanese and Korean expatriate managers and communities in the United Kingdom. He has conducted extensive research on *karaoke* singing in Japan, and has recently completed fieldwork on the adaptation of *karaoke* in the United Kingdom. Recent articles include 'The adaptability of *karaoke* in the United Kingdom' in *Karaoke Around the World: Global Technology, Local Singing* (edited by T. Mitsui and S. Hosokawa, Routledge) and 'Japan's empty orchestras: echoes of Japanese culture in the performance of *karaoke*' in *The Worlds of Japanese Popular Culture* (edited by D.P. Martinez, Cambridge University Press).

John Knight is lecturer at the School of Anthropological Studies, Queen's University Belfast. He has carried out field research in mountain villages on the Kii Peninsula in western Japan, and has written on a variety of topics to do with rural Japan, including the changing relationship to the natural environment. He is the editor of *Natural Enemies: People–Wildlife Conflicts in Anthropological Perspective* (London and New York: Routledge).

Sepp Linhart is professor in the sociology of Japan at the University of Vienna, Austria. He has carried out fieldwork in various prefectures of Japan including Hokkaido, Toyama, Tokyo, Kanagawa, Kobe, and so on, since 1967. His publications include *Ken no bunka-shi* (The cultural history of the *ken* game), Tokyo 1998 and *The Culture of Japan as seen through its Leisure* (co-editor), New York 1998.

Wim Lunsing is a research fellow at the graduate school for sociology at the University of Tokyo and has been an associate research professor of Japanese

Studies at the University of Copenhagen. He has conducted fieldwork on sexuality, gender and on sexual activity in urban Japan. His publications include *Beyond Common Sense, Negotiating Constructions of Sexuality and Gender in Contemporary Japan* (London and New York: Kegan Paul International) and 'Japan: finding its way?' in *The Global Emergence of Gay and Lesbian Politics: National Imprints of a Worldwide Movement* (edited by Barry D. Adam, Jan Willem Duyvendak and Andre Krouwel, Philadelphia: Temple University Press). Currently, his major research interest is in emotions and questions of employment in the current economic crisis.

Okpyo Moon is a professor of anthropology at the Academy of Korean Studies. She has carried out fieldwork in Gunma-ken and Kawasaki City in Japan as well as in Korea, and her publications include *From Paddy Field to Ski Slope: The Revitalization of Tradition in Japanese Village Life* (Manchester University Press) and 'Marketing nature in rural Japan' in *Japanese Images of Nature: Cultural Perspective,* (edited by P. Asquith and A. Kalland, London: Curzon Press). Her current interests are with the comparison of family and gender among the urban middle class in Japan and Korea.

Ulrike Nennstiel is associate professor in Sociology at Hokusei Gakuen University (Sapporo, Japan). She has carried out fieldwork almost all over Japan, concentrating on Chiba-ken, Tōhoku and Hokkaido. Her publications include *Widerstandslos in Japan? Sozialwissenschaftliche Theorien und ihr Beitrag zur Erklaerung des Scheiterns von Buergerbewegungen* (Japan without opposition? Social theories and their utility in explaining the defeat of social movements in Japan (Munich: Iudicium) and 'Citizens' movements in Japan. Differing Issues – Differing Responses' in *Diversity, Change and Fluidity: Perspectives on Japan Perceiving Itself* (edited by P. Ackermann and E. Schulz, Bern: Peter Lang).

Massimo Raveri is professor of East Asian religions at the University Ca' Foscari of Venice. As an anthropologist, he has done field research on Shintō tradition and on Shugendō ascetic practices. His recent publications include *Il corpo e il paradiso: le tentazioni estreme dell'ascesi* (The body and paradise: the extreme temptations of the ascesis) (Venice: Marsilio), and *Del bene e del male* (On good and evil) (Venice: Marsilio).

Aviad E. Raz is senior lecturer in the sociology of organizations at Ben Gurion University of the Negev (Israel). He has carried out fieldwork regarding the structure of play, leisure activities and organizational culture in Tokyo Disneyland. His publications include *Riding the Black Ship: Tokyo Disneyland and Japan* and *Emotions at Work: Normative Control in Japanese and American Organizations,* both published by Harvard University Press (Asia Center), as well as various articles concerning the hybridization and flow of culture in Japan (and elsewhere).

María-Dolores Rodríguez del Alisal is an associate professor at the Escuela Oficial de Idiomas, and President of the Instituto de Japanologia, Madrid. She was co-founder of the Spanish Association for Japanese Studies. During a stay of almost ten years in Japan affiliated to Keio University she researched mainly rural society and Shugendō Festivals, doing fieldwork in Kyushu, Wakayama, Shikoku, Iwate and Miyagi prefectures. She has collaborated, edited or co-authored volumes on mountain festivals, lunch boxes, advertising in Japan and on Japanese emigration to Latin America. Her current interests are in comparative studies, such as Japanese and Spanish material culture, Spanish and Japanese pilgrimages and tourism.

Carolyn S. Stevens is a senior lecturer in Japanese Studies at the Melbourne Institute of Asian Languages and Societies at the University of Melbourne, Australia. She is the author of *On the Margins of Japanese Society: Volunteers and the Welfare of the Urban Underclass* (Routledge) and other articles on public welfare and social marginality. Her current research focuses on Japanese popular music and its consumption, an interest which arose after working in the Japanese pop music industry in the early 1990s.

Jan van Bremen worked in the Department of Anthropology in the University of Amsterdam (1975–86) and joined the Centre for Japanese and Korean Studies in Leiden University in 1987. He specializes in the history and theory of anthropology, Japanese and Southeast Asian anthropology, Japanese religion, and Japanese society. Recently published volumes include *Ceremony and Ritual in Japan: Religious Practices in an Industrialized Society* (edited by Jan van Bremen and D.P. Martinez, London: Routledge), *Anthropology and Colonialism in Asia and Oceania* (edited by Jan van Bremen and Akitoshi Shimizu, London: Curzon Press).

Yamaguchi Masao is the President and professor of Social Anthropology at Sapporo University. He has experience of fieldwork in various parts of the world, including West Africa, Indonesia and Mexico. His recent publications include: *Haisha no seishinshi* (Intellectual history of losers in modern Japan) (Tokyo: Iwanami Shoten) and *Uchida Roan no Sanmyaku* (The impact of Uchida Roan in Taisho Japan) (Tokyo: Shobunsha).

Series editor's preface

Foreign perceptions of Japan since around 1980 have been in turn euphoric, apprehensive, dismissive and sober. If the 1980s was an age of spectacular economic growth (leading to widespread concern about the international impact of Japanese economic expansion), the 1990s was often dismissed as the 'lost decade'. After the emergence of severe problems with the Japanese financial system in the early 1990s, those who had urged other countries to learn from Japan came to be ridiculed as purveyors of misleading nostrums. Japan seemed unable to bring about much-needed reform to its systems of economics and politics. Many observers thought that the State interfered too much with the market, that there was far too much "cronyism", government wasted huge sums on poorly costed and unneeded infrastructure projects, large swathes of economic activity were massively protected from competition, and democratic accountability was there in form but hardly in substance. A very few so-called "Japan-enthusiasts", such as Ronald Dore, continued to maintain that there was merit in the way Japan organized things, but they were voices crying in the wilderness.

Whatever the rights and wrongs here, it is important to remember that the 1990s was the first decade following the collapse of the Soviet Union and the ending of the Cold War (at least in Europe). The Western alliance, led by the United States, had triumphed, and that triumph was not just a matter of relative military strength, it was a triumph of ideology. For a few short years the strange notion of Francis Fukuyama that the end of the Cold War meant the end of history, was in vogue. The fact that Japan still marched to a different tune was inconvenient to those who thought in this way, if they thought about it at all, and when the Japanese economic and political model started to go wrong, it was easy to argue dismissively that Japan would recover only if she submitted to globalizing (meaning Americanizing) forces and moved over in essence to the unique model capable of delivering success.

Meanwhile, in Japan itself, a huge literature emphasizing the uniqueness of Japan and the Japanese people had developed as a means of establishing and reinforcing a sense of national identity under threat from these very forces of Americanization. The more extreme versions of this literature were of dubious intellectual pedigree, and the genre as a whole hardly shone with methodological rigour. At its worst, it was grossly chauvinistic, paranoid and meretricious, at its best it was at least seeking Japanese solutions for Japanese problems. As a phenomenon, it is important and repays study.

Perhaps, however, the key point to understand is that Japan is at a turning point in her history, even comparable with those of the late nineteenth and middle twentieth centuries. Japan remains the second-largest economy in the world, and by far the largest economy in Asia (still several times larger than that of China). There is evidence that scepticism is on the rise about the assumption prevalent in the 1990s that there was only one path to be chosen for everybody, and that that path was designed in the United States. Radical reform is indeed crucial for Japan, but somehow the ship of state needs to be steered between the Scylla of blindly following American models and the Charybdis of obscurantist and exclusive nationalism. Enlightened leadership is essential for this task.

The Nissan Institute/Routledge Japanese Studies Series was begun in 1986 and has passed its 50th volume. It seeks to foster an informed and balanced, but not uncritical, understanding of Japan. One aim of the series is to show the depth and variety of Japanese institutions, practices and ideas. Another is, by using comparisons, to see what lessons, positive or negative, can be drawn for other countries. The tendency in commentary on Japan to resort to outdated, ill-informed or sensational stereotypes still remains, and needs to be combated.

When we look back over the academic literature on Japan that has been written over the past 15 or 20 years, it is interesting to note the richness and variety of literature based on the discipline of social anthropology. Happily, if there is competition between the academic disciplines of those studying Japan, it is (usually) friendly competition. But it is worth speculating why it is that the social anthropologists should have contributed so much to our understanding of Japan and the Japanese. This is emphatically not because the anthropologists concentrate on the exotic. That is an outdated assumption. Rather, it is because they have evolved a discipline that is at once rigorous and imaginative, theoretically sophisticated and comparative, micro-concentrated and laterally extensive. Unlike the tendency in some other disciplines, social anthropologists have long ago given up the idea of imposing a single model of how human beings behave (or should behave), while recognizing that we all have in common at least the characteristic of being human.

This is well demonstrated in the present book. The universal human phenomenon of play is here explored in the Japanese environment. This exploration is on the one hand a study of the deep meanings of play in human societies and their contingent manifestations in the case of Japan. From playing soccer to hiking in the forest, from *onsen* to *karaoke* to *inakazumō*, from tattooing to rock music to the gay scene, we see a wonderful blending of traditional and modern, global and particular, in a rich and tasty soup that can be regarded as symbolic of the creative complexity of Japan today. This book will surprise those who do not automatically associate Japan with laughter.

J. A. A. Stockwin

Acknowledgements

The papers by Eyal Ben-Ari and Jan Van Bremen in this book are reproduced by kind permission of *Social Analysis* and *Florilegium Japonicum* respectively.

The photographs and figures were taken or made by the author of the chapter in which they appear.

The editors would like to thank the Japan Anthropology Workshop for hosting the initial conference on which the book is based, and for supporting them throughout the process of getting it into press. They would also like to thank the contributors and ultimately the readers for their patience with the rather lengthy nature of the exercise.

CONVENTIONS

Japanese names are used throughout this book in the normal Japanese order, with surname first, and given name second.

Macrons have been omitted over the long vowels in place names commonly used in English, such as Tokyo and Osaka.

Introduction

Massimo Raveri

Play seems to be such a simple activity. But the more we think about it, the more we analyse it, the more complex and elusive it reveals itself to be. It seems at first to be superfluous, but on the contrary it is fundamental: all humans play in different ways at any age. It can be described as a carefree and joyful activity, but nevertheless sometimes discloses a secret, fierce violence. It can be sheer pleasure, and cruelty. We so often use the word 'play', but it is a poor description because it covers events and performances with the most varied, and often opposed, characteristics.

We in fact find ourselves confronted by a vast range of situations that codify the interweaving of two conflicting tensions: the valuing of the player's aggressive subjectivity, or its dramatic devaluation, its annulment. There is play that turns fantasy and quick decision making to better account, and games that require rationality and strategy. Agonistic games place maximum value on the ability, strength, and determination of the competitors, but in many forms of play the crucial factor is luck, which implies a complete deprivation of the power of players. Games force us to rethink the meaning of terms such as 'freedom', 'dominance' and 'chance', and to examine closely the complexity of their interaction.

Starting to play means keying acts, words and thoughts to a different tune. It means entering freely and passionately into an 'other' reality – a parallel and abstract world – delimited in time and space as if between inverted commas: 'this is play'.

Play – as Bateson has pointed out (1955; 1978) – is marked by a make believe quality, but made real by its un-reality. This is not the only paradox. Scholars like Csikszentmihalyi (1981) and Loy (1982) have asked how it is possible that play, apparently unrelated to any useful aim, so free from ordinary life, at the same time has such an influence on it. What has to be redefined is the concept of 'serious', 'real' behaviour seen in antithesis to the 'ludic'. Often what is created in play is as 'real' as what is produced under the pressure of life's needs. Besides, play can be quite 'serious', when it deeply affects the personality of the players or it involves their economic or social interests. On the other hand, many people do 'serious' activities with a ludic spirit. In some cases it is indeed work that isolates particularly men and sets a kind of moratorium on their familiar world: exactly what we think of as a peculiarity of play. 'Reality' is a relativistic dimension and play offers the possibility of 'restructuring' it, constantly modifying its perspectives and aims.

With all its subtle and varied forms – from games of chance that involve an almost demonic passion, to a sudden flash of wit in the middle of a conversation – play means always a change of scene, a diversion of course, a switching of the glance. And it implies a risk. Because in the self-deception of play one experiences a different way of being that perhaps expresses, in those short moments, one's most secret, but truest nature. From this derives the peculiar ludic temptation of putting everything, even love, or power, at stake. In Latin *inlusio* means 'entering into play'. But this 'illusion' is perhaps the real wisdom.

For the first anthropologists, play was a subject too light to be worthwhile studying. Edward B. Tylor in his *Primitive Culture* (1871) wrote about children's games as mysterious store-houses in which ancient and forgotten rites, beliefs and institutions survived without any apparent sense. Games were nothing more than silent, fragmentary 'memories of the infancy of mankind'.

The insight of Huizinga (1872–1945) gave play back its value. In *Homo Ludens* (1938), he elaborated an original concept of play that implied culture in every possible form. Not only did he say that every culture has its own specific ludic expressions, but he also had the theoretical courage to affirm that the characters of play were those of culture, and that the ways of culture, since the beginning of mankind, manifest themselves in the logic of play. 'Related to the suggestions of positivism, from Spencer to Lelo's "sociological" aesthetics', writes Umberto Eco (1973: 8), 'the notion of play as the origin and constant of cultures did fascinate at least because it was outrageous: it seemed indeed a "pseudo-concept" that was violently grasping the power, and conquering the Winter Palace arrogantly inhabited until then by Aesthetics, Metaphysics, Ethics, Economy'.

In recent times, thinkers like Wittgenstein, Lyotard, Morgenstern and von Neumann set play at the core of a new hermeneutics, with their interpretations of the nature of the game which governs the rules of language, as it governs the formulations of logic, the mechanism of the psyche and the dynamics of economic strategy. In fact, since Saussure, the chess game has been a paradigm most congenial to the theories of structural anthropology. Nevertheless, when von Neumann and Morgenstern (1944) affirm that fundamental structures of socio-economic phenomena consist of a self-sufficient combinatorial matrix which obeys rules that are just those of a game, an anthropologist like Geertz (1983) takes a critical stand against what he thinks to be a cynical and hyper-rationalistic interpretative model that expresses only the utopia of power to control and dominate social reality.

Wittgenstein too, in *Philosophical Investigations*, often utilizes chess as a metaphor for clarifying the nature of the language. But at a certain point in his reasoning, he accepts the fact that play cannot be imprisoned in a single definition, and that in many cases the chess metaphor does not work at all. He writes about 'language games' and realizes how often the language choices, the 'moves' in the everyday conversation, are guided by a flux of rules that are constantly transformed, abandoned, innovated, or rules that hide themselves even to the player himself. 'And is there not also the case' – he notes – 'where we play and "make up the rules as we go along"? And there is even one where we alter them – as we go along?' (1968: 39e).

This book was conceived at the Sixth International Studies Conference of the European Association for Japanese Studies, which took place in Berlin, 16–19 September 1991. The choice of theme was motivated by the desire to continue a debate initiated at the Fifth Conference of the Japan Anthropology Workshop (JAWS), held in Leiden, on ritual behaviour in Japanese culture (Bremen and Martinez 1994). We thought that the discussion could be resumed from a new perspective because the fundamental problems involved in ritual performance on the one hand and in play on the other were not so distant from each another. Some of the interpretations and theoretical approaches which had emerged on that first occasion could constitute the beginning of a new debate. This book contains almost all the papers presented in Berlin, revised and brought up to date, and other contributions to the new debate.

As was found with ritual, ludic performance demonstrates the same difficulty of drawing that fine line which separates behaviour that is genetically conditioned from that which is culturally learnt. Observations by ethologists on animal games and the analysis of human games by anthropologists, psychologists and semiologists oblige us to rethink the terms of the relationship between culture and nature. A more articulate and sophisticated interpretation of the dynamics of culture and nature has come to oppose the too clearly cut dualistic analysis so dear to the first structuralists; because also among animals play is a free, conscious and pleasant activity, of fundamental importance for learning and innovation (Bruner, Jolly and Sylva 1981).

In comparison with ritual, play apparently expresses a freedom of imagination, the improvisation of fantasy. But up to what point? On a more profound level, the nature of the game is revealed, with its binding structure of rules and combinatorial matrices. We could say that rites and play are performative actions of the same nature, but that they differ in the strategic margin given either to a deterministic course or to a probabilistic range of choices.

Rite and play moreover have the power of connecting metahistory with history. As performative actions they can re-enact an ideal and relatively stable normative order, re-defining it through the mutable psychological and social choices of the participants (Harris 1981). But what kind of relationship is there between ludic patterns and symbolic classifications in any given culture? Huizinga's idea of the harmonious balance between what he thought to be the two cardinal principles of civilization (the serious and the playful) in a certain sense sums up the classic opposition of twentieth-century anthropology between function and structure (Norbeck 1977). Of course the structuralist temptation is to answer that every culture reflects its patterns in the logic of its games, so that the two schemes are symmetric. As a performance delimited in time and space, the ludic would be the actualization of an abstract model of social dynamics, almost a utopian moment that reproduces the variables of competitive interaction, perfect harmony, risk, chance and the security of control. As well as the rules that in some sports release a circumscribed violence follow the patterns that sanction aggressivity in society.

The chapters in this book reflect a certain uneasiness of the authors towards theories that tend to constrain social experiences into holistic schemes, based on harmonious and static sets of oppositions. They are more in tune with contemporary hermeneutics and its relativistic, multi-perspective approach. Many pages of the book reveal a fresh sensibility in trying to capture the dynamic aspects of play, caused by the tensions between conservation and fracture. The authors accept the fact that culture can play ambiguously, that often there could be games that do not reflect its real functioning at a deep level. Indeed there may be an ideological phase when culture lies to itself and in a period of crisis alienates itself in ludic experiences that feign perfect functioning and create a pleasant evasion from the distress of the present. For this reason the timeless fixity of game is only a reassuring presumption. Its forms alter with time as the interpretations given to them superimpose themselves.

Play is the ground on which traditional ideas could be experienced and learnt, but it is also a delimited context to try out alternative and innovative fantasies that could be a source of inspiration for new forms in culture (Sutton-Smith 1977: 226). This is why power is continuously interfering in the world of play, trying also to control its weight in the society at large. Indeed, when ludic expressions become excessive – as Huizinga pointed out – they represent a threat to the stability of society. When, on the contrary, ludic performances are severely repressed, culture risks stagnation.

The studies of Huizinga, Caillois and Csikszentmihalyi suggested to Turner (1983) the idea that play could be interpreted as a liminal situation in which received ideas, conformist sentiments and traditional norms are fragmented and rearranged in a bricolage of fascinating and fragile combinations. Every example of play would be a powerful commentary on life. In the 'hypothetical' way of re-enacting the world that pertains to the nature of play, man invents, undoes and remakes 'reality' without fear of becoming imprisoned within it.

The body is at the core of play: because play means senses, emotions and, above all, deep desire. Joy Hendry chooses the traditional Japanese art of tattooing as a way of making the body itself the object of play through a complex interlacing of symbolic meanings. The ideology that establishes the symmetries and hierarchies of the limbs through the norms of purity and the interdictions of impurity sets the human body as a powerful *signifiant*, a basic paradigmatic model for structuring other social 'bodies' or configurations. The tattoo is a transgressive form of play because it superimposes on the physical body other imaginary bodies that confuse its lines. The deceitful forms, animated by the movements of the limbs, produce an ambiguous image of the body, in contrast with the logic of power which tends to impose only one form of the body, in order to legitimate a monothetic model of symbolic classification, and to encourage conformist behaviour.

It is not therefore by chance – underlines the author – that tattoos (forbidden by the Japanese authorities until 1945) flourished among people at the margins of society, so as to become an integral part of their language. Tattooing became a refined artistic expression chosen by the concubines of the pleasure quarters as a pledge of love and devotion to their master; tattooed also were the wandering *samurai* with no leader, second sons of merchants with no business to inherit. Since the Second World War, tattooing has become associated with the *yakuza*, the gangsters who control the forbidden areas of play (gambling, prostitution, drugs), who carry a somewhat ambiguous aura of terror and of that romantic admiration reserved for the chivalrous bandits. Tattooing is play, but also, at a deeper level, a challenge to the common feelings of mainstream society. The *Nihonshoki* (720) suggests that tattooing was used by the authorities as a form of punishment and exclusion, being interpreted as a sign of 'savagery'. But still today tattoing commands respect among prisoners.

By the same logic, the traditional tattoo's designs often represent ambiguous beings like the dragon (*tatsu*) or sacred figures of spiritual mediation, such as Jizō, Fudō and Kannon, who stand at the margins between the Pure Land and hell and mediate the transition between life and death.

There are in Japan great masters of the tattoo, who live almost apart, surrounded by the respect – almost veneration – of their *deshi* (apprentices) and clients. Their artistic techniques, which are felt as vaguely 'impure', have grown in a world of silence and secrecy. Also the splendour of the most magnificent full-body tattoo is concealed under the clothes of its owner. Its beauty is revealed to few and in intimacy. The sensuous spell of the forms of bodies shading one into the other is achieved through prolonged voluntary suffering, and submission. Tattooing is a cruel game.

The ludic interpretation of games – writes Sepp Linhart – constitutes a performance which, in a closed context, reflects the rules and tensions of society and irreverently makes fun of them. Towards the end of the Tokugawa period (1600–1868), prints representing the game of *ken* became quite popular. They showed three antagonists, in various shapes or dresses, winning in turn one over the other, each antagonist being stronger but at the same time weaker than one of the others. The prints were *ryōkō* (fashionable), often *dōke* (foolish), and there was no serious subject that could be saved.

In the *kitsuneken*, for example, there were three characters around a chess board: the head of the village (representing the old government) had political power, the hunter (incarnating the new political forces) had military power, and the cunning and magical fox (symbol of the aristocracy of the old capital) had supernatural power. Religion too was put at stake: *ken* prints made caricatures of the three gods especially popular around Edo at that time: Okina Inari, Datsueba, and Otake Dainichi Nyorai.

The humour, the satire, offers the possibility, at least for those brief moments of laughter, to be free, because irony rearranges the trivia of daily life so that it appears in a different, estranged light. A burst of laughter is the recognition of the familiar made paradoxical. *Ken* could be seen as a ludic evasion, an ideological mask that hides the harshness and anxieties of life (Harootunian 1989). In fact *ken* flourished in a period which was also one of much wishful *yonaoshi* (world renewal) thinking.

The pattern of *ken* play is related to the *mitsutomoe*, the Daoist circular symbol that expresses the eternal dynamism of *yin* and *yang* and the Five Elements – opposed and united in a perennial process of generation and destruction. The *sansukumiken* game, for example, did not represent the social forces in the Tokugawa period (the *samurai*, the peasants, and the merchant-citizens) fixed in their hierarchical roles – as the

Confucian utopia would dream them to be – but, with a smile of irony, as involved in an obsessive and unending whirlpool of power: the *samurai* having the supremacy over the peasants because of their swords, the peasants having supremacy over the citizens because of their production of food, but in their turn, the citizens having supremacy over the *samurai* because of their wealth. And so each social entity wins and loses in a vicious circle, that – maybe – could be translated into the 'real' game of life.

The great philosophical traditions of Daoism and Zen have made of this kind of mocking, anarchical humour a way to a deeper wisdom. Laughter suddenly upsets the perception of reality and sets free the mind, just as does a *kōan*, where the search for enlightenment sets itself up in the guise of a game of enigmas.

The logic of play is in a continuous and tense relationship with the ideology of power. In the case of the *ken* game, those who bear the heaviest pressure of society free themselves through play and teasing, in an inward moment of amusement. But in another, almost opposite, case – that of the Japanese gays discussed by Wim Lunsing – it is social power that does not accept their diversity and frees itself of what it judges to be a potential threat, confining them to the margins, in a separate world that gay men describe as *kono sekai*, a realm of play and laughter, a world of *asobi*.

Although Japan has no laws discriminating against homosexuality explicitly, the social structure leaves little space for public gay lifestyles. The situation cannot be compared with the experience of gay communities in the US and elsewhere. The cultural premises are so different, as are the actual ways of living and experiencing a homosexual identity in social relations.

In Japan there are places – certain bars, cinemas and hotels – where gay men may meet freely. But the possibility for a gay person to be really at easy without shame in a normal social environment lasts only for a few hours and under the conditions of being self-restricted to a dimension of 'play'. And not even in these tacitly accepted places of suspended reality, can gay men truly be themselves: some informants told Lunsing that they avoid entering these bars in their own town because they could risk their anonymity as gay. Others said they did not dare to go because the image they had of them was sombre (this compounded by the image the mass media give of these bars as places for transvestites). Still others say that they do not like these places simply because they are boring. This is perhaps the sharpest judgement: it unmasks a social experience which is, by its intrinsic logic, reduced to superficial acquaintance and stereotypical behaviour; an experience which is often – maybe inevitably – deprived of any authenticity. The gay man, who relaxes in these bars, enjoying these occasions of 'play', does nothing else but justify the cultural process that denies dignity and respect to his diversity.

The very same logic of interaction between ideology and play is the focus of Yamaguchi Masao's article on *karakuri ningyō* in the Tokugawa period.

The advent of Western technology in Japan in the sixteenth century inspired many artisans to create a new machine culture. As in Europe, the clock in Japan was the machine that struck in depth the social imagination of the age, both as a complex mechanism with its apparatus of springs, gears, cams, and cranks, and as a metaphor of a world of orderly precision, and self-regulating harmony.

But the Tokugawa government forbade any industrial or military use of machinery, distrusting the scientific innovations of the new technology and fearing the potential of its systematic exploitation. As a result, specialists in mechanical technologies were not recognized as members of a real profession (as medical doctors were, for example). They were treated like magicians, creating odd, eccentric and useless things. Regarded with suspicion, they were confined to the ambit of play. However, notwithstanding the fact that their activity was kept at the margins, and concentrated in the world of entertainment, in the eighteenth century they reached a high level of technical achievement. Among the artisans who made clocks, automatic puppets and other machinery for *kabuki* theatre, Ono Benkichi is often mentioned as comparable with Leonardo da Vinci.

It was in the Meiji period (1868–1912), when the process of modernization and industrialization began to change the country radically, that these conjurers of technological fantasies finally entered the 'real' game – that of the economy and production – at the core of the new society. Tanaka Giemon, who in 1853 had opened a 'House of *karakuri*', in 1875 founded a company that later became the Toshiba Manufacturing Company. Another example is the family of Tsuda Sukezaemon who inherited the position of clock engineer in Owari province. Scholars maintain that the trademark of Toyota Motors was already being used by the engineers working under Tsuda in the Edo period and that the family production system was easily transformed into a Western-style factory system.

It was just this ludic spirit of experimenting and entertaining – argues Yamaguchi – that made possible the easy and ready acceptance of Western applied sciences in Japanese culture. It echoes Vittorio Lanternari's notion of play as a 'mental laboratory' in which previously unorthodox scientific ideas could be freely 'played' and tried (Lanternari 1988: 117).

In the case of Japan, the link between the playful gusto that illuminates a passion for technological knowledge has deeper implications. Starting from an overall view of the multiple ways in which Japanese culture has always valued this-worldliness, the desire of the senses and an intense pleasure in working, María Rodríguez del Alisal's article sheds light on the various religious roots of the creative strength and vitality of the Japanese in many fields: their painstaking curiosity, the fresh pleasure of experimenting and constructing things.

The ludic is not outside religious experience. It is an integral part of Japanese ritual tradition. Partaking of the harvest's first fruits with the ancestral tutelary gods is a feast for all the community. In sacred play (communal banquets, *kagura* dances, theatrical performances, competitions, and processions) there is always a symbolic exchange of gifts, expressing a ritual recognition of dependence, and to be drunk and easy during the feast reveals the deep pleasure of being one with the community of gods, ancestors, and men. The sacred dance is often a performance connected with fun, joy of life and gratitude to the god for the gift of fertility to the fields, and to humans. In Kyushu, during a wedding ceremony, it is a tradition that a man, wearing the smiling mask of the *Ta no kami*, the god of the paddy fields, dances a comic and obscene pantomime in front of the married couple and the honoured guests. Then husband and wife are obliged to play – amidst the laughter of their parents and friends – with the phallic statue of the god.

The gods speak in the transgressive language of play, as they do also in the language of suffering, because both are parallel states that fracture gestures and meanings, rules and emotions. The ecstasy of a shaman through which the divine spirit communicates his will to humans is said to be *kami asobi*, the 'play of a god'.

The idea of god at play is an intuition that solves the crucial problem of why god creates. It explains the contradiction of a supernatural power who is free, unconditioned in his will, without defects and without desires, and who nevertheless decides to act because he is simply playing. Gods act and create as artists do, or children, for the sheer pleasure of their fantasy. The nature of their play is often subversive and dizzily mysterious because the spontaneity of a god knows no limit, but it is pure, because it is infused with love (Kinsley 1979; Raveri 2000: 305–8, Sax 1995).

The idea is fascinating and disquieting: it could imply also that the world has been created only for pretence, for the enchantment of illusion. The play of a god gives to the believers a sense of joy in life, of positive acceptance of this world's experience. But on the other hand it discloses the subtle 'deceit' of a god, disillusionment with all forms of existence. It is easy indeed to believe that what is good in the world is the result of divine amusement. Much more difficult to accept is the idea that suffering and evil also obey the mysterious laws of chance – like a dice game of god.

One of the results of this book might at least be the exploding of the myth, so abused by the mass media, that the Japanese are a grey, anonymous mass of efficient, obedient workers. The articles here reveal a Japan outside officialdom, a lively Japan of tumultuous and independent thought, inefficient and aesthetic, pleasure-loving, aggressive and wasteful, creative and anti-authoritarian.

But to smile at a laughing Japan is not enough. By studying the ways in which the young Japanese play – their games, their music, the contradictory images of their amusements like *manga*, *anime*, video games – one may be able to determine the subtle ways in which, in contemporary post-industrial society, their imagination, personality and creativity are conditioned and developed.

Carolyn Stevens's chapter examines the cultural production and consumption of pleasure found in the Japanese rock fan context. Abandoning the many negative stereotypes (that fans are 'deviant', 'disreputable', 'dangerous', passively created by the modern celebrity system) the author analyses the processes by which fans of a Japanese rock group – the Alfee – take pleasure from their activities. The chapter recognizes the importance of the relationship between the icon's meaning and its following and how fan identity affects the young's perception of their place in the world around them, at school, in the family, and then at their workplace.

Fan identity is not only based on a perceived connection with the band but also on the interaction among fans. Especially in a concert – with its strict rules of subversive fun – they have a good time and they share the same hopes and dreams. 'Fandom' is a sort of communication between young people, with special semiotic codes based on a love for the group and a deep familiarity with its artistic history.

The Alfee as dialogue could be the key to success in a social relationship not only at school but even at work, because even when a fan has become a full member of society – and work and family appear to be given priority over fandom – the fan thinks that to listen to the Alfee music and to talk about them is a relief from work's stress.

One might argue that playing the fan's role is a method of prolonging one's youth through adulthood and refusing the stress of adult responsibilities, bringing the individual back to a carefree, relaxed state. The author's suggestion is that fandom could be the integrating factor for one's multiple personal identities that change over time. Fandom, with its increasing store of memories, is a way to describe certain points in a person's life and can provide a facet of unity to these changing identities. It is in this juxtaposition between change and constancy that nostalgia works to integrate an idealized past with the present, in a pleasurable way. Much has been written about nostalgia in the case of Japan. It is a romanticization of the past that can assume the performative character of a play in order to create emotional ties for those who probably never experienced it directly. Nostalgia is not a product of the past; it resides in the present. It is a key to the Alfee's concerts. The old fans are the precious market of the group and the management does what it can do to appeal to their nostalgic feelings.

These first chapters propose a kind of optimistic interpretation of the innovative potentialities of play, in arts as in the field of sciences. This may be fine, but we also have to consider that play could create new forms of alienation and anxiety, with negative consequences for the social context, as demonstrated by 'new' aggressive tendencies rife among soccer hooligans and players of violent video games.

We have to admit that, more or less latent, there is violence in play. What is the reason? This is the question at the core of Michael Ashkenazi's chapter, which asks why in Japan various aspects of violence are culturally appreciated in the context of play.

The fantasy of violence is funny. In the world of *manga*, for example, physical cruelty is depicted in a very vivid way, often connected with sexual abuse, whose brutality seems to know no limits. Various Japanese magazines specialize in arms, being either true instruments of war or toys, with a narrative background of imaginary scenes of death and destruction.

In religious ceremonies, too, violence seems to be a founding element. As test cases, Ashkenazi analyses the traditional *sumō* fight (*inakazumō*) and the orgiastic procession of the sacred palanquin during a *matsuri* (festival). These situations of play show well-tried and tested techniques in the formation and sublimation of aggression. By the use of ritualized violence, whether physical or psychological, in a continuous, tense interrelation between rule-building and rule-violating, they experiment with the social processes of dominance and rebellion (Dal Lago 1990; Giulianotti, Bonney and Hepworth 1994). Violence 'seems' to be spontaneous and unrestrainable, so as to make the spectators shudder, but in reality it is controlled and almost never bypasses the schemes of play. The normative pressure of a vertical society loosens through the well-calculated – and delimited – bursts of violence.

Anthropological studies on the relationship between play, sport and violence have come up with divergent interpretations (Blanchard 1977; Mergen 1986). Some scholars explain that sport tends to reduce the levels of violence in society, because it allows both the players and the spectators to live a deep cathartic experience. On the contrary, other scholars have reached the conclusion that sport increases the incidence of unstructured aggression.

David Le Breton, in analysing high-risk sport, uses the definition of 'modern ordeals' (Le Breton 1991: 48). An ordeal is a divine judgement obtained through stochastic – and often very dangerous – procedures that testify to a passage from a private to a public justice. Nevertheless Le Breton's metaphor holds up. Putting one's own life at stake in a game means to find out if it is still worthwhile living. The 'extreme' sport is a challenge, and an oracle of the signs of fate. It could be seen as a kind of revenge of the anonymous 'man without qualities' of contemporary society, who risks his life for a few moments of media celebrity (Duthie and Salter 1981; Verden and Sewart 1986).

The ludic is not an end in itself. The agonistic game is not that which society plays, but is rather the foundation of social relationships, the meaning of power itself. Games are serious because they are necessary to any society. They are not free because they are governed by the pressure of power interests. Violence is deep in their nature, because the real game is played on a deeper level. Even behind the light-hearted spontaneity of an evening drink one catches a glimpse of a silent, refined struggle, whose logic is connected with the structure of authority, the ties of obligation, and ways in which different roles and different genders are balanced during the day.

Precisely from this perspective, Eyal Ben-Ari analyses the complex interplay of group dynamics in a *bōnenkai*, a drinking feast so typical of Japanese society.

Much of the anthropological literature contains strong functional assumptions about the relation between drinking occasions and the wider social context. Linhart (1986; 1988) talks of the opportunities provided by such gatherings for the reduction and relief of the stress due to the often excessive tensions and obligations of interpersonal relations in Japan. Vogel (1963: 105) emphasizes how going drinking together serves to mantain camaraderie within the workgroup. Rohlen (1974) shows how *bōnenkai* are related to the solidification of group identity. But there is a tendency to leave the internal dynamics of these occasions unexplored. Ben-Ari instead analyses the peculiar mix of performance and improvisation which unfolds within such situations and sheds light on ways in which these occasions evolve according to strategies to manage conflict and promote social harmony.

The logic of the *bōnenkai* is first of all to create a special situation ('the drinking frame') organized at a restricted time (Saturday evening, holiday, end of the year) and in a separate space (restaurant, guest room). Then it commands a switching of behavioural codes, the most important of which seems to be the levelling of statuses. The social distinctions, which keep people apart in everyday life, are apparently disregarded and a relative equality is temporarily established. When intimacy within the drinking frame is taken further, it results in what Lebra (1976: 110) has termed 'social nudity', or what Hendry (1993) in different terms has called the process of 'unwrapping'. Yet social nudity entails more than a violation of norms or the expression of tenderness and affection. It is a risky situation. So there are often *mamasan, geisha* and bar hostesses, who can facilitate the unfolding of such processes and the 're-creation', in harmony, of a new social group characterized by a certain temporary identity, intimate behaviour, and a sense of fellowship.

This is a process by which organizational disagreement is transported to an interpersonal level. It is the most effective and legitimate means used in Japan to keep conflict under control. That is, the conflict is circumscribed within a social frame that facilitates the expression of certain problematic issues on the basis of a temporarily created group within which trust is gradually demonstrated. It is precisely the different quality of relations between individuals that can unfold during drinking occasions that may be utilized in order to manage conflict.

The *bōnenkai* also activates a certain number of social mechanisms that seem to be crucial, in the Japanese context, for creating ties within heterogeneous gatherings, or between existing collectivities whose relations may be marked by tension or opposition. These mechanisms of transient grouping which operate in the interstitial spaces between different permanent organizations make possible the creation of solidarity among people with different backgrounds, diverging allegiances and diverse external ties.

These mechanisms of *asobi* – Ben-Ari argues – point to a culturally constituted facility among many middle-class Japanese to move rather smoothly from one social frame to another. In a vertical society, at the metalevel of play, they get acquainted with the internal dynamics of other groups, and learn to relate horizontally with them.

Seriousness tries to exclude play – as Huizinga wrote – while play can very well include seriousness. Bill Kelly clearly shows how *karaoke* in Japan is a kind of play that hides very serious traits. This might seem odd, because in Europe a good *karaoke* performance to be enjoyable has to be extemporary, candid and spontaneous – just to have a good laugh. This is why the performances are often embellished with stage theatrics and 'hamming it up' in front of an audience. *Karaoke* provides a chance for many people to stand out, to become for a few minutes a film or singing star. Taking the microphone turns an individual into the centre of the group's attention. The *karaoke* singer, revealing his or her humanity, hesitations and shyness, is more easily accepted into the group.

Just because of these characteristics, *karaoke* performance in Japan has to be 'perfect', not only from a technical point of view; it must also be socially faultless and careful of the rules of etiquette, so as not to interfere badly in the complex web of interpersonal relationships of those present. The choice of the 'right' song, the correct movement of the arms, the modesty of one's composure, the way to appreciate another's performance, everything has to favour the soft flow of emotions and feelings of harmony among friends. So *karaoke* performance can neither be too original (not to provoke jealousy) nor too spontaneous (not to discover excessively one's own true sentiments at the risk of hurting someone else's feelings).

To avoid errors, the performance must be highly conventional. So people 'train' in *karaoke*. Professional singers and other 'experts', found in the pages of specialized newspapers or in special television programmes, give meticulous instructions on every possible detail, from the vocal techniques to the correct enunciation of words, from the posture of the body to the way of holding the microphone. This way of learning is based on imitating and copying the actions of the master, a trait that also tends to characterize the traditional Japanese educational ethos. The emphasis on painstaking repetition, and assimilation of patterns, as a way – first of all – of really mastering one's own mind, is central to the learning of all the classical arts. The seriousness with which *karaoke* is experienced does not imply for the Japanese a lack of amusement. To stay in the right place in disciplined order and smooth harmony – as Hosokawa (1995: 152) has noticed – gives a Japanese person a sense of security, of excitement, and great satisfaction in his leisure time.

An interesting question is whether it is possible to define a peculiar Japanese way of playing. For Rupert Cox the answer is yes. The implication is that there may be a model of learning and practising play that also makes sense of the experience of play. Such a concept is contrary to common sense perceptions of play in the West, which emphasize its unstructured and spontaneous nature.

Cox suggests that play in Japan is based on the absence of a clear distinction between creativity and order. There is also a fundamental ambiguity in the Japanese way of playing which always seems to be a mixture of opposing categories: the sacred and the secular, the aesthetic and the ascetic. Play could for the Japanese be an activity involving concentration and hard work, infused by a deep sense of religious experience, of self-oblivion and of enlightenment. All the different Japanese ways of playing are subject to constraints: by religious traditions, by ideological discourses and by socio-economic forces. But on the other hand, even in structured and disciplined pursuits, the sense of play is a fundamental aspect.

Some common themes underlie all the historic shifts in the meaning of play in Japanese culture, and for Cox it is possible to connect the medieval concept of *asobi* with the modern idea of *rejā* (leisure). He reflects on the fact that the vertigo of play is inherent even in the most austere religious practice. The traditional idea is that through continual and repetitive performance of ecstatic techniques, the self of everyday experience would be discarded and the adept would undergo a radical psychological change that will enable him to become one with the god.

Towards the end of the Heian period (794–1185), the Buddhist theory of self-cultivation and its psychophysical techniques of concentration were incorporated into the practice of the arts. Play became a spiritual 'path' (*dō*) of high intellectual sophistication, in which the ideal condition of aesthetic appreciation was sought in an analogy with the religious experience of enlightenment. The ambiguity of a word like *miyabi* meant that it could refer both to a spiritual withdrawal from the world as well as to an idealization of the aesthetic values of leisure and refinement of the Heian court.

During the Tokugawa period there was a huge expansion in the number and classes of people practising the arts. The 'arts' included activities of entertainment (*yūgei*) and self-cultivation (*bugei*, martial arts), but the distinction was soon eroded to the point where all these activities were known as *geidō* (artistic ways). New aesthetic terms – *hari* (strength of character), *bitai* (allure), *iki* (refined consciousness of the sensations,) *tsu* (stylish behaviour) – were created to structure and identify the feelings and emotions of the new 'social world of play' (Nishiyama 1997:54).

The *iemoto* system – continues Cox – emerged after the Genroku era (1688–1704), replacing the *dō* metaphor and reinventing its religio-aesthetic tradition by treating the transmission of the way as 'filiation'. Through the metaphor of kinship, the 'playing' of arts became constrained within the institutional matrices of power and authority. The new system stressed the politico-economic dimensions of the art. The realm of 'culture/general education' (*kyōyō/ keikogoto*) in the Tokugawa period overlapped with 'play/entertainment' (*asobi/yūgei*) for the notion of play presupposed the learning of an art.

This very positive attitude towards entertaining pastimes was considered immoral by the Meiji intellectuals and pedagogues: to study the arts as a form of play (*asobi*) was against that 'authentic Japanese spirit' which was becoming the powerful myth of a reinvented past. The term *yūgei* took on a vulgar meaning.

The emergence of a consumer society brought significant changes. Arts began to be regarded as items of mass culture, something that may be possessed by achievement and certification within a hierarchical system, rather than a matter of skill and taste. As a consequence of the 'leisure boom' of the 1980s, the arts became more and more the product of a pervading industry of entertainment, formed by large media organizations like Sony, NHK and Asahi, by Hankyu or Mitsukoshi department stores, and, last but not least, by the *karuchasentā* (the cultural centres). The rigid hierarchical social structure and the exclusivity of the *iemoto* system has relaxed in favour of a 'culture industry' which has transformed arts into leisure, open to a wider social market, a less refined taste, and lighter practice.

Simone Dalla Chiesa, too, studying school football, notices, as Cox does, how thin the line of demarcation is between the Japanese way of practising this sport and an ancient 'way' of self-cultivation.

Soccer in school is governed by a hierarchical organization (*sakkā dōkōkai*), modelled on the traditional *iemoto* system, that is to say it is structured into different statuses and roles depending on seniority and gender, and has at the top a captain, who has not been voted in by the group but nominated directly by his predecessor.

The sporting activities are organized following the *dōkōkai*'s code of rigid and severe rules, issued by the school and applied by the teachers. Autonomous or spontaneous behaviour could risk being condemned as 'individualistic'. From a strictly sportive point of view, affiliation to a *dōkōkai* implies an intense and sincere involvement, because it imposes exhausting training sessions and repetitive drills.

Sport is a ludic game, but in Japanese amateur football agonistic pleasure seems to be absent. For Dalla Chiesa, the secret purpose of football training is not to defeat the adversary, but to play with a perfect style in a harmonious synchronization of the players, as if in an elegant ballet. Maybe it is just in this selfless flow of movements, executed in a condition of *muga* (without *ego* consciousness), that could be discovered the hidden dimension of pleasure.

This end is unreachable, for evident technical reasons. And the school – or the small company sponsoring the *dōkōkai* – is well aware of this inevitable failure. But they continue to encourage this way of playing soccer because it is essentially of an ethical nature and serves to shape the student's mind, to strengthen his will and his attitude of conformism and dedication to the group. Since 'the goal is not the goal', to play means to accept the challenge of fighting together in a heroic way, to spend all one's energies for the team. A player is of value not so much for his goals but for his zeal, and is rewarded with a sense of warm protection and understanding from the team. It is the same ideal of sacrificing one's physical integrity discussed by Whiting in his books on Japanese professional baseball (Whiting 1977, 1989).

The *dōkōkai* is in fact a closed group, whose existence is self-sufficient. The training sessions – the time of labouring together – realize its purpose. The team does not need to face the teams of other *dōkōkai*. In the simple weekly match, the 'adversaries' are always friends, because they are members of the same *dōkōkai*: more than a game, the weekly match seems to be a 'representation' of a game. In the rare cases when the team accepts the challenge of an 'external' tournament, the event is followed with sparse interest and ironic hilarity, as if it could not be a serious matter.

John Horne's chapter demonstrates how this 'ascetic' interpretation of sport – almost as if it would be a 'way' – is changing in contemporary Japan. The test case is again soccer, but this time it is soccer played at a professional level.

In the 1990s football truly became a 'world game'. Following the 1994 World Cup Final in the US it became clear just how much global interest had been generated by the tournament. So much so that Ian Taylor (1998) has described the World Football Championship as 'the largest mass marketing of happiness ever'. Japanese entrepreneurship also understood the possibilities of economic profit offered by what was until that time a marginal sport.

In 1993 full-time professional soccer – in the shape of the Japan League – was launched with a massive injection of capital and a large marketing campaign. Spectators may have been experiencing soccer as a consumer event, rather than as a sports match. The initial boom of the first years was followed by a slow but continuous decline of spectator numbers in subsequent tournaments. With the qualification for the FIFA World Cup (France 1998) by the national team, however, and the prospect of co-hosting the 2002 World Cup with South Korea, football seems to be back in fashion as an exciting spectacle.

The case of soccer sheds light on the ever-growing interdependence of the world of play with economic and ideological interests. In the balance between internationalization and nostalgia, professional football is the result of an unavoidable process of economic globalization that sells to different countries new 'transcultural' myths and symbols, that often do not fit with the traditional values connected with sport (MacClancy 1996).

For example, the fundamental traits of Japanese school football or of professional baseball 'samurai style', are:

1   the inculcation of *bushidō* values through severe training which promotes endurance, and aims to strengthens the spirit;
2   anti-individualism, and a stress on the importance of complete dedication to the team, without caring for results;

3   hierarchical manager–coach–player relations, which gives the manager total control over the life of the subordinates; and

4   a 'mechanical' style of play which promotes 'automatic' movements.

However, in contemporary Japanese society, all these ideas and values are passing through a deep crisis. The 'new' sport of soccer imposes the continuous trial of innovative schemes, the aggressive fantasy of the players, individualistic behaviour not only during the match (in the adoption of what is called the European or South American styles) but also out of the stadium (with long and dyed hair, earrings and supercars). It is based on competition, aims at a result, and wants victory. It has been transformed into consumer leisure, created and controlled by the media.

Here maybe is the demarcation line between the old and the new. Soccer as a fruit of international show business can accommodate new demands and suggest new (international) ways of thinking and acting in society. In the soccer stadium, the West is manifested, the world is manifested, and the star system ignores the *Nihon no kokoro* (Japanese spirit) but proposes as new paradigms of success some champions from Brazil or Italy.

In baseball the motto *wakon yosai* (Japanese spirit, Western skill) has been preserved and Buruma (1996: 244) observes how the world of baseball is more conservative than other parts of Japanese life and how few signs of change there are. But whether this 'pure Japanese spirit' would be enough to compete adequately in sports at an international level, is the question. Maybe this is where professional soccer, in constituting a deliberate effort to reshape its basic principles, has in turn started to determine changes in other sports and, through them, to influence changes in traditional social values. As Horne rightly concludes: 'Soccer may be a "funny old game", but it is never *just* a game'.

Jan Van Bremen in his chapter stresses the need to pay careful attention to the process of the transformation of play into consumer leisure. In post-industrial societies there may be a movement away from the stress on the liturgical to an increase of ludic frames in religious rituals.

Between the 1970s and the 1980s, in different parts of the world, a revitalization of public celebrations and ritual was noted. New rites were made and old ones revived in places of prospering economy. It has been argued (but this position has also been criticized) that the driving force behind the recovery or reappearance of many rites was an increase in the ludic element, at the expense of liturgy. It infused old rites with new life. In other words, the fireworks became more important than the patron saint. In many aspects, also in Japan, play has come to prevail over liturgy.

Although praising the importance of Huizinga's studies, Van Bremen notes that his ideas are not any longer sufficient to interpret changes in the meaning of play in contemporary societies. They must be superseded by an innovative hermeneutics able to translate the new languages of play.

For example, the entertainment and communication business, in the logic of economic expansion, tends to reach multinational dimensions. The creators of entertainment products – in offering the same ludic forms (film, videoclip, and bestseller book) on different national markets – take for granted that ludic inner states are universal. But this is not so sure, notes Van Bremen.

First of all, forms of ludic behaviour in play or in games are not necessarily symptomatic of inner states. In other words, the fact that the performative language of play tends to induce emotional states does not signify that it achieves its purpose. One might think that there are enough outward signs such as gestures or facial expressions to be able to 'read' an inner state. But it is very difficult to understand an exotic psychological classification on its own terms, grasping the silent connections conventionally established in any culture between bodily posture, words on sentiments and sensations, and inner states.

Some ethnographers presume that different inner states have been adequately distinguished by the psychological vocabularies of their own languages. Yet research finds no universal inner state corresponding to a particular word or phrase (Needham 1981). That is why it is difficult, if not impossible – Van Bremen concludes – to translate sentiments and meanings from one language into others.

Yet the capacity of persuasion of the contemporary mass media is so powerful, the techniques of seduction of the advertizing world so sophisticated, that the multinationals of entertainment have already succeeded in creating leisure products which stir up the same pleasant, appeasing and conformist emotions in different part of the world (Canevacci 1995).

Other authors too – Okpyo Moon, Ulrike Nennstiel, John Knight and Sylvie Guichard-Anguis – centre their articles on cultural changes in contemporary Japanese society seen through problematic aspects of the world of play.

All of them start from the established fact that the Japanese rural world is in a very bad economic, as well as demographic, decline: in the 1920s the rural population amounted to 70 per cent of the total; in the 1990s it represented only 20 per cent of the population. The development of a tourist and entertainment industry has been one of the most widely adopted strategies, initiated in the 1970s, to revitalize the rural economy and society.

The development, in different epochs, of a way of interpreting and utilizing hot springs (*onsen*) – as described by Guichard-Anguis – could be considered paradigmatic. During the Tokugawa period, to go to a hot spring meant to have a spiritual itinerary: it was partly a pilgrimage and partly a way of relaxing the mind. It was also a way of recreating the energies of the body and reinvigorating one's health. From the Meiji period, regular trips were institutionalized in 'modern' organizations such as schools, and firms, for the purposes of learning. After the Second World War, Japanese internal tourism ideology has changed: since the 1960s it has increased in quantity and family holidays emerged as a new leisure style around the 1970s. Tourism for learning or for spiritual or physical health decreased and tourism for recreation and play (ski, golf, mountaineering) burgeoned. Places like the *onsen* were transformed into sophisticated organizations for physical enjoyment, where the body is satisfied in all its desires. A stronger concern with leisure and quality of life rather than with work and efficiency is probably one of the consequences of social change in the so-called post-industrial Japan.

It is possible to detect two main directions in the 'leisure' exploitation of the country. The first is the creation of opportunities for new experiences and pleasures for local people with the idea of making villagers feel that to remain in the country no longer means to be 'backward' economically and culturally. The second trend aims at the enhancement of a 'regional character' – lifestyle, nature, special products, traditional artefacts, folklore – everything that could be considered 'unique', *mezurashii* (rare) and deeply connected with the history and identity of the place, that might attract urban tourists.

Rural villages are no longer seen as places of hardworking farmers or as suppliers of rice, vegetables and unending migratory labour force, but rather as a source of unpolluted water, fresh green forests, health, ancient culture and real 'good' life. The comparison with the stress of the metropolis is made in a way satisfying to the tastes of urban tourists, whether it be through nostalgia, a concern for nature, a historic flavour, exoticism, traditionalism or authenticity.

For the dreams of urban people about 'old Japan', the rural world has been transformed into the ultimate source of Japanese identity. In this process of creating memory, the key myth is the *furusato* (the home village). It is dreamt about as an isolated world, with distinctive imagery – old houses, straw roofs, paddy fields against a mountainous backdrop – a holographic souvenir of 'the good old' way of life, of an old Japan that does not exist anymore and that, maybe, never existed.

With the development of leisure time, illegal fishing has become a frequent phenomenon and a serious economic problem in Hokkaido as well as in other parts of the country. Ulrike Nennstiel clarifies how tourists could be a source of, but at the same time a threat to, income. Opposing interests are at stake: the traditional economy is based on lobster fishing, a labour considered *kiken* (dangerous), *kitanai* (dirty) and *kusai* (smelly), but flourishing in revenue; on the other hand, the village authorities, travel agencies and hotels, through advertisement campaigns, invite tourists to discover the splendour of the natural world of the lake and enjoy with their families its good fish. In so doing they legitimate an illegal fishery not of a few but of thousands of tourists. The conflict is inevitable, and between fishermen and tourists a subtle game of reciprocal exclusion has begun, polite on the surface, but tough in substance.

John Knight sheds light on a situation still more paradoxical, that of the conflict between ways of playing. Mountains too have recently become a place of rivalry between recreational activities of villagers, and the new recreational activities of the tourists.

On the one hand there is the old world in decline with its traditions of hunting wild boars, trapping small birds, catching snakes for *kanpoyaku* (traditional medicine), fishing in the torrents and searching for mushrooms and curative herbs. On the other, there is the urban world of green tourism, which is on the increase. Enormous rural areas have been transformed into golf courses, ski slopes, theme parks, hotels and marinas. Wildlife tourism is becoming more and more organized (deer parks, monkey parks, bear parks, etc.). Hiking in the mountains is very popular, especially among younger Japanese, and hikers also gather wild herbs and mushrooms, pick flowers, birdwatch and observe forest animals.

So the locals dispute the outsiders' right to such forest goods, but hunting can also endanger the tourists' activities in the mountains. The locals are destined to lose: upland dwellers are more and more estranged from the forest around them and there is a widespread perception that the contemporary generation of young in the countryside, who spend their free time in front of the television or playing computer games, have lost the routine familiarity with the forest. The new social imaginary that affirms the 'love for nature' and seeks to go back to 'ancient roots' is the result of the cultural hegemony of the metropolis.

Moon discusses the regional movements that seek to reconstruct a local 'unique' tradition. They serve as a means of attracting 'nostalgia tourists' as the authenticity thereby created often has a great appeal to modern urbanites (since the early 1970s more than two hundred folk museums have been opened throughout Japan). If the process of industrialization has brought a wave towards cultural homogeneity at the global level, the emphasis upon regional character found in 'leisure in the country' movements may be understood as a wave in the opposite direction, namely towards rediscovering cultural difference (and the so often discussed 'Japanese uniqueness').

In reinventing their past for the tourists, rural people have reinvented a new past and a new identity for themselves in an attempt to redefine the meaning of their existence in a post-industrialized society. This newly constructed identity will help them to overcome not only the material disadvantages of rural decline but also their self-conception as losers in industrialized and urbanized modern Japan. But the reproduced past is often as alien an experience to the modernized locals as it is to the urban tourists.

Play and ideology are deeply connected in contemporary interpretations of play, as Aviad Raz's chapter clearly demonstrates. His case study is Tokyo Disneyland (TDL), an extremely successful transplant of the original theme park from the US, which was opened in April 1983.

The scholars of the International Play Association (IPA) – interviewed by the author – distinguish between *rejā* (leisure) and *asobi* (play). *Rejā* designates playful activities which in reality do not foster play: they are merely 'fun'. The opposite word – *asobi* – carries a wide semantic array of 'traditional' concepts, from freedom and indulgence to ritual worship and ecstasy, and is made to stand for the Japanese tradition of children engaging in creative, free play. *Rejā* is executed indoors, hinges on technology (TV, *famicon*, playstation), and consists of prescribed activities. *Asobi*, in contrast, is usually outdoors, in natural settings, and is considered to be promoting imagination and creativity.

Tokyo Disneyland was considered by the IPA members to be a totally controlled artificial environment in which nothing was left to the freedom and creativity of the guests. They said that Tokyo Disneyland had sold off the spirit of the *matsuri* (festival) and replaced the carnevalesque with the predictable. In fact TDL is certainly not a place which encourages visitors to break away from social control. Disney strategy is based on planned efficiency, safe illusion and controlled family entertainment: the guests merely take part in the show, becoming two dimensional like in a big Nintendo game. TDL is light culture, trendy, playful, nothing ideological and nothing original. It is cute, all bright colours, mediocre and clean, poignantly inhuman.

The IPA members judged TDL as pure 'American *rejā*', the site of American cultural imperialism, forgetting that TDL was planned and is managed by Japanese companies. Raz is right when he unveils the dichotomy of '*rejā/asobi*' as a self-serving ideological construct, implying further ideological contradictions such as 'modern/traditional', 'fake/authentic', and ultimately 'America/Japan'. One could be impressed and uneasy in front of Disneyworld, but to say – as IPA scholars do – that it is a phenomenon extraneous to Japan, is sheer prejudice, useful only to avoid the problem, because the Disney magic works, in Japan as in the US. In 1997 TDL was visited by 17 million Japanese making it the most successful theme park in the world.

TDL speaks a new language of play which, whether good or bad, is meaningful to contemporary society. It is up to the anthropologists to be sufficiently free and lucid to be able to understand it and decode its grammar. What gives light to many pages of this book is this same search for the nature and meaning of play and its sometimes contradictory relations with other symbolic languages of society. The authors have tried to be, in Wittgenstein's sense, translators of the logic and polythetic relations of these semantic games, these 'forms of life', knowing that the ludic experience, in its multiform reality, could be the test case that can lead us to a clearer understanding of the meanings and the dynamics of culture itself, the game that plays us.

Bibliography

Bateson, G. (1955) 'A theory of play and fantasy. A report on theoretical aspects of the project for study of the role of paradoxes of abstraction in communication', *Approaches to the Study of Human Personality*, APA Psychiatric Research Reports 2: 39–51.

Bateson, G. (1956) 'The message "this is play"', in B. Schaffner (ed.) *Group Processes*, New York: Josiah Macy Jr. Foundation Proceedings, pp. 145–242.

Bateson, G. (1978) 'Play and paradigm' in M.A. Salter (ed.) *Play. An Anthropological Perspective*, West Point, NY: Leisure Press, pp. 7–16.

Blanchard, K. (1977) 'Team sports and violence. An anthropological perspective', in D.F. Lancy and B.A. Tindall (eds) *The Study of Play. Problems and Prospects*, West Point, N.Y.: Leisure Press, pp. 106–19.

Bremen J. van and Martinez, D.P. (eds) (1994) *Ceremony and Ritual in Japan: Religious Practices in an Industrialized Society*, London: Routledge.

Bruner, J.S., Jolly, A. and Sylva, K. (eds) (1981) *Il gioco. Ruolo e sviluppo del comportamento ludico negli animali e nell'uomo* (Play, role and development of the ludic behaviour in animals and humans), Rome: Armando Editore.

Buruma, I. (1996) *The Missionary and the Libertine: Love and War in East and West*, London: Faber and Faber.

Canevacci, M. (1995) *Antropologia della comunicazione visuale* (Anthropology of visual communication), Ancona-Milan: Costa e Nolan.

Csikszentmihalyi, M. (1981) 'Some paradoxes in the definition of play', in A. Taylor Cheska (ed.) *Play as Context*, West Point, NY: Leisure Press, pp. 14–26.

Dal Lago, A. (1990) *Descrizione di una battaglia. I rituali del calcio* (Description of a battle: the rituals of soccer), Bologna: Il Mulino.

De Sanctis Ricciardone, P. (1994) *Antropologia e gioco* (Anthropology and play), Naples: Liguori.

Duthie, J.H. and Salter, M.A. (1981) 'Parachuting to skydiving: process shifts in a risk sport', in A. Tylor Cheska (ed.) *Play as Context*, West Point, N.Y.: Leisure Press, pp. 167–81.

Eco, U. (1973) '*Homo Ludens oggi*' (*Homo ludens* today), introduction to J. Huizinga, *Homo Ludens*, Turin: Einaudi, pp. 7–27.

Geertz, C. (1983) *Local Knowledge. Further Essays in Interpretative Anthropology*, New York: Basic Books.

Giulianotti, R., Bonney, N. and Hepworth, M. (eds) (1994) *Football, Violence and Social Identity*, London: Routledge.

Harootunian, H.D. (1989) 'Late Tokugawa culture and thought' in M.B. Jansen (ed.) *The Cambridge History of Japan*, vol. 5, *The Nineteenth Century*, Cambridge: Cambridge University Press, pp. 168–258.

Harris, J.C. (1981) 'Beyond Huizinga. Relationships between play and culture', in A. Taylor Cheska (ed.) *Play as Context*, West Point, NY: Leisure Press, pp. 26–36.

Harris, J. and Park, R. (eds) (1983) *Play, Games, and Sports in Cultural Context*, Champaign, IL: Human Kinetics Publishers.

Hendry, J. (1993) *Wrapping Culture: Politeness, Presentation and Power in Japan and Other Societies*, Oxford: Clarendon Press.

Hosokawa, S. (1995) 'Singing not together: *Karaoke* in São Paulo', in W. Straw (ed.) *Popular Music. Style and Identity*, Montreal: Duffering Press.

Huizinga J. (1949) (orig. 1938), *Homo Ludens. A Study of the Play Element in Culture*, London: Routledge and Kegan Paul.

Kinsley, D.R. (1979) *The Divine Player. A Study of Kṛiṣṇalīlā*, Delhi: Motilal Barnassidas.

Lanternari, V. (1988) 'Fra natura e cultura' (Between nature and culture), *Mondoperaio* 12: 109–36.

Le Breton, D. (1991) *Passion du risque* (The passion of risk), Paris: Métailié.

Lebra, T.S. (1976) *Japanese Patterns of Behaviour*, Honolulu: University of Hawaii Press.

Linhart, S. (1986) '*Sakariba*: zone of "evaporation" between work and home?' in J. Hendry (ed.) *Interpreting Japanese Society*, London: Routledge, pp. 231–42.

Linhart, S. (1988) 'From industrial to post-industrial society: changes in Japanese leisure-related values and behaviour', *Journal of Japanese Studies* 14 (2): 271–307.

Linhart, S. and Frustuck, S. (eds) (1998) *The Culture of Japan as Seen Through its Leisure*, Albany, NY: SUNY Press.

Loy, J.W. (ed.) (1982) *The Paradoxes of Play*, West Point, NY: Leisure Press.

MacClancy, J. (ed.) (1996) *Sport, Identity and Ethnicity*, Oxford: Berg.

Mergen, B. (ed.) (1986) *Cultural Dimensions of Play, Games and Sport*, Champaign, IL: Human Kinetics Publishers.

Needham, R. (1981) 'Inner states as universals', in *Circumstantial Deliveries*, Berkeley, CA: University of California Press, pp. 53–71.

Neumann J. von and Morgenstern, O. (1944) *Theory of Games and Economic Behaviour*, Princeton, NJ: Princeton University Press.

Nishiyama M. (1997) *Edo Culture. Daily Life and Diversions in Urban Japan, 1600–1868*, Honolulu: University of Hawaii Press.

Norbeck, E. (1977) 'Johan Huizinga and modern anthropology', in D.F. Lancy and B.A. Tindall (eds) *The Study of Play: Problems and Prospects*, West Point, N.Y.: Leisure Press, pp. 13–22.

Prebish, C. (1993) *Religion and Sport: The Meeting of the Sacred and Profane*, London: Greenwood Publishers.

Raveri, M. (2000) '*Le vie di liberazione e di immortalità*' (The paths to liberation and immortality), in G. Filoramo, M. Massenzio, M. Raveri, P. Scarpi, *Manuale di Storia delle Religioni* (History of religions), Rome-Bari: Laterza, pp. 298–436.

Rohlen, T.P. (1974) *For Harmony and Strength: Japanese White-Collar Organization in Anthropological Perspective*, Berkeley, CA: University of California Press.

Sax, W. (ed.) (1995) *The Gods at Play. Līlā in South Asia*, New York: Oxford University Press.

Scholz-Cionca, S. (ed.) 1998, *Japan. Reich der Spiele* (Japan. The empire of play), Munich: Iudicium Verlag.

Sutton-Smith, B. (1977) 'Towards an anthropology of play', in P. Stevens Jr. (ed.) *Studies in the Anthropology of Play. Papers in Memory of B. Allan Tindall*, New York: Leisure Press, pp. 222–32.

Sutton-Smith, B. (ed.) (1979) *Play and Learning*, New York: Gardner Press.

Taylor, I. (1998) 'Contradictory aspects of contemporary football', in *The New Economics of World Football, FIFA Conference*, Paris: International Media Centre.

Turner, V. (1983) 'Liminal to liminoid in play, flow and ritual: an essay in comparative symbology', in J. Harris and R. Park (eds) *Play, Games, and Sports in Cultural Context*, Champaign IL: Human Kinetics Publishers, pp. 123–64.

Turner, V. (1983) 'Play and drama: the horns of a dilemma', in F.E. Manning (ed.) *The World of Play*, West Point, NY: Leisure Press, pp. 217–24.

Tylor, E.B. (1871) *Primitive Culture. Researches into the Development of Mythology, Philosophy, Religion, Language, Art and Custom*, London: J. Murray.

Verden P. and Sewart, J.J. (1986) 'Trash-sport: socio-cultural implications of the pursuit of thrills, fame and fortune', *TAASP Newsletter*, XII, 2, Winter, pp. 18–23.

Vogel, E.F. (1963) *Japan's New Middle Class*, Berkeley, CA: University of California Press.

Whiting, R. (1977) *The Chrysanthemum and the Bat. The Game Japanese Play*, Tokyo: The Permanent Press.

Whiting, R. (1989) *You Gotta Have 'Wa'*, New York: Vintage Books.

Wittgenstein, L. (1968) *Philosophical Investigations*, translated by G.E.M. Anscombe, Oxford: Blackwell.

1 The Japanese tattoo

Play or purpose?

Joy Hendry

Introduction

The tattoo is associated with play in many countries, and this frivolity has recently spilt over into Japan in a big way, especially among young people. In Japan, tattooing has a deadly serious side too, however. Defining the boundaries of play is a difficult enterprise, of course. One person's play is another's toil, and 'play' often incorporates a serious purpose beneath the apparent fun. Moreover, activities that amuse members of one society, or one sector of a wider society, may well offend a different one. The association between play and tattooing is highly ambiguous in Japan, complicated by a global resurge of interest in the subject, and this chapter will seek to explore the meaning of this curious example of Japanese playfulness.

Japanese tattooing attracts the attention of artists far and wide for its beauty, and for the skills of its creation. Although tattoos are found in various parts of the world, in various degrees of elaboration, the Japanese version is undoubtedly among the most aesthetically developed. Years ago historian of tattooing, W.D. Hambly, wrote, 'no other style can compare in colour, form, motion, or light and shade of background' (1925: 312; cf. Morris and Marsh 1988: 84), yet the reaction of many Japanese people to the whole idea of tattooing is still negative. A friend with whom I was staying when I began this investigation, in 1991, looked sickened when I mentioned the subject. Others warned me very seriously against it.

The two opposing attitudes stand, of course, for different points of view, and there are several others that could be mentioned, but they introduce the theme by way of epitomizing the ambivalence that surrounds the nature of Japanese tattoos and the people who wear them. A Japanese tattoo, in its full glory, covers the back and several other adjoining parts of the body. It depicts folk heroes, religious figures and a variety of flora and fauna, outlined, first in the blue-black of ink beneath the skin, and then coloured in with a combination of brilliant dyes. There is usually a main character depicted on the back, but the design will be picked up, or offset, with other smaller figures on the arms, chest and thighs. More limited Western-style tattoos, sometimes called '*wan-pointo*', though they may cover several square inches of flesh, have recently gained popularity.

All this is often entirely obscured by clothes, however, and people with tattoos are barred from many public bathhouses, so the full effect may be reserved for a privileged few on a limited number of occasions. Some of these occasions are specifically associated with 'play', such as a contemporary example found in 'club culture', where it is possible to admire tattoos that glow in their full glory only under ultra-violet light.[1] Other such occasions are far more serious in their purpose and may indicate quite sinister intent. Let us first examine some of the historical reasons for this propensity to hide what may in effect be works of art little different from the famous Japanese woodblock prints liberally on display in galleries around the world.

A short history of tattooing in Japan[2]

First mention of Japanese tattooing is to be found in the third-century Chinese chronicle, the *Wei Chih*, where the Japanese, 'the Wa', are described as follows:

> men, young and old, all tattoo their faces and decorate their bodies with designs
> . . . The Wa, who are fond of diving into water to get fish and shells, also
> decorated their bodies in order to keep away large fish and waterfowl.
>
> (McCallum 1988:114)[3]

Later reports emphasize the decorative nature of the designs, rather than their protective qualities, and the fact that the position and size of the patterns indicated differences of rank (*ibid.*).

However, the Chinese disapproved of tattooing, and indeed any puncturing of the skin, and in the first Japanese chronicles, which were written from the seventh century, it was evident that these Chinese attitudes had been adopted in Japan too. References to tattooing in the *Nihonshoki*, for example, were about its use as a form of punishment and showed indications of the barbarism and savagery it was supposed to represent. Otherwise, tattoos were associated particularly with the people who inhabited the peripheries of Japan, namely the Ainu, who tattooed their faces and arms, and the Okinawans who tattooed their hands and feet (McCallum 1988: 116–7).

For mainland Japanese, over the centuries, tattooing was used as a punishment for heinous crimes such as murder, betrayal and treason. It was also used to brand slaves and to distinguish groups of outcast people. Such tattoos seem to have been much more limited in size and elaboration, however, composed merely of a line or a series of lines, depending on the severity of the punishment. In a 1716 code, tattooing was associated with relatively minor offences such as 'flattery with ulterior motives' (van Gulik 1982: 10), fraud and extortion, and there is some evidence to suggest that by this time people with tattoos had begun to band together and also to have more elaborate tattoos done over the ones which marked their catalogue of crimes. Tattooing as a punishment was finally abolished in 1870 (*ibid.*: 12).

During the Edo period (1600–1868), tattooing became evident in the context of play, with reference in the writings of Ihara Saikaku, and depictions of the full-body tattoo in the wood block prints of Utamaru (Richie and Buruma 1980: 14–21). It seems to have flourished in the pleasure quarters, first in a small way as a mole or a name – for a concubine to pledge devotion and loyalty to her master, likely as not

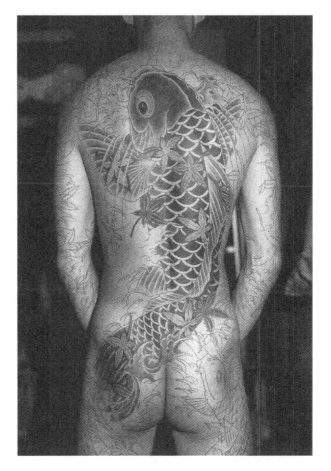

Figure 1.1 A full-body Japanese tattoo, with main theme on the back, picked up again on other parts of the body. This example is a *koi* (carp), and illustrates the process of making a complete 'canvas' before gradually filling in the colour. As the bearer of such a tattoo moves, the fishes depicted on his body may appear to be swimming

married officially elsewhere (*ibid*. cf. McCallum 1988: 118) – and then as a kind of full-body rejection of the wider, highly organized society into which some people just did not fit. Those with tattoos would be in clearly marginal positions: the wandering samurai with no leader, second sons of merchants with no business to inherit, or people associated with transition such as palanquin bearers, firefighters and construction workers.

Many commentators point to a connection between full body tattoos of the time with the Suikoden, a Japanese translation of the fourteenth-century Chinese story now known in English as the Water Margin, legendary tales of a Robin Hood type figure called Sung Chiang and his 108 followers. These stories were popularized in

Japanese in ninety volumes by Bakin, illustrated by Hokusai and, later, with even more impact, in 108 individual prints by Kuniyoshi.[4] Some of the favourite characters wore splendid tattoos, and several of these characters have since been chosen as the centrepiece of tattoos in real life.

During this period, tattoos were actually banned several times, along with restrictions on other activities such as *kabuki*, woodblock prints and elaborate clothes, in the repeated official condemnation of the world of pleasure. In response, merchants developed elaborate linings for their austere coats, subtly to display their wealth, and others expressed their rejection of the rules by elaborately decorating their bodies, which they then concealed with clothes. The wider society disapproved – partly expressing a notion of sin attached to the piercing of the skin – but like the outlawed heroes of the popular legends, those with tattoos may well have seen themselves as forces for good in an overly authoritative world.

One group of people who wore tattoos, and whose designs distinguished their particular associations, were the firefighters of the time. They were, of course, absolutely vital because of the serious threat fire was and is in a country where most of the houses are built of wood, but they were a rough and rowdy crowd, and ordinary people were wary of them. Nevertheless they provided an important service, and tattooed or not, people were obliged to seek their help. This relationship typifies the ambiguous attitude of the wider society to tattooing, and the marginal position those with tattoos often held.

From 1868, under a perceived notion of Western disapproval, tattooing was again prohibited as a barbarous custom and many of the chapbooks used by the artists were forcibly burnt. However, foreigners often liked the tattoos they saw and they even sought out people with tattoos to employ as palanquin bearers. Furthermore the tattoo artists began to receive foreign customers, some as illustrious as King George V of England, when he was Duke of York, and Nicholas II of Russia, when he was Tsarevitch, cousins who were serving together a period as sailors (Brain 1979: 52; McCallum 1988: 124). In fact, many European tattoo artists have been influenced by Japanese techniques and designs since that time, some even travelling to Japan to learn more about them.

In Japan itself, tattooing remained prohibited until 1945, but several groups of people continued to practise it covertly. The various skills had been divided between different artists, as with woodblock printing, but during this period individual artists learnt to master all the techniques required in order to diminish the likelihood of revealment. Unlike in Europe, their customers were not soldiers and sailors, who were rather part of mainstream society, but members of the underworld and people in other marginal positions.

After the Second World War, tattooing became associated particularly with the *yakuza*, or gangsters of the Japanese mafia, who themselves carry a some-what ambiguous image – partly of terror, partly romantic, through their por-trayal in films and television dramas, and their self-styled chivalrous path of *ninkyōdo* (see, for example, Kaplan and Dubro 1986; Raz 1992). Their activities are definitely associated with the world of play, but in forbidden arenas of gam-bling, prostitution, protection and drugs. There are other occupational groups who are said to wear tattoos, such as construction workers, steeplejacks, *sushi*-makers and prostitutes, but the predominant image was until very recently with the *yakuza*.

Since I first presented this chapter at the Berlin conference in 1991, tattoos have become increasingly popular with young people in Japan, many of whom choose Western motifs, which are thereby distinguished from the more traditional Japanese variety and apparently carry less opprobrium. They are called 'tattoo', using the English word, and some artists confine their work to these smaller examples of the genre, offering a range pretty much like those found in Western countries. Their clients are influenced by Western rock artists who sport tattoos, and one of my Japanese students mentioned the US band *Motley Crüe* as having inspired his own interest. The main focus of this chapter is concerned with the more specifically Japanese tattoos, however.

A contemporary impression

With this historical overview as background, I would like to turn now, first, to the world of tattooing as I observed it during a period of field research in 1991, and from that albeit very limited experience, examine some of the rationale behind its practice. My contacts in this world were rather few, but they were good ones in the sense that they were extremely co-operative. As might be expected, there were no official figures about the numbers of people involved, but estimates of my contacts put the number of artists in Japan at that time between 120 and 300, mostly men, and mostly located in a few urban centres.

At that time, there was no advertising, very few entries in the yellow pages, and the artists hung no signboards over their studios. In the last few years of the 1990s artists specializing in Western tattoos began to appear and advertise themselves quite openly on the streets of many Japanese cities, but in order to meet my best informant in 1991, things were a little clandestine. A personal introduction from an artist in Oxford provided me only with a telephone number, and when I called I was instructed to take a taxi from the nearest station to a specific street corner, where I should phone again. I was then collected by the *deshi* (apprentice), who led me through several back streets and eventually up an outside staircase into a first-floor apartment.

There are two chief words for tattooing in Japanese. The first, *irezumi*, literally the insertion (*ire*) of ink (*sumi*), is the one associated with punishment and the general disgust of the wider public for the practice. The second, *horimono*, is based on the verb *horu*, to engrave, puncture or incise, also used for carving, engraving and sculpture, so that this word has much more positive, artistic connotations. The character for *horu* appears in the adopted names of the artists. Some examples are Horicho, Horiuno, Horibun and Horigoro, names that are passed on through the generations. The one I found in the first-floor apartment was Horiyoshi III, a man who by the end of the decade was to become probably one of the best regarded tattoo artists in the world. A photograph on the wall depicted his predecessor and mentor, Horiyoshi I.

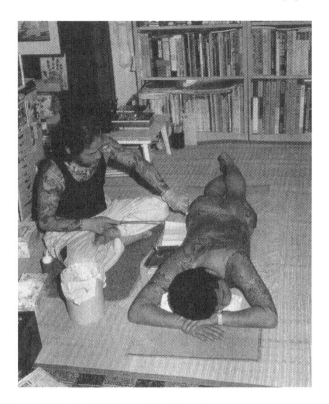

Figure 1.2 The artist Horiyoshi III at work in his studio

Horiyoshi III claimed to have some 2000 clients, on whose bodies he was working, but he had by then completed 20 full-body tattoos and these customers met two or three times a year, with the artist, in a sort of reunion. A photograph of this group also hung on the artist's wall, alongside a polished plaque with the names of some of his earliest creations, who apparently purchased it for him as a way of showing their gratitude. The *deshi* described the feelings of these men in buying the plaque almost in terms of worship, and neither argued when I suggested that the artist was on his way to becoming a sort of *kami-sama* (deity).[5] It certainly became clear when I asked if I could photograph his work, and therefore the bodies of his clients, that the decision to allow me was his, totally without reference to the canvas, except where I asked!

The process of acquiring a full-body tattoo is a long and complicated one requiring between 150 and 200 hours of work, usually carried out at the rate of one or two hours weekly and costing (in 1991) some 10,000 yen a time, adding up to a total basic cost in the region of 2 million yen. It is thus not a project to be undertaken lightly, and a potential customer must first be introduced to the artist and make a request to be tattooed. If they seem serious enough, a discussion will follow to plan the design, using books with adaptations of illustrations from popular stories and legends, perhaps some existing sketches, and a series of flower designs for the peripheries.

During one afternoon, I saw a girl dump-truck driver have her first outline of a Kannon imprinted on her back, a man have his fifth session on a huge tiger, another have some colouring work done on a collection of nine carp swimming all over his torso, and a period of detailed colouring-in carried out on the bottom of a man whose shoulders and back already displayed a solid array of intricate design. During this time, the *deshi* was busily drawing up his own collection of designs inspired by the library of books. A particular advantage of this artist's studio, however, was a record he had kept of the names, ages, occupations and other details of his clients for the previous two years, including their motivation, and reasons for choosing a particular design. This he allowed me to study.

I was struck already then by the predominance of youth amongst the ages. Most of the clients were in their late teens or early twenties, so this did not seem to be a dying art.[6] The occupations were not surprising: the vast majority had entered *jiyūgyō*, apparently a euphemism for *yakuza*, with the odd driver, carpenter, construction worker and 'hostess'. Approximately one-fifth of the clients had relatives with tattoos; most of the others had become interested in the idea in their teens. Their stated motivations, and reasons for choice, were largely playful: *kakkoii kara* (they are 'cool' or 'cute'), *sukidatta kara* (because I like them), *geijutsu to omou kara* (I think they are artistic), *oshare toshite* (personal adornment), although a few were more directed in that they followed a family resemblance, or expressed a religious conviction.

The clients were friendly enough, but at least on this first occasion, they were not particularly talkative. They were not exactly reticent, but they tended to defer to the artist, who suggested that a strong motivation for acquiring tattoos also included the idea of strengthening one's psychological or spiritual outlook (*seishin*), which they conceded was a factor.

A former member of a *bōsōzoku* biker gang I interviewed more recently confirmed this theory, saying that he decided to have some tattooing to make him look tough, and although he knew he was the same, it made him feel stronger, as well as commanding respect among his friends and associates. His mother was deeply disapproving, however, and it took him two years to confess to his father what he had done. At the time of our interview he had not told his grandmother about his adornment at all, though it covers his shoulders and part of his back, and is clearly visible when he wears a T-shirt. As for the mother of his girlfriend, she was trying to persuade him to have the tattooing removed.

Another informant, a publisher who specializes in books and magazines about tattooing, himself boasting of a complete full-body design, reported on the negative effect he had caused when he was admitted to hospital. However, he noted that for *yakuza* who spend time in prison, tattoos are a form of protection, and some will try to speed up the acquisition of their tattoos if they are likely to be convicted of a crime. He claimed that they would then not only be admired by the other prisoners, but looked after by the guards, who would not want to spoil the work!

The designs and their meaning

An examination of some of the designs chosen will at this point shed further light on the attraction of tattoos, for the central figures are very often characters who display or displayed qualities which are highly prized in certain areas of Japanese society. Often mythical figures, they sometimes had special abilities. Chōgoro Konjin, for example, was known for defeating demons, Harunosuke Aoyage could change himself into a snake, and Kinnosuke Hime-matsuri learnt to fly (Morita 1966: 115). The popular Robin Hood style heroes of the Water Margin stories were brave and stoical, demonstrating qualities of perseverance and steadfastness, prized for boys throughout Japan.

Dragons were popular with the firefighters of the nineteenth century because of their dual associations: with fire, but also with water, in particular, rain clouds and thunder. They are seen as opposed to danger and therefore acting as a protective force for the firemen. The Dutch anthropologist, Van Gulik, carried out a detailed structural analysis of dragon symbolism, seeing it as a mediator between life and death, and a reconciler of opposites, notably fire and water, in the manner of yin and yang. For the owners of dragon tattoos, then, these benevolent creatures were thought to confer strength, wisdom, wholeness and bravery (1982: 115–78), and this is the motif chosen by the 'biker' mentioned above. The dragon, or parts of it, also seems to appeal to Western tattoo artists and their customers.

Another popular beast to be seen in tattoos is the colourful Japanese carp, or *koi*. This is also associated with strength and stoicism, for the fish is said to climb waterfalls, swim against the current, and, when caught, to lie unflinching on the cutting board, bravely awaiting its fate. It is depicted in the huge flags which hang above houses in late April and May, announcing to the world that a baby boy has been born to the family, for its qualities are those which it is hoped the boy will emulate as it grows up. Sometimes the carp in tattoos is seen ridden by a small boy, known as Kintarō, or Koitarō, another popular mythical character whose strength is great despite his diminutive size.

Another category of figures is religious, very often associated with Buddhism. Fudō, for example, is the guardian of hell, a fierce-looking figure surrounded with flames, and wielding a sword to smite down his enemies and a length of rope with which to bind them up. As Donald Richie argues in his book about tattooing, however, Fudō is not bad, like the imps and devils of Western tattooing. He is a force for good, a guardian of morals who punishes transgressors. He may live in a bad neighbourhood, but he works hard for a good cause. He may be ugly, but he is good at heart. Richie suggests that some of the Japanese who sport tattooed bodies may see themselves in a similar light (Richie and Buruma 1980: 49).

Japanese women who wear tattoos are often associated with men who do the same. The wives of the artists provide some especially fine examples. There are even cases where a couple will ask to have their tattoos co-ordinated so that the picture will only be complete when they are locked in an embrace. Kintarō's mother is a figure sometimes chosen by a woman, perhaps engaged in the act of breast feeding her son (Morita 1966: 25). As motherhood is held in high regard amongst

Figure 1.3 Horiyoshi's *deshi* (apprentice) carefully preparing designs later to be used in tattoos

Japanese women, this parallels the choice of male qualities for men's tattoos, and the case of Kintarō's mother is even more appropriate since it is especially desired to be the mother of a successful boy. The Kannon chosen by the female dump truck driver mentioned above is a Buddhist figure, known as the Goddess of Mercy, particularly worshipped by women.

Tattoos undoubtedly have erotic overtones as well, however. The famous Tanizaki novel about tattooing, *The Tattooer*, is a particularly sado-masochistic story which illustrates this tendency, but there are references in several other literary works as well. The wider world may disapprove of tattooing, but there is a hint of the attraction of forbidden fruit about it. The publisher mentioned above gave me a collection of photographs he had prepared in the form of a brochure, each depicting a tattooed girl in an erotic pose, complete with a name and telephone number. He noted also that girls with tattoos are a special feature of some soapland establishments.

Play or purpose?

What then can be concluded from this summary consideration of the subject of the Japanese tattoo? It is evidently associated with play in several respects, but it is clear that we need to look further than the *kakkoii kara* explanation of motivation for a full understanding. Within the underworld, I have little experience to draw upon, but a tattoo is evidently a source of some considerable power and status, as we saw in the case of the former biker, who explained that many members of his group 'graduated' to the *yakuza*. We have also discussed the case of the prison inmate, but

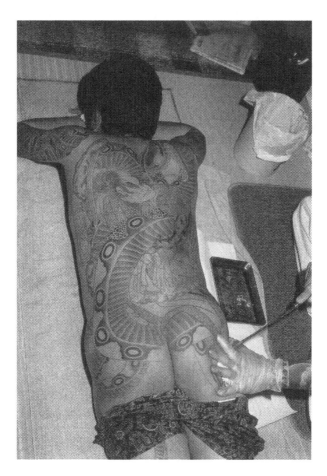

Figure 1.4 Detail of the tattooing process

in the wider world, its essentially hidden nature, and the generally ambiguous attitude towards it, allows tremendous potential for the impact of sudden revealment.

Owners of tattoos may also display overt aspects of status and rank within their own circles, just as political leaders have done at other times and in other societies of the world (see, for example, Gell 1993). Jacob Raz has identified a list of what the ownership of a tattoo signifies for the *yakuza*: first, it is part of an initiation rite to enter the order; second, it is proof of perseverance and manliness to go through the painful process and third, it demonstrates the irreversibility of entering the *yakuza* world, and fourth it provides a trade mark to bear on the body (Raz 1992: 219). In recent times, a symbol of the particular *gumi* (branch) is very often included in the design, just as a symbol of the fire-fighting group used to be in the past.

According to the publisher referred to above, however, there are some further, more subtle distinctions to be made within the world of tattoo owners. His opinion, of course, represents only one view, but he explained that a tattoo with some space showing, known as a *dannabori*, is of a higher class (*hin ga aru*) than a more solid one, in the same way that space is regarded as an essential part of other forms of Japanese art. He added that for some people the acquisition of improvements becomes a kind of addictive pleasure, so that knowing when to stop is a demonstration of taste, restraint and therefore some refinement. A *nukibori*, or partial tattoo, sometimes in a totally Western style,[7] has a completely different meaning, although always expressing something of the rejection of the wider moral order since one damages the body received from one's parents.

Amongst the *yakuza*, however, he notes that the *oyabun* are often free of tattoos, and their children would not need to run out and get them. It is the lower orders who find it useful to express their commitment in this way. It is like a uniform, he added, though Raz reports that only about half of the *tekiya* (gangsters who set up stalls at festivals) he worked with felt the need to wear one (personal communication). It would be interesting to know whether there are alternative ways to acquire the same kind of status.

As for the tattoo artists, themselves, the ones I met did not seem to agree with the publisher's view, nor did they even make much effort to hide their decorated bodies. Horiyoshi III, for example, had solid tattooing right down to his wrists and, again, creeping appealingly up his neck beneath his longish hair, and he is among the best respected in Japan, according to several informants, not including his clients. This man clearly loved his work, with a joy and intensity that could also qualify it as 'play' (cf. Rodríguez's chapter in this volume), and he regarded his skill as highly creative. When not engaged in earning his living, he amused himself by decorating the bodies of his wife and assistant, a budding successor in case his still young son did not inherit his enthusiasm.[8]

My research on this subject is been very limited, and it would be interesting to find out a lot more about the possibilities of communication within the world of the tattooed, but my guess is that the game goes on. In anthropological terms, tattooing is itself symbolic of marginality, since the puncturing of the boundary between the inside and the outside of the body is a metaphor for the breaking down of parallel boundaries between inside and outside within the wider society. In Japanese society this is a boundary which is particularly marked in all sorts of ways (see Hendry 1995; Bachnik and Quinn 1994), so the metaphor is likely to be very powerful.

Those who are particularly associated with tattoos in Japan – the *yakuza* – are certainly marginal by the standards of the wider society, and the ambiguity of their roles is in keeping with the liminal position they inhabit. But others who choose to be tattooed could similarly be rejecting the world in which they live – playful young rebels, such as members of the biker *bōsōzoku*, who make noise too to express their revolt, artists whose work keeps them outside an establishment they may feel is ossified, women employed in industries surrounding 'play' and entertainment instead of bringing up children in tightly-knit families, even construction workers, whose lives are especially subject to the vagaries of economic change.

As the author of a splendid book of colour photographs of Japanese tattoos has commented, they represent 'power bestowed at the price of submission', and 'elegance obtained by way of violence' (Fellman 1986: 12). Although the wider society represents the tattooed as somehow outside the boundaries of acceptable behaviour, they also carry on their bodies living illustrations of the legends, mythology and symbolism of the whole nation. As one writer puts it 'their bodies are a living showcase of Japanese mythology' (Macintyre 1981: 149). Perhaps the very ambiguity of tattoos provides a purpose in helping to define an alternative world of play, where they have some quite specific roles in delineating a discourse of power which goes beyond the too-oft discussed rhetoric of economics.

Notes

1 I would like to thank Helena Burton (2001) for much useful information relating to tattooing in early twenty-first century Japan, especially in 'club culture' and other areas of which I have no experience at all. I am also indebted to my student, Shigeto Tsujii, whose explanations of his experiences contributed greatly to my contemporary understanding of the subject.

2 The best source I have found for the history of tattooing is Van Gulik 1982, but this section is derived from several sources including McCallum 1988, and Richie and Buruma 1980.

3 Van Gulik (1982: 246–9) has a detailed discussion about the context and interpretation of this source.

4 One of Kuniyoshi's prints was reproduced on the cover of my book *Wrapping Culture* (Hendry 1993).

5 Since that time, the artist's reputation has grown and grown. He is singled out in a recent American publication (Kitamura and Kitamura 2001), his photograph attracted a Japanese student to my university who was surprised that we should know such an eminent person, and, sadly, a student who recently tried to gain an interview with him was turned away. I would like to thank Lionel Titchener at the Tattoo Museum in Oxford for putting me in touch with Horiyoshi III. With hindsight, I am sure that his introduction was more valuable than I realized at the time.

6 This would also seem to contradict Kaplan and Dubro's idea (1981: 274) that young *yakuza* are restricting themselves to much smaller Western-style tattoos – but this research was carried out before the 1992 changes in the law with regard to gangs, and things may have changed again now.

7 Another of my informants in 1991 had enough work to specialize entirely in Western-style tattoos, however, so this was clearly a growing fashion.

8 According to Kitamura and Kitamura (2001), his son has now been designated as Horiyoshi IV.

Bibliography

Bachnik, J. and Quinn, C. (1994) *Situated Meaning: Inside and Outside in Japanese Self, Society and Language*, Princeton NJ: Princeton University Press.

Brain, R. (1979) *The Decorated Body*, London: Hutchinson.

Burton, H. (2001) 'Oriental Irezumi and occidental tattooing in contemporary Japan', unpublished undergraduate dissertation, Oxford University.

Ebin, V. (1979) *The Body Decorated*, London: Thames and Hudson.

Fellman, S. (1986) *The Japanese Tattoo*, New York: Abbeville Press.

Gell, A. (1993) *Wrapping in Images*, Oxford: Clarendon Press.

Hambly, W.D. (1925) *The History of Tattooing and its Significance*, London: Witherby.

Hendry, J. (1993) *Wrapping Culture: Politeness, Presentation and Power in Japan and Other Societies*, Oxford: Clarendon Press.

Hendry, J. (1995) *Understanding Japanese Society*, London: Routledge.

Kaplan, D.E. and Dubro, A. (1986) *Yakuza: The Explosive Account of Japan's Criminal Underworld*, Reading, MA: Addison-Wesley.

Kitamura, T. and Kitamura, K. (2001) *Bushido: Legacies of the Japanese Tattoo*, Atglen, PA: Schiffer.

Liggett, J. (1974) *The Human Face*, London: Constable.

McCallum, D. (1988) 'Historical and cultural dimensions of the tattoo in Japan', in A. Rubin (ed.) *Marks of Civilization: Artistic Transformation of the Human Body*, Los Angeles, CA: University of California, Museum of Cultural History, pp. 109–34.

Macintyre, M. (1981) *The Shogun Inheritance: Japan and the Legacy of the Samurai*, London: Collins.

Morita, I. (1966) *Irezumi: Japanese Tattooing* (in Japanese with English introduction by D. Richie), Tokyo: Zuhushinsha.

Morris, D. and Marsh, P. (1988) *Tribes*, London: Pyramid Books.

Raz, J. (1992) 'Self-presentation and performance in the yakuza way of life: fieldwork with a Japanese underworld Group', in R. Goodman and K. Refsing (eds) *Ideology and Practice in Modern Japan*, London: Routledge.

Richie, D. and Buruma, I. (1980) *The Japanese Tattoo*, New York and Tokyo: Weatherhill.

Van Gulik, W.R. (1982) *Irezumi: The Pattern of Dermatography in Japan*, Leiden: E.J. Brill.

2 Interpreting the world as a *ken* game

Sepp Linhart

Sake should be *kenzake*

Sake wa kenzake	*Sake* should be *kenzake*
iroshina wa	but there are various methods:
kairu hitohyoko mihyokohyoko	The frog jumps one, two, three,
hebi nura nura	the snake comes slippery.
nameku de mairimasho	Let us try with the slug!
/ sore / janjaka janjaka janken na	Dingdong dingdong – stone *ken*!
basama ni	It was by his old mother,
Watōnai ga shikarareta	that Watōnai was scolded.
tora wa hauhau	The tiger comes a-crawling
totetsuruten	to the sound of the *shamisen*.
kitsune de sā kinase	Now come with the fox!

This song may seem difficult to understand, but it forms the core of the short *kabuki* interlude *Warau kado niwaka no shichifuku*, written by Sakurada Jisuke III (1802–77) and first performed at the Kawarazaki theatre at Edo on the twelfth of the first month of the year Kōka 4 (1847). The performance by Matsumoto Kōshirō VI (also Kinshō, 1812–49) as boatman, Ichikawa Kyūzō II (1800–71) as *manzai* dancer and Nakamura Utaemon IV (1798–1852) as bath house servant met with such success that it was played continuously for 95 days. According to the *Kōgai zeisetsu*, which describes manners and customs from 1789 to 1859, 'This funny *ken* . . . was so popular, that single-sheet prints were issued, and many variations of the song were made' (Jinyaō 1970: 273). Saitō Gesshin in his famous Edo chronology *Bukō nenpyō* states: 'The spring play at the Kawarazaki theatre brought forward a dance with *mushiken*, *kitsuneken* and *toraken*, and people everywhere imitated it at parties' (Saitō 1968: 111).

A more lively description of the enthusiasm during the spring months of 1847 is contained in the famous diary of Fujiokaya Yūzō:

> Kōka, year of the sheep, second month
> I also went to see the cherry blossoms in Yoshiwara. At that time the play
> *Totetsuruken* was an overwhelming success at the Kawarazaki theatre in

Figure 2.1 Ken no keiko (*Ken* exercise). Anonymous woodblock print, *ōban* size, probably issued during the first month of 1847. Censors' seals Mera and Murata, hitherto unidentified publisher. This is the first or one of the first *ken* pictures, not signed because of the Tenpō restrictions, but probably drawn by Kuniyoshi. Each one of the three animals stands for a certain actor, as can be easily recognized by features of the face, and actors' crests on their robes. Each animal symbolizes a certain kind of *ken* game, and two animals present a certain pose of the fox *ken*. Nakamura Utaemon IV as a frog represents the *ken* of the small animals while posing as a fox. Matsumoto Kōshirō VI as fox stands for the fox *ken*, while funnily taking on the pose of the hunter who wins over the fox, and Ichikawa Kyūzō II symbolizes the tiger *ken*. His gestures cannot be clearly identified as those of a certain *ken* game.

Saruwakachō. Everybody who came to see the cherry blossoms, old biddies included, considered it a great shame not to know that *ken*. Therefore they bought an exercise book to learn the *Totetsuruken* for 16 *mon*, and all, all those going home practised this *ken* game.

(Suzuki and Koike 3: 128)

The great success obviously motivated the other two big Edo theatres in the next two years to start the season with *ken* interludes too.

Before continuing, a short explanation of *ken*, probably the most popular drinking game of the Edo period, seems appropriate. Actually the dance and song given above also included *janken*, still very important in Japanese society, and therefore contained all four major forms of *sansukumiken* or 'ken of the three who are afraid of one another': *mushiken* or '*ken* of small animals', *janken* or 'stone *ken*', *toraken* or 'tiger *ken*', and finally *kitsuneken* or 'fox *ken*'. All these *ken* variations are based on the same principle. Any of the three figures which one can show with one hand, two hands, or the whole body, is stronger than another one but weaker than the third one. *Mushiken* and *janken* are performed with the right hand only. The snake (forefinger) eats the frog (thumb), which eats the slug (little finger), but the snake never creeps over a trace left by a slug. In *janken* the stone (fist) wins over the scissors (spread thumb and forefinger), but the scissors can cut paper or a *furoshiki* (open hand), which again can be used to wrap a stone. *Kitsuneken* is played while sitting on the floor, and here the fox (two arms held upwards) with his magic power wins over the village headman (*shōya*, kneels in official position), who of course is superior to the hunter (imitates holding a gun), but the hunter has the power to shoot the fox. The most dramatic *ken* is the 'tiger *ken*', in which Coxinga (Watōnai, imitates a warrior holding a lance), the Sino-Japanese pirate of the Ming period, wins over the tiger (crawling on arms and legs), which of course is stronger than Coxinga's mother (going on a stick), but according to the norm of filial piety the mother is superior to Coxinga. All these variations of *ken* apart from *janken*, which seems to be the newest form, were known in Japan in the eighteenth century. With this basic knowledge of *ken*, a game which already in its land of origin, China, was usually played as entertainment at drinking parties, it is no longer difficult to understand the initial song.

My interest in the subject began in 1988 after I read an article by Mitamura Engyo '*Dentō shita Meiji shonen no totetsuruken*', which had been originally published in May 1925. In this interesting essay Engyo gives fourteen examples of single-sheet woodblock prints which were issued between 1847 and 1885, the texts of which were all modelled after the cited *Sake wa kenzake* song (Mitamura 1976). Since this song contains a line *totetsuruten*, which imitates the sound of the *shamisen*, it is also called *Totetsuruken*. Having begun to study the *ken* game shortly before, I became curious why there were so many similar prints and whether there were still other ones, not mentioned by Engyo. In this chapter I would like to give an overview of my search for other pictures and texts, present some examples not mentioned by Engyo, and try to put forward a hypothetical explanation for the immense popularity of the *ken* theme in the time before and after the events usually called the Meiji Restoration (1868).

An overview of *ken* prints in the bakumatsu and early Meiji period

Included in this overview are only the *ken* prints which were obviously in one way or another modelled after the *Sake wa kenzake* song of 1847, but not woodblock prints with *ken* subjects, but without song texts. I found the prints by looking through a great number of published works on *ukiyoe*, by investigating the *ukiyoe* collections of Österreichisches Museum für Angewandte Kunst, Vienna, the National Museum for Ethnology, Leiden, the Royal Museum of Scotland, Edinburgh, the Tokyo Daigaku Shiryō Hensansho, the Tokyo Toritsu Chūō Toshokan, and the Waseda Daigaku Engeki Hakubutsukan.[1] One problem when doing this kind of research is that the *ken* prints of this category were obviously regarded as rather lowly and are therefore hardly ever included in *ukiyoe* collections of European and American art museums. If they are, they are usually not included in publications of representative *ukiyoe* works.

Of the 14 examples given by Engyo, eight are from the period 1847 to 1851, in which the influence of the theatrical performances was probably strongest, one is from 1859, and five are from the Meiji period. In the course of approximately five years since I began this study I have been able to find 148 prints with song texts as well as 28 texts only, for which prints should exist or at least should have existed. They are related to more than 50 different themes and there are many more different texts. Although there are many prints with different pictures but the same text, I found only twice pictures which were identical but had a different text. Of one picture, I located a black and white as well as a colour version.

As for artists, 128 of the prints were signed, 20 were anonymous, and of the signed prints, 82 were designed by artists of the Kuniyoshi school and 39 by those of the Toyokuni III school, two by artists belonging to neither of these schools, while 4 are by artists otherwise unknown, who probably used another name to hide their identity. Three signatures could not be read. Of the 82 prints of the Kuniyoshi school, 44 are by Kuniyoshi himself, and all these were done between 1847 and 1849. Of his pupils Yoshitsuya and Yoshifuji drew at least 9 pictures each; Yoshitora made 6. Yoshiiku designed 5, Yoshikazu 3, Yoshifusa and Yoshimori 2, and Yoshitoyo and Yoshitsuru produced one. Toyokuni III, the great rival of Kuniyoshi, designed at least 16 *ken* pictures, Kunichika 8, Kuniteru and Sadafusa 3 each, Kunimori II 2, Kunimasu, Kunisada II, Kuniteru II and Kunitsuna II 1 each, while Chikashige, pupil of Kunichika, drew 3 pictures. This list is by no means complete. Hitherto unknown or unpublished *ken* pictures may become known in the future, but I stress the fact that the Utagawa Kuniyoshi school with Kuniyoshi in the forefront clearly took the initiative in introducing and promulgating this theme during the bakumatsu period. This is of relevance, as it seems to be clear today that Kuniyoshi was also the artist who initiated the production of the *namazue*, popular prints issued immediately after the great earthquake of Edo in 1855, which praised the earthquake as a great social leveller and for providing good jobs for many of Edo's artisans (Takada 1995). It has also to be added that Kuniyoshi during and after the Tenpō reforms (1842–4) continuously made fun of the various strict measures issued by the authorities against the luxurious consumption behaviour of the town's people by drawing a considerable number of caricatures of these measures. Interestingly, though, he did not come into conflict with the authorities until the landing of Perry in 1853 (Minami 1997: 107–140). The humour, ridicule, and derision in many *ken* pictures thus can be seen in direct relation with Kuniyoshi's civil disobedience. But we also have to note that *ukiyoe*, apart from private editions, were only issued when they promised commercial success. This means that the anti-authoritarian values and attitudes expressed in the *ken* pictures were those of a considerable number of *ukiyoe* consumers in the last years of the Tokugawa and the early years of the Meiji period.

What do I mean by *ken* pictures? What are their common characteristics? Pictures with people involved in a game of *ken* can be traced back as far as 1730. They can usually be categorized as *bijinga*, or 'pictures of female beauties'. In these pictures the game of *ken* is only one of the accessories of the beauties displayed. In the pictures which I define as *ken* pictures, the persons involved in the game are not beautiful women, but all kind of characters, even animals and objects. Often rather than two of them competing, as is the usual number in a *ken* game, three persons are exhibiting the three figures of fox, hunter and village headman of the 'fox *ken*' or the figures of another invented *ken*. The aim of these pictures is not to portray reality or at least idealized reality, but to make the viewer laugh.

Most of the *ken* pictures have a title ending in *ken*. Out of the 148 pictures of my sample they amount to 90. To cite just a few examples: *Dōke kenburiken* (Foolish *ken*-figures *ken*), *Tsuku monoken* (*Ken* of things sticking together), *Dōke okuyama ken* (Foolish *ken* next to the Asakusa Kannon temple), *Yūgureken* (Twilight *ken*), *Dōke Daruma ken* (Foolish Daruma *ken*), *Yoshiwaraken*, *Sangokuken* (*Ken* of the three countries), *Jiisan bā san anesan ryūkōken* (Fashionable granny, grandpa and older sister *ken*, see Figure 2.3), *Sanbutsuken* (*Ken* of the three Buddhas), *Asakusaken*, *Yonaoshiken* (Reforming the world *ken*), *Jishinken* (Earthquake *ken*, see Figure 2.4), *Ryūkōken* (Fashionable *ken*), *Yokohamaken*, *Shin monku senri no tora ken* (Thousand miles tiger *ken* in new words[2]), *hatsuumaken* (*ken* of the first horse-day in the second month), *Ryūkō hashikaken* (Fashionable measles *ken*), *Sangoku abochin-ken* (*Ken of the fools from the three countries*), *Ryūkō oni no me ken* (Fashionable *ken* of the devil's daughter), *Ryūkō kaichō ken* (Fashionable *ken* of temple exhibitions, *Ryūkō usagi ken* (Fashionable rabbit *ken*).

Many titles include words such as *dōke* (crazy, foolish, eight times) or *ryūkō* (popular, fashionable, 28 times), and many of the pictures are signed as *giga*, comic or witty pictures. *Ryūkō* signalizes the potential buyer of the print, that he is marching along with the trend of the time, while the chiffres *dōke* and *giga* make clear to him that he deals with caricatures.

Some prints, 25 in number, are without a title, some (23) have the word *ken* somewhere in the middle of the title, like *Ken no keiko* (*Ken* exercise, see Figure 2.1), *Dōke kenawase* (Foolish *ken* combination), *Dōkeken nandemo kandemo* (Crazy whatsoever *ken*, see Figure 2.2), *Asakusa okuyama dōke kenzake* (Foolish *kenzake* within the Asakusa temple), and some (12) have titles without the word *ken*, but obviously belong to the same genre, like *Shunkyō sannin namayoi* (Three drunkards in spring), *Ryūkō mitsu byōshi* (Fashionable simple triple), *Daijishin* (Big earthquake), *Sannin musume no minage* (Three girls who drowned themselves), *Ekōin kedai ni oite* (Within the Ekōin temple precincts),

Figure 2.2 Dōkeken nandemo kandemo (Crazy whatsoever *ken*). Woodblock print, *ōban* size, signed *matakoto* Ichiyūsai Kuniyoshi *giga* (witty picture, again by Ichiyūsai Kuniyoshi) and red *kiri* seal, probably issued in 1847. Censors' seals Yoshimura and Muramatsu, publisher Ebiya Rinnosuke. Judging from the similarity of the depiction of the three animals in Figure 2.1 we can assume that the anonymous print *Ken no keiko* was also drawn by Kuniyoshi. There exist other prints with the depiction of the same three animals. They can be found on at least three other prints by Kuniyoshi, and on at least one each by his pupils Yoshitora and Yoshitsuya. The latter ones are drawn differently, though.

Neko sanbiki no uta (The song of the three cats), *Tegoma nashi tsume shōgi* (A Japanese chess problem without a captured chessman), *Ryūkō sannin* (Three fashionable people)

Apart from the picture, all prints have song texts, and some have instructions of how the *shamisen* has to be played to accompany the song. Still others contain further instructions of how to dance to the song, giving detailed dancing figures.

As for the illustrations, the most typical ones, as stated, are depicting three persons, animals or things, each of them in one posture of the *kitsuneken* game. In variations there are only three people but no longer in typical *kitsuneken* positions. Other pictures show two people drinking *kenzake* together. And finally there are prints with small dancing figures only. Of the 148 prints which I could check 134 were single-sheet *ukiyoe*, 7 were diptychs (2 anonymous, 4 by Kuniyoshi, 1 by Kunichika) and 7 were triptychs (2 by Kuniyoshi, 1 by Toyokuni III, 4 by Kunichika) which were of course more expensive, but became more common in the Meiji period.

Many prints have nothing to show the year when they were published like a censor's seal of a certain year or a publication date, and the events to which they refer are sometimes obscure. Nevertheless I tried to classify all the prints according to their publication date into four groups: from 1847, when the first prints appeared to the sixth month of 1852, which is the period when no date censor's seals were in use, the seventh month of 1852 to 1859, 1860 to 1869, and 1870 to 1904, when the final print with a *ken* theme on the Russo-Japanese War was published. The outcome is

1847 to 1852.6	84 prints	15.3 prints per year
1852.7 to 1859	21 prints	2.8 prints per year
1860 to 1869	26 prints	2.6 prints per year
1870 to 1904	17 prints	0.5 prints per year

More than half of all the prints were issued during the five-and-half year period, which witnessed the great *ken* boom brought forward by the funny *kabuki* interlude. During the 1850s and 1860s there were time and again certain occasions to publish *ken* prints. These include: the great earthquake of Edo in 1855, the opening of Yokohama to foreigners in 1859, the measles epidemic of 1862, and of course, the Meiji Restoration and the accompanying civil war in 1867/68. Therefore during this period the average number of issued prints hardly decreases. It is only during the Meiji period when woodblock prints entered a stage of crisis, and especially after the war against Satsuma in 1877, that their number decreases significantly. If we count only until 1879, then the yearly average is still 1.3 pictures.

The functions of the prints seem to have been various: some were clearly instructional sheets for songs, texts and melodies, and dances popular from *kabuki* performances. These prints seem to have been issued by various publishers at the same time, often drawn by the same artists. In my sample there are 22 prints of the *Sake wa kenzake* song, 5 anonymous, 7 by Kuniyoshi, 4 by Yoshitora, 2 by Yoshifuji, and 1 each by Yoshitsuru, Yoshitsuya, Sadafusa, and Kuniteru I. The 19 prints with a publisher's logo were from 16 different publishers, which shows that many publishers were eager to issue their own *ken* prints. Of these same 22 prints, 13 contain dance figures and 4 *shamisen* notations. A similiar success as the *Totetsuruken* was the *Sangokuken* (*Ken* of three countries) which was included as a dance in the *kabuki* play *Shinki ikken tori no hatsugoe*, which was successfully performed as first play of the year in Kaei 2 (1849) at the Ichimuraza (Ihara 6: 519). I found 17 prints (11 by Kuniyoshi, 2 each by Yoshifuji and Toyokuni III, 1 by Kunimori, and 1 unidentified), of which 8 prints carry dance figures and 2 *shamisen* accompaniment. Similar examples can be enumerated from other theatre performances. But there are also some other prints with dance figures or *shamisen* notations, like the *Neko sanbiki no uta* by Yoshifuji from around 1850, the *Shinkyoku teisei hyōban Yokohama tora ken* by Yoshiiku from 1860, the *Ryūkōken no zu* by Yoshitora from the time of the measles of 1862, the *Ryūkō oni no me ken* by Yoshimori from 1867, and the *Ryūkō tora ken* by Kunichika from 1869. Some of these seem to have a very similar function to the German *Bänkelgesang*, ballads which report in a funny way recent sensational events that were thought to be of interest for many people.

Another group of prints is formed by those which imitate other *ken* songs, the so-called variations (*kaeuta*). These *kaeuta* sound very funny for those who know the original text, as for example, when a song imitating *sake wa kenzake* (*sake* has to be *kenzake*) starts with *take wa kanchiku* (bamboo has to be solid bamboo, Figure 2.2). This art of funny imitation was highly developed in the *gesaku* literature and was especially popular at the end of the Edo period as the so-called *jiguchi*. Of course, it makes many of the *ken* prints difficult to interpret, because today we do not have the knowledge of an average Edo citizen of the 1850s.

A third group of prints deals with events of great importance for society, like earthquakes, epidemics or political changes. They belong to one of the three groups of prints commonly called

1   *namazue* which appeared in 1855 immediately after the big earthquake in Edo, about which Ouwehand has already reported briefly (1964);
2   *hashikae* which describe the measles epidemics of 1862, recently analysed by Rotermund (1991, 1995);
3   *awatee*, pictures dealing with social and political events from 1862 until the Meiji Restoration (Yoshida 1974: 1:37–8).

The last group has the same function as *kawaraban*, the modern newspapers. Interesting events are reported on woodblock prints with texts and illustrations. It seems that to make the news still more interesting, some artists or publishers published them in the form of *ken* pictures. Needless to say, this categorization is not unilineal. There are many areas of overlap. Therefore, it is rather a grouping for convenience's sake than one based on clear-cut logical principles.

It seems that in Japan nobody cared about the *ken* prints after Mitamura Engyo who himself interpreted them only as a curiosity. None of the standard reference works for *ukiyoe* makes mention of them, even though the notion of *ken* picture, *ken no e*, was already in existence in popular Japanese language during the late Edo period, as can be seen from a verse in a *chonkina* song of 1860:

Hangi suru hangi suru	A printing plate is printed, is printed
han han hangi suru	A prin-, prin-, printing plate is printed

han wa nani o suru	What is to be printed?
ke ken no ken no e da	It is a *ken*, a *ken*, a *ken* picture!

(Linhart 1992a: 287)

Some examples of *ken* prints and songs

Roughly one month after the dance *Sake wa kenzake* had been successfully performed at the Kawarazakiza, the arrogant *samurai* Nonoyama Shikibu, after demanding an umbrella from a young apprentice passing by when it started raining, was decapitated at Misujichō, Asakusa, by Iijima Kasan, who wanted to help the youth and for this deed became very famous. According to the *Fujiokaya nikki* shortly after this murderous case a print with the following text appeared:

Sake wa kennon inkyosan	*Sake* is dangerous, old man.
kubi wa hitohyoko mihyokohyoko	The head jumps one, two, three
chi wa nuranura	and the blood is streaming.
kenshi de mairimasho	Let's go with the sword fighter!
ame wa zarazara zanzara da	The rain rains *zarazara*,
tokoro wa Asakusa Misujichō	the place is Misuji in Asakusa.
goban e sā kinase	Come all to number 5!

(Suzuki and Koike 3: 126)

Two weeks later two thieves broke into the Daishū temple in Edo to steal the eyes of a five-metre high Enma figure, but unfortunately for them one fell down from the big statue and his companion became so afraid that he called for help whereupon many people came and the thieves were caught. At least three different prints were issued to report this happening, all showing Enma, a temple priest and the thief playing *ken*. The accompanying text runs as follows:

Sate wa Enma no me o tori ni	Only to take the eyes from Enma
hairu hito koso shiyoko shiyoko to	thousands of people enter.
yoru sorosoro menuki ni mairiyasho	Let's come again at night to take it!
sore janjaka gangan nenbutsudō	But ding-dong, cling-clang in the Amida hall
bōsama ni dorobō ga shikarareta	the thief was caught by the priest
tama wa haihai kaeshimasho	Of course I shall return the jewel!
sā oide yukinase	Please come all!

(Kodama 1994: 179)

On the tenth day of the fifth month in the same year Yone, the 18-year-old daughter of a *sake* merchant, Chika, the 18-year-old daughter of a fishmonger, and Hisa, the 19-year-old daughter of a vegetable shop owner, drowned themselves by jumping into the Sumida river, their arms tied to each other. Their corpses were found at

Eitaibashi, and many people went to see them. There were many interpretations of why they did this, and before long a print with the following text was issued:

Sate mo Kanda no Inari kawagishi	Near Kanda's Inari shrine
onna no minage o hiite kita	a drowned woman is about to be fished from the river.
kenbutsu dorodoro yama hodo da	So many people went to see that it looked like mountains.
kawa kara agarimasu	Now she is coming up from the river.
Dandan tazuneriya sannin da	After asking you hear that they were three!
otoko wa bantō ni shikarareta	The man was scolded by the clerk,
tora wa heiki de gomen nase	but the tiger, undisturbed says 'Excuse me!'
minage de sā kinase	'Come with the drowned one!'
	(Suzuki and Koike 3: 164)

That *ken* in 1847 was so popular that even reports about the Shinshū earthquake were made in the *ken* picture song style astonished even Saitō Gesshin, the compiler of the *Buke nenpyō* (Saitō 1968: 112). On a *namazue* with the title 'big earthquake' (*Daijishin*) a *namazu*, a prostitute and Amida Nyorai are playing *kitsuneken*, while a prose text in the upper fifth of the print gives a short report on the earthquake which occurred in Shinshū on the evening of the twenty-fourth day in the third month of Kōka 4, at a time when the Amida Nyorai statue of the famous Zenkō temple was exhibited to the public (*kaichō*), and when therefore many pilgrims were present. The song's text runs as follows:

Sate wa Shinshū Zenkōji	Now let us two make a pilgrimage
kaichō mōdete	to see the exhibition
futari tsure tsure	of the Zenkō temple in Shinshū
nagusami de mairiyasho	to drive away our boredom
Sore jishin jakajaka taihen da	This earthquake – ding dong – is really terrible
Amida ni jishin ga shikarareta	It was scolded by Amida Buddha
ryojin hauhau shokoku no	The travellers were crying!
mukai ga sā kinase	Come to meet them from the various provinces!
	(Katō 1995: 240)

What is really astonishing is that apart from high politics no topic seemed to have been too holy to be turned into a *ken* song. As for politics, such prints depict their theme only very indirectly so that a lot of imagination and knowledge of contemporary symbols is needed to understand the print's meaning. But there are also some *ken* prints treating politics quite openly. The first one refers to the arrival of commodore Perry, the second one, a two-sheet print, is from the time of the Meiji Restoration and bears the title *Tegoma nashi tsume shōgi* (A Japanese chess problem without a captured chessman). It shows the three figures of *kitsuneken* around a giant chess board: the hunter, representing power, as symbol for the Satchō coalition, the village headman, the traditional authority, standing for the *bakufu*, and the clever, supranatural fox symbolizing the Kyoto aristocracy; and makes fun of the *bakufu* which lost the battle of Toba Fushimi, even though it had more troops than the enemy. But the short text of this print is no longer in a *ken* song tradition, as is also the case with a two-sheet print *Satsumaken* issued in March 1877 and reported on by Mitamura (1976: 196–98). It is of course a description of the events which led to the Seinan War in 1876–77, told in the *kawaraban* style, typical of Edo period.

One group of *ken* prints has no relation to particular events and no news value. The aim of those prints seems to be in their funny presentation of a certain well-known theme. For example, in 1847, Kuniyoshi published a print *Dōke Daruma ken* (Funny Daruma *ken*), on which three Darumas are posing in *ken* positions. The Darumas are certainly the same actors as those on the first *ken* pictures about the *Sake wa kenzake* song. The accompanying text tells us:

Sake wa kinshu de iroke made	Sake is not allowed nor are women
yameru kokoro de mi o kimeyo	Let us purify our body with a renouncing heart!
bibinaru kabe nagamete	We shall live looking at the humble
kurashimasho	wall!
sore kandemo nondemo zazen mame	Biting and drinking small beans
bonzan ga wachō e watararete	the bonze came over to Japan
sore de hōbō hiromuru ten	thereby broadening the heaven.
shūshi o sā hiromeyo	Let us propagate our faith!
	(Robinson 1963: 48)

Kuniyoshi seems to have been especially fond of such *ken* prints and we can speculate that he also wrote most of the *ken* songs on his prints himself, since no name of a poet or songwriter is mentioned in these prints, as is the case in other ones.

Since *Warau kado* had been such a success, the Nakamuraza opened its new season on the seventh day of the first month in the fifth year of Kōka (also first year of Kaei, 1848) with a *jōruri Iroshina kaete kenzake* (*kenzake* with other methods), a title which clearly shows that a sequel to the previous year's success was planned. Two of the actors were also the same as the previous year's actors: Nakamura Utaemon IV and Ichikawa Kyūzō II, who were joined by Seki Sanjūrō III (1805–70). This time they performed 'Crane, turtle, pine *ken*', in which the turtle, because it lives 10,000 years and the crane only 1000 years, wins over the crane, which again wins over the pine tree because it uses it to house its nest. But the pine wins over the turtle on the back of which it grows (Fujiokaya 1927: 216; Ihara 1961: 510). This *ken* of longevity seems to have lacked the enormous popularity of its predecessor, and I could find only four single–sheet prints and one triptych related to it, three drawn by Kunisada and one each by Kuniyoshi and Yoshifuji.

But nevertheless, a year later, the third great Edo theatre, Ichimuraza, from the seventeenth of the first month of Kaei 2 (1849) again showed a *kenjōruri*, *Shinki no ikken tori no hatsugoe* (a *ken* game to new rules until the cock crows). This new *ken*, again performed by the enormously popular Nakamura Utaemon IV, Seki Sanjūrō III and the owner of the theatre, Ichimura Uzaemon XII (1812–51), was called 'Three countries *ken*' (*Sangokuken*) (Fujiokaya 1927: 228; Ihara 1961: 519), being a comparison of India, China and Japan, and just as the Japanese like international comparisons today they seem to have liked them even 150 years ago. *Sangokuken* became popular in a similar way to the *Sake wa kenzake* song two years earlier. The original text says:

Omae onna no na de oIsesan	You are a woman and your name is Ise,
kagura ga osuki de toppiki pii no pii	you like *kagura* dances and the sound of flutes.
shishi wa Morokoshi Kōshisama	The lion is from China as is Confucius.
tenten Tenjiku o Shakasama	From In-, In-, India is Buddha.
maruku osamaru sankokuken	The *ken* of the three countries forms a circle.
nan no kotta jabujabu ohige o nadenade	What does this mean? Dabble, dabble, stroke your beard,
kururi to mawatte ikken shiyo	turn around and play one *ken*!
	(Suzuki and Koike 3: 456)

Seen from today this song, in which the three great Japanese religions, Shinto, Buddhism and Confucianism, symbolize their three countries of origin Japan, India and China, and in which Japan wins over China, China over India and India over Japan, sounds a little blasphemic, but for the citizens of Edo it was great fun. The same phenomenon as 1847 occurred: prints with the actors and prints for training purpose were issued and many *kaeuta* appeared.

At this time three gods were especially popular around Edo: Okina Inari of Nihonbashi, Datsuebā from Yotsuya and Otakesan, Otake Dainichi Nyorai, and at once the text of the *Sankokuken* was changed to fit these three *hayarigami* in various ways. In Kuniyoshi's *Jiisan, bāsan, anesan ryūkōken* it runs:

Okina no na de Inarisan	Your name, old man, is Inari.
aburage o suki de katte kite kuu	You love fried bean curd, buy and eat it.
Musume monogoshi koi kimono	Good mannered girl in blue dress.
tende ni negai o obā sama	To the many individual prayers
karuku kanaeru nandemo gan	the old woman answers mildly:
donna kotte mo tabitabi	If you pray stubbornly and continuously
urusaku negatte ippen kikō	then I shall hear you once.

Figure 2.3 Jiisan, bāsan, anesan ryūkō ken (Fashionable grandfather, grandmother and older sister *ken*). Woodblock print, *ōban* size, signed Ichiyūsai Kuniyoshi *giga* (witty picture by Ichiyūsai Kuniyoshi) and red *kiri* seal, probably issued in 1849. Censors' seals Murata and Mera, publisher Bunseidō. The three depicted popular gods Okina Inari from Nihonbashi (right side), Datsuebā from Yotsuya (left side) and Otakesan (back) make the typical gestures of the *sangokuken* for India, Japan and China. Of this print there exists a second version with totally different words.

For the Edo citizens who knew the texts of *Sake wa kenzake* or of *Sangokuken* these *kaeuta* must have sounded very funny, especially so since they are even funny for the scholar doing research about them today. That they were received with great enthusiasm by the public can be concluded from the number of similar prints that were published.

On the second of the tenth month in the second year of Ansei (1855) the earthquake that occured in Edo was, according to *Bukō nenpyō* (Saitō 1961: 147), the biggest since the Genroku period. At least five prints, two signed by Enjū,[3] about whom nothing else is known, and three anonymous, appeared under titles like *Jishinken* (Earthquake *ken*), *Dōke jishin ken* (Crazy earthquake *ken*), *Yonaoshiken* (World renewal *ken*) and *Sanshoku yonaoshi ken* (World renewal *ken* for the three professions) depicting for example, the thunder god, the fire god and the *namazu* playing *ken*. On one print an older man – the father – is sitting beside them drinking *sake* and completing the four things to be feared: *jishin* (earthquake), *kaminari* (thunder), *kaji* (fire) and *oyaji* (father, see Figure 2.4). On another print the artisans who make great

Figure 2.4 Jishinken (Earthquake *ken*). Anonymous woodblock print, *ōban* size, probably issued in the tenth month of 1855. No censor's seal, no publisher's logo.

profit from the earthquake and the disaster it created are shown. Similar *ken* prints of professions which make much money are especially typical after this date: the postman after Japan's forced opening, the doctor at the time of the measles epidemics, the rickshaw man after the Meiji restoration.

Yonaoshi, reforming the world, was not only one interpretation of the results of the many earthquakes, but also a phrase in many peasant uprisings of the time (see Linhart 1992b). In the New Year's *kabuki* performance of the Nakamuraza in Edo from the fifteenth of the first month of Ansei 6 (1859) there was again included a *ken* song under the title *Yonaoshiken*, but in this case *yonaoshi* meant only that certain professions would make much money and it cannot be connected with revolutionary changes. Although at least nine prints were issued to make this *yonaoshiken* popular, I could not find a single *kaeuta*, which is certainly a good indicator of the popularity of a song. Of the *Jigokuken* or 'hell *ken*' of 1860 I found only one print, and of the *Hatsuumaken* of 1861, included in a play at the Ichimuraza from the twenty-seventh day of the second month of Bunkyū I (1861), I could locate six. The *Hatsuumaken* seems to have been the last *ken* dance and song which was incorporated into a *kabuki* performance, but *ken* prints for singular events were issued until at least 1885, some of them still as *kaeuta* of the *Sake wa kenzake* song of 1847, like the *Totetsuriken* of 1871 which deals with the change from old Edo to new Meiji coins:

Sate mo kondo no zeni sōba	Now this new Sen market!
kaeru hitobito mina komari	All people have problems with change
kosen zarazara	Small coins sound *zarazara*,
nabe sen de mairimasho	let us try with pan coins!
zarasen na bitasen to	But even if you throw away
hyakusen ga nagerarete	a hundred shabby old coins,
zara o hōbō de totte kuru	people will come from afar to pick up that trash.
ten otsuri de sā kinase	Oh come with the old Tenpō coin!
	(Miyao 1967: 179)

Other Meiji events in *ken* prints report a tiger which was shown in 1869, the good business of rickshaw men in 1870–71, the popularity of rabbits in 1872–73, the three most popular figures in the world of entertainment and the best *yose* entertainers in 1881. The final print which is mentioned by Mitamura Engyo (1976: 199–200) treats a typical Edo theme: three temple exhibitions (*kaichō*), a theme which also occured several times previously (see Figure 2.5).

The world – a *ken* game

We need now to look for a reason why the *ken* prints were so popular, why the *ken* songs and the three figures playing *kitsuneken* even constituted something like a *nishikie* subgenre of their own for about forty years.

As I have shown elsewhere (Linhart 1995b), during the seventeenth and eighteenth centuries, and well into the Kasei era of the nineteenth century, the main

Figure 2.5 Ryūkō kaichō ken (Fashionable temple exhibition *ken*). Woodblock print, *ōban* size, signed *konomi ni tsuki* Kuniteru *giga* (witty picture by Kuniteru according to his taste), issued third month of 1871. Censor's seal *aratame hitsuji* 3, publisher Horinoya Taisuke. The three figures each symbolize one shrine or temple that in the spring of 1871 had prepared a special exhibition of their treasures. The bull stands for the Ushijima Shrine in Mukōjima, Tokyo, the fox for the Inarisan in Oji, and the *tengu*, a wood goblin with a long nose, for the Saijō temple near Odawara.

form of *ken* in Japan was *honken*, a game of numbers quite unrelated to the *sansukumiken*. *Sansukumiken* was probably known in Japan as *mushiken* since the Nara – or Heian – period, but it was mainly a children's game. 'Fox' and 'tiger' *ken* were already known in the eighteenth century, as can be shown from woodblock prints, but it was only after 1847 that 'fox *ken*' became a mainstream version, and it seems that the *Sake wa kenzake* song's popularity was partly responsible for this change. It was also known as *Tōhachiken* – after the medicine peddler whose announcement '*Tōhachi – gomon – kimyō*' (Tōhachi pills – five *mon* only – wonderful effect) seemed to have been so interesting that *ken* players began to use it instead of shouting 'one, two, three' at the start of the game. *Kitsuneken* kept this position until the disappearance of all *ken* but 'stone *ken*' after 1945.

Adapting the structure of the *ken* game to various events and depicting the participants in those events as *ken* players was of course great fun, fun which can best be seen in the various prints of Kuniyoshi. These funny pictures, *giga* with attributes such as *dōke, fūryū* or *ryūkō*, were part of the late Tokugawa culture which H.D. Harootunian (1989) has called a 'culture of play'. According to him *gesaku* authors rearranged 'the most mundane, familiar, and trivial activities that townsfolk encountered in their daily life' and

> by rearranging them so that they appeared unfamiliar, by forcing readers to look at activities that they performed habitually and objects they took for granted, writers could jar them into seeing customs in a new and different light. Laughter was recognition of the familiar made to appear strange and even alien.
>
> (Harootunian 1989: 175)

This was exactly the case with most of the *ken* pictures.

The fact that the *ken* in the *ken* prints referred to in this chapter is always 'fox *ken*', a form of *sansukumiken*, is important. Of course one could answer this question by simply saying that for about forty years there was a fashion, and for several years even a craze, of *Tōhachiken*, which found its expression also in woodblock prints. But even then we must ask why there was such a fashion. Do fashions not tell us much about the consciousness of people, about their collective ideas?

Let us take a look at the special characteristics of *sansukumi*. Each one of the three elements has one stronger and one weaker opponent, a constellation which is only possible with at least three elements. As Kurt Singer already pointed out more than sixty years ago, *sansukumi* is related to the *mitsutomoe*, a universal symbol of East Asian cultures expressing dynamism as well as a state of equilibrium (Singer 1938: 15). In the well-known *futatsutomoe*, on the other hand, the weak and strong elements are contained in both parts, leading to a state of equilibrium without dynamism. *Sansukumi*, of course, expresses a paradox, an antithesis to our everyday life, in which we are used to unilinear hierarchical rankings, and there are speculations that it belongs originally to the Daoist tradition of unexplainable things. If we start to analyse it logically, we will soon discover that the various figures are strong and weak in different realms. By looking at the *sansukumi* figures in this way the riddles they constitute can be explained easily. In *sansukumi* there is the same reasoning at work as when a schoolchild dilutes fear of a teacher at an examination by thinking of how he might look in underwear, or when a child offsets weakness in mathematics by being very good in athletics.

So if we return to the *kitsuneken* we see that: the village headman has political power over the hunter; the hunter has mechanical power over the fox; the fox has supernatural power over the village headman. Every *sansukumi* group can be analysed in that way, and the power exerted over the others can never be of the same kind in all three relations. In *toraken* for example, Watōnai has physical power over the tiger; the tiger has physical power over Watōnai's mother; and the mother has moral power over her son Watōnai. But to analyse the *sansukumi* constellations in such a way takes all their fascination from them. And, it has to be added, there is of course a certain relevance in the different kinds of power in a *sansukumi* group. Superiority in one realm and inferiority in another one do exist and can have important meaning. Today we see that there are countries which are economically strong and militarily weak and vice versa, a situation which can lead to difficult relations. It would be easy to construct a modern 'three nations *ken*', like the Japanese did in 1849.

During the Edo period Japanese society was divided into three big classes: the military, the agrarian and the townspeople. These classes can be said to have constituted a kind of *sansukumi*, too. The *samurai* had political power over the *nōmin* (farmers), on whom they enforced taxes; the *nōmin* produced food for the townspeople, and the townspeople were economically in a superior position to the samurai, and thus each class was dependent on the others. In other words, we can say that the rigid Tokugawa class structure produced – the longer it existed – more and more status inconsistency. The popularity of *sansukumiken* might be partly explained by the fact that it vividly expressed – without sociological tools difficult to describe – this state of society. That this is not mere speculation can be seen from an untitled *surimono*, a privately published and in this case anonymous print, on which a *samurai*, a peasant and a craftsman are playing *kitsuneken* (*Tabako to shio no hakubutsukan* 1984: 249, plate 1143).

But what can best explain the popularity of *sansukumiken*, is the fact that *sansukumi* contains a certain hope for the oppressed. Even for the oppressor there are human or supernatural beings stronger than he is. *Ken* flourished in a period which was also one of much wishful *yonaoshi* (world renewal) thinking, and as I already mentioned, there are quite a number of *ken* illustrations combined with *yonaoshi* texts. *Yonaoshi*, often criticized as regressive or backward looking 'for the good old times', is an expression of the people's desire to live a good life, based on a primitive egalitarianism. On the print entitled *Yo no naka yonaoshi arigata ken* (*Ken* of thankfulness for the renewal of this world), issued in the eleventh month of the year Meiji I (1868) on occasion of the gift of free *sake* given to the inhabitants of Edo by the *tennō* after his transfer from Kyoto to Edo, we can read:

Teten ten kara tamawaru osake	They drink this *sake* received from
o nonde	he-, he-, heaven
hyakushō akindo shokunin mo	Farmer, merchant and artisan.
minna dontaku oiwai de	To celebrate this Sunday, let's make
	a *ken* game
osake no kigen de ikken sanjimashō	in *sake* spirit!

kondo chōdai Tanchōshu	Now we receive Tanchō *sake*
kame wa mannen Yōrōshu	the 10,000 years old turtle, how wonderful
kamiyo no osake wa Jindaishu	the *sake* of the age of gods is Jindaishu
Kenbishi Masamune Masayoshi mo	And to end with Kenbishi, Masamune and Masayoshi
maruku osamaru omedetaya	how happy we are!
chochongayoyasa	Chochongayoyasa!

Figure 2.6 Yo no naka yonaoshi arigataken (*Ken* of thankfulness for the renewal of this world). Woodblock print, *ōban* size, signed Utashige *giga* (witty picture by Utashige). Issued eleventh month of 1868. Censor's seal *aratame tatsu* 11, publisher Iseya Kanekichi. Utashige is most likely another name used by Hiroshige III (1843–94), who designed a great number of caricatures in a similar style.

To take a little rest from work, to drink *sake* as one pleases, and to play a game of *ken* – such simple pleasures are hiding behind the people's search for world renewal.

I again would like to stress the fact that *kitsuneken* was the most popular form of *ken* from the 1840s onward. In this game the figure of the village headman, *shōya* or *nanushi*, is a symbol of the official authority, of the power of the ruling class, of the state system. He is a representative of those who have the say, those who usually win. It is no problem for the village headman to win over the hunter, probably the figure with which the common people could most easily identify themselves. But the power of the village headman was limited. First of all, the hunter had a rifle – and we know from the research of Tsukamoto Manabu (1993) and others that there were many rifles in the villages, and if the headman did not act according to the rules of the game, the rifles could also point at him, as was the case in the many peasant uprisings at the end of the Tokugawa period. Without a rifle the headman does not have the power to win over the fox like the hunter, like the people. The fox is, of course, not only an animal, but also a being with supernatural forces, feared by everybody. At the same time the fox at the omnipresent Inari shrines is also a holy messenger of the important Inari deity to whom the common people pray everywhere in Japan. It is not necessary to repeat here that the last years before the Meiji Restoration were a period in which supernatural forces among the common people enjoyed a special popularity, that their *Weltbild* (word picture) contained many supernatural features which can easily be seen from woodblock prints, theatre plays and stories of that time. Hirota Masaki (1987) has convincingly explained the reasons for the development of this *Weltbild*. For me *kitsuneken*, which was only rarely called *teppōken*, *shōyaken* or *nanushiken*, forms a part of this *Weltbild*.

The consolation and hope, the egalitarianism and final retributive justice contained in the principles of *sansukumi*, the dynamics and the equilibrium of *mitsudomoe*, and the very easily understandable symbols of *kitsuneken*, which fitted perfectly into the *Weltbild* of the common people around the Meiji restoration, were probably responsible for the lasting success of *kitsuneken* and of the *ken* pictures drawn in a spirit of playful fun. The world and the dramatic worldly events were interpreted as a *ken* game in the *ken* pictures and the *ken* songs. With Michail Bachtin (1995) we can speculate that the laughter which these interpretations provoked might well have brought a certain relief to a people suffering under social and political contradictions.

Notes

1   My thanks are due to Kimura Yaeko (Tokyo Toritsu Chūō Toshokan), Professor Kōno Junichi (Yokohama Shiritsu Daigaku, Yokohama), Kuwabara Setsuko (Ostasiatisches Museum, Berlin), Matsuyama Kaoru (Waseda Daigaku Engeki Hakubutsukan, Tokyo), Ken Vos (National Museum for Ethnology, Leiden), Johannes Wieninger (Österreichisches Museum für Angewandte Kunst, Vienna), Jane Wilkinson (Royal Museum of Scotland, Edinburgh), and Professor Yamamoto Hirofumi (Hōsei University, Tokyo) for their kind permission to see their respective collections and/or for their help.

2   *Senri no tora* refers to the famous saying 'like setting free a tiger's child in a field of a thousand miles' (*senri no nobe ni tora no ko o hanatsu ga gotoshi.*).

3   According to Endō Takeshi (1980: 135) and Katō Mitsuo (1995: 324–25) the signature
     of this otherwise unknown artist has to be read as Enjū, while Hayashi Yoshikazu
     (1989: 73) reads it as Yajū.

Bibliography

Bachtin, M. (1995) *Rabelais und seine Welt. Volkskultur als Gegenkultur* (Rabelais and his world.
    People's culture as counter culture), Frankfurt: Suhrkamp (Suhrkamp-Taschenbuch
    Wissenschaft 1187).

Endō T. (1980) *Genshoku ukiyoe daihyakka jiten 5: Fūzoku* (Great ukiyoe encyclopedia in colour:
    Manners and customs), Tokyo: Taishūkan shoten.

Formanek, S. and Linhart, S. (eds) (1995) *Buch und Bild als gesellschaftliche Kommunikationsmittel
    in Japan einst und jetz* (Books and pictures as means of social communication in Japan,
    formerly and today), Vienna: Literas 1995 (Reihe Japankunde).

Fujiokaya, Y. (1927) '*Tengen hikki*' (Notes from the centre of the universe), in Asakura Musei
    (ed.) *Shin enseki jūshū 1* (Ten new collections of imitations), Tokyo: Hiroya kokusho
    kankōkai, pp. 126–232.

Harootunian, H.D. (1989) 'Late Tokugawa culture and thought', in Marius B. Jansen (ed.)
    The Cambridge History of Japan 5: The Nineteenth Century, Cambridge: Cambridge University
    Press, pp. 168–258.

Hayashi, Y. (1989) *Chinpan. Garakuta sōshi* (Strange publications: rubbish storybooks),
    Tokyo: Kawade shobō shinsha (Kawade bunko).

Hirota, M. (1987) '"*Yonaoshi*" ni miru minshū no sekaizō' (The world view of the people to be
    seen in the movements for world renewal), in Asao Naohiro *et al.* (eds) *Nihon no shakaishi
    7. Shakaikan to sekaizō* (Social history of Japan 7: views of the society and the world),
    Tokyo: Iwanami shoten, pp. 261–98.

Ihara, T. (1961–63) *Kabuki nenpyō 6–8* (Kabuki chronology), Tokyo: Iwanami shoten.

Jinyaō (1970) '*Kōgai zeisetsu*' (Comments on the luxury of the capital), *Kinsei fūzoku kenbun shū*
    (Collection of reports on manners and customs during the early modern period) 4,
    Tokyo: Kokusho kankōkai, pp. 1–379.

Katō, M. (1995) '*Namazue sōmokuroku*' (Index of catfish pictures), in Miyata and Takada
    (1995), pp. 237–363.

Kodama, K. (ed.) (1994) *Tokubetsuten Edo no shijuku* (Special exhibition: the four stations of
    Edo), Tokyo: Tokubetsuten Edo no shijuku jikkō iinkai.

Linhart, S. (1992a) '*Chonkina – 19 seiki kyokutō ni okeru "me no hoyō"*' (The chonkina 'a
    recreation for the eyes' in the nineteenth century Far East), in T. Yokoyama *(ed.) Shikaku
    no 19 seiki. Ningen, gijutsu, bunmei* (A vision of the nineteenth century. Man, technology,
    civilization), Kyoto: Shibunkaku, pp. 269–326.

—— (1992b) '*Bauernaufstände für "Weltverbesserung" im Japan des 19 Jahrhunderts*' (Peasant
    uprisings for world renewal in nineteenth century Japan), in P. Feldbauer and H.J.
    Puhle (eds) *Bauern im Widerstand. Agrarrebellionen und Revolutionen in Ländern der Dritten Welt
    und im vorindustriellen Europa* (Peasants' resistance. Agrarian rebellions and revolutions in
    third world countries and in pre-industrial Europe), Vienna, Cologne Weimar: Böhlau
    (*Beiträge zur Historischen Sozialkunde Beiheft 1*).

—— (1995a) 'Kawaraban – die ersten japanischen Zeitungen' (Kawaraban – the first
    Japanese newspapers), in S. Formanek and S. Linhart (1995) pp. 139–66.

—— (1995b) 'Some thoughts on the ken game in Japan: from the viewpoint of comparative
    civilization studies', in T. Umesao, B. Powell and I. Kumakura (eds) *Japanese Civilization*

in the World XI: Amusement, Suita: National Museum of Ethnology (Senri Ethnological Studies 40), pp. 101–24.

Machida shiritsu hakubutsukan (ed.) (1995) *Bakumatsu no fūshiga. Bōshin sensō o chūshin ni* (Caricatures of the late Edo period, especially on the civil war of 1868–69) Machida: Machida shiritsu hakubutsukan zuroku 95).

Minami, K. (1994) '*Naitō Shinjuku no hattatsu to hanei*' (The development and prosperity of Naito Shinjuku), in K. Kodama (1994), pp. 220–4.

—— (1997) *Edo no fūshiga* (Caricatures of the Edo period), Tokyo: Yoshikawa kōan (Rekishi bunka raiburarii 22).

Mitamura, E. (1976) '*Dentō shita Meiji shonen no totetsuruken*' (The tradition of the Totetsuruken from the early Meiji period), in *Mitamura Engyo zenshū* 19, Tokyo: Chūōkōronsha, pp. 188–200.

Miyao, S. (1967) *Nihon no giga. Rekishi to fūzoku* (Comic pictures of Japan. History and manners), Tokyo: Daiichi hōki shuppansha.

Miyata, N. and Takada, M. (eds) (1995) *Namazue. Shinsai to Nihon bunka* (Catfish pictures. earthquakes and the culture of Japan), Tokyo: Ribun shuppan.

Ouwehand, C. (1964) *Namazu-e and their Themes. An Interpretative Approach to Some Aspects of Japanese Folk Religion*, Leiden: E.J. Brill.

Robinson, B.W. (1963) *Kuniyoshi. Ein Meister des japanischen Farbholzschnitts* (Kuniyoshi: a master of the Japanese colour woodblock print), Essen: Burkhard Verlag Ernst Heyer.

Rotermund, H.O. (1991) *Hōsōgami ou la petite vérole aisément. Matériaux pour l'étude des épidemies dans le Japon des XVIIIe, XIXe siècles* (Hōsōgami or measles made easy. Materials for the study of epidemics in eighteenth- and nineteenth-century Japan), Paris: Maisonneuve and Larose.

—— (1995) '*Krankheitsbilder in Krankheits-Bildern. Zu den sozial-historischen Bezügen der Darstellungen der Masern (hashikae)*' (Portrait of a disease. On the social-historic relations of depictions of measles (hashika-e), in S. Formanek and S. Linhart (1995) pp. 107–37.

Saitō, G. (ed. Kaneko, M.) (1968) *Zōtei Bukō nenpyō 2* (Enlarged chronology of Edo 2), Tokyo: Heibonsha (Tōyō bunko 118).

Sakurada, J. (1942) '*Warau kado niwaka no shichifuku (Totetsuruken)*' (The sevenfold luck dance at the door where one laughs), in T. Takano (ed.) *Nihon kayō shōsei 10* (Collection of Japanese songs 10), Tokyo: Tōkyōdō, pp. 411–15.

Singer, K. (1938) '*Das Bild der kreisenden Drei*' (The image of the circulating three), *The Transactions of the Asiatic Society of Japan*, Second Series, vol. XVII: 1–152.

Suzuki, T. and Koike, S. (eds) (1988) *Kinsei shōmin seikatsu shiryō. Fujiokaya nikki 3, 18–26, Kōka 3 nen – Kaei 3 nen 6 gatsu* (Materials on the life of the people during the early modern period: the Fujiokaya diary from 1846 to the sixth month of 1850), Tokyo: Sanichi shobō.

Tabako to shio no hakubutsukan (ed.) (1984) *Ukiyoe*, Tokyo: Tabako to shio no hakubutsukan.

Takada, M. (1995) '*Namazue no sakushatachi – gakō o meguru bakumatsu bunka jōkyō*' (The creators of the catfish pictures – the cultural circumstances of painters during the late Edo period) in N. Miyata and M. Takada 1995, pp. 34–51.

Tsukamoto, M. (1993) *Shōrui o meguru seiji. Genroku no fōkuroa* (Politics of living things. the folklore of the Genroku period), Tokyo: Heibonsha (Heibonsha raiburarii 18).

Yoshida, T. (1974) *Ukiyoe jiten. Teihon* (Ukiyoe encyclopedia. A standard text), 3 vols, Tokyo: Gabundō.

3 *Kono sekai* (the Japanese gay scene)

Communities or just playing around?[1]

Wim Lunsing

Originally, the idea for this chapter developed from my growing uneasiness about the way in which a number of Japanese and British scholars reacted to my explanations of the research I was conducting on categories that include gay and lesbian people.[2] These reactions can be represented by the phrase: 'So, you are studying the gay community' (in Japanese, *gei konmyuniti*). In England, Scotland Yard used this same term when warning 'homosexuals' to take care when a series of murders of gay men occurred in the spring of 1993. What the term 'gay community' is supposed to mean is, however, not very clear. An article in the *Gay Times* (Simpson 1994) asked the question whether such a thing exists in England and the majority of those questioned about it reacted by saying that they thought or hoped that it did not exist. This of course depends very much on how the term 'gay community' is defined.

As the Dutch lesbian researcher Judith Schuyf (1992) wrote, views on what lesbian communities are changed enormously during a relatively short period of time in the 1970s and 1980s: from groups of people who support each other, through ideological entities of people who share the same political beliefs, to spatial structures that are accessible to women only. Schuyf discerned five different lifestyles in the Netherlands during the 1950s and 1960s – that of butch–femme relationships, bar dancers, ordinary people (who think that they are not much different from anyone else), romantic friendships (in which sex plays a minor role) and intermittent lovers of women – and adds three more that developed in the 1970s and 1980s – lesbian-feminists, lesbian mothers and anarcho-squatters. By the term 'communities' she refers to categories of people who share a particular lifestyle.

Stephen Murray (1992), likewise, pointed out that there is an enormous variety in what he calls 'the gay community of San Francisco', mainly produced by differences in ethnic background. However, he discerns territory, that is certain areas in cities where gays and lesbians are concentrated, as the foremost component of a community. In addition he mentions the following features:

> . . . a concentration of interaction among those who identify themselves as gay into gay primary groups, concentration in space (of residence, but more importantly of community institutions) in specifiable territory, learned (though

not monolithic) norms, institutional completeness, collective action, and a sense of shared history.

(*ibid.*: 113)

If this is what a gay community is supposed to consist of, then there are not many gay communities outside the US. In the Netherlands, such a community that has a specific territory can hardly be discerned. Schuyf's lifestyles may in the Netherlands come closest to Murray's concept of gay communities. However, their nature differs immensely.

The Japanese scholars mentioned above had in general little knowledge of homosexuality in Japan. Their thinking on homosexuality was largely determined by experiences in the US. I felt that by using the term 'gay community,' they tried to fit my research within the American discourse, which is definitely dominant where gay and lesbian issues are concerned, and thereby ignored particular features characterizing gay life in Japan. Of prime importance is the feature that although Japan has no laws discriminating explicitly against homosexuality, the social structure, which is largely based on marriage as the smallest social unit (Hendry 1986), leaves little opportunity for public gay lifestyles. This goes for any alternative lifestyle to marriage and hardly prevents living a gay lifestyle discreetly (Lunsing 2001). Living a discreet gay lifestyle is often not seen as very serious business: many Japanese gay men talk of their gay life, using the term *asobi* (play).

This chapter considers the question of whether, in the case of Japan, speaking of a gay community makes any sense, and if so, what can be said about it. I limit myself largely to the male side of the story. The most obvious place in Japan to look for gay men are the many gay bars, which can be seen as the major centres of gay life in Japan. Therefore this chapter will first focus on the functions these places serve and the extent to which they live up to demands gay men have. How do men gain access to these places? Why do some go there and others not? After this, I shall discuss what Japanese gay organizations have to say about the term 'gay community' and how that relates to the gay bar circuit. Finally the discussion concentrates on the question of whether the term 'gay community' has any significance with regard to the Japanese situation, and if so, what this consists of and how it relates to the concept of gay life as 'play'.

Kono sekai: gay bars and other meeting places

Kono sekai is the word many Japanese gay men use when talking of the gay world in phrases like: *Kono sekai ni haitte kara* (since I entered this world). This indicates that they consider the gay world to be separate from the rest of society. Most central to *kono sekai* are the gay bars. In Tokyo the largest concentrations are located in Shinjuku, Ueno and Asakusa. The *Otokomachi Mappu* (men's city map), a guidebook for gay men (Kaimeikan 1998), identifies about 250 gay venues in Shinjuku alone. In Osaka one finds gay venues concentrated in Doyamachō in Umeda (popularly also called Kita (north), 148 places, fifty-nine in Nanba (also Minami (south) and forty-five in Shinsekai (the 'new world', a name the area acquired after it was rebuilt in the 1950s), the area with the largest concentration of day labourers in Japan (*ibid*). This division between north and south is stressed mostly by those who prefer the south. According to them, the south is the real Osaka and the north is for newcomers. The north is visited relatively more by people travelling from the area north of Osaka, Kobe and Kyoto, while some visitors come from much further away. Moreover, the visitors of bars in the north tend to be younger on average, which together makes the north/south division in Osaka comparable to the Shinjuku/Ueno and Asakusa division in Tokyo. In the case of Tokyo, anthropologists and Japan specialists have made a major issue of the *shitamachi/yamanote* division, 'low city/high city' coined by Edward Seidensticker (1983). Typically the bars can be found in areas near major railway stations and in areas that have a low market value, such as Shinjuku Nichōme, which until the prohibition of prostitution was an *akasen chitai* (red light, literally 'line' district, Ōtsuka 1995: 14–19).

Other major towns also have quite a number of gay bars. Even in smaller provincial towns one can find them. The *Otokomachi Mappu* includes seventy-one towns, and after Tokyo and Osaka, sections on Yokohama, Nagoya, Kyoto, Hiroshima, Sapporo (in Hokkaido), Hakata (in Kyushu) and Naha (in Okinawa) are large. Informants from remote areas mentioned bars in their towns that do not appear in the *Otokomachi Mappu* and I found additional ones in Osaka as well as in Shinjuku, which indicates that the total number of over 1200 entries in the *Otokomachi Mappu* is by no means exhaustive. As gay bar owner Ōtsuka Takashi wrote, estimates of the number of bars in Shinjuku vary from 200 to 400. Nobody knows how many there are because they are nowhere registered as gay venues (Ōtsuka 1995: 9–10).

Most venues are bars, where one can have a drink with a little snack on the side. Often a *karaoke* installation is present for those who want to sing their hearts out. Prices vary, but usually the first drink costs between 1,500 and 1,800 yen and from the second drink the price varies between 600 and 800 yen for the cheapest drinks. The high price for the first drink pays for the snacks that are always provided and for the ambience. This system of a high-priced first consumption leads to much misunderstanding among foreigners, who may think that they are cheated, which is one of the reasons why bartenders tend to become anxious when foreigners enter. Problems are likely to arise only when the drinks are to be paid for, which customarily does not happen until the patron leaves. Additional fees are charged for the use of the *karaoke* installation. A simple night out with three beers can easily cost about 3,000 yen.

In a style in keeping with the size of Japanese housing, gay bars come in two sizes, small and tiny. Small bars can accommodate up to fifty persons, if many do not mind standing. The tiniest bar I visited could accommodate six persons sitting at the counter and another six in the second row. Then there would be no space left to stand and if the person farthest from the entrance had to leave everyone had to file out. About twenty seats is usual. At the centre of the tiny bar is the *masutā* (master), or the *mamasan* (mamma), depending on how the man behind the bar identifies himself or is identified by his clientele. Lately *masutā* has won ground over *mamasan*, which is a female title and is also used in regular establishments, where the *mamasan* as a rule is a woman. Other bars employ young staff whose wages are on a par with general *arubaito* wages, at about 700 yen per hour.

One often finds a number of bars in one building, some on every floor, or, if the building is narrow, one on each floor. One may even find a lift with a door at street level that stops at a different bar on every floor. I found the largest number of bars in one building in Shinjuku, where the six-storey high Yamahara Haitsu[3] contains fifteen bars as well as a gay book and pornography shop in the basement.

In areas like Shinjuku and Doyama, bars are characterized by the sort of clientele they cater to. In Shinjuku, there are bars for young people (*wakasen*), for older people (*fukesen*), for fat people (*debusen*) for culturally interested people, for foreigners and those who like foreigners (*gaisen*), and, to give an example, for those who like to sit dressed in nothing but a *fundoshi*, the Japanese-style loincloth. *Wakasen*, and so on are words Japanese gay men employ to indicate the type of man that dominantly frequents a bar. Thus, a *debusen bā* attracts fat people as well as people who are interested in meeting fat people. *Gaisen* bars are often exceptionally large and do not have the usual pricing and paying system but let their clientele pay the same for every drink each time they are served.

Ageism is very conspicuous. The *Otokomachi Mappu* indicates for the bars it describes the age of its customers (20–25, 25–40, 30–50, above 50) and what sort of love relationships can be found in terms of age (both young, young/middle aged or old, both middle aged, both old, anything).[4] This coincides with the most frequent subject when the type one seeks is being discussed: age is the first denominator, typically represented by the question: *toshiue-toshishita*? (older or younger?). During in-depth interviews with gay men individually, however, age turned out to matter less. The personality of the other was central and most people believed this not to be related to age in a linear way. In the particular case of a love relationship, difference in age may even be sought.

About 5 per cent of the bars appearing in *Otokomachi Mappu* are *hosutopabu* and *urisenbā*. Here the cover charge is much higher to pay for boys who are present for the patron's convenience. They may give shows, including dancing, singing, telling jokes, cross-dressing, striptease and masturbation acts, and they are available for chatting with the patrons. These bars are, thus, comparable to the hostess bars catering to straight men (for example, Allison 1994; Louis 1992; Mock 1996). Besides this, they are present to comply with a customer's wishes in the field of sex, in which case every activity is added to the bill. *Urisen* means specializing in selling (in this case sex) and these are the explicit prostitution places, but *hosuto sunakku* (host snacks) usually also have hosts engaging in prostitution. Usually boys can be taken to a private room upstairs or to a hotel or the house of the patron on various schedules, ranging from one hour for 12,000 yen to all night for 25,000 yen. Not many people can afford this on a regular basis. Patrons are divided between relatively few regulars and a larger number who come only once. *Hosuto pabu* are only found in Tokyo (Shinjuku), Osaka (Doyama), Nagoya, Kyoto, Hakata, Naha and Sapporo.

Hattenba are places where gay men can meet and have sex. Those listed in *Otokomachi Mappu* include such diverse locations as gay beaches, parks, film theatres (mostly straight pornographic film theatres), and toilets, mostly in department stores and railway stations. The number of entries of *hattenba* is less representative of what there is than that of gay bars. I found by chance a number of *hattenba* in Osaka that are not mentioned in *Otokomachi Mappu*. *Hattenba* may develop and disappear overnight, while others have existed ever since the end of the Second World War and possibly even before that. Remoter places, in particular in western Japan, where it is warmer, have fewer bars and relatively more *hattenba*.

A third category of places that is not always included in the *hattenba* sections is that of hotels. Most widespread is a chain called Kirakukaikan, with twelve branches, of which most can be found in western Japan, in provincial towns rather than in the largest cities. Two can be found on Shikoku, in Takamatsu and Tokushima, but Osaka has no Kirakukaikan. In Osaka one finds a number of other hotels instead. These places usually include saunas, *mikkusu rūmu*, rooms where a large number of men can find a place to rest, to have sex or both, private rooms, swimming pools and gymnasiums. Besides these, there are also a number of specialized gay saunas and gymnasiums. A new development in the late 1990s are the *yaribeya* (literally, 'do-rooms'), which can even consist of small regular apartments, where people pay an entry price for the opportunity to have sex with other patrons. Altogether, it appears that Japan has such a widespread variety of meeting places for gay men that the vast majority of gay men in Japan have easy access to them and thus to meeting other gay men.

To visit or not to visit

Not all gay men visit gay bars or *hattenba*. About a third of the sample of 300 gay men responded to a questionnaire issued by the gay activist group Occur (*Ugoku Gei to Rezubian no Kai* 1992) that they do not visit gay bars.[5] In a survey of ninety-seven readers by the gay magazine *Za Gei* (*Za Gei Henshūbu* 1992), the sample of which is more varied in age but probably more biased towards men who frequent bars, 44 per cent visited a gay bar once or twice monthly, 31 per cent once or twice weekly and 15 per cent more often. No answering space is provided for those who never visit gay bars and those who visit them thrice monthly, but it is safe to conclude even from these figures that considerable numbers of gay men seldom or never visit gay bars.

Informants who did not visit gay bars said that they did not like the atmosphere, which is largely described below, that it was too expensive, or that they felt insecure about visiting gay bars in the town where they lived because acquaintances might see them enter or exit. They feared for their anonymity as gay. This phenomenon was widely reported even in a major city like Kyoto, which was supposed to have only a small number of gay bars because gay men from Kyoto felt it was safer to go to a bar in the more anonymous Osaka.

On two occasions, when entering a gay bar and when entering a gay bookshop in Osaka, I noticed a person fleeing to the door. Both persons were known to me and were working at a university I visited regularly. They apparently felt that their anonymity would be endangered if I knew of their gay interests. This agrees with the story of an informant who was sitting in a gay bar when his boss came in. He quickly turned his back but felt he could not get out past his boss without being recognized, so he sat silently until his boss made clear that he was recognized by addressing him. He had known of his boss's homosexuality, as he had more than once seen young men entering and exiting his boss's house in the evening and in the early morning. Nevertheless he felt awkward about his boss discovering his homosexuality. However, nothing changed in their professional relationship.

Visitors to gay bars are predominantly of younger age groups, usually in their 20s, 30s and 40s, while there are few in their 50s and over. Major preconditions for visiting gay bars are having money and time to spend as one pleases, which can be very limiting, as incomes can be very low and when they are high enough, time is likely to be limited. Thus, one finds on the one hand students who spend hours on one drink, and on the other, middle-aged men who drink as much as they can in one hour. For the first group money is the constraining factor and for the latter time. Among the reasons given for why people do or do not often visit gay bars, however, money and time were seldom mentioned. Those who cannot afford to go drinking can also be found standing around on the street or, in the case of Nichōme, in and around the gay shop Rumière (Lumière). They are called *rumiko* after the name of the shop (Ōtsuka 1995: 21–2).

Some informants said that they did not feel like going to gay bars because the image they had of them was very *kurai* (sombre, dark). This is compounded by the image the mass media has presented until recently of gay bars as transvestite bars, which is a total misrepresentation – and one that is reinforced by Robertson (1998) who writes that gay magazines list hundreds of advertisements for transvestite places, which is a gross distortion. This image is so influential that young gay men may not dare to go to gay bars. They may even think that they have to dress up like a woman because they are gay, notwithstanding the fact that in the majority of gay bars one hardly ever finds a transvestite.

A particular category of visitors to gay bars are women, mostly heterosexual, although in Osaka, where, unlike Tokyo, hardly any lesbian bars exist, lesbian women frequent some gay bars as well. This phenomenon of women visiting gay bars was picked up by the women's magazine *Crea* (1991) with a special that turned out to be the beginning of the *gei būmu* (gay boom), a phenomenon of enormous media attention for gay men that developed in Japan from the early 1990s. The image many people have of gay bars has improved since the media depictions have become increasingly realistic (Lunsing 1997).[6]

In a few cases women accompany their gay husband to a gay bar. They tend not to be open about this, however. Gay husbands are passed off as heterosexual or the couple would keep silent about their relationship. In these cases the *masutā* said what the real relationships and sexual preferences were, after the couple left. While some gay bars do not admit women unless they are in the company of a gay man, others do not mind who enters the bar as long as they behave. In some cases this leads to gay bars being dominated by heterosexual female customers.

While a much-cited reason for the popularity of gay men and gay bars with heterosexual women is that they do not have to fear sexual advances from them, fear of harassment does play a role with especially young gay men in relation to visiting gay bars and especially *hattenba*. The word that is used to describe harassers is *hen na ossan* (Kansai dialect), or *hen na oyaji* (Tokyo dialect), which literally means 'funny old man' but here best translated into 'dirty old man'. These *hen na ossan* seem to think that they can do anything they like with those who are younger, and being gay, they harass younger men, analogous to Japanese heterosexual men who think it is normal to harass women.

Functions

When visiting Japan in 1988, I contacted Minami Teishirō, at the time representative of the Japanese section of the International Lesbian and Gay Association (ILGA). He told me a story about gay men in Japan that I would hear again and again. In short it is as follows: gay men try to maintain a 'standard' heterosexual lifestyle as much as they can, including marriage,[7] and visit gay bars only to release their stress (*sutoresu o hassan suru tame ni*) when they have the time on the way home from their offices. This story is obviously limited to the category of gay men who work in offices. For those who are in freer positions, like artists, or more binding ones, like family businesses, things are often different. The fact is that the patrons of gay bars in Osaka's Doyama, as well as in Tokyo's Nichōme, are in the majority white-collar workers.

Relief from the stress of living in a heterosexual world all day and often at night as well is obviously an important function of gay bars in Japan. Here is a place where gay men can actually be gay. However, as Linhart (1986) has pointed out, relief from the stress accumulated in the workplace is a function of all bars in Japan. The difference is that for gay men regular bars do not provide the relief straight men find there because everyone is expected not to be homosexual. For gay men, accompanying their colleagues to a straight bar may even increase their stress (Lunsing 2001).

In order to attain this relief, alcohol plays its role. Alcohol functions to make the patrons mellow, so that they may proceed to sing *karaoke*, which is also a good way to relieve stress. By singing *karaoke* people step into the shoes of another person, another role, and can release themselves temporarily from the role they play during the day. This is the ultimate *henshin* (transformation), the singer is a star for the time the song lasts (Linhart 1986). Songs sung in gay bars are not necessarily much different from those sung elsewhere. The style of the bar is the major determinant. While in some places, especially *fukesen* bars, Japanese *enka* (traditional sentimental songs) form the main menu, in bars that are visited by younger men (*wakasen* bars) a more modern repertoire dominates. Many gay men appear to be able to relieve their stress and get mellow without alcohol; they have soft drinks or, for instance, the very popular cold *ūroncha* (oolong tea). It seems that gay men may even have the gene that prevents them from digesting alcohol relatively often.

Though many informants cited the wish to find a lover as a reason for visiting gay bars, this does not happen very often. Oikawa (1993) discussed what he called '*Nichōmebyō*' (the illness of *Nichōme*) which is the block in Shinjuku where gay bars are concentrated. Gay men who lived through a period of one-night stands (*wan suteppu*: one step) and became dissatisfied with that life suffer this mental condition. While I also encountered such cases, the majority of gay men in Japan do not have many one-night stands and are on the cautious side when embarking on a sexual or romantic adventure. Having many partners or one-night stands is generally seen as bad behaviour. It even happened that I was warned about people who change lovers all the time. They are thought not to be serious, honest or reliable because they 'just play around (*asobu*)'.

The situation in most bars does not allow one to move about freely. Usually the *masutā* points out a seat for the guest and if the persons next to him happen to be grumpy, he can only talk with the *masutā*, who, indeed, in such cases is likely to entertain the patron himself. Unlike bars in Europe, where bartenders in general hardly pay any attention whatsoever to the well-being of the patrons, Japanese bartenders try always to make sure that their patrons are talking with someone. If a patron should be interested in talking to someone on the other side of the bar, it is not uncommon for him to ask the bartender to be introduced and moving seats may be organized to facilitate the new acquaintance. Thus, one may be asked to move seats repeatedly. Whenever I went to a gay bar in the company of a group of Japanese they would stick together and hardly ever talk to strangers. On one occasion the *masutā* of a bar in Osaka told two of my company of six to go to the pornographic film theatre and find a lover for the night. They had come all the way from Tokyo and were staying in a hotel, making it easy to take someone to their rooms. They accepted the reduced tickets for the theatre but did not go.

This episode suggested two things. One, the *masutā* of this bar thought that it was unlikely that they would meet a lover in the bar, in particular since they were in a group, and two, the film theatre was considered to be a good place to pick up a lover for the night. The film theatre combines several theatres, one of which specializes in gay pornography with a continuous programme alternating between a Japanese and an American film. The American films show mostly mosaics that cover the genitals totally. This is a result of the Japanese law that prohibits the exposure of 'pubic hair', which is legal jargon not only for pubic hair – shaving does not help – but for genitals as well. As a result, Japanese films are very different. They do not focus on genitals. Instead, facial expressions of pleasure and pain are important means to excite the audience. Watching the films was clearly not the main reason for those visiting the theatre, however. Sitting in the theatre, I noticed several people looking around (cruising) to the point of peering closely into others' faces, which was probably necessary to discern something in the dark.

Outside in the hall stood a small bench and some vending machines selling drinks. A couple of people often sat there, ranged in age from 17 to 48. They turned out to be regular visitors who discussed their latest lovers and such. People were coming in and going out of the theatre continually to go to the hall or to the toilet on the other side. In the hall was a door with *Tachiireikinshi* (No Entrance) on it, but it was entered and exited continually. As it turned out, this door led to the back staircase where sex took place, mostly in the form of *fellatio* or mutual or one-way masturbation.

The fact is, however, that even here one finds regulars, who come neither to watch films nor to have sex but rather to talk with other regulars. This suggests that sex is not the major issue for many gay men in Japan. Sex can be found in many places but someone to talk with regularly, a friend with whom one can discuss one's personal life, including problems with one's family and one's relation to lovers, is what is most needed. In bars, people are less likely to discuss such things, as the *masutā* or other guests may know who one's lover is and telling them could thus complicate matters, or at least that is what they think. This is further exacerbated by the fact that most Japanese do not consider it good behaviour to trouble others with one's problems, unless they are close friends. *Meiwaku o kakeru*, as 'causing trouble' is called, is a distinctly negative term. It incurs debt, which has to be repaid sooner or later. This can be very bothersome, as one never knows when the creditor may want his repayment and in what way he may want it. Hence, it is often considered to be preferable not to incur debt (Hendry 1992).

Gay bars may provide a place where homosexual men can talk about their personal problems and a minority certainly finds this there. Many, however, do not. A man who was wholly isolated as a gay man – initially he claimed that I was the first he ever spoke with about it – had been going to a bar in Shinjuku regularly for a period of ten years before I met him. Eventually he had grown tired of all the casual chit-chat every night and decided not to go any more. Concerned telephone calls from the *masutā* failed to change his mind. An informant who frequents gay bars said he felt he could not discuss his personal problems there. When a lover broke up with him he placed an advertisement in a gay magazine to find a new lover. He received numerous replies from people who wanted to be friends with him and a network for people to discuss their *nayami* (troubles) has developed.

As late as 1992 I overheard a discussion in one of the more progressive gay bars in Shinjuku about AIDS. People wondered how one gets infected. Notwithstanding the AIDS Protection Law, which requires that the government inform people about HIV and how to avoid contamination (Ōhama 1988), basic information had not even spread among gays in Japan, let alone other groups. The gay bar circuit is underutilized in spreading information about AIDS, partly because many *masutā* think it bad policy to confront their patrons with unpleasant subjects. This illustrates the limited nature of the role of gay bars in discussing social issues of relevance to gay men.

Nevertheless, bars do pay much attention to building up a continuing relationship with their patrons. A usual method of binding them is the *bottoru kiipu* (literally, bottle keep) system. Bottles of whisky, brandy and the like are sold to customers and kept in the bar to be used at the customer's convenience. Hundreds of bottles being kept is no exception: in a bar in Doyama I counted over 700. The bartender was surprised when I said that I had counted this number and said he had no idea whose bottles they all were. As rarely more than ten persons were present in the bar and it usually was quite empty, I surmise that many who kept a bottle there did not come back for it, as, indeed, happened to me on an occasion when I bought a bottle together with a friend. We never found the time to go again together and did not wish to go alone. The *masutā* of another bar in the same building said that he kept bottles for only a couple of months after which he would pour them to regular patrons free of charge.

Being recognized by the *masutā* in a bar is considered to be very important. When being taken for a bar crawl in Shinjuku by one of my informants, he made a major point of being recognized by the *masutā* in each bar we visited and in the one case in which the *masutā* had no idea who he was, he was terribly upset. We stayed for one short drink only, while in other bars we at least had had some food with the drink. At the same time, however, it is common for people not to use their real name in gay bars. Some *masutā* seem to have real elephant memories. In a bar where I had been once in 1993 and returned, looking quite different, for a second time in 1996, the *masutā* recognized me. He even remembered with whom I was that time and where we had been sitting. In one case, a *masutā* found it so important to be a good socializer that he even learnt sign language in order to speak to deaf patrons.

Apart from this, many bars have special parties on one of the New Year days, when most Japanese do not work and spend time with their families. Those who do not wish to see their families can go to these gay bars, which may have boisterous parties, often including drag and of course *karaoke*. Lately, bars also organize sports competitions, ranging from volleyball tournaments to a tennis matches. In the latter, which was organized by bars in Nichōme, as many as 160 people competed some years ago (Ōtsuka 1995: 201), and volleyball tournaments have recently drawn over a thousand participants.

Two books by gay authors show a large difference in attitudes towards gay bars. While one admits that they are not everything, the role played by gay bars was important to its author in making friends and establishing a gay lifestyle (Nishino 1993). While he admits that they form a limited world, he insists that they have much to offer:

> At that time I fully recognized that Nichōme was little short of having a wired fence around it, nothing more than a ghetto and that the me wandering around this tiny block night after night was nothing more than a Diane Keaton looking for her mister Goodbar, but that was all right for me. Because we did not despair of anything. Because it was great fun to sally forth boisterously all of us together.
>
> (*ibid*. 99, my translation)

The other is rather vindictive. Gay bars to him are of no use. He found it impossible to make friends and eventually ended up paying boys for sex, even though he found this a very base activity (Itō 1993). He found friends and lovers much later, making use of the personal advertisement sections in gay magazines.[8] Among my informants, I found the same variety in attitudes. While one liked to go there and regarded gay bars as an important part of his life, the other loathed the places and would never be seen in them. The following quote from a gay man in his late 20s indicates the limitations of gay bars:

The reason I hardly ever go to gay bars, is that I do not like bars, no matter whether it is a gay bar or a *nonke* (straight) bar. When I want to drink sake,[9] I go to an *izakaya* (traditional style Japanese drinking place, where one usually sits on the floor and a large variety of food is on offer), and when I want to sing, I go to a *karaoke bokkusu* (a rental room with a *karaoke* installation), so I hardly ever go to a bar . . . But if there would be an *asshu* (gay)[10] *izakaya* or *karaoke bokkusu*, I would go there. I do not like to go to places I find uninteresting, just because *asshu* are gathering there.

(Kantorii Rōdo [Country Road] 1993, my translation)

Gay communities, gay bars, gay movements, gay networks

Comparing Japanese gay bars and the other zones that constitute *kono sekai* to Murray's definition of a 'gay community', it is obvious that *kono sekai* does not fit the bill. Those who frequent bars may not define themselves as gay and they usually are not part of gay primary groups. Although bars tend to be concentrated in particular sections of major cities, the people who visit them live anywhere. Community institutions are virtually non-existent.[11] Though some norms may exist, they are not different from general norms in heterosexual circles even up to the point that many think it is *hazukashii* (shameful) to be gay. The only collective action related to *kono sekai* that I found was a rumour that in 1993 signatures were collected to protest against bulldozing down the whole Nichōme area in favour of new high-rise buildings, which would have meant the end of the gay area in Shinjuku.

The gay activist group Occur[12] insisted during their Gay Rights Rally in 1991 that what Japan lacked was a gay community and that it was necessary for them to form one. To them, the meaning of *kono sekai* is:

> In the past (. . .) everybody, including homosexuals (*dōseiaisha*) themselves, thought that homosexuals lived in the world of the *fūzoku sangyō* (the industry of immoral entertainment), the city of the night. There are many young homosexuals that ended up thinking that in the future they had to enter the *mizushōbai* ('water trade' – the industry of sex and entertainment).
>
> (*Ugoku Gei to Rezubian no Kai* 1992: 396)

Occur's idea of what a gay community consists of is modelled on San Francisco. What they intended to build was 'a community (*chiiki kyōdōtai*) where homosexuals live together and support each other in everyday life' (*Ugoku Gei to Rezubian no Kai* 1992: 270). Many Japanese gay and lesbian people are critical of this idea. A lesbian informant involved in networking activities in Osaka found the whole idea ridiculous. Seeing the American example she decidedly thought this not worthy of following up in Japan. 'In America it all went wrong (*Amerika ni wa shippai shita*),' she pronounced. While she thinks lesbian and gay networks are much needed, a community in the sense proposed by Occur is not.

The longest-lasting gay organization in Osaka is Osaka Gay Community (OGC). Gay as well as straight people attend their meetings, and discussions include a wide variety of topics related to gender and sexuality. It combines a high degree of integration with a philosophy that is directed at changing society as a whole rather than building a gay community. Therefore places where gay and lesbian people can regularly meet, which are not of a closed nature but open to anyone who wants to participate, are needed. Hirano Hiroaki, who invented the name of OGC, wrote in relation to this discussion that he had not given much thought to the meaning of the word 'community' when choosing a name for his group (Hirano 1993).

Adding to the scope of *kono sekai*, recently gay and lesbian club parties can be found in Osaka, Kyoto, Tokyo and elsewhere. Further, there are growing numbers of gay circles at universities, and groups that come together to discuss problems related to sexuality. In the last case, the advent of AIDS played an important role. Even secondary school students increasingly attend such study groups. They wish to know more about AIDS and sexuality for themselves or they may be interested in doing voluntary work in the field. Some even aim at studying medicine and hope to be able to fight AIDS through their studies; others are doing a project on homosexuality at their school and thus want to interview gay people for it. Such secondary school students are always welcomed warmly (no pun intended).

Networking between various groups has developed fast. OGC for instance has contacts with groups as far from Osaka as Sapporo and Kyushu. These groups have strong relations with AIDS activist groups that again include heterosexuals. They are open to anyone who wants to join at any time and even advertise in regular newspapers, facilitating a discussion with heterosexuals, which has been growing very fast since the beginning of the 1990s. If a gay community is supposed to consist of gay and lesbian people only, these groups cannot be called gay communities either. The term 'gay community' came from the American situation which is quite specific. The obvious reason why American terminology has been able to enter the global English-language discourse seems merely to be that Americans are dominant where it comes to gay and lesbian studies. This has led to an unfortunate and confusing imposition of American discourses on the situation in Japan. It may very well be the case that if a culture is not as homophobic and violent as the American one is, there would not be much need for a gay community in Murray's sense. Schuyf's lifestyle definition of communities fits the Japanese situation better. There are gay and lesbian people who share a variety of lifestyles. This definition of community, however, is one that hardly exists in Japan. I believe that it is more appropriate to speak of networks, which in Japanese is *nettowāku*.

The existence of the gay bar scene and the sex-oriented parts of *kono sekai* seem to have little to do with the development of all the other groups. While there are a few bars where activists and the like tend to go, these are rarely occasions for organizing anything, even if they may get involved in serious discussion. The newer developments in the direction of activities such as sports tournaments could be explained as a communal development but just as well be seen as an extension of the 'play' of gay men. From the viewpoint of Occur the gay bar scene contributes very little to furthering the living circumstances of gay people in Japan. Other people find gay bars uninteresting because the level of discussion there is alien to them or because they do not like to do things in a purely gay context. Many others, however, find in the bar scene a welcome outlet and as such it cannot be denied that they perform a very important role in the lives of many gay people, even if that role is marked by the word *asobi*. It is important to be able to play.

Notes

1 The Austrian government (*Ministerium für Wissenschaft und Forschung*), the Japanese government (*Monbushō*) and the Japan Society for the Promotion of Science gave support for the research on which this paper is based. Most of all I wish to thank the many Japanese who, while volunteering to be research subjects, often picked up the bills for me while showing me around a variety of gay bars.

2 The variety of manifestations of homosexuality in Japan makes using the nouns gay and lesbian problematic, as many people engaging in homosexual activities or experiencing homosexual feelings do not identify themselves as such. Therefore I have made it a habit to use the terms gay and lesbian only attributively in a manner that includes all those who experience feelings towards their own sex, regardless of how they identify themselves. Constructions of homosexuality (Greenberg 1988) in Japan are changing swiftly and the same applies to the understanding of the meaning of words used to describe homosexuals (Lunsing 1995, 1997, 1998, 2001). The project focused not only on gay and lesbian people but also on other people whose ideas, lifestyles or feelings are not compatible with the marriage system. Therefore I was even more discontented with scholars who showed their misunderstanding by using the term 'gay community'.

3 *Haitsu* comes from the American term 'heights' and in Japan it indicates a type of building one step up from plain wooden structures.

4 This division is printed on every page in *Otokomachi Mappu*. Each category has a number that is placed by the entries on the various bars.

5 37.1 per cent does not visit, 64.3 per cent does (*Ugoku gei*: 371). This survey was conducted among members of Occur, who tend to shun gay bars and among gay men visiting bars, mostly in their 20s, which makes the outcome not very useful.

6 Part of this boom were a number of Japanese films and novels. These included especially *Okoge* (Nakajima 1992), which is the Japanese equivalent of fag-hag and as a film and a novel deals with the relationship of a gay couple and a female friend and *Kirakira Hikaru* (Ekuni 1992) which deals with a triangular relationship of a gay couple one of whom marries a depressed, alcoholic woman. Both drew large audiences. The message is that gay men are romantic, handsome and charming, a positive image, which is depicted partly in scenes in gay bars or *hattenba*. *Okoge* even starts on a gay beach. In addition the autumn of 1993 saw the advent of very realistic gay characters in a number of hōmudorama (soaps), of which especially *Dōsōkai* (alumni association), which peaked with an audience of 20 per cent, deserves mention (Lunsing 1997).

7 See Lunsing (1995, 2001) for discussions of homosexuality in marriage.

8 See Lunsing (1995) for a discussion of gay magazines.

9 *Sake* here means alcoholic drink, not only the Japanese alcoholic drink *sake*. In fact in gay bars the latter is hardly ever for sale.

10 '*Asshu*' is a term that I found to be used exclusively among a particular gay network centred in Osaka. It is the Franco-Japanese pronunciation of the French letter 'H', which stands for homosexual (Lunsing 2001).

11 The scale of what exists is extremely limited, such as a small clinic where men can be tested for venereal diseases and office space of activist groups.

12 Occur is probably best known for suing the metropolitan government of Tokyo, after

having been denied access to the *Fuchū Seinen no Ie*, a youth facility in suburban Tokyo. See Lunsing (1998) for a more detailed account.

Bibliography

Akā, Ugoku Gei to Rezubian no Kai (1991) *Fuchū seinen no ie: dōseiaisha sabetsu jiken to wa* (The Fuchū Youth Hostel: a gay discrimination incident), *Inpakushon* (Impaction) 71, August, 52–61.

Allison, A. (1994) *Nightwork: Sexuality, Pleasure, and Corporate Masculinity in a Tokyo Hostess Club*, Chicago and London: University of Chicago Press.

Crea (1991) *Tokushū: gei no runessansu '91* (Special: gay renaissance 1991) in *Kurea* (Crea), February.

Ekuni, K. (1992) *Kirakira hikaru* (Twinkle), Tokyo: Shinchōsha (first published 1991).

Greenberg, D.F. (1988) *The Construction of Homosexuality*, Chicago and London: University of Chicago Press.

Hendry, J. (1986) *Marriage in Changing Japan: Community and Society*, Tokyo: Tuttle.

Hendry, J. (1992) *Understanding Japanese Society*, London: Routledge.

Hirano, H. (1993) '*Kono sekai, kono michi, kotchi no hō etc. etc. unzari*' (This world, this way, this side etc. etc. fed up with it), in *Musubikko*, November, p. 15

Itō, S. (1993) *Otoko futarigurashi: boku no gei puraido sengen* (Two men living together: my gay pride declaration), Tokyo: Tarō Jirō Sha.

Kaimeikan (eds) (1998) *Zenkoku otokomachi mappu '98 nenban* (The nationwide men's map 1998), Tokyo: Kaimeikan.

Kantorii Rōdo (nickname: Country Road) (1993) '*Chōdo ii kikai na no de*' (As it is just the right opportunity), in *Magazine Don!*, November.

Linhart, S. (1986) '"Sakariba": zone of "evaporation" between work and home?' in J. Hendry and J. Webber *Interpreting Japanese Society: Anthropological Approaches*, (eds) Oxford: JASO, pp. 198–210.

Louis, L. (1992) *Butterflies of the Night: Mama-sans, Geishas, Strippers and the Japanese Men They Serve*, New York and Tokyo: Tengu Books.

Lunsing, W. (1994) '"*Homo senshinkoku*" *oranda ga boku o sodateta*' ("Gay frontline state" the Netherlands brought me up), *Fujin Kōron*, February, pp. 358–63.

Lunsing, W. (1995) 'Japanese gay magazines and marriage advertizements', *Journal of Gay and Lesbian Social Services* 3 (3): 71–87; published simultaneously in G. Sullivan and L. Wai-Teng Leong (eds) *Gays and Lesbians in Asia and the Pacific: Social and Human Services*, Haworth: The Haworth Press, pp. 71–87, and New York and London: Harrington Park Press, imprint of the Haworth Press: New York and London.

Lunsing, W. (1997) '"Gay boom" in Japan: changing views of homosexuality?', *Thamyris: Mythmaking from Past to Present*, 4 (2): 267–93.

Lunsing, W. (1998) 'Lesbian and gay movements: between hard and soft', in Claudia Derichs and Anja Osiander (eds), *Soziale Bewegungen in Japan* (Social movements in Japan), Hamburg: Mitteilungen der Gesellschaft für Natur- und Völkerkunde Ostasiens e.V., vol. 128, Ostasien Gesellschaft, pp. 279–310.

Lunsing, W. (2001) *Beyond Common Sense: Negotiating Constructions of Sexuality and Gender in Contemporary Japan*, London and New York: Kegan Paul International.

Miller, N. (1992) 'Japan: the emperor's new clothes', in *Out in the World: Gay and Lesbian Life from Buenos Aires to Bangkok*, Harmondsworth: Penguin Books, pp. 144–81.

Mock, J. (1996) 'Mother or mama: the political economy of bar hostesses in Sapporo', in Ann Imamura (ed.) *Re-imagining Japanese Women*, Berkeley, CA: University of California Press, pp. 177–91.

Murray, S.O. (1992) 'Components of gay community in San Francisco', in G. Herdt (ed.) *Gay Culture in America: Essays from the Field*, Boston: Beacon Press, pp. 107–46.

Nakajima, T. (1992) *Okoge* (Fag hag), Tokyo: Magajin Hausu.

Nishino, K. (1993) *Shinjuku nichōme de kimi ni attara* (When I meet you in Shinjuku Nichōme), Tokyo: Takarajimasha.

Ōhama, H. (1988) *Nihon no Eizu: Sekaiteki 'Shibyō' to no Tatakai* (AIDS in Japan: the fight against a global 'lethal disease') Tokyo: Saimuru Shuppankai.

Oikawa, T. (1993) *Nichōmebyō: gei sekkusu no otoshiana* (Nichōme disease: a pitfall for gay sex), *Imago* 4, (12): November 1993, pp. 165–77.

Onitsuka, T. (1993) '*Komyuniti wa tsukuritai, de mo gettō wa iranai*' (I want to build a community but I don't want a ghetto), *Musubikko* (Little connector), November, pp. 14–15.

'*Otoko dōshi, onna dōshi: aijō dake de tsunagaru*' (Among men, among women: connecting only with love) (1994), *Asahi Shinbun, nikkan* (morning edition), 3 January, p. 19.

Ōtsuka, T. (1995) *Nichōme kara uroko: Shinjuku gei sturiito zakkichō* (The scales from my eyes in Nichōme: miscellaneous stories from Shinjuku's gay street), Tokyo: Shōheisha.

Robertson, J. 'It takes a village: internationalization and nostalgia in postwar Japan in S. Vlastos (ed.) *Mirror of Modernity: Invented Traditions of Modern Japan*, Berkeley, CA: University of California Press, pp. 110–29.

Schuyf, J. (1992) 'The company of friends and lovers: lesbian communities in the Netherlands', in Ken Plummer (ed.) *Modern sexualities: fragments of lesbian and gay experience*, London and New York: Routledge, pp. 53–64.

Seidensticker, E. (1983) *Low City, High City: Tokyo from Edo to the Earthquake*. New York: Knopf.

Simpson, M. (1994) 'Is there such a thing as a gay community?', *The Gay Times*, January, pp. 30–2.

Takamure, I. (1991) *Nihon koninshi, Nihon rekishi shinsho* (A history of Japanese marriage, new books on Japanese history), Tokyo: Tōbundō (first published 1973).

Ugoku Gei to Rezubian no Kai (Akā) (ed.) (1992) *Gei ripōto: dōseiaisha wa hatsugen suru* (Gay report: homosexuals speak out), Tokyo: Tottori Shinsha.

Za Gei Henshūbu (ed.) (1992) '*Daigokai Za Gei ankeito*' (The fifth gay survey), in *Za Gei* (The gay), July, pp. 42–52.

Magazines

Adon, Barazoku, Kurea, Magazine DON!, Sabu, Samuson, Takarajima, Za Gei

4 *Karakuri*

The ludic relationship between man and machine in Tokugawa Japan

Yamaguchi Masao

In our assessment of the development of mechanical technology, we tend to focus primarily on the productive aspects of the industry. For this reason we generally hold the misconception that there was no development of mechanical technology in Tokugawa Japan. Everyone knows that the Tokugawa government forbade the military and industrial use of machinery. As a result, specialists in mechanical techniques were not recognized as members of a real profession, as medical practitioners were, for example. They were treated like magicians and regarded with suspicion. They were considered to belong to the world of entertainment. Indeed, mechanical specialists – artisans of *karakuri* – were confined to the world of play, fuelling spectacles, theatre, and mechanical toys: all activities and objects set free from the world of utility.

Because of this exclusion of machinery specialists, there was almost no industrial culture in Tokugawa Japan, in spite of the fact that architecture, weaving, engineering, and artisanship maintained high standards. People are thus amazed at the speed with which Japan developed a mechanical culture within just half a century after opening her doors to the West and beginning to learn Western technology. One reason for her rapid progress is that she grafted the newly introduced Western mechanical culture on to '*karakuri* culture', which had already been fully developed in the Edo period.

Karakuri craftsmen utilized wood to construct most of the parts of their devices because there was a scarce supply of mineral material available during the Edo period. The cogwheel is no exception. Wood cannot be used for cogwheels, because the softer parts wear out easily if they are used as gears. A carpenter had to join six triangular fragments to construct one wheel, using only the harder and coarser parts of the wood. By building on such a tradition of resourceful craftsmen, modern Japan was able to industrialize rapidly in an amazingly short period.

Although some mechanical devices had been constructed in ancient and medieval Japan, they were not as complex as those created by *karakuri* specialists after the sixteenth century. It was due to the advent of the Western clock in the sixteenth century that the Japanese artisans of the machine were inspired to create a new machine culture. For the first time not only in their lives but in the history of the country, they discovered such apparatus as the spring, gear, cam, crank, speed controlling machine such as the controller; the crowned machine for reducing speed with a balance wheel, etc.

It is said that the very first clock to arrive in Japan is the one that St Francis Xavier dedicated in 1551 to Ouchi Yoshitaka, then Lord of Suho. This clock did not survive the peril of Ouchi, however. The oldest extant mechanical clock is the one that the Spanish king, Philip III, presented as a gift to Tokugawa Ieyasu in 1612. The original is preserved at Toshōgu on Mt Kudo in Shizuoka City.

Unlike in China, where imported clocks were preserved only as luxury goods and no attempt was made to localize them, Japanese artisans tried to Japanise the Western clock. What they did was to transform the Western clock, based on a star calendar, into a clock based on a lunar calendar.

When the mechanical clock arrived in Japan, the Japanese were using an irregular time counting system. They used to lead their lives according to the changes and rhythms of nature. Consequently, the span of daylight between sunrise and sunset constituted the basic unit of daily time. Daytime, as well as night was divided into six units. Units of time varied according to the four seasons as well as locale. Thus, in summer, one time unit was longer in the daytime and shorter at night. The case was reversed in winter. These early mechanical specialists transformed the Western clock to meet the requirements of Japan's irregular time counting system.

Tsuda Sukezaemon, a blacksmith from around Nagoya in Owari province, is believed to have fabricated the first clock in Japan. According to *Owarishi* (Descriptions of Owari), written in 1832, Tokugawa Ieyasu called upon Sukezaemon to repair a clock that had been presented to him by Korea. Not only did Sukezaemon repair the original, he also built a copy based on the clock he repaired (Tsunoyama 1984: 49).

Karakuri in the Edo period is said to have started when Takeda Omi opened his *karakuri* puppet theatre in Dotonbori in Osaka. Takeda Omi was a clock specialist. Ihara Saikaku bears witness to the work of Takeda Omi in his *haikai*: 'cha no hakobu ningyō no kuruma hatarakite' (How interesting it is to watch the march of the automaton puppet carrying tea). He included this poem in a collection called *Dokugin hyakuin* (One hundred solitary writings of Hokku), published in 1675, commenting as follows:

> Harima in Edo and Takeda in Osaka, applying their knowledge gained from the Chinese, have fabricated a wheeled mechanical doll with a main spring that can move in any direction. It holds a teacup. The movements of the eyes, mouth and feet, the motion of the extending of the arms as well as its bowing gesture are remarkably lifelike.
>
> (cited in Tachikawa 1980: 54)

The Edo Harima in this quotation refers to Harima Shōjō. Takeda Omi I is said to have created an automaton puppet inspired by children who were playing with sand. According to the *Settsu kenbun fudebyōshi* ('A description of news around Settsu'), he constructed a precise eternal clock. Omi I passed on his techniques to Kiyotada – Takeda Omi II – whose Takeda Karakuri Theatre was considered as legitimate as the *kabuki* theatre. There were three other puppet theatres in Osaka at the beginning of the seventeenth century.

In 1705, Takeda Izumo, Omi I's younger brother, replaced Takemoto Gidayu as the head of the Takemotoza on the occasion of the theatre's production of *Yomeitennō shokuninkagami*, a play that included many carnivalesque and spectacular scenes. From this production onwards, the *karakuri* of the Takeda family was adapted for the *joruri* stage. Chikamatsu wrote a number of texts for *joruri*, such as *Kokusenya kassen* (The battle of Coxinga, 1715), *Yuriwaka daijin nomori no kagami* (The epic of Yuriwaka, the Japanese Ulysses), *Keisei sutendōji* (1718), and *Heike nyogogashima* (1719), etc.

Takeda's troupe made their first visit to Edo in 1741. They were so popular that they came again in 1757. A record of their visit was published the following year as *Okarakuri ezukushi* (Illustrated Grand Karakuri). Morishita Misako (1988: 160–90) has written an analysis of the image of children in this book. The first programme, 'Ten months in the Mother's Womb', depicts the process of conception corresponding to images of Buddhist deities representing the months of the year. There is also a puppet of a three-month-old child, which plays the flute and defecates. People were fascinated by its clumsy movements. The clumsiness reminds adults of their infancy, a period of their lives which they push aside to the margins of their memory. In this puppet people witnessed the emergence of the buried possibilities of the human body by exposing themselves to primordial movements, which can be termed 'metastability' (Gandelman and Gandelman 1989: 191–213). Because of their lack of practicality, the movements of the child puppet render the human body an object of play.

Karakuri shows featuring child puppets were called *kodomo kyōgen* (child pieces). Morishita explains the significance of *kodomo kyōgen* in the following way:

> The *karakuri* puppet appears on the border where man and puppet make precarious contact. The figure of the puppet resembles the human figure. However, the moment that it starts to move, it reveals a decisive divergence from human movement; it makes rapid shifts difficult to capture with the naked eye, while simultaneously exposing its clumsiness. Each moment that its naive movement is inscribed, the expected modes of everyday performance and standard narrative patterns are dislocated. This disillusion is compensated for by our attraction to the movements and changes which that strange body, distinct from the human body, enacts to a greater or lesser degree than normal . . . in a sense, the child's body made its debut on the stage of entertainment, exposing its strangeness (1988: 187–8).

In 1741, the year that they appeared in Edo, the Takeda family organized a large-scale *karakuri* spectacle that was a tremendous success. At this time, the main focus of *karakuri* started to shift from the puppet to the mechanism of the stage itself. With Namiki Shōzō I's invention of the *seri* (the stage lift) in Osaka, the mechanization of the stage began. Seichi, Takeda Omi VI, sold his title of Omi Taijō and left the Takeda Theatre.

Nakayama Mikio, a specialist on Tsuruya Nanboku IV, writes that it was the playwright who carried out stage designs in the Edo period. It was natural for the playwright, who wrote the text, to act as the director of the stage machinery. Nakayama writes that a piece of drama was first conceived in terms of the use of space, to which the text was then accommodated; apparatus was either built in or pulled out to meet the space needs of the production (Nakayama 1987: 222). Some of the *karakuri* mechanical stage techniques which were still in use after the decline of *karakuri* puppets in the professional theatre include the *mawaributai* (revolving stage), *seriage* and *serisage* (elevating and descending mechanism), *gandōgaeshi* (machine for turning upside down), *yataikuzushi* (roof-turning device) and *chūnori* (a machine for making actors fly above the audience).

At the beginning of the nineteenth century, a *kabuki* dance called *hengeodori*, or 'dance of transformation', became popular. In the *hengeodori*, the actor's body itself came to be used, in a sense, as, mechanical apparatus. The *hengeodori* required that the actor perform acrobatic movements. It featured tricks and *tromps d'oeils* of the stage made possible by *karakuri* installations. With the introduction of *hengeodori*, *kabuki* performance became fast paced and extremely acrobatic. The body was used like a *karakuri* mechanism – there was no longer any distinction between the human body and the trick apparatus. For instance, in 1794, Onoe Shōsuke invented a trick to change abruptly the face and hairstyle (*pelloque*). Tightrope performances and acrobatic feats made their way on to the *kabuki* stage.

However, it was Tsuruya Nanboku IV who perhaps made the most extensive use of mechanical tricks, such as the ones used in his *Tenjiku Tokubei: Karabanashi* ('Korean Stories of Tenjiku Tokubei'). Tokubei, a pirate who has returned from Tenjiku, comes before the village headman and relates tales of his journey abroad. He receives a special sword from his father, who, as a general in Korea, was defeated by Mashiba Hisayoshi. After teaching his son the magic of the toad, and instructing him to take revenge on his enemy, Tokubei's father commits suicide. When Tokubei finds himself surrounded by the police, he begins to use his magic. He hides behind a cloud that descends from above. In the next moment a giant toad appears. As it marches, the toad opens its eyes and mouth, then splits into two. Tokubei emerges from the crack. There follows another trick in which the sword, bent into three, instantly becomes straight as Tokubei steps out of the toad's body.

Onoe Shōsuke was the ideal actor for a playwright like Tsuruya Nanboku IV, who made extravagant use of absurd and fantastic plots. Shōsuke himself invented many tricks to surprise audiences, turning a skeleton into a ghost, transforming a beauty into a demon by turning her face white and her hair red, and growing two horns on her head (Hattori 1988). Shōsuke was able to train himself to perform all sorts of unnatural and acrobatic gestures (see Yamaguchi 1991).

In addition to mechanical tricks, Nanboku made extensive use of ludic elements – the carnivalesque, grotesque humour, punning and farce. These ludic structures allowed Nanboku to destroy the stereotyped image of reality and verisimilitude and to introduce marginal elements rarely found on the conventional *kabuki* stage. In his production, he realized a cosmological structure through the dislocation of elements

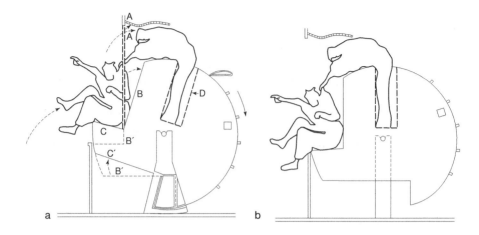

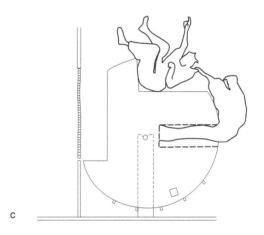

Figure 4.1a, b and c Butsudangaeshi

from everyday life. He dismembered these elements from one other, mixing and turning them into signs with a touch of the symbol, then rearranging them, structurally, according to the cosmic scheme of good/bad, light/darkness, beautiful/ugly, right/evil, sanctuary/deep valley, palace/whore's den, fidelity/betrayal, life/death, etc.

In Tōkaidō *Yotsuya Kaidan*, Nanboku fascinated audiences with his extensive use of *karakuri* such as *butsudangaeshi* (turning over backwards in the style of a Buddhist altar, see Figure 4.1), *chōchin nuke* (sliding apparition from the wall behind a lantern), *kabe no kiekomi* (disappearance into the wall), among others.

As mentioned above, because the machine was forbidden in the world of production, its use seems to have been concentrated in the world of entertainment. Thus, the theatre of Edo Japan reached a high level of technical achievement compared to that found on contemporary Western stages. In spite of the fact that the European theatre employed various mechanical devices after Inigo Jones and in the Baroque theatre, the first use of the revolving stage at the Munich Royal Theatre was 100 years behind Namiki Shōzō who in 1758 invented and used it in Osaka. In the eighteenth century, there appears to have been no Western device comparable to an apparatus like the *yatai kuzushi*, which turned the roof upside down during the play *Nansō Satomi Hakkenden* (Eight royal dog heroes of southern Awa).

One of the genres that fascinated *karakuri* engineers was the *chahakobi* or *chakumi ningyō* (tea carrying automaton puppet – see Figure 4.2). Some of the earliest detailed information on the *chahakobi ningyō* is given in a book called *Karakurizui* (*Karakuri* illustrated), published in 1796. It consists of three volumes: the first is devoted to Japanised clocks, the second and third to various *karakuri* fabricated by applying springs and weights. The *chakumi ningyō* is described in volume 1. If one puts a cup on the plate held by the puppet, the puppet begins to move in the designated direction. It stops when one removes the cup. And when one puts the cup back on the plate, the puppet turns around and returns to its original position. Apart from the *chakumi ningyō*, the following types of mechanical puppets are known to have been made, among others: *godangaeri* (a puppet that descends a staircase and does a somersault), *kotekijido* (drummer boy), *uotsuri ningyō* (fishing puppet).

Among the artisans who made automaton puppets and other machinery, Ono Benkichi is often mentioned as comparable with Leonardo da Vinci. Born in Kyōto in 1801, he revealed his talent from a very early age. He first trained in drawing with the Shijo school and apparently went to Nagasaki when he was 20 years old, where he studied medicine, physics, engineering, Western painting and sculpture. It appears that he then mastered astrology, the calendar, mining, the art of navigation and a number of other natural sciences. He also learnt a variety of crafts, including wood carving, bamboo work, gold work, lacquer, leather, cloth and glass handiwork, pottery, *makie* enamel painting and fireworks. After his sojourn in Nagasaki and a visit to Korea, he settled down in Kanazawa where he was friends with Zenia Gohei, an extremely rich merchant who was eventually destroyed by the local government. Ono learned the art of photography around 1841, only three years after the invention of the Daguerreotype.

Tanaka Giemon, born in 1799, was a much more practical mechanical artisan. He was the first son of an artisan in tortoiseshell work. Giemon was so skilled in making *karakuri* that he came to be known by the nickname 'Karakuri Giemon'. In Kaei 5 (1853), in Kyoto, he opened a 'house of *karakuri*', a shop called Kikodo. There he repaired all sorts of clocks. He made his living producing well-made curiosities, such as lighters, or stands for *sake* cups in the shape of a tortoise. In 1875, after the Meiji Restoration, Tanaka Giemon founded the Tanaka Seizōsho in Ginza, a company that later became the Toshiba Manufacturing Company. Toshiba was taken over in the Meiji period by the Mitsui Trading Company. Tanaka Giemon's

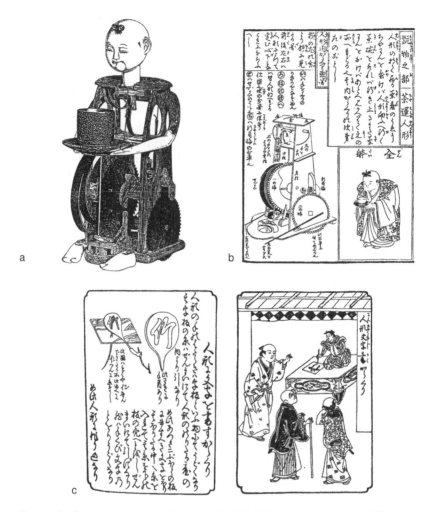

Figure 4.2a Contemporary reproduction of a *chahakobi ningyō* (tea-carrying doll)
   b *Chahakobi ningyō* from '*Kikō Zufu*'
   c Writing puppet

engineering career demonstrates one case of the continuity between the traditional technology of machinery – *karakuri* – and modern technology.

It goes without saying that the automaton puppet was a prototype of the robot that is said to be flourishing in industrial Japan today. In a sense, we can say that the Japanese learnt to tame the machine by means of the *karakuri* puppet because they considered the puppet an extension and copy of the human figure, not as something sent by demons or animated by the divine. In a society where mechanical figures are thought to be pure material, people are always potentially suspicious that they may go beyond human control. This secret fear of the mechanical being is expressed in Fritz Lang's film, *Metropolis*, where an automaton agitates labourers slaving away in a factory underground. Suspicion of the mechanical being is justified in the ambiguous feelings in Jewish thought toward Golem.

In Japan, it was in the world of entertainment, in a ludic ambience, that the automaton puppet made its appearance. As playthings, the puppets did not threaten human competence or existence; they remained charming copies of the human figure. They were considered in a way like domestic animals, or strange animals such as elephants that had been made objects of curiosity in the milieu of spectacle, as seen in the *kabuki* piece *Zōbiki* (Pulling an elephant). Peasants expressed comparable sentiments towards their domestic animals – horses or cattle – and gave them human names.

A similar attitude is manifested towards the robot hero in postwar Japanese comic books such as Tetsuan Atomu (Iron-armed atom) by Tezuka Osamu, Tetsujin Nijūhachigo (Ironman no. 28) by Yokoyama Mitsuteru and Doraemon by Fujiko Fujio, to name only a few (see Figure 4.3). Robots are either treated as welcome guests in the human world (Doraemon) or as figures trying hard to become human themselves (*Atomu*). These comics reflect the traditional attitude of the Japanese toward the automaton, which began with the first Westernization of their machine technology.

It was in Nagoya, home of Tsuda Sukezaemon, the founding father of the Japanese-style clock, where the first clock industry in modern Japan came into existence in the early years of the Meiji period. The Toyota Automatic Weaving Machine Company still has a cogwheel made of wood that Toyota Sakichi invented. It is assumed that there is a close relationship between this cogwheel and that of *karakuri* puppets.

Takanashi Ikuma suggests that the collective manufacturing of the Japanese clock, invented by Tsuda Sukezaemon, seems to have been revived in the manufacturing system of the first car fabricated by Toyota Jidō Shokki in 1935. The Automobile Section of the Toyota Automatic Weaving Machine Company succeeded in manufacturing the historic no. 1 test car of the A1 type automobile in 1935. In fact, however, the municipal government of the City of Nagoya created and began to sell the first Japanese-made automobile in 1932 – three years before Toyota – under the patronage of I. Ohya, then mayor of the city. Ohya had arranged for four manufacturing companies to produce the different parts and one to sell.

This style of manufacture represents an application in a modern context of a traditional regional production system. This Owari case is highly illuminating in demonstrating the relationship between *karakuri* technology and the development of modern industry. The family of Tsuda Sukezaemon inherited the position of clock engineer and chief blacksmith in Owari province; Tsuda was in charge of all the shipwrights and agricultural toolmakers in the province. So that outsiders could not steal the secret of the clock, Tsuda developed a system whereby he allocated the manufacture of the different parts of the clock to a number of craftsmen in the region. A variety of artisans, such as carvers, painters, and *makie* painters, joined the clockmakers in the production of the clock. Takanashi maintains that these clock engineers working under Tsuda in the Edo period were already using the *kanban*,

Figure 4.3a Tetsujin 28-go
　　　　b Tetsuwan Atomu
　　　　c Doraemon

or trademark, of Toyota Motors, now known throughout the world (Takanashi 1990: 41–9).

Tsuda's technology was transmitted to the modern industry of Toyota by Toyota Sakichi, who invented the wooden gear for the automatic weaving machine. Wooden gears were commonly used in *karakuri dashi*, carts bearing mechanical puppets (Takanashi 1990: 185–6). The Owari or Nagoya area has long been known as a centre for these *dashi*. The earliest *karakuri* in the region appears to have been created in 1618, on the occasion of the *Tōshōsai*, the festival of the Tōshō shrine in Nagoya. There was a strong influence from such eminent Kyoto artisans as Takeda Omi and Yamamoto Hidanojō on the construction of the *karakuri* on the *dashi* used in the festival. Many were made by Tamaya Shō bei, however, who seems to have been the central figure among cart *karakuri* puppet makers. Due to limited space and time, we cannot go into a full description of these *karakuri dashi*.

Hitachi, in Ibaragi prefecture, is known today as one of the industrial centres of Japan. It is of great interest to us that here too developed a tradition of *dashi* with *shikake*, or mechanical devices. *Fūryūkasaboko*, as these *dashi* are called, are extravagant constructions. The highest exceeds 15 metres. It consists of two parts, a front *yama* and a rear *yama*. The front *yama* represents a five-storied Chinese pagoda of *hahuu*. When the palace splits in two, *karakuri* puppets emerge on five levels. The cart is also equipped with a central watchtower, or *tenshū*. After performing some theatrical pieces, the puppets turn upside down and change into beautiful young girls at the end. The stage of the cart is constructed in such a way as to rotate. The scene changes to a rocky hill, before which stories based on children's folk tales are performed (Akiyama and Mizuniwa 1985).

Water was one of the few power sources skilfully exploited in production in the Edo period. As we noted, during this period, industry for mass production was not encouraged. However, use of the water mill was permitted in agricultural production. A book entitled *Nōgyōbenriron* (Notes on convenient agricultural apparatus), written and published by Okura Nagatsune in 1822, describes an apparatus called a *gekiryūsui* (Water of a violent dragon) used to lift water to elevated levels (see Fig. 4.4). The *gekiryūsui* was invented by a certain Kume Gisaemon, who exhibited it as entertainment at Asakusa in Edo. Once again, we find a scientific invention first appreciated in the world of entertainment rather than in the academy (Uno n.d.).

Figure 4.4 Gekiryūsui.

The water mill was used in the puppet theatre of Chiran, in southern Kyushu, at the festival of the Toyotama shrine. A hut was built along the stream in front of the shrine. A mill on the stream powered the mechanical apparatus located under the stage (*yatai*). *Karakuri* puppets set in motion from under the *yatai* enacted stories based on myths and folk tales. Their movements were to recall for the spectator the movements of the divine, called *kamiasobi*.

Suishi karakuri is a typical example of *karakuri* used in a folkloric context. The miracle of the *karakuri* enhanced the divine atmosphere of the shrine during the festival. Other devices used to evoke the divine in the folkloric context included *sōsengi* (cord play), where objects such as serpent marionettes were moved in the air, controlled by means of a cord (Figure 4.5).

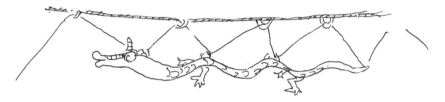

Figure 4.5 Sōsengi – cord play

The *tsunabi* is another device that uses string. In the case of *tsunabi*, however, fireworks are attached to the object to make the play even more exciting and brilliant. During the *Dengaku matsuri* in Nishiura there is a ceremony called *ofunewatashi*, in which a miniature boat is pulled along a cord through the air towards a pile of firewood. A small fire is lit on the boat, which kindles the firewood when the boat hits the pile. The boat then returns to its original position. Pulleys are used in ingenious ways for this performance (Uno n.d.).

The cases of Nagoya and Hitachi suggest that there is some coherent continuity between the ludic techniques of *karakuri* and modern technological developments in these cities, although further research would be needed to draw any definite conclusions.

One of the reasons why the Japanese feel sentiments of familiarity, rather than animosity, towards machines, and robots in particular, is explained by the fact that the significance of mechanical technology was degraded when it was first introduced in the Tokugawa period. Confined to the world of entertainment, machines were integrated into the ludic logic of corporal movement. The Japanese could incorporate the machine without experiencing the horror of its possible divine or demonic character. In a word, Japan industrialized through the spirit of play, and not through calculated economic logic as is usually assumed both by the Japanese themselves as well as by foreign observers.

Bibliography

Akiyama, T. and Mizuniwa, H. (1985) *Ibaragi no ningyōshibai* (Puppet theatre in Ibaragi), Nagareyama: Chiba.

Gandelman, T.D. and Gandelman, C. (1989). 'The metastability of primitive artefacts', *Semiotica* 75, (3/4): 191–213.

Hattori, Y. (1988) 'Kaseiki zengono butai' (Theatre productions from around the Bunka Bunsei Period), *Nihon geinōshi* (History of performance in Japan) vol. 6, pp. 100–64.

Morishita, M. (1988) *Edo no biishiki* (Eyesight on minimal things in Edo), Tokyo: Shinyōsha.

Nakayama, M. (1987) 'Karakuri ryaku nenpyo' (Simplified chronicle of *karakuri*), Kotōshidan, 222.

Tachikawa, S. (1980) *'Jidōningyō: sono sei to shi'* (The automaton puppet: its birth and death), in S. Tachikawa (ed.) *Ningyō karakuri*, Tokyo: Hosei University Press.

Takanashi, I. (1990) *Karakuri no bunkashi* (The culture of *karakuri*), Tokyo: Gakugei-Shorin.

Tsunoyama, S. (1984) *Tokei no shakaishi* (Social history of the clock), Tokyo: Chūōkoronsha.

Uno, K. (n.d.) *Nippon no karakuriningyō* (Puppets in Japan), Kawasaki: Kanagawa.

Yamaguchi, M. (1991) 'Cosmological dimensions of the Japanese theatre', in Y. Ikegami (ed.) *The Empire of Signs*, Amsterdam.

5 Ludic elements in Japanese attitudes to *tsukuru*

María-Dolores Rodríguez del Alisal

Introduction

This chapter explores Japanese attitudes to creating and producing something. These attitudes may well have influenced accepted social thought on work and production in Japan, and it is proposed that research on this subject could help to clarify changing attitudes to work among Japanese young people. I should like here to revise ideas both of work and play in a Japanese context, and for this purpose, I will examine these concepts with a particular focus on Japanese *manga* and *anime* creation, represented by the work of the famous *mangaka*[1] Miyazaki Hayao. Through research carried out into his way of creating, it soon became clear to me that his creation is a mixture of fun and hard work.

There is a general perception abroad that Japanese people are hard workers. In Japan, too, the *shigoto no oni*, or 'work ogre', is well accepted. The phrase refers to a type of person who works terribly hard, and a wife will show more pride than dismay in telling her friends that her husband is a real *shigoto no oni*. I have often wondered what part playfulness might have in all this hard work, and the question led me to this investigation. I am interested in seeking the driving force behind the Japanese relentless striving towards *tsukuru*[2] and how it might be influencing modern Japanese society.

My own Spanish culture, in contrast, gives high priority to the ludic for ludic's sake, and that means enjoying oneself without any purpose. Being able to do nothing has traditionally attained social recognition in Spain. 'A business that does not allow you to get up at 10 a.m. every morning is not a real business', it is said in Spanish. Traditionally, work and manual labour were never highly regarded in Spain. I do not want to reiterate the old saying that Spanish people are always having a *siesta*, and would even suggest that Spaniards probably do not enjoy themselves as much as most of them pretend to when doing nothing. Likewise, many Japanese can really have a lot of fun at work.

Classical Spanish literature is full of references to how happy life could be for shepherds living in fertile fields, happy just to lie on the grass the whole day, drinking water from clear streams, and eating delicious fruit that grow naturally everywhere. In the most famous Spanish novel ever written, not only the protagonist himself, Don Quixote, but also Sancho Panza, affirm the goodness of an ideal shepherd's life (Cervantes 1998: 58). Moreover, after listening to his master's speech about the marvellous life they both would have remaining in a beautiful place (that they consider similar to the mythical *Arcadia*), Sancho Panza says that many other people would join them, including the village priest, since he likes enjoying life so much (Cervantes 1998: 645).

The traditional perception about Spanish attitudes to work and play demonstrates a visceral disdain for all kinds of manual work or economic activity, and a real passion for gambling and for doing nothing. But, according to Veblen (1899), these attitudes were also to be found in most other European countries at the beginning of the nineteenth century. Dislike of work and production, and a strong preference for ludic activities are nowadays also an essential part of Western culture. We must play and enjoy ourselves. These attitudes are mainly supported by economic forces, but they used to be considered completely apart from economic purposes (Seara 1998). In fact, it has become commonly accepted that an activity of 'pure play' cannot be included in circles of economic production. But maybe it is time to reconsider that attitude, when pure play activities are supported by structured organizations such as the Olympic Games, tourism and so forth, where they can become even more economically productive than activities that are generally accepted as being strongly connected to economic production.

Japanese classical literature from the Heian era reflects a similar attitude when it describes how the nobility and the courtiers used to spend their time attending flower viewing parties, listening to birds singing, writing love letters . . . Not everybody was lucky enough to spend life in that way, but I just mention the system of values. With the increase of *samurai* power and the institution of the *ie* family system, priorities were given over to hard work and endurance and new values were incorporated into Japanese culture; the old hedonistic traits did not disappear completely but they were re-oriented for more fruitful results. From that time onwards, not only work but also play and games are not well considered in Japan unless they have been achieved with great effort, preferably by enduring some serious hardship.

A Spanish father or mother will be extremely happy to explain the high marks of their children by saying: 'Oh, my child does not study at all. I cannot explain it to myself either', the best result for the least effort. In Japan, people show greater happiness in getting what they want if they had a hard time achieving it. As if in evidence for the social value it carries, hardship (*kurō*) is always mentioned when something has been successfully achieved. And this pattern can be seen at work, at play, and in all games.

In fact, to do a good job in Japan can be, in many cases, strongly connected with playing games. If a man is really human in the full sense of the word when playing (Schiller 1968: 72–3), it could be said that Japanese people really do perform as 'economic animals', when they become infatuated with their work, considering it half as a drug, half as a game. Huizinga stated that the evolution of human beings is closely related to the capacity for and the activity of playing, and that play is older than culture (Huizinga 1972: 16). But the act of playing has not generally been connected to production. Moreover, play has usually been considered as an alternative to productivity, just generating satisfaction.

It is true that in many cases play is not productive, but in other cases it is strongly connected to economic production. This is not a consequence of modernity, because Greek and Roman games or festivals were closely connected to economic activities. The point is to know when a game is just pure play, and when it, or any playing activity, can also be considered as a main generator of economic productivity. The lust for public games in classical Rome was quite strong. Emperors, like Nero or Titus frequently organized and patronized different types of games which would last for several days, including lotteries with presents consisting of home utensils, tickets for wheat, gold, pearls and precious stones, paintings, pets and domestic animals, even houses and ships (Friedlander 1947: 514).

Mangaka, the new artisan and the ludic of digital creation

In Japan, people belonging to the artisan or artistic domain (traditionally undifferentiated in Japanese society) still maintain most of the old ludic attitudes to production which were always found in that country. A good example is provided by the figure of Miyazaki Hayao, the famous *manga* and *anime* creator. Born in 1941,[3] he graduated from the Department of Politics and Economics at Gakushuin University. While there, he became affiliated with a study group dedicated to children's literature. He decided on drawing *manga* under the influence of Osamu Tezuka, starting his activity as an animator in 1963, when he worked for Toei Doga, one of the biggest companies in Japan. After becoming famous with works such as *Nausicaa of the Wind Valley* and other movies, he founded Studio Ghibli in 1985 with a colleague, Takahata Isao, and has been producing his own films ever since. He has been primarily an animator, drawing many of his works in pencil, using no ink. He liked to render backgrounds, costumes and props in great detail, in a style reminiscent of the French artist Jean 'Moebius' Giraud.

Miyazaki stated from the very start that he was determined not to create *manga* that people would read while they were eating soba noodles (Shodt 1996: 277–8). The form used by Miyazaki is very Western, both in settings and in representing people, props and customs. Inside, however, he is very Japanese, and makes frequent allusion to Japanese religious myths and legends. Like Osamu Tezuka, Miyazaki has always been attracted by giant insects. The protagonist of his first famous *manga*, *Nausicaa*, was inspired by a Heian legend about a princess who loved insects. Nevertheless, she is called Nausicaa, after the famous Greek heroine of Homer.

Miyazaki was born into a big family with several brothers and sisters. His father was an engineer involved in building planes for the Japanese army during the Second World War. He is fascinated by flying artifacts, and different flying objects are to be found in his films,[4] but, probably because he knew well the destructive power of of human artifacts, he has always shown a real concern about nature and its preservation. All his works show a retro-future vision and an ecological, anti-industrial attitude. In 1984, when sixteen episodes of *Nausicaa* were serialized in the magazine *Animage*, Miyazaki temporarily stopped drawing and went back to his real interest in animation. Since then, he has seldom worked on comics. Especially since founding Studio Ghibli, he has dedicated himself to the creation of animated films.

There are now around 100 people working in Studio Ghibli. Miyazaki's last film, *Mononoke Hime* (Princess Mononoke[5] or the phantom princess), made with a budget of $24 million, surpassed the film *ET* that held the record for fifteen years, to become the highest-earning film in Japanese history, until it gave way to *Titanic*. The film had more than 13 million viewers and earned $150 million less than one year after its release. Around 2 million videos were sold. Moreover, the film received the Cultural Agency's grand prize at the First Media Arts Festival Awards. The award 'recognizes achievement in new artistic fields that have developed techniques which make new forms of visual expression possible' (*Japan Economic Newswire*, 13 January 1998).

The story of *Mononoke Hime*, a feminist, ecological and rather dark film based on the conflict between industrial progress and nature, is set in the Muromachi Era, around the time of the War of Onin (1467–77). Its main emphasis is the need to live in harmony with nature, a theme transmitted in other films by Miyazaki. In spite of being an animated film, it has a very complex script, more for adults than for children. In fact, it was produced for people between 15 and 40 years of age.[6] Miyazaki said that by making this story, he wanted to show his concern for the future of the environment. Besides, the Muromachi Era mirrors the present era, in the sense that changes and confusion that took place in that period, as well as the attitudes to nature and the environment, are similar to the changes and crises of our civilization today. During that dynamic period of Japanese history, iron production burgeoned, but threatened the environment. A new type of society emerged in which women had even more freedom than they do today and many new arts were born, leading to the formation of a solid Japanese civilization.

Pure nature is recreated in this film, which shows the scenery of Japan when there were no roads and no dams – high, wild mountains, streams of cristalline water, plenty of birds, insects and animals, and a sparse population. A strange creature appears from time to time in the depth of the forests, called the *Kodama* ('echo', but its literal meaning is a tree spirit and the sound of the word *kodama* could also be translated as 'small spirit'), a kind of ancestor's spirit of the forests. One of the most interesting aspects of the film, however, is the detail used in depicting the everyday lives of the people of the time. The iron-making people worked in the *tataraba* (lit. 'iron-making place') where iron sands and charcoal were put in a furnace made of clay and burnt for several days to release the iron ingot. Because of the charcoal needed to melt the iron sands, trees were important for the process, and the *tatara* people keep cutting down trees while the forest gods fight against them. In *Monoke Hime*, iron-making means human civilization. The manufacturing of weapons represents war, and the tools made of iron represent agriculture, another more pacific aspect of human civilization. The conflict between the forest gods and the main characters shows the irresolvable conflict between humans and nature.

People working in the Studio Ghibli with Miyazaki are encouraged to commute by bicycle, as part of their personal campaign to preserve nature, but there are now several silicon graphics workstations at the studio, and computer graphics were used extensively – more than three cuts – for *Mononoke Hime*. Computers were used in three ways: digital painting, digital composition, and computer-generated images. New technologies are used naturally, and do not seem to conflict with traditional drawing.

Miyazaki's work was followed by the cameras of Studio Ghibli during the whole process of his creation. A tape was produced entitled *Mononoke Hime kōshite umareta* (That's how Princess Mononoke was born). The tape is a complete documentary record showing not only Miyazaki at work, but also his team, their everyday life and activities in the studio during the three complete years spent making the 133-minute film. One of the most interesting points is the way Miyazaki planned, explained and discussed his project with all the members of his team. At one of the meetings, for example, he tried to explain how he sees the other world, and the close relationship between living beings and the deceased. As most of the members of his team are young people, he had to explain even simple details about Japanese folk beliefs and about Buddhism. In this case, and while at work, it is amazing to see how Miyazaki enjoyed what he was doing, even when things did not go so well. The project also had a downside: too many hours of work every day and the hard pressure of time scheduling brought Miyazaki to real exhaustion, and he even thought of retiring completely from his job. Fortunately for his fans, he will keep on drawing although no longer taking on difficult projects.

The members of Miyazaki's team seemed as enthusiastic as the animator, enjoying the common project. For three years, everybody worked from 10 a.m. to midnight from Monday to Saturday, sometimes even on Sunday. In the recording tape, it is possible to see Miyazaki cooking *soba* noodles for the whole team, or training during a regular earthquake drill. Miyazaki and some of his closest co-operators helped in Kobe after the earthquake, and he noticed that not only a lack of food could be a problem, but also the lack of a toilet. He has designed in Studio Ghibli a special toilet for emergency use in case an earthquake should occur, and the tape shows the moment when Miyazaki introduced the invention to the whole team.

In order to represent accurately a real setting with woods, mountains and waterfalls, as they are seen in *Mononoke Hime*, Miyazaki and his team travelled to a distant island near Okinawa. There they observed the landscape, the sea and the waterfalls. Lots of sketches were made and the group had plenty of time to discuss and comment on their future work. Back on the main island, Honshū, they used a weekend to visit an old *tataraba*, where iron used to be made. Humans in *Mononoke Hime* destroy forest to make iron, and it was very important for Miyazaki to represent such a place accurately. The samurai also have an important role in the animated film: Miyazaki asked his close co-operator and manager Suzuki Toshio to bring a real Japanese sword (*katana*). He displayed it, holding it in his hands in order to draw it later; sometimes he would repeatedly do himself the actions he had to draw, imagining what the position of the body could be in every movement. Or he would ask one of the younger collaborators to perform a special action in front of him, paying attention to each and every one of his movements.

For the recording of the voices, as in other well-known Miyazaki films, famous film and stage actors were used for the cast.[7] Miyazaki directly supervised the recording. He was assisted by Hisaishi Joe, the music director, and Suzuki Toshio, Studio Ghibli's manager. Their enjoyment of the recording of voices is contagious, although sometimes both actors and Miyazaki's team had to repeat lines again and again. In these cases, when the actors were finally able to perform as they were requested, the three supervisors rejoiced in a lively way. In other cases, the actor's opinions influenced the final result, as in the case of the *Song of Mononoke*, which was changed a little due to the opinion of the singer, Mera Yoshikazu.

Miyazaki said that probably *Mononoke Hime* would be his last feature-length film: he could not go on physically, since directing a film is such exhausting work. He will leave Studio Ghibli to make way for young people, assisting in some capacity in the future, such as producing and writing scripts. He is building a 'Senior Ghibli', near Studio Ghibli, as his retirement place. As he can afford it now, he said he will probably be making films to please two people out of 100. He said he felt happy to be able to do many more things.

When the film was released on 12 July 1997, its success was greater than expected. It was then that Miyazaki spoke about his thoughts on *tsukuru* or producing *manga* and *anime*. He used conventional, very formal words: *Tsukuritai sakuhin wo, tsukuru hito tachi ga kanōna kagiri no tōtatsu ten e to, nijiriyotte iku. Sono zenkateiga sakuhin wo tsukuru to iu koto nanoda* (The person producing a work is trying as hard as possible to do his/her best, progressing little by little. We could say that this whole process is what we think about when producing something). People attending the ceremony of the release of the film and listening to his words nodded when Miyazaki explained his idea of creating or *tsukuru*. This word has traditionally had a great deal of emotional connotation for Japanese people.

In fact, during the process of drawing *Mononoke Hime*, Miyazaki received many applications from young people wishing to join Studio Ghibli. After carefully screening the applicants, Miyazaki concluded that most young people today do not have a positive inner attitude (*kokorogamae*) towards work, and that they are just looking for fast results and an effortless quick promotion. Words like hard work and effort (*kurō*) are almost unknown to the young generation. Miyazaki considers that creative work must reflect the worries of the artist. Through his/her creation, an artist must contribute a little to changing this world. And, at the same time, an artist's creation must influence his/her life (*Mononoke Hime kōshite umareta*: video tape).

In his speech at the release ceremony, Miyazaki mainly spoke about the hardness (*kurō*) of the whole process and about his and his team's endurance, about his physical extenuation and the tight schedule he and his team were obliged to follow. But they do not reflect completely the attitudes of Miyazaki nor of his team colleagues. It had to be really very hard work to make a film as difficult as *Mononoke Hime*, conveying both the serious message and an enjoyable one. The other side of the situation is that Miyazaki and his team showed a playful attitude at work, as can be seen in the tapes recorded during the process. Without this, possibly *Mononoke Hime* would not have become the product it is.

Tsukuru and its religious background

Miyazaki Hayao has become the most international of all Japanese *manga* and *anime* creators. His personality and his attitude to creative work can be easily understood, not only in Japan but in the rest of the world. Nevertheless, his attitude to producing (I use this term for *tsukuru*) his work is rooted in an older Japanese ethic.

Tsukuru is a Japanese term that could be translated into many different forms, all of them similar: to do, to make, to build, to produce, to create, to perform, and other related terms. The word also has religious origins, and an understanding of these could help to clarify the universe of Miyazaki's *manga* films. In spite of their Western style, they evidence a deeply Japanese influence, mainly of religious and mythical characteristics. I think that Japanese religion has influenced Miyazaki's work and his whole attitude to creating (*tsukuru*). Japanese religion has influenced the attitudes of most of Japanese people, and can be seen in the internalization of their own popular beliefs or folk religion (*minzoku shinkō*, or *minzoku shūkyō*), sometimes referred to as 'primitive Shintō'.

Shintō comprises a set of beliefs that rely upon the *kami*, supernatural beings with immense powers beyond any human control. *Kami* may be described as the set of powers and elements of Nature controlling the very subsistence of humans. These *kami* lack, as far as is known, any moral or philosophical code or judgement, but were usually kind and helpful towards humans who in turn treated *kami* with awe and respect. Defilement (*kegare*) especially offended *kami*. To clean this *kegare* from the human world it was necessary to offer frequent rituals and sacrifices, so that the *kami* would return kindly to bless and help the humans in their endeavours. According to Shintō beliefs, human life potentially generates *kegare*. That does not mean that everyone and everything is impure, but that impurity emerges from human life, so that *kami* must visit this world frequently to regenerate everything, and not allow *kegare* to stay for long. To clean defilement from this world is the main task of the *kannushi*, or Shintō priest. For Japanese people in general, the basis of Shintō religious observance and practice is mainly to visit shrines and undergo *harai*, a cleaning ritual performed by the priests (*kannushi*).

Ritual control

All Shintō rituals require propriety and control. It is highly important to perform the rituals in a proper form and things must be done in the right manner. From early times, *kami* were expected to come when properly requested. Any place could be temporally transformed into a divine place, therefore the role of the priest was critical, to ensure the strict observance of the ritual. This situation has not changed much and nowadays too a Shintō priest is a real expert who is in rigid control of the immediate ritual environment. The relationship between the *kami* and the ritual community he serves is crucial (Ashkenazi, 1990: 43–4). The kind of careful preparation practised not only lies at the very heart of most of the agrarian festivals or *matsuri*, but has permeated many aspects of Japanese social attitudes, both to work and to play. Of all *matsuri*, the shrine festivals that take place during the yearly ritual cycle are most relevant, probably because not only the shrine and *kannushi* are involved, but parishioners and the whole community as well. The *kami* must be properly invited, correctly entertained and seen off. This periodic festival activity serves to deflect defilement and prevent ill fortune from entering the community (see Nelson 1992). People's attitudes when attending a *matsuri* can vary from mere curiosity or even pure recreational experience to an enthusiastic religious stance. In general terms the sole word *matsuri* meant to perform a role in the best possible manner to achieve *kami* satisfaction. Identification with *kami* also indicated that human satisfaction was a reflection of divine satisfaction. From this point of view *kami* should be treated as people themselves would like to be treated.[8]

Technology and tools

Since early times Japanese technology has been adapted to nature. As humans considered *kami* uncontrollable forces of nature from which many benefits but also evil could come, good relations with the gods were necessary to guarantee the very subsistence of human life. This attitude also meant a close empathy with the natural environment. The producer or creator was considered a real mediator between human kind (the users and customers) and God. Getting people satisfied meant getting *kami* satisfied. Extracting beauty from nature and incorporating it into people's lives to make both humans and the gods content became a real ludic experience.

The process of creating something beautiful and useful depended first on how the creation was started. The tools used in producing the final product were treated with the same respect and fearsome reverence as the product itself. The artists, builders or artisans also identified themselves with the tools used to produce their work, considering their instruments a part of themselves. Tools used to create were imbued with a divine quality, a divinity present in every process of creation and production. Human beings are also prospective *kami*.[9] The audience in the old *kagura* (ritual religious dances) was considered to be the embodiment of the divinity. At the same time, the performer was the real mediator between *kami* and the audience. And, as a *medium*, the performer was the recipient of the *kami* spirit.

Feudal past

Japan remained almost completely isolated from the rest of the world for about 250 years, from the early seventeenth well into the second half of the nineteenth century. At that time, Japan was basically an agrarian country. The political isolation and the strongly centralized social control brought a closed autarchy as well as a lack of internal and external conflicts. This peculiar course of history brought a development of technology in the production of food and the manufacturing of tools, as in every aspect of creation, with almost no external influences. Another key point in the formation of attitudes on *tsukuru* was the policy of austerity imposed by the government to all social classes, especially to peasants, but also to artisans and traders. For all of them it was compulsory to use a certain type of fabric for their clothes, or a certain type of furniture in their homes. Gradually everybody developed ingenuity and a sharp sense of creation in order to make the best of their lot.

At this point, any differences between artist and artisan almost vanish. In China it was said that the artist used his genius to create a prototype and the artisan used his skill to produce that prototype in any given quantity. In Japan that distinction did not exist. In fact every mechanical worker tried hard to bring his work as nearly as possible to technical and artistic perfection, following well-established techniques, norms and models. Any modification was only slowly introduced, in almost an imperceptible manner.[10] In their turn, peasants also achieved an increase in agrarian production, with rice production increasing by 1.7 times and attaining much better quality. To achieve a sheer increase in volume was not an end in itself, however, if it went against achieving a better quality.

The family system and its influence on tsukuru

The traditional base of Japanese social organization is to be found in the *ie*, an extended family system or family line, taken in the sense of ancestor/descendant relations. The heir to the house, usually but not necessarily the eldest son, was in charge of preserving and ensuring the existence of the family and bringing prosperity to the house. This very same structure was duplicated in the system of production and creation.

The heir of an artist or artisan was obliged to continue his master's skills or abilities. To improve previously learnt skills was one of his main tasks, and this was achieved generally without introducing any drastic changes. Let us examine the situation in the *ie* of a carpenter.[11] The eldest son was heir to the tools and to the peculiar skills of his father, who acted with a long-term view in mind and even planted trees so that descendants could someday use that wood. The heir tried to continue his master's professional activity. When a beautiful and useful object was produced, the object functioned as a connection between producer and user. This attitude is similar to the religious attitude to preparing a site for a *matsuri* to please the *kami*. The results might not always be as expected, but most important was the personal attitude or *kokorogamae*. Production starts with the external form (*katachi kara hairu*) and has to go all the way through final results, passing through the tools and instruments. The final object must reflect this attitude, bringing real satisfaction to the user. And the user's satisfaction could be considered the base for the producer's satisfaction too.[12]

In Spain, Greek and Roman classical tradition has provided models for the ludic attitudes of people. In ancient Greece, slaves did manual work, and male citizens had the opportunity to enjoy philosophy and conversation without the obligation to do any kind of work. This attitude to free and ludic time was also adopted by the Romans, who created plenty of free time to enjoy games, festivals and gambling. This attitude pervaded later cultures in the Mediterranean area. In northern countries of Europe, there were similar attitudes, but these gradually changed because of religious influences, especially Protestantism. Work started to be considered a respectable treasure.

From tradition to modernity

The Japanese *ie* system has managed to survive in some aspects, and can be found in Japanese companies and factories trying to combine tradition and innovation while remaining faithful to the principles of their companies' founding fathers. People in their 40s or over who grew up with the traditional work ethic (especially if they belong to the artisan milieu) certainly feel that way. Itami Jūzō reflects the idea in his film *Tampopo* which depicts the life of a widow with a son in his teens. She has to run the small noodle restaurant of her deceased husband, but the shop is crumbling under a heavy load of debts, and her son is always bullied at school. One day, two truck drivers stop at the restaurant, trying to get a good meal of noodles, but get rather messy food instead. The young widow confesses that she cannot cook and the drivers decide to help her by visiting each and every famous noodle restaurant to try and capture the best recipe. They invoke the unusual help of someone said to have been one of the experts in the field who died many years ago, but who agrees to return from the other world to teach them the secrets of the art. Finally refurbished and painted, the restaurant reopens and the three men show their satisfaction when eating the new noodle recipe. When the truck drivers depart, a long queue of people wait their turn outside the small shop.

Most interesting in this example is the attitude of the woman and those who help her. This attitude, again *kokorogamae*, is kept up throughout the whole process and leads them to the success of making the best noodle restaurant in town. Success means happiness for everybody and this is the fun of the game. All the people in the team were struggling to improve the restaurant in order to achieve the pleasure of customers (and that meant success for the restaurant). This attitude is similar to the one people adopt during preparation for a *matsuri* when the question is how to please *kami*. In Japanese there is the proverb: *O kyaku sama wa kami sama desu* (the customer is god, not king), and this is quite meaningful.

In real life, a similar case may be seen in the case of a couple of *tōfu* artisans who had a small *tōfu* shop in Kyoto where they used a traditional recipe. The shop had very low popularity. One day, the owner tasted his homemade *tōfu* and he discovered that it tasted bad. Again, this couple followed an intense search, trying to find the best recipe. Their quest was almost in away half ludic, half religious. At last, they managed to produce a *tōfu* that has gained this couple a solid reputation and fame in Kyoto, where the owner is now known as 'the god of artisans'. The way was long and difficult but rewarding, and he himself agrees that both of them enjoyed themselves very much during the whole process.

Most of the artisans I knew in Kyoto produced their works as if they were unique masterpieces. Although traditional crafts are not so much in demand in modern Japanese society, these craftsmen worked with total dedication and it looked as if they were not thinking so much about their economic reward. This was the case with an artisan of *fūrin*, the traditional little bell that decorates almost every Japanese house in the summer. I met him in Osaka, during a craftsmanship fair in a department store. He explained to me that the type of *fūrin* he made was an unusual one, and he could not sell big quantities. When he inherited the business from his father he was thinking of producing a different type of bell in order to reach a larger sector of the market. But he eventually decided to keep his father's style, introducing some curious (he used the word *omoshiroi*) innovations. He now has a fixed market for his product and although he does not sell as much as others, he says he feels happy making something he really knows and enjoys. He probably lacks public recognition or economic reward, but he gets satisfaction through keeping his family business going. Moreover, he is proud of having a 'speciality' among the specialized *fūrin* makers, and this makes his work rewarding. And the fact that he is able to offer a different style of bell to his customers reassures him on his identity and brings sense to his existence.[13]

During research visits to the prefectures of Wakayama, Aichi and Iwate, and also in Okinawa where I formed part of a research group lead by Professor Miyake Hitoshi, I had many opportunities to attend *matsuri* (festivals), always finding myself amused by the seriousness of the preparations. Everybody got up very early in the morning; the people in charge of preparations were divided into different teams performing almost ritual tasks. All of them made every effort to ensure the success of the festival. A festival is a ludic activity but the whole community works as hard as if they were doing a job.

Similarly, on several trips to the town of Kajimadai, near Sendai, where I visited agrarian villages and farms, peasants proudly displayed their main products to me: apples, spinach, strawberries or melons, showing an intimate pleasure and pride that they had achieved a better quality or a bigger size. Each apple was carefully wrapped into a special type of paper to be protected against insects, too much sun, heat or cold. Each of these apples seemed to have a distinct personality. Like robots on an assembly line who are given names, I thought that each and every one of these apples might have also a name. Farmers I met seemed to be rejoicing at the prospect of seeing their products displayed and admired, which made all their work and efforts ludic and pleasant.

In the modern company domain, the president of a famous Japanese beer manufacturer showed a similar attitude when he tried to change the brand image and people's perception of the product – even the very taste of the beer produced in the factory (Higuchi 1993). It happened that, although the brand had always ranked second in the list of top beers, its sales had decreased and it was losing popularity day by day. The newly appointed president decided to visit the presidents of other top beer companies, asking their advice in order to find out what they thought a good beer should be. At the same time, the company started a nationwide campaign among consumers to try and get feedback. Much information was collected and the process of change was under way. No time or money was spared. A team of people worked in close contact with the factory until a completely new taste was developed. The next step was to work in co-operation with the advertisers for a publicity campaign. The new product was a real success, and not only did that beer brand recover, but it even surpassed that of the former competitors.

This president, even without being conscious of it, had an almost religious attitude. He acted with a spirit of mission when he decided to follow a learning path (*shūgyō*) similar to a rite of passage. He also showed a ludic attitude: exultant and amused like anyone can be in a game. Here again we find a pride characteristic of people producing something with their hands, using their skill or devoting themselves to the pursuit of a goal. The origin of this attitude could be in the already mentioned fact that from old times the social status of these people was low (in the case of merchants/artisans) or their real weight in society was not recognized (in the case of farmers). Separated from the circles of power and decision-making, they have developed an identification with the most traditional aspects of their country. They identify themselves with the real spirit of Japan. Similarly, in modern companies producing commodities, competition is strong and managers must be careful not to be surpassed by their competitors.

Change and continuity

Together with economic up-and-downs, and influences from other countries, an increasing tendency to enjoy more free time has been growing in Japanese society since the end of the 1980s. When the bubble economy became a real problem and fewer hours of work were needed, public campaigns were started for more hours of free time and less of work. It was commented then that many mature people, especially men, could not fully understand the pleasure of doing nothing. Different programmes were organized to instruct mature people on how to use and enjoy their free time. The reason was that most of these men were unable to think of using their time in something different from productive work.

Younger people do not seem to have the same problem. They have grown up in a different type of society. They are said to belong to the *shinjinrui* (new race) of Japanese. They try to avoid hard work, and hate the three *ki: kitanai, kitsui, kibishii* (dirty, strict, difficult) tasks. It is hard to think that these young people could easily get used to a full commitment to their working activities. Neither do they identify themselves so completely with their production. In fact, like their Western counterparts, many young Japanese people look for enjoyment in activities not at all connected with their job: travel, shopping (in the case of young women), car driving. Parallel to this trend, companies try to make jobs more attractive and pleasant, as can be seen in the following text:

> *Jidai no henka de mōretsu kara 'beautiful' e; korekara wa 'business' wa asobi gokoro wo motte, 'enjoy' suru 'business beautiful' to demo iu yōna hōko ni susumu koto ga mottomo daijina keie 'policy' no hitotsu ni naru.* (Because of changes in our times, let's have fun at work. From now on, business must be done in high spirits. We must switch to a style of job that could be called 'beautiful business': this is a matter to be encouraged)
>
> (*Chichi*, April 1989)

Another executive director recommends that products should have the characteristics of being *tsukaiyasui* (easy to use), *wakariyasui* (simple to understand) and must reflect the following attitudes: *tanoshisa* (enjoyment), *asobi* (fun), *yorokobi* (merryness), *yōkisa* (quality), *akarusa* (brightness). This statement reflects the great efforts being made by company directives in order to make job atmosphere and working attitudes more ludic and pleasant. This could be a consequence of new tendencies shown by the younger generation, the *shinjinrui* who, as said, prefer to consider work completely apart from their ludic time, finding their real pleasure in activities other than work. To consider a job, whatever it could be, an artisan's creation has been one of the tendencies for many working people in the past, but these traditional sentiments seem to be not so widespread today, particularly since the postwar tendency to identify workers with their company is declining (cf. Nakamaki 1990, 1992).

Traditional attitudes have been adapted in some cases but not in others. It is difficult for companies to offer their employees a meaningful, collective goal, as well as economic stability and a real base – both for individual and corporate identity building. Religious attitudes still permeate Japanese society and this fact can help in maintaining traditional attitudes, although many young people's tendencies are for a more individualistic approach. Perhaps only creative producers like Miyazaki Hayao are able to maintain both their modern artistic individuality and their roots based on the traditional Japanese ethic.

Conclusions

As in the past, when many artisans' work was not especially well-regarded by society, modern *mangaka* have had to struggle today against public prejudice. Only a real perfection and creativity led them to success. *Mangaka* are obliged to prove that they are not acting as simply *dilettante* or *amateurs*. As well as creating a positive and playful attitude, they have to try hard, showing a superior skill.

Ludic attitudes to work seem curiously rather productive. This may be the reason why companies encourage their young employees to have a joyful attitude when performing their job. Moreover, a certain laziness at times can later become very productive, especially nowadays, where leisure occupies a very important place in society, both as people have more spare time and as a generator of economic income.

The main point of the Japanese personal attitude known as *kokorogamae* and of the positive playful spirit (*asobi gokoro*) is to emphasize that the purpose is important, but the attitude has to be a ludic one. This will have a great influence on the results. When finally the product is enjoyed by the users, it is as if, through the inspiration of the divinity (*kami*), the maker, producer or creator acted as a mediator: he/she became – in a sense – a *kami*, through creating the best object possible for a prospective user . . . also considered a *kami*.

Maybe the final conclusion should be that ludic sense and satisfaction are embodied in the thought that 'we could all become *kami*, by the Way of *Tsukuru*'.

Notes

1   *Mangaka* means 'creator of Japanese comics' (*manga*), but recently the same term has been used for creators of animated films as well.

2   The Japanese word *tsukuru* in its phonetic sound can be translated as 'to do', 'to create', 'to make', 'to build', 'to produce' or 'to achieve'. As often happens in the Japanese language, a single phonetic sound can have many different characters for writing, and the meaning of each also has different connotations.

3   A complete account of Miyazaki's life and work can be found in Miyazaki 1996.

4   Miyazaki's work, *Kurenai no buta* (also known as *Porco Rosso*), depicts the story of an adventurer in a biplane. This work was serialized in *Animerica*, vol. 1, nos. 5–7, with the title *The Crimson Pig*.

5   *Mononoke* means 'the spirit of a thing'. It can be attributed to any inexplicable thing. It can also be the spirit of an inanimate object, such as a tree. It may be applied to the spirit of a dead person, a live person, an animal, goblin or monster. In English it is translated as 'phantom'.

6   As Frederic Shodt says: 'Modern *manga* began as a children's medium, as a subculture, but *manga* are now read by adults of nearly all ages and are part of the cultural mainstream. Yet no matter how hard artists try to create 'grown up' material, *manga* still betray their origins – in their continuing emphasis in 'cuteness' and in the way the distinction between material for children and adults is still much more blurred than in other entertainment media'. *Mononoke Hime* seems to have the purpose of pleasing adults more than children.

7   Ishida Yuriko, a very popular young actress who appears in a lot of films and trendy dramas, played Mononoke Hime and Matsuda Yōji played the role of the male protagonist, the young Ashitaka. Other roles were played by Morishige Hisaya, Miwa Akihiro, a transvestite famous for his perfomances of mysterious females, Mori Mitsuko, and Tanaka Yuko, one of the most popular actresses in Japan.

8   The myth of Amaterasu shows perfectly the importance of play and hilarity to gain the favour of the divinity. Having been offended by her brother Susanoo, Amaterasu shut herself up in a cave, leaving the whole world in darkness, until a minor Goddess, Ame no Uzume danced a grotesque and fairly obscene dance that aroused general laughter and shouting. The noise finally pushed Amaterasu into peeping out of her hiding place, and she was then pulled out of the cave amidst general laughter and content.

9   Ian Reader explains that: 'The continuity between humans and *kami* means that human beings, too, can become *kami*, retaining an influence in this world, generally through a continuation of the qualities that marked them out in this life' (Reader 1991: 25).

10 Yamaguchi Masao's chapter in this same book explains how mechanical technology was devalued or not well-considered and how this had a great influence on the attitude of those creating mechanical objects. These people had to achieve a high degree of perfection to get social and popular recognition.

11 The ritual involving the selection of tools has been described by Coaldrake (1990). He mentions that there were two different types of tools: 'for the mind' and 'for the hand'. All of them were imbued with special significance, because 'the carpenter could follow the right path only if he used the appropriate tool in the correct way for each task' (1990: 11).

12 This attitude on the part of master carpenters of traditional Japanese shrines and temples has not changed, as mentioned by Coaldrake (*ibid.*), and in the case of the famous Nishioka Shōichi, who became the protagonist of a video in the year 1990.

13 Dorinne Kondo takes a critical approach about artisanal work as self-realization in her book *Crafting Selves* (1990).

Bibliography

Ashkenazi, M. (1990) 'Ritual experts in Shintō and Judaism', in *Japanese Civilization in the Modern World: Religion*, Senri Ethnological Studies, Osaka, 29, pp. 37–46.

Coaldrake, W. (1990) *The Way of the Carpenter*, New York: Weatherhill.

Cervantes, M. (1969) 'Rinconete y Cortadillo', in *Novelas Ejemplares*, Madrid: Alfaguara.

—— (1998) *El Ingenioso hidalgo, D. Quijote de la Mancha*, colección centenario, Madrid: Espasa.

Durkheim, E. (1960) *Les formes élèmentaires de la vie religieuse*, Paris: PUF.

Friedlander, L. (1947) *La sociedad romana*, Mexico: Fondo Cultura Económica.

González, S. (1998) *El Laberinto de la fortuna, juego trabajo y ocio en la sociedad española*, Fundación Estudios del Ocio, Madrid: Biblioteca Nueva.

Higuchi, H. (1993) *Nen zureba hana ga hiraku*, Tokyo: Shotensha.

Huizinga, J. (1972) *Homo Ludens*, Madrid: Alianza.

Kondo, D. (1990) *Crafting Selves*, Chicago: University of Chicago Press.

Martín, A. (1975) '*El arte paleolítico español*', in Menéndez Pidal (ed) *Historia de España*, vol. 1, Madrid: Espasa-Calpe.

Miyazaki, H. (1996) *Shuppatsu ten, 1979–1996*, in T. Suzuki (ed.) Studio Ghibli.

Nakamaki, H. (1990) 'Religious civilization in Modern Japan, as revealed through a focus on Mt Koya' *Japanese Civilization in the Modern World: Religion*, Senri Ethnological Studies, Osaka, 29, pp. 121–36.

Nakamaki, H. (1992) *Mukashi daymyō, ima kaisha (Kiguiō to shūkyō)* Kyoto: Tankōsha.

Nelson, J. (1992) 'Shinto ritual: managing chaos in contemporary Japan', *Ethnos* 57: 77–104.

Read, H. (1972) *Imagen e Idea*, Mexico: Fondo de Cultura Económica.

Reader, I. (1991) *Religion in Contemporary Japan*, Honolulu: University of Hawaii Press.

Schiller, F. (1968) *La educación estética del hombre*, Madrid: Espasa-Calpe.

Seara, Luis Gonzalez (1998) *El laberinto de la fortura*, Madrid: Biblioteca Nueva ed.

Shodt, F.L. (1966) *Writings on Modern Manga*, California. Stone Bridge Press.

Veblen, T. (1951) *Teoría de la clase ociosa*, Mexico: Fondo de Cultura Económica (first English edition 1899).

Wohrringer, W. (1953) *Abstracción y Naturaleza*, México, Fondo de Cultura Económica.

6   Saved by the love song

Japanese rock fans, memory and the pursuit of pleasure[1]

Carolyn S. Stevens

Introduction

> The sensibility of the consumer operates by producing structures of pleasure
> ... there is the satisfaction of doing what others would have you do, the
> enjoyment of doing what you want, the fun of breaking the rules, the fulfill-
> ment – however temporary and artificial – of desires, the release of cathar-
> sis, the comfort of escaping from negative situations, the reinforcement of
> identifying with a character, and the thrill of sharing another's emotional life,
> and so on ...
>
> I am suggesting that our most common relationship to popular culture is
> determined by the cultural production of pleasure.
>
> (Grossberg 1992: 55)

This chapter examines the processes of 'pleasure' found in the Japanese rock fan
context. Following on from Grossberg's stipulation that fandom is defined as the
consumption of the 'cultural production of pleasure', an analysis of these processes
show how fans of a Japanese rock group, the Alfee, take pleasure from their activities
and how fan identity affects their perception of their place in the world around
them: in school, family and/or workplace relationships. Particularly noted are fans'
concert attendance and their interaction with one another in that context. There
are obstacles which must be overcome when attending an Alfee concert (for
example, school, work and family obligations). Part of the pleasure of attending a
concert is overcoming these adversities, or 'beating the odds'. However, once
achieved, rock concert attendance has very strict rules, despite its 'free-for-all',
festival atmosphere. Looking back on social interactions according to these rules,
Alfee fandom provides a scale by which fans can view their own life course process
in a pleasurable way as paced by the band's twenty-year history.

Lisa A. Lewis' volume, *The Adoring Audience: Fan Culture and Popular Media* (1992),
sets forth definitions of fandom and the processes by which people become fans. Fans
are 'positively' defined by their intimate knowledge of a subject (Jenson 1992); their
relationship to the consumption and production of popular culture (Fiske 1992); and
the empowerment of the individual through participation in 'fandom' (Grossberg
1992). These definitions counter the negative stereotypes that many of us are familiar

with: fans as 'deviant', 'disreputable', and 'dangerous' (Jenson 1992: 9). Other negative definitions include the idea that the fan is passively created by the 'modern celebrity system, via the mass media' (Jenson 1992: 10). The fan is often seen as someone who is not a part of 'normal' society, as the fan's priorities are skewed towards values that are embodied in pastimes not valued by the majority or by those in positions of power. Yet, there are rules that guide fan consumption of popular culture. This is primarily a question of the legitimation of taste and the establishment of boundaries: how 'meaningful' are popular cultural representations, and how far should we go in consuming them or discussing the consumption of them? One may argue that the cultural and economic processes that surround these products, rather than the products' content, are important areas of investigation in their own right. Therefore, fandom may be seen as both integrated and separate, both bound and freed from the cultural icon to which it attaches itself. This chapter recognizes the importance of the relationship between the icon's meaning and its following but does not attempt to critique the Japanese rock band artistically. Rather, I am interested in looking at fandom's value as it stems from its function as an integrating process of multiple personal identities in other contexts over time, and how nostalgia works to integrate the fan's past with the present in a pleasurable way. Thus, fandom expresses a valuable social process. Raveri has noted that, 'The ludic is not an end in itself, but the foundation of social relationships'. Alfee fans find in fandom a set of meanings by which they mark time over the individual life course.

Lebra Takie, in her now classic study of Japanese women, specifically embraced a life-cycle approach because she felt that a subject's 'life pattern, role repertoire, status and values tend to change radically over her life stages' (1984: 3). This is true for men as well as women. Though fans may be seen as marginalized from mainstream taste, life stage definitions for Alfee fans are not radically different from other Japanese. Student, friend, worker, spouse, parent – these categories are set by the individual's relationships to others both inside and outside the family. I argue that Alfee fandom may be used as an emic interpreter of life stages that is layered upon the more general roles assigned to most members of society.[2]

Introducing the Alfee

An examination of rock fans may help to settle some of these issues in a Japanese context.[3] This rock band has an established fan base that allows the band to continue an active performing and recording career even after their peak of popularity in the 1980s. Who are the Alfee? The Alfee, or '*Arufii*' as they are known in Japanese, are Takamizawa Toshihiko (electric guitar), Sakazaki Kohnosuke (acoustic guitar) and Sakurai Masaru (bass guitar). This guitar-based trio hires other musicians to play drums and keyboards during recording sessions and concert tours, but the three guitarists constitute official membership in the group.

Takamizawa and Sakazaki were born in 1954, and Sakurai in 1955; all are natives of the Tokyo metropolitan area. All are *jinan*, or second sons, of middle- to upper-class families (Takamizawa's father is a retired school principal while both Sakazaki and Sakurai are sons of liquor shop owners). The band formed in

1973, while the three members were classmates at Meiji Gakuin University in Tokyo. It first performed under the name 'Confidence' and these early performances and recordings reflect the influence of Japanese folk music movement in late 1960s and early 1970s, notable as this was the first time Japanese popular artists recorded vocals in Japanese rather than in English.[4] Their early style also accounts for their current composition: a folk band did not need a percussion section, so the group consisted of only two acoustic guitars and a bass. All three members contributed vocals. Their first full-length album was released in 1975 by Victor Records under the name 'Alfie'[5] but it found little audience and their contract was soon allowed to expire. The three young men later signed a new contract with Canyon Records (later, Pony Canyon) in 1979 and released their first album under the name they currently use, 'Alfee'.[6] They released two albums and seven accompanying singles, but these met with little commercial success, though their concert tours were gathering a following. In 1981, under pressure from their manager and the Canyon recording executives, they changed strategies. Takamizawa, one of the acoustic guitarists and the group's songwriter, changed to electric guitar and took over the band's leadership from Sakazaki, who remained on acoustic guitar. The band released their first rock album in 1981 and continued to produce albums and singles with Pony Canyon. In January 1983, the Alfee commenced their first national tour, despite the fact they had no national hit single.

In October 1983, the Alfee broke the national hit chart for the first time with their single 'Marie-Ann'. It was their fourteenth single with Pony Canyon (not including their work with Victor), and this gave them a reputation of being a hard-working band who had earned their success. They released another single, '*Hoshizora* no distance', in 1985, which outperformed 'Marie-Ann'. From then on, the Alfee made their way successfully in a competitive pop industry through hard work. From 1983 to 1994, they performed an average of ninety shows a year, released twenty-two full-length albums, twenty-eight singles, twenty-one concert videos, and presented thirty-nine outdoor and special events (The Alfee 1995). Their concert tours are so well attended even today that they ranked number nine in 1997 concert attendance records (*Nikkei Entertainment* 1998: 39). When asked what concerts they had seen in the last year, a random sample of university students rated Alfee performances as the eleventh most frequently attended (Inamasu 1994: 90).

Other Alfee achievements include 1989 concert appearances with Jean Paul Gaultier fashion shows, the opening of the 1990 Osaka Flower Exhibition (*Hana no Banpaku*), an appearance on the American Music Awards ceremony in 1991, the performance of the national anthem at an NBA exhibition game in 1994, the opening of the Tokyo Dome in 1988 and the Tokyo International Forum in 1997, and even international concerts (Forest Hills, New York in 1998 and Berlin, Germany in 1999). In 1997, the band's long-term contract with Pony Canyon Records expired and they signed up with Toshiba EMI, Japan, where they are currently located. Their 1998 concert video, 'Tokyo one-night dream' hit number one on the video charts, as evidence of their continuing presence in the Japanese pop/rock music scene.

The Alfee fan

Because the band has been active for over twenty years, Alfee fans' age varies from early teens to early 40s. At times one even sees small children at concerts, accompanied by their fan parents. Alfee fans are both male and female (though women predominate) and they come from both rural and urban regions. I have yet to confirm that the Alfee appeal to one particular social class rather than a range of middle and upper classes. However, we can assume that Alfee fan identity is restricted to middle and upper classes because consumer behaviour involved requires a certain amount of expendable income.

Signs of fandom: the language of the Alfee

A linguistic analysis is helpful here in defining fan identity from the fans' perspective. Identification with the Alfee can be seen as divided into two levels: general and specific. First is their identification as 'Alfee fans', distinct from other Japanese groupies. They give their 'condition' a name to distinguish themselves from fans of other musical groups: they are '*aruchū*', a pun on the phrase *arufii muchū* (meaning in an 'Alfee daze', or an 'Alfee trance') and the word *arukōru chūdoku* (often shortened to *aruchū*, meaning 'alcoholic'), so that one could quite literally translate their condition as 'Alfee-aholics'. *Aruchū* fans go to *arukon*: a term derived from *arufii konsāto*, or 'Alfee concerts'. This clearly fits into Fiske's category of 'enunciative productivity', a characteristic of fandom defined as the 'use of semiotic system (typically, but not exclusively, verbal language) which is specific to its speaker and its social and temporal context' (1992: 37–8).

Fans' identity construction is self-conscious in the writings of fans in magazines: fans write to the official fan club magazine and other music magazines, always introducing themselves in the following manner: '(name), (age), Alfee fan history: x years'. Alfee fandom also overcomes personal and cultural differences. After discussing problems of racism in Japan, an Alfee fan wrote to me in English: 'You are my *arutomo* [a combination of the first syllables of the words 'Alfee' and 'friend', in other words, an 'Alfee pal'], we talk about The Alfee and enjoy their music. It is enough to be *arutomo*'.[7] This conciliatory message was sent in the belief that our mutual feelings for the Alfee could conquer cultural differences. Fandom is thus considered powerful and universal.

Fandom as life-stage: the student, the **shakaijin**, *the 'Alfee mama'*

Alfee fan identity is based not only on a perceived connection with the band but also on interaction among fans. Fandom is a form of communication between young people; they share their hopes and dreams about their idols with each other. They also just have a good time, using the Alfee as an excuse to go out and enjoy themselves in each other's company. Sometimes Alfee fans will gather and end up discussing anything but the Alfee.[8] Yet it is their passion for the band that brings them together. Concerts are just such an impetus for gathering. Fans buy tickets to the concerts and meet each other both before and after the concert; they might share a snack or a drink, or just sit outside the arena until the concert begins, talking about the band or anything else that comes to mind. The concert is an event that marks the fans' interaction at a particular date and place. This event, with all its associations, is filed away in the fans' cache of memories. However, as concert tickets are not inexpensive (usually about 6000 yen) and competition for seats can be fierce in smaller venues, not every fan can attend every concert. Barriers to concert attendance are a common theme in letters to the fan club magazine. These obstacles shift over time. Interestingly, this is precisely the departure point for the discussion of 'rules of game': the rules of the rock concert often collide with rules for family, school and company life. The life-stage model is useful to point out that these non-fan identity rules tend to change with time during an individual's life course.

Alfee concerts are not considered dangerous, but some young fans have difficulties getting permission to go out on school nights, especially during exam season. Some are just deemed too young to attend; a fan who was unable to go to a 1993 concert implies the reason is her age as she introduces herself, her letter printed in the original childish hand: 'As a fifth grader, I've never been to an Alfee concert, and I thought I would definitely go to [this one] . . . but as I expected, it was impossible [*yappari muri deshita*]' (*Alfee Mania* 1993: 8). Another entry, this time in a music magazine published at the height of the group's popularity, offers advice to the young Alfee fan:

> To the fan . . . who wrote in the no. 11 issue: If your parents object to the concert, then get them to go with you!
>
> First, you must get them to recognize the Alfee's worth (*arufii no yosa*). If they go to a concert with you and approve of the Alfee's great songs and the other fans' good manners, then they'll relax. That's the best way! . . .
>
> But, because you're a ninth grader,[9] you've got to study properly. You should think about . . . the position you're putting [your parents] in . . . If you fail your studies, the Alfee wouldn't be happy either!
>
> (*Best Hit* 1985: 131)

A young student writes:

> Since I've started talking about the Alfee at my school, gradually I've made more and more friends who are 'intimate' (*shitashimi no*) with the Alfee . . . Having friends around to whom I can always talk about the Alfee is the *best*. Life at school has become fun.
>
> (*Alfee Mania*, 1994: 9)

Parents, it appears, need to be educated about the Alfee's good points in order to give permission for their children to attend concerts. In fact, the Alfee themselves can be seen as parental figures as well (since they too would be disappointed in a fan's failure at school). In the last case, the Alfee function in a different way to support a student's educational experience. The stress of the Japanese competitive educational system becomes manageable to this fan who finds that telling others she is an Alfee fan makes her feel more popular and eases the tedium of classroom life. Her love for the band facilitates other social relationships in her peer group.

Another fan tells of her first conscious identification as an Alfee fan, again related to the educational system:

> My first contact with the Alfee was when I was in junior high school, the time of 'Marie-Ann' and '*Hoshizora* no distance'. Because I was so busy with school, I didn't have any time to listen to the Alfee. But, later I experienced a setback with my college entrance examinations. Every day was painful. At times, I thought there was nothing more I could do . . . then I listened to '19' [an Alfee song released in 1988; at that time, the fan was aged nineteen], and I was saved. After that I began going to concerts and making new friends through the Internet [Alfee fan] mailing lists. I ended up being completely entranced by the Alfee [*aruchū*].[10]

Merry White's ethnographic study of Japanese teenagers (1993) notes that '[s]chool is a place where . . . everything significant happens – and not always in the classroom' (p. 71–2). School becomes the child's institutional identity; furthermore, the student *per se* is a constructed image that is specifically tied to status in the community (p. 75). The image's content is primarily attributed to academic excellence (or lack thereof), but there are other kinds of status involved in the construction of studentdom. How students interact with each other is also important. Primary school is thought to be generally carefree, while schooling becomes increasingly competitive and serious in nature as one goes up the ladder to the university examination after senior year. Tracking in secondary school may separate students from their primary and junior high school peers, leaving them to make new friends in a new environment. This process can occur earlier if the student attempts entrance at prestigious junior high schools as well. Creating a common discourse for friendly interaction is important, as things may become difficult when '[l]earning what is cool and what is not . . . takes place in an atmosphere pressured by the examinations' (p. 78). The fan quoted feels that the Alfee as dialogue is the key to success in social relationships at her school.

It is notable that all of the expressions of student identity in fan letters and interviews refer to the years before university entrance, or specifically to the period leading up to the university entrance exam. Not all young Japanese attend university, and those who do not might experience different kinds of pressure (to find employment, for example). College students often find it easier to attend Alfee concerts as they have a more flexible schedule. However, without part-time jobs or other financial support, college students may not have the steady income required to pay for the frills of fandom (repeat concert attendance, travelling across the country to see special events, buying Alfee souvenirs and CDs, and so on). Being an Alfee fan is not inexpensive and students are often prohibited from activities for financial reasons.

After graduation (whether from high school, junior college or university), Japanese young people find themselves in a new environment with a new identity: as a *shakaijin*, or 'a member of society'.[11] In this respect, the individual is turned out into society; this brings on new worries to the Alfee fan who might have to choose between being a responsible member of society or *aruchū*:

> I thought the summer event would probably be held on a Sunday . . . [When i]t was scheduled for Saturday and Sunday – though I was thinking 'All right!' – I was also worried because I work in a department store and I was afraid I couldn't get time off. As a new employee (*shin-nyūshain*), I thought it would be impudent for me get off work on Saturday. I asked my senior colleague and it turned out okay. I was really lucky!
>
> (*Alfee Mania* 1993: 15)

Work appears to be given priority over fandom (because it would be rude to shirk her responsibilities at the department store) but the pleasure at being 'lucky' to get that particular day off is important enough to the writer that she sends the story into the fan club newsletter.

Although working Alfee fans have incomes that support their fan behaviour, they may have troubles attending concerts held on weekdays because of the six or six-thirty performance start. I often noticed at concerts that though the ticket office posted 'Sold out' signs on the day of the performance, there were always empty seats scattered throughout the arena when the lights went down for the first number. However, when the lights came up after the first set, all seats were filled. This was because many working fans could not make it to the concert arena by the time the curtain rose. Missing the first few songs is the price the working fan has to pay, but it is worth the price of the ticket to see the rest of the set.

Work-related stress is a concern for many Japanese. The mass media has taken the phenomenon up in its most extreme form (*karōshi*, or death from overwork), causing concern for insurance companies and corporate institutions that might be held responsible.

Though certainly not all Japanese workers find themselves in such a dire situation, the daily grind of a salaried worker in Japan is part of the popular vernacular, and it is acknowledged as a real source of anxiety. Fandom is one outlet for this kind of tension. A fan writes that participation in the concert has relieved her of 'stress from work' (*Alfee Mania* 1993: 15). One might argue that rock fan identity, long associated with teenagers, is a method of prolonging one's youth through adulthood. Fandom combats the stress of adult responsibilities, bringing the individual back to a carefree, relaxed state.

Marriage has often been described in larger Japanese society as a true sign of adulthood, more so than that of finding employment. This is because marriage implies responsibility for others, both financial and emotional. It can also be another life course step that changes the way the Alfee fans view their participation with the band and other fans. The fan club plays up a member's wedding by facilitating a congratulatory message from the band at the wedding: the fan magazine calls this programme 'Happy Wedding'; if members send the details of the ceremony, the club delivers a recorded tape or autograph to the new couple. However, for some, this is a point of departure. To 'graduate from the Alfee' (*arufii o sotsugyō suru*) is a common way to describe this change in self-identification: the fan is no longer 'into' the Alfee. This is more frequent in cases where the spouse is not an Alfee fan. However, marriages between Alfee fans are not infrequent.[12] On an Internet bulletin board associated with the Alfee's official home page, a 36-year-old woman writes

> 8 August 1998 was our first summer event since our marriage. We went together. Our seats on the first day were number 1 and 2 in the first block. It was just like a wedding present. I will save these tickets as a souvenir of our love [*futari no kinen*].
>
> (The Alfee Official Home Page 1996)

However, not all married couples see the Alfee concert as a celebration of their marriage. Costs of fandom might impede on a young household's tight budget. An especially acute problem is childcare. A female fan told me that the only fan letter she had ever sent to the Alfee was a request for child-minding facilities at Alfee concerts. Because childcare is often still considered the sole responsibility of Japanese women, many older, married female fans have problems attending concerts. Some bring their small children to the concerts but worry about the effect of the loud music on infant ears.

Another scenario is that of the young mother, unable to go to *arukon* because of an objecting spouse or other responsibilities such as caring for an elderly family member. In one letter, a fan writes that she misses Alfee concerts because she cannot yet leave her five-month old daughter, but she compensates for her absence by buying Alfee concert videos and watching them at home. She finally obtained permission from her begrudging husband to attend the Christmas concert series, going with her two children: she calls herself an *aruchū mama* (*Alfee Mania* 1993: 25).

In sum, we see that though individual fans lead various lives under different social and economic pressures; there are different expectations attached to these manifold personal roles that regulate people's behaviour. Students are supposed to stay home at night and study. Workers should fulfil company obligations before knocking off for the evening, and mothers should not leave their children or take them out late at night. Observing these restrictions general categories of fandom emerge. These categories are predominant in fan utterances (in interviews or in print). The student, the worker and the parent are three life stages that appear most distinct because of the quite different behaviour expectations associated with each. There may be liminal spaces between the categories (a *rōnin* waiting for entrance to a university, for example). These generalized categories which span childhood to adulthood are applicable in many contexts other than fandom, as they are often used in Japanese society to describe personal identity. Japanese people see their lives in a continuum, but as a process passing through markers which delimit identities in relation to others as well as the discrete self.

Consuming fans: the rules of pleasure

The previous section informs us about three general life stages that carry with them social expectations that can either facilitate or block the Alfee fans' participation in a valued fan activity, the concert. Overcoming obstacles colours the way a fan perceives the concert experience: it becomes a victory of sorts (as illustrated in the naming of the 1993 Alfee national tour, 'Victory'). In this section, I discuss the concert experience itself and how different kinds of fans negotiate with the rules of concert attendance as a form of pleasurable consumption.

Callois's differentiation (1962) between the *paidia* and the *ludens* was one of the first works that identified the separate but overlapping spheres of 'fun and freedom' versus 'the rules of the culture' (see Hendry, this volume). There are certainly strict rules, enforced order and constructed boundaries in concert attendance.

Interestingly, concert attendance is related to some extent to several of the five forms of play identified by Callois.[13] *Agon* (competition) is fierce when fans compete for concert tickets: competing for good seats close to the stage and in some cases, for seats at all (sold out shows are common in small, crowded urban arenas). The first strategy to improve one's chances (*alea*) of getting concert tickets is knowing when and where the concerts will be held at the earliest possible date. Early access to information allows the fan to apply for concert tickets as soon as they go on sale. This information is available in general music and entertainment magazines, but the first information is sent to fan club members. Members receive the tour schedule, mailed directly from the management company. Tickets go on sale about two months before the concert date. A fan has several options to obtain tickets. The first option a fan has is buying tickets through commercial ticket agencies, which are located in department stores or other public places, and tickets may be bought at site or reservations can be made over the telephone. In the case of reservations, financial transactions are made by electronic bank transfer. The fan may reserve tickets over the telephone, and is told to deposit the correct amount in a specified the bank account number. Tickets are then received in the mail.

If the fan wants to buy tickets for concerts held in other regions, he or she may contact one of the many promotion companies employed by the Alfee's management company. Fans who want to travel to other regions for tickets may contact one of the dozen companies that roughly divide Japan into seven regions: Hokkaido, Tōhoku, Kantō, the western coast, the central area (Chūgoku), the Kansai area, and Kyūshū and Okinawa. Another possible method of reserving tickets concerns personal connections: the national Alfee e-mail mailing lists ('Alfee Patio' and 'Alcoholic', for example) and pen pals may buy tickets for friends. In buying the tickets together fans will be assured of seats together.

When times are desperate, fans rely on each other. Outside the concert halls on the day of the event, fans without tickets for that night's concert, or those soon, will gather early, holding signs with messages such as: 'If you can, please give up a ticket for tonight's concert – Please!' They are looking to buy tickets from other fans, not from the *dafuya*, or 'scalpers', who buy them in bulk from the commercial agencies. There are also small shops, called *kinken shoppu* or 'discount ticket shops', which sell concert tickets along with department store gift certificates, train tickets and phone cards. These stores sell tickets at sometimes inflated prices, depending on availability and demand.

Fans in different life stages will deal with the ticket purchasing process in different ways, employing different strategies that are available to them at that time. Young fans are hampered by their lack of funds to buy tickets, though they have the free time during the day repeatedly to dial ticket agencies to try to get an early order in for a particular concert (which also means they can obtain good seats). Working fans might be unable to spend much time on the phone during working hours, but their access to expendable income may allow them to take advantage of other methods of ticket purchasing, such as through *dafuya* and secondhand ticket sellers.

No matter how old the fan is, all Alfee fans must follow the rules of the concert hall during the event. Fans may not move freely; they are not allowed close proximity to the stars on stage or back stage. Furthermore, concert halls have strict rules about the use of photography and video cameras and tape recorders and forbid their use in the auditorium. Despite these regulations, the mimicry (simulation) of a fantasy experience transports the audience to an extraordinary world of bright lights and loud music. This encounter with the stars and other fans is highlighted by smoke bombs, laser shows, cherry pickers and, in the case of outdoor events, fireworks, adding to the vertigo (*ilinx*) experience of the concert.

After the concert ends, the fans are enjoined to leave the arena quickly, quietly and in an orderly fashion, though many want to prolong the concert experience by lingering. For those who are determined to get a last glimpse of their idols, waiting for the band members' exit is the final stage in the concert process. 'Seeing the star off' (*miokuri*) takes time. Young fans who have a curfew or fans who live in distant suburbs and might miss the last connection home cannot participate in this activity. Anywhere from a dozen to fifty fans, usually women, may gather outside the stage door waiting for the band members. The members' exit from the hall is not immediate; first they shower, change and confer with crew and management regarding the next engagement. At concerts in urban centres, small receptions are held backstage for band's guests (usually record company and other related business associates, the press, celebrity guests and so on). On these nights the fan may have to wait more than an hour before the band members emerge.

Sharply defined boundaries construct the emotional space between fan and idol; these boundaries define the real relationship between them (separated and inaccessible) but the boundaries exist to invite testing. Fans do not treat these barriers as absolute. Alfee fans see the boundaries as lines drawn for investigation: they push up against the temporary fencing; arms waving, they squeal when the star motions in their direction. Security is not oppressive, as fans do not try outright to destroy rules; fans seem to know exactly how far they can go before security steps in. For the most part, stage door greetings are focused on fans' verbal rather than physical expressions. Others inside the arena can always tell when the most popular member has left the building because of the burst of high-pitched shrieking. In 1992 I observed long scratches in the paint on the bonnet of the electric guitarist's car, a result of fans' exertions; sometimes rules do get broken.

Despite the various regulations that govern fan behaviour at concerts, the personal pleasure that the fans experience is spontaneous and individual. In fact, it is so individual that sometimes the fans themselves cannot agree on what actually happened at a concert, as illustrated in the fan reactions to a 1996 outdoor event.

Consuming memories

The following is an anecdotal example of fan life-stage identity and memory as influencing the successful perception of a concert. What is pivotal here is the age of the fans involved and their level of participation in the past; the definition of a 'good' concert; and the validity of memory. If there are rules to physically attending a concert (as we have seen in the previous section), what are the emotional rules for concerts?

Nostalgia appears key. Naturally, newer fans have less experience to wax nostalgic; however, as the band ages, their fans age too and the majority of Alfee fans have an increasing store of memories by which to measure their fan identity. In a random sample of twenty-eight fans, for example, I found the average age to be 29 and the average length of fandom to be twelve and a half years (one respondent claimed an eighteen-year fan history). This means that many fans are committed to the Alfee in the long run, and see their consumption of the band as a constant in their lives.

The desire to seek nostalgic pleasure in consuming the Alfee is one draw for fans, but it can also create conflict. In August 1996, the Alfee performed two outdoor concerts in Yokohama as part of their annual summer event series. For some fans, this concert had special meaning as it was the fifteenth summer event the band had performed, and it marked the ten-year anniversary of the 3 August 1986 'Tokyo Bay-Area' event. The 1986 event was considered 'special' partly because of the emotional impact one of the songs performed then had on the audience ('Rockdom – *Kaze ni fukarete*', a personal review of personal relationships during the songwriter's youth). This was the first time the song was performed in public (the single was released in September 1986, approximately a month after the Bay Area event). It is also likely that the scale of the 1986 performance magnified the impact, boasting an audience of 92,500 members. It was said to be the largest ever outdoor concert performed by a Japanese artist at that time (The Alfee 1986: 77; The Alfee 1996).

Another distinctive aspect of the 1986 concert is the fact that one band member allegedly made a verbal promise to the audience. What constituted this promise, however, seems unclear. Some said that the promise was to sing (that same song) at a concert ten years later (*Alcoholic* 14/8/98). However, other fans (who either did not attend the 1986 concert or those who did attend the concert but just did not remember the interaction) could not understand the connection between the two concerts.

At the 1996 concert, the singer fulfilled his 'pledge' and performed the same song. He became so nostalgic that he shed tears during the performance (broadcast live on the multi-screen stage setting to all seats in the audience). After the concert, Takamizawa recalled the difficulty in singing certain songs at concerts because of the emotions they entailed, and changes he felt over time made him hesitant to perform them in public. However, he felt he could not avoid singing certain songs forever and eventually acquiesced (The Alfee 1996). Fans who had attended the 1986 concert relished the member's tears, and identified with his nostalgic expression themselves, recalling their own personal situations upon hearing the song ten years previously.

> Having [the Alfee] perform songs that contain so many memories like . . . 'Rockdom – *Kaze ni Fukarete*' . . . it was like a flashback of memories. I ended up thinking, 'Ah, I have to fight to go forward'.
>
> (Female, 24)
> (The Alfee Official Home Page 1996)

Other fans felt confused and a bit annoyed, however, to see Takamizawa and other fans crying at a concert, an event that they thought was supposed to be 'fun'. This was because the newer fans (or those who simply did not remember) did not identify the current experience with the 1986 concert. They had been excluded from the emotion.

> It seems to me that the fans' varied reception of this year's concert depends on whether they participated in the [Tokyo] Bay Area [1986 concert]. That seems to be the key. Are there many out there who actually heard the promise Takamizawa made ten years ago at the end of the Bay Area [concert], and who really know the content and context of that promise? I felt this year's concert had too many elements and was unsuccessful in pulling them all together. That's why [the concert] left a bad aftertaste.
>
> (*Alcoholic* 14/8/96)

Even a fan who had participated in the 1986 event did not seem to understand the problem.

> I don't remember any promise from ten years ago! It's not that he promised something like 'we'll keep on going for another ten years'. They also didn't promise to do another all night concert the following year. Surely, at that moment, the idea of ten years later seemed to them full of spirit (*sei ippai*). After all, the members were performing a concert in front of an endless stream of 10,000 people! I don't think they had the luxury of time to think ahead![14]

Another tried to explain the others' dissatisfaction to members who defended the concert's success. This writer is more concerned with the *paidic* aspect of concert attendance. To him, having a good time is enough. He down plays the idea that the ten year 'promise' makes or breaks the concert's outcome:

> I, who selfishly believe that the summer event is like a festival where one releases tension by making a lot of noise, think it's all right that a concert doesn't have

a theme [shared by all]. There were a lot of different elements, including fulfilling a silly promise [*kudaranai yakusoku*] . . .

(Alcoholic 23 / 8 / 96)

Another fan tried to play down the rift by blaming it on the fans themselves: 'We expect too much from events. If they were just regular concerts, we'd be completely satisfied' (*Alcoholic* 23/8/96). Other fans retaliated with the criticism that the 'newer' fans did not really understand the Alfee or the meaning of summer events: nostalgia here did not unite but served to divide.

Much has been written about nostalgia in the case of Japan. It is not so much a sense of 'loss and the desire to recover that loss' (Ivy 1995: 57) but a romanticization of the past for those who most likely never experienced it directly and thus have no strong emotional ties to the symbols and dominant meanings associated with them: '[n]ostalgia is not a product of the past, for what occasions it resides in the present, regardless of the sustenance provided by the memories of the past' (Robertson 1997: 118). If fan nostalgia is to be pleasurable, it is as an emotion shared by a small, reasonably bounded community, focused on a shared time and space (for example, 1979 to the present, Japan, or a summer concert event). Furthermore it must be constructed in a way that 'those who most likely never experienced it' can relate to it in some way. That is probably where the Alfee concert broke down. The references were too obscure and the change in atmosphere (from 'fun festival' to 'sober reflection' time) was too broad for some fans to follow.

Conclusion

Just as the continuous state of Alfee fandom can measure time, in cases where fandom is abandoned, fan identity still acts to mark out personal history. A former fan can look back at the period of fandom as a way to describe a certain point in that person's life. In fact, there is empirical evidence that the Alfee do lose fans as they grow older. Inamasu and others asked high school students 'what kind of music did you like in primary school?' and the Alfee were number six on the list of most abandoned musical stars. This is interesting considering the five entries above them were disbanded groups or 1980s idols who had lost their momentum. University students asked the same question also ranked the Alfee as number six, behind two disbanded groups, a deceased singer and two other current acts, making them the third most abandoned contemporary group! (Inamasu 1994: 87)

Aside from this information, it is clear that the Alfee's long-standing success relies heavily on a solid, continuous fan base. Though new buyers are always sought for Alfee products, it is the old timers who stabilize the management company's income and allow them to innovate and perform unusual and expensive events (like the overseas concerts in 1998 and 1999). The management company is aware of this precious market and does what it can to appeal to the nostalgic aesthetics of these fans.

In early 1993, the Alfee performed a short series of concerts where they reprised their role as a folk band. During these 'acoustic live special' concerts, they performed many of their very early numbers which had long been abandoned since they adopted an electric sound. One woman (probably a *shakaijin!*) wrote about this event:

> I arrived at the concert thirty minutes late, and the nostalgic sounds of 'Days gone by' greeted me as I entered. My encounter with the three – Mr Sakurai. Mr Sakazaki and Mr Takamizawa – 20 years of following the Alfee seemed collapsed into only four minutes. The three men on stage appeared not to have changed their fundamentals since their student days. I, who followed them through their 'live house'[15] days, . . . felt as if I had been transported back in time.
>
> (*Alfee Mania* 1993: 9)

At the beginning of this chapter, I proposed the concept of fandom as an integrating process of multiple personal identities that may change over time. Fandom can provide one facet of unity to these changing identities. It is this juxtaposition between change and constancy where nostalgia works to integrate the fans' past identities and experiences with the present in a pleasurable way.

Notes

1   The first part of the title refers to the song 'Saved by the love song', lyrics and music by Takamizawa Toshihiko. The author wishes to acknowledge the help of Mineta Shoko and all members of the Alfee web site project, 'Liberty Bell 21st' and the 1996 members of the Alfee fan mailing list, 'Alcoholic'.

2   Lebra notes the methodological problems this approach entails, such as relying on the memories of subjects (1984). As Alfee fandom is a relatively new phenomenon, subject memory is not stretched over very long periods of time. I have gleaned material from various individuals in different life stages, making each utterance current to the speaker. The information used for this chapter was gathered from personal and e-mail interviews with Alfee fans, fan letters published in the Alfee Mania monthly newsletter and other fan magazines and books; the Official Alfee home page (http://www.alfee.com) and the 'Alcoholic' Alfee fan mailing list.

3   Other interesting fan populations, 'notorious' for their intense fandom in the music industry, include fans of X-Japan (a hard rock 'visual' group which disbanded in late 1997). The apparent suicide of X-Japan's lead guitarist, Hide, the following year, generated a record-breaking observance of celebrity funerals, outperforming the funerals of other public figures such as Hibari Misora and former prime ministers.

4   For a more detailed explanation of the Alfee's role in the larger music scene in the 1960s and 1970s, see Stevens (1999).

5   The band acquired its name from a record company executive who had enjoyed the 1960s' pop single, 'What's it all about, Alfie?'

6   The second record company changed the spelling of the name of the band to avoid copyright infringement. In 1986, the band began using the article 'the' preceding the name 'Alfee', in an attempt to anglicize their image (as in ('The Beatles'). However, 'The Alfee' (in roman letters) tends to be a written sign for the band and the Japanese term '*Arufī*' is used generally in speech.

7   Personal communication with fan, 29/7/96. All Japanese translations are by the author.

8   Another form of leisure is Alfee fans gathering to criticize the Alfee (e.g. 'I didn't like what Takamizawa wore at the last concert; didn't you think it was a bit showy?' and 'Wasn't the tour last year better?' etc.)!

9 The original Japanese here is *chūsan*, meaning *chūgaku san'nensei.*
10 Personal communication with fan, 9/1/96.
11 Another popular term for *shakaijin* in their first year is *fureshuman*, or 'freshman', borrowing the American term for a first-year student.
12 I was invited to a wedding of two Alfee fans in July 1998. The wedding invitation was shaped like an Alfee concert ticket, complete with wording to evoke a sense of participation in a musical event, not a social ceremony.
13 See Linhart 1998 for an application of Callois's model to Japanese society.
14 Personal communication with fan, 27/10/98.
15 'Live house' refers to nightclubs and other venues where amateur and semi-professional musicians play for small audiences.

Bibliography

Alcoholic (mailing list for Alfee fans). Postings from 11–30 August 1996. URL address: alcoholic-info@pa.yokogawa.co.jp.

The Alfee (1986) *8.3. Tokyo Bay-Area.* Tokyo: Jiyūkokuminsha.

—— (1995) *Progress* (souvenir pamphlet from the 1995 spring tour). Tokyo: Eight Days, Co. Ltd.

—— (1996) 15th *Summer 1996 Yokohama Red Bricks,* Tokyo: Ongakusenkasha.

The Alfee official home page (1996) 'The Alfee home page/summer event '96 (fan's impressions)', URL address: http://www/alfee.com/databox/live/event_96/fun_ imp/index.html. Date created: 15 August 1996.

Alfee Mania (1993) Official fan club magazine, vol. 59.

—— (1994) Official fan club magazine, vol. 60.

Best Hit (1985) Tokyo: Gakushūkenkyūsha, December issue.

Cahoon, K. (1993) 'Popular music in Japan', in *Japan: An Illustrated Encyclopedia,* Tokyo: Kodansha, pp. 1284–5.

Caillois, R. (1962) *Man, Play and Games,* London: Thames and Hudson.

Fiske, J. (1992) 'The cultural economy of fandom' in L. Lewis (ed.) *The Adoring Audience: Fan Culture and Popular Media,* London: Routledge, pp. 30–49.

Grossberg, L. (1992) 'Is there a fan in the house? The affective sensibility of fandom', in L. Lewis (ed.) *The Adoring Audience: Fan Culture and Popular Media.* London: Routledge, pp. 50–65.

Inamasu, T. (ed.) (1994) *Gendai no wakamono to ongaku* (Contemporary youth and music), Tokyo: Gendai no Wakamono to Ongaku Kenkyūkai (Contemporary youth and music research group).

Ivy, M. (1995) *Discourses of the Vanishing: Modernity, Phantasm, Japan,* Chicago, IL: University of Chicago Press.

Jenson, J. (1992) 'Fandom as pathology: the consequences of characterization' in L. Lewis (ed.) *The Adoring Audience: Fan Culture and Popular Media,* London: Routledge, pp. 9–29.

Lebra, T. S. (1984) *Japanese Women: Constraint and Fulfillment,* Honolulu: University of Hawaii Press.

Lewis, L.A. (1992) *The Adoring Audience: Fan Culture and Popular Media,* London: Routledge.

Linhart, S. (1998) 'Introduction: the Japanese at play: a little-known dimension of Japan', in S. Linhart and S. Frühstuck (eds) *The Culture of Japan as Seen through its Leisure,* Albany, NY: State University of New York Press, pp. 1–26.

Nikkei Entertainment (1998), '*Shijōsaikyō no raibu āteisto o sagase!*' (Find the artists with the highest concert attendance in history!), July, pp. 36–55.

Robertson, J. (1998) 'It takes a village: internationalization and nostalgia in postwar Japan' in S. Vlastos (ed.) *Mirror of Modernity: Invented Traditions of Modern Japan*, Berkeley, CA: University of California Press, pp. 110–29.

Stevens, C.S. (1999) 'Rocking the bomb: a case study in the politicization of popular culture', *Japanese Studies* 19(1): 49–67.

White, M. (1993) *The Material Child: Coming of Age in Japan and America.* New York: Macmillan.

7 *Inakazumō*, fun, and socially sanctioned violence[1]

Michael Ashkenazi

Introduction

Violence is often portrayed in sociological and anthropological literature as a breakdown of social order (Coser 1967; Siegel 1973; Taylor 1993), or a regulated means of social control (for example, Chagnon 1968), but, altogether, something serious, often deleterious, and an indication that something is 'wrong' in the society concerned.

Whatever the moral issues concerned (most of the readers of this chapter will no doubt pride themselves on being members of non-violent societies, or at least those that have 'outgrown' or no longer resort legitimately to violence), I would like to suggest that the use of violence in some societies is socially legitimated and institutionalized for other reasons. In Japanese society, in this case, many aspects of violence are culturally valued, and belong in that broad realm of we can call 'entertainment' or 'play.' Moeran's 1986 paper is seminal to what I write here. It crystallized some of my own thoughts regarding the peculiar paradox of violence in modern Japanese society. In 'The beauty of violence' (Moeran 1986), the author argues that the prevalence of violence – torture, rape, and graphic killings – is related less to the functionalist explanation that showing such scenes promotes harmony and togetherness, since the alternative is frightening, than to the fact that graphic displays of violence reawaken fundamental aesthetic and tradition-laden principles inherent in Japanese society. Taking Moeran's article as a starting point, I want to illustrate a further thesis: the idea that violence, participated in or observed, is fun for many people (largely men) for rather complex reasons. Violence as entertainment is of course endemic in most societies, whether in the form of gladiator performances of various sorts, or watching a Friday night punch-up. In Japan, violence as fun connects subtly and not so subtly with both traditional and modern, the individual and the state. This can be seen both in traditional *asobi* (play) during *matsuri* (festivals) and in the context of modern leisuretime activities.

The pursuit of violence in relaxed settings

To start with, my concern here is with the exhibition of violence and its display in relaxed settings. I am not concerned with the use of violence to settle political differences, violence as an aspect of illegal business (for example, *yakuza*), or violence in the settling of daily disputes: rare but not unheard of in Japanese society. The most prosaic forms of violence people come into contact with, sometimes to the point of participation, are within the framework of entertainment – *asobi* – activities, some of which I shall document here as examples. I would like to go further, and to argue that violent leisure activities are present throughout Japanese society. I will illustrate this by looking at forms of leisure in Japan, some traditional, some more contemporary.

Inakazumō

Several hundred people had gathered in the grounds of the shrine in the village. The building itself was open, and people, mainly men, sat in the shade or on the shrine platform watching the action in the ring. The ring itself was an imitation of the formal *dohyō* of Grand Sumō. It was a low mound of packed earth and clay, in which had been set a circle of straw bales laid on their sides so that only a low ridge showed over the earth floor. A roof held up by four wooden poles surmounted the dohyō. The contestants were local lads, from the ages of five to their late teens. Competitors are usually arranged by age, and attempts are made to follow selection rules similar to those of *ōzumō* (grand sumō)[2], which serves as the model for *inakazumō*.

The competition took up most of the morning, with spectators coming and going as the spirit took them. The platform of the shrine served as one vantage point, and spectators completely ignored the rituals that took place within. Competitors, all amateurs, or at most members of a local sports club, compete wearing linen loincloths. In contrast to *ōzumō*, there is little posturing before the match. The referees are dressed for the most part in tracksuits.

A match starts with the referee (there are no *shimpan* or judges) announcing the bout and the contestants and their background, for example, 'So-and-so-*kun* of such-and-such village'. The contestants square off on the ring, squat and clap hands in the traditional set of starting postures. They then crouch and charge at one another, attempting either to get a hold on the other's sash, or to push them out of the ring or slap them down on the earth. Many of the matches are hard fought, and the contestants hard pressed to show the impassivity in the face of effort, pain, defeat and victory that is supposed to be expressed by *sumotori*. The referee eggs them on, wielding either a folded towel or a folding fan in lieu of the professional *gyōji*'s stiff Chinese fan. Eventually one of the contestants succumbs, either by being pushed out of the ring, or by being thrown.

Takenouchi *and* bonden

Earlier that year, I had gone to the city of Omagari to watch the *takenouchi matsuri*. Hundreds of underdressed youths (some wore nothing more than a *fundoshi* or loincloth in the freezing cold) stood wearing hard hats and holding bamboo staves in their hands in two large, opposing gangs 'North' and 'South'. After a lengthy period of mustering in the heavy snowfall, a time utilized for drinking local sake, and hurling epithets and snowballs at one another, the two sides marched forward. Poking the four-metre bamboo staves at each other had been forbidden by the police a few years previously. Instead, members of each gang brought their staves down heavily on the heads of those before them, hoping (sometimes not in vain) to hit members of the other party on the head.

One man in the second row, too inebriated to note with whom he was fighting, simply laid out with all his might in every direction, putting those immediately beside and in front of him to flight until some stewards cornered him and forced him off the pitch. After a lengthy series of thumps and rattles, the two sides parted, drank some more, and then they were marshalled once again for a repeat performance. No one died and most injuries were quickly dealt with, and only one person was taken to hospital. That year, an older man casually remarked as we made our way homewards that *takeuchi* these days was very mild, almost innocuous. In the old days, he said, men were sometimes killed, and the resulting feuds could go on for years.

The following day, in a shrine high in the nearby snowy mountains, I watched teams of men carrying *bonden*, tall poles topped with basketware bale-like objects wrapped in colourful cloths. After a brief ritual, the teams started a contest, trying to force their way into the crowded shrine against a force of opposing defenders. The struggle involved mere shoving at the outset, but soon grew heated. Blows were exchanged, the *bonden* ripped, and only by the intervention of the onlooking policemen was a semblance of order restored.

The examples above demonstrate two fundamental properties: they involve violent contests, and they are highly ritualized. An additional feature is worth noting: they are confined almost exclusively to males. Now, rituals are not the only social activity in Japan (or elsewhere) in which violence is given a prominent and lauded place. But the ritualized violence of country *sumō* and related contests, however explained or justified in religious or ideological terms, requires further examination, because it re-occurs in far broader contexts in other areas of Japanese life.

The elaboration of vicarious violence: boys magazines

The average individual in Japan is swamped with violent images, whether he or she wants to observe them or not. Children's comics are violent, portraying, on the whole, violent activities and their results, sometimes in highly graphic form. This phenomenon is extended to feature prominently in adult comic books, which are read by a large proportion of the populace (Schodt 1996).

Japan has a lively and active fiction press (in contrast to its informative press, which is often restricted, censored, and tends to be controlled by bureaucratic and capitalist interest, see Hall 1997), which allows, indeed encourages, the lively expression of imagination, preference and the unthinkable.

Manga

Manga are particularly interesting in this regard. *Manga* are ubiquitous in Japan, with circulations running in the millions per month for some of the more popular

(Schodt 1983). *Manga* cater to all tastes and fashions, ranging from semi-pornography to popular explications of business matters. Violence in *manga* is extensive, whether it is used to carry the story forward (for example, in a historical novel or an illustrated classic such as the Chinese classic 'Tale of three kingdoms') or whether the *manga* is dedicated, in essence, to slaughter and mayhem, as are some of those reviewed. Any kind of violent pursuit is permitted. Limbs can be cut off, people eviscerated and slashed to bits, eyes gouged out. *Manga* style differs from most American and European comics in that the viewpoint is often very personal, even intimate, and the reader's viewpoint is quite often that of the protagonist, or, in some cases, the protagonist's weapon. Gory details are rendered with sometimes clinical exactitude.

It is to my mind particularly significant that sex, on the other hand, is restricted and censored. Roughly speaking, censorship in Japan forbids the portrayal of the genitals and of any pubic hair. Publishers of illustrated magazines have pushed at these limits by shaving the hair on models' bodies, and, in *manga* by using euphemisms: a snake head for the male organ, splashes for the female or by portraying sexual organs in vague outline, without details.[3] What has to be highlighted here is the different attitudes towards violence and sex. The first may be displayed in great detail, the other may not. Interestingly enough, displays of rape are permissible providing the actual sexual organs are not shown. And while *manga* violence is fantasy violence, violence also occurs as a leisuretime activity in other expressive forms.

Magazine adverts

The display or carrying of offensive weapons is forbidden without a licence in Japan. Access to firearms is strictly controlled, and even bladed weapons such as swords and knives require police permission. Perhaps as a consequence, the model gun business flourishes, as can be seen in the advertisement pages of most men's magazines. Perfect replicas of assault rifles, pistols, police and military equipment are heavily touted. Men's magazines – *Tarzan* and *Popeye* – as well as the more overt such as *Pistoru* (Pistol), legitimate the pursuit of violence as a vicarious activity. These displays come in three main forms: as advertisements for weaponry, usually mock-ups of military and other weapons, and as stories in which the use of such weapons feature.

Magazines provide a fertile and accessible source for examining features of modern society in Japan. The prevalence of such magazines, and their widespread readership provide a reflection of what the publishers feel the public wants. The advertisements, in particular, reflect the commercial demand side of a reasonably large sector of the population (Moeran 1986) and can be taken as an expression of public preference. Advertisements for firearms abound. These include disabled copies of military firearms and usable (but non-lethal) gas- and airguns. Shops throughout the country provide these weapons, which can also be bought by mail order. Significantly, most of these shops are to be found in *sakariba*, the zones of bars and entertainment places that can be found around most major railway stations. They sell both traditional weapons, such as swords, staves and throwing knives, and the most modern machine guns and assault rifles in replica, webbing, and other military and paramilitary equipment.

In fact, the access to firearms goes much further than mere displays. In the same magazines, many firms advertise opportunities for travel to foreign countries (former Eastern Bloc countries in Europe and the US are favourites) where individuals can participate in live firing of everything from small pistols to anti-tank weapons. Many of these magazines run photo essays detailing the weapons fired, and the pleasures of the experience offered. Here the emphasis is on the actual, rather than vicarious pleasures of exhibiting and participating in simulated violence. There are tours in which participants merely fire on firing ranges, and others in which they have the opportunity to try out a range of exotic military weapons (anti-tank rockets, for example, in Eastern Europe) and combat hand-gunning courses in the US. I have heard, though without firsthand evidence, of a firm that offers tours to world hotspots such as the former Yugoslavia, with an opportunity to try out the weapons used in the local conflict.

Discussion

Several issues are raised by the forgoing. At a global level, it is perhaps useful to ask why violence is so attractive. Why is it pursued, and associated with the irreducible concept of having fun? At a more local level, it is useful to ask why and how Japanese society controls violence, and access to it as a means of entertainment. Some of the answers are to be found in central social concepts: the re-utilization of manhood and struggle, the mutual effects of spectators and actors, and the preservation of tradition and traditional values. But these must also seen against a background of the relationships of power that define the nature of Japanese society as a whole.

It is useful to return, briefly, to the overall public perception that many Japanese express about their own social arrangements: that of the *tateshakai* or vertical society. How does such a perception retain its vitality in the face of alternative examples, and, in fact, in the face of alternatives within Japanese society? *Tateshakai* has two sides to it: the public acceptance and even support of hierarchical relationships, and the real relationships of unequal power embodied in such a concept. It is to be supposed that such a system will generate a certain amount of inconsistency, and that it needs to be supported by public consciousness on the one hand, and the inconsistencies ameliorated in some form on the other. I would argue that the public expression of violence-as-fun serves to promote both these aspects. The real locus of power within Japanese society – unequally distributed, often hidden beneath layers of appearance, and often inaccessible to the average individual – has managed to sustain the system through a combination of economic success and cognitive appeal. Japan not only is powerful, but its leaders and people repeatedly tell themselves so. The 'vertical', thus inherently unequal and rigid, power distribution has also led to the sorry social, economic and political impasse Japan finds itself in at the end of the twentieth century, since by its very nature, such a system is unable to critique, and thus improve, itself.

From the perspective of violence as fun, or violence as entertainment, several socially acceptable mechanisms seem to be operating in tandem to support the national *status quo*.

Manhood and tradition in the practice of violence

Manhood in Japan is inextricably tied to the concept of struggle. The violent entertainment in Japanese society is not confined to men because they are the only ones clearly capable of violence: political gangs of the 1960s and 1970s, female *sumō* wrestlers and other examples clearly refute that. But in the world of legitimate violence which *sumō* and the *takenouchi matsuri* illustrate, women have no part. Women and children, being but incomplete men, are not expected to display the ability to struggle in anything but embryonic form. They 'do not have the physical ability', 'would look bad doing it', 'don't understand what it is all about,' to cite but a few of the reasons provided by participants and spectators alike. Moreover, for many, both spectators and participants, *sumō* wrestling – as many other 'masculine' and 'struggle' pursuits within the traditional realm – exemplifies one additional aspect of the masculine and mythological history of modern Japan, when supposed martial virtues reigned triumphant.

Spectators as legitimators of violence

The role of spectators, and their distinction from competitors, is crucial to understanding sports (Avedon 1979; Caillois 1979; Cheska 1978), which often re-enact for participants crucial aspects of their culture (Montague and Morais 1976). Both categories are obvious actors in a shared drama. Competitors practise their sport to and for spectators, and these are expected not to be passive, but active connoisseurs of the sport (Harris 1983). Spectators react to the competitors with expressions signifying approval or disapproval; competitors act out their roles, showing stoicism or triumph (never, if possible, the burden of defeat) as appropriate. But this is violence we are concerned with here. Significantly, it is controlled violence. The spectators intend, vicariously, to skate on the precipice of participation. It is the *spectators* who provide the legitimization of the activity. Without them, while violence might continue (as for instance, in the form of a battle, or of a ritual), it is unlikely to flourish and may well decay, as many traditional activities have. A violent attack by political extremists I witnessed at Waseda University, took place not by accident in the centre of the campus. It was, from this point of view, a theatre, in which the participants (at least, the victors) were trying to establish not only their political success, but to legitimize it before the student audience. *Sumō* and other violent activities skate close to that extreme but are legitimized by the constraints they allow to have placed on themselves by police and other organs of public order. Spectators are thus a necessary part of violence as fun, for, by being before spectators, the violence is made manifestly and explicitly legitimate. Since these forms of violence are 'fun' – essentially an irreducible – it is also 'play': essentially a harmless activity, not serious, and thus legitimate in public contexts where the public participates as spectator. The legitimacy here is in a way off-handed: it adheres to the activity because many people, by participating in it in a non-serious way, show it to be fun.

Tradition and traditional values

Sporting contests often act out a major myth in the society concerned (Burnett 1983; Cheska 1978). The myths that are being enacted are not impenetrable mysteries for the participants. At a certain level they are aware that the games are re-enactments of a myth reality, to coin a phrase. Their interpretation is important, because for many participants, the games are 'local traditions' whose justification is upholding an example set by their forefathers. The myth itself, so far as I could see, is rarely objectified. What is objectified is the need to preserve tradition as worthwhile in and of itself, to institutionalize it. Tradition includes such values as are expressed by religion. *Inakazumō* is a religious event, recognized as such both in *ōzumō* and in the association of *sumō* matches with shrine festivals. Moreover, this particular religious and ritualized aspect is part of a generalized attempt to compete, with more or less success, with other attractions, in the cities and in Japanese techno-culture in general.

This re-enactment of myths is even more prominent in the other examples presented. Participants in *bonden matsuri* are aware of, and re-enact agricultural sexual myths. But daily myths are re-enacted, created and recreated in the published media, as *manga* which tell myths-of-choice tailored to fit the most ludicrous and frantic dreams of the dullest *sarariman*. These myths take form, are manifest, for those who care to pursue or can afford to pursue them, through the firearms holidays (at one extreme) or regulated *sumō* (and other violent sports such as rugby, karate, and so on) at the other. The foundation of this myth: the myth of masculinity expressed through violent action, the popular myth of the samurai is one that is far from discouraged by the powers that be, ever intent on using these created myths for their own concerns. It is thus institutionalized and has a place of its own within other aspects of the concatenation of meanings that is society.

Fun

Let us get back to the global level and ask why people participate in such activities: actively as in *inakazumō* or *takenouchi*, or passively, as readers or spectators. It is all very well to say that people attend festivals and suchlike 'to reaffirm their cosmology' or to re-enact community solidarity, or, in our case, to legitimize violence or some such anthropological approximation of what we think they are really doing. This approach suffers from some weaknesses, however. Is it for example reasonable to say that people who do not attend are not interested in community solidarity?

Instead, I want to suggest that people participate in such activities because they are fun, and to examine the concept. Webster's dictionary defines 'fun' as 'for amusement' which hardly covers the entire spectrum of meaning. People go to have fun not only because it is 'amusing' but because it is enjoyable (though many things are enjoyable but not 'fun' – I enjoy my work, but it's hardly 'fun'). Huizinga (1955), notwithstanding an exhaustive treatment of the issue of play, has great difficulty once he reaches what appears to be an irreducible element (and perhaps it is, and should be so), and thus avoids treating fun.

So let us examine what people are doing (without, perhaps asking them) at a country *sumō* match. The statements of community worth and cultural significance we can take for granted. I want to go a little bit beyond that, and examine fun from a different perspective. Where can we find it? Well, one of the places to find it is, paradoxically, in violence, violence of a particular kind, granted, but violent none the less.

The role of violence

Sumō evolves from a tradition of struggle. Moreover, from a tradition of struggle which was essentially rule-less, until codified by agreement. It is true that *sumō* itself, as a matched competition, was codified fairly early in Japanese history, from the Heian period (Cuyler 1985), but it existed within the ambit of the emergent military picture of historic Japan. Any brief examination of the histories of struggle provides a lesson in ruthlessness, murderous behaviour, lawlessness, and other expressions of the subjugation of rules to expediency. *Sumō*, on the other hand, is an epitome of rules; without them, the game does not exist.

The paradox of course needs no elaboration, nor are people ignorant of it. Struggle is embodied in the struggle of man against man, in *sumō*, with barred holds, in other cases of struggle, with almost no holds barred. Japanese possess a host of social and cultural media and methodologies for dealing with conflict (see, for example, Eisenstadt and Ben Ari 1990; Krauss *et al.* 1984). This is not to say that conflict is absent, clearly not the case, but conflict can be limited (in everyone's mind, at least) so why not enjoy the delicious frisson of danger? The Japanese ability to control violence is well documented. It relies partly on ritualized formulations of rules governing the violence (Ashkenazi unpublished; Goodger 1985), and partly on massive displays of force by the police. Thus mob scenes which could easily erupt into violence (for example, *takenouchi matsuri* or *bonden*) never erupt into something totally uncontrolled. In *takenouchi matsuri*, large groups of inebriated young men armed with bamboo poles belabour one another in a frenzy until one group gives in and retreats. Wildness exemplified is controlled, largely by heavy infusions of alcohol which ensure, at least, that neither side can do too much damage to the other; but, more importantly, by the imposition of rules from the outside by the arbiters and legitimators of violence, the organs of the ordered community or the state, as both Davis (1967) and Kalland (1995) have noted in other *matsuri*. This form of controlled violence, controlled wildness and struggle, appears to be universal among human beings. The oldest reference to such activities is in Herodotus (1966: 126), and others abound. *Sumō*, particularly grand *sumō*, which serves as a model for modern *inakazumō*, is an elaboration of this form. Wildness is personified, allowed limited freedom in the exercise of struggle. It serves as the background against which other social effects and social myths can be manufactured.

Violence appears to be in itself 'fun' for at least some people. This is also intimated in other anthropological studies, for example, Freilich's study of urban Mohawks (Freilich 1977), Chagnon's work on the Yanomamo (1968), and Montague and Morais's treatise on football crowds (Montague and Morais 1976). 'Battle' and 'fun' seem to be here synonymous, and we should ask why this is. Part of the answer is release. Not the cathartic release talked of in psychology, but the release from rules on the one hand, coupled with the assurance that rules exist for protection on the other. Licensed violence, like licensed foolishness, any kind of licence, skirts on the edge of danger, hopefully never to actually fall in.

Walking on the edge

The violence and disorderliness of which *inakazumō* and other violent entertainment is the refined edge, are as dangerous as they are attractive. It is not merely the symbolic danger of controlled violence spilling over into uncontrolled violence, nor the fact that these activities represent a 'controlled' end of uncontrolled violence. It is also that danger, to the individual, is palpable, if only vicarious. Rozin (1987) has commented about eating peppers that perhaps people do so because of the thrill of danger inherent in eating a poison and getting away with it. In the Japanese context, the same may be said for eating *fugu*. Controlled violence presumably has the same thrill for human beings worldwide.

It is also the thrill of being permitted, with licence, to break some of the rules. *Inakazumō* is here only the most formalized example of rule breaking. As one examines other events, such as the mock battles staged between villages and neighbourhoods, the wild carrying of *mikoshi*, and other such activities, one is brought to the conclusion that it is the breaking of rules – violently or in more benign ways – that characterizes one element of fun. Such broken rules can be brought about in a number of ways.

Drinking and drunkenness are related to the issue of the thrill of violence. Drinking is masculine (and also attracts women) as it releases from inhibitions and from many rules of conduct. Alcohol is encouraged in *inakazumō*, by the prevalence of beer booths and advertisements, and the frequent distribution of cold *sake* from barrels. None the less, it is limited by custom: spectators do not fight amongst themselves. But these activities represent controlled violence, from which the fun emerges. Drunkenness and violence and maleness are intrinsically combined, and letting any one of them loose brings the others along.

One way of taking the edge off violence as a source of fun is by redirecting it. Fun, in other words, can be generated by means other than excitement and violence. The juxtaposition is not intentional, I believe. It is more in the nature of a control over the violent possibilities inherent in having men compete and drink before spectators. The fairgrounds that accompany many *matsuri*, the housewives who wait under the trees with the family picnic while 'the men' go off to watch *sumō*, all provide a balance for the vicarious violence of the competition.

The role of women

The role of women is a particularly interesting one in *inakazumō* and in other violent activities as well, largely because of its passivity. While in some instances in Japan women have come to acquire male roles (Koyama 1964; Lebra 1981; Robertson 1989), on the whole their presence in male-dominated events is looked on with suspicion. In *sumō*, certainly *inakazumō*, women's roles are confined. They do not compete (I exclude the rather anomalous case of *onnazumō* in Shikoku, about which I have no direct evidence), they do not judge, and their role is a background one. Women's role is to encourage the participants, and to supply the comforts necessary for the warriors. In the 'modern' examples raised here, women are given more prominence (there are female heroines no less bloodthirsty than their male counterparts in *manga*, and firearm holidays often feature women, though they usually fire 'feminine' weapons: elegantly styled, or lower-calibre weapons).

What women say about these activities is also revealing. Responses range from 'boys will be boys' to the standard cultural responses of 'supporting our traditions'. Even though women, by their assigned role in society are excluded from much of the activity, the objectives are internalized among them as well.

It should be added that women do participate in some apparently male occupations, such as carrying *mikoshi* during *matsuri*. However, notwithstanding the apparent similarity between male and female carriers, here too there are anomalies. Women rarely serve as fan bearers (the role that directs the passage of the *mikoshi*), in addition to encouraging the carriers, and they do not carry the *mikoshi* as wildly as men do. In other words, notwithstanding the assumption of an apparently male role, it is carried out in an expressly 'feminine' manner: there is, after all, no reason why women cannot toss a *mikoshi* into the air, get drunk or otherwise behave like male *mikoshi* carriers. The proprieties of life are maintained rather than threatened by female participation, no matter how ambivalent it is becoming elsewhere (Ueno 1987).

On restrictions, permissions, and the channelling of fun

All societies ritualize violence to some degree. In many this is a major outlet for energies, and, in some celebrated cases, a major source of entertainment. Thus the Yanomamo, celebrated by Chagnon's (1968) work, have weighty social drives which propel fist, staff and axe fights. In an environment poor in social stimulus these provide a major source of entertainment. The same is true of the Nuba in Sudan (Riefenstahl 1976). But what causes Japanese – saturated with visual, auditory and tactile cues and stimulation to engage in violence, even vicariously?

The Japanese individual in Japanese society is peculiarly placed. On the one hand he (and 'he' is strongly operative here) lives a restricted, circumscribed, strongly prescribed life. On the other hand, the same individual has licence to indulge himself in ways that in other countries would be strongly limited: acting childish is not negatively sanctioned, public drunkenness is tolerated, even encouraged, indulging in egoistic behaviour is tolerated. Violence in traditional societies, whether the Yanomamo or Edo period Japan, has major social functions. These have disappeared with the emergence of modernity. But the model of violence remains as a potential, ready to be exploited for other ends.

It is a truism in political science that the state maintains a monopoly on the regulation and allocation of violence within its boundaries. That, in fact, is one of its defining characteristics. In terms of the sorts of violence discussed here, it is useful to consider that the regulation of this monopoly occurs within two framing considerations: institutionalization and legitimization. Violence can occur in different contexts in which different degrees of institutionalization or legitimization can occur. Certain violent acts are institutionalized in that there are more or less regularized roles for the exchange of violence: police and armed forces are examples. Legitimization occurs where 'the public' (whomsoever and wherever these may be) accept violence as reasonable and even expected. Police activity in arresting a violent suspect, for example, is both legitimate and institutionalized. Armed robbery, or personal physical attack are neither legitimized nor institutionalized. But what of those acts that lie in between? The *yakuza* for instance, are not legitimized, but they certainly are well institutionalized in Japanese society. Violent abuse of wives (Lunsing 1998) is legitimized in Japanese society, but probably not institutionalized. These differences are crude pointers, but they are useful for understanding the place of the phenomena described above, of 'violence as entertainment.'

Of the examples given above, *sumō* is legitimized and institutionalized in the form of *ōzumō* (grand *Sumō*), where it is an activity that is absorbing to thousands, having a high degree of legitimacy, and a set of interlocking institutions which embrace a fairly large proportion of Japanese society. Similar, though lesser degrees of legitimacy are accorded to other forms of legitimized violence, such as *Muai Thai* (kick boxing) and wrestling. *Inakazumō* is an element in the institution of *sumō*, which derives its legitimacy partly from its religious and cultural association, partly from the legitimacy of grand *Sumō*. It is institutionalized to a weaker degree in the ritual and social activities of some communities, though in many it has vanished as an institution.

Manga violence can be differently identified. While *manga* themselves are institutionalized in Japanese society, the violent aspect has become completely legitimized. Graphic descriptions of violence can be highlighted against the elliptical, illusory and bowdlerized depictions of sex: where violence in adult and even children's *manga* is explicit in all its goriness; men and women have sex in *manga* with blanked genitalia and a picture of a banana between their conjoined bodies. Clearly then, violence is legitimate; sex is not: a curious state of affairs unless we recognize that in both cases the government is maintaining its monopoly, and staking an interest in people's lives.

The *takenouchi* and similar *matsuri* display another example of the legitimatization of violence within an institutionalized framework. There are plenty of *matsuri* in which there is no violence whatsoever. But in the atmosphere of fun and licence that pervades many *matsuri*, violence, particularly, as Davis (1977) and Kalland (1995) have both noticed, that which appears uncontrolled but is finally overcome and 'domesticated', is very attractive. Like surviving *inakazumō* these are institutionalized because they are an element in the whole complex of community *matsuri*, community rituals, and the survival of the community that are so valued in Japan. They also tend to support the structure of the state, and help in legitimizing the publicly accepted ideology of hierarchy (*tateshakai*), which has helped maintain the state system for so long.

In a modern society, more concerned about its entertainment than even the bread and circuses of Imperial Rome, such rituals of violence are particularly attractive, perhaps because there is some need for individuals to break the rules just for fun, just for the hell of it. Be that as it may; vicarious violence is prominent in all modern societies via television. The Japanese make controllable violence a part of their repertoire of 'things to do', one that is acceptable even to the controlling forces of society.

The Japanese government is conceivably an element in all this. For all the specific failings of specific governments (particularly in the past ten years), the regime of modern (post Second World War) Japan, has proved remarkably successful. It is the sole example in East Asia of a stable government not run by *diktat*, dictator, or revolutionary council. It has been (at least, until the past half decade) remarkably successful economically. It has provided for one of the broadest distributions of national wealth in the world. There have been many reasons for this state of affairs, but certainly one of them has been the ability of the regime to seize on those essential institutions which preserve and enhance this state of affairs, and which, of course, also preserve the regime. Clearly the clever regulation of violence, in what was once, it ought to be remembered, an extremely fractious and violence-prone culture (see Borton 1976; Blomberg 1976), is what should be desired.

Conclusions

Fun and violence seem, at least here, to be inextricably linked together. I think, however, that it is not the violence that is addictive (except, perhaps to some: those best equipped to enjoy it). Rather, it is the frisson of walking on the edge. Perhaps some of the hammer syndrome is there somehow as well. It feels so good when one stops. Barbara Myerhoff (1975) has suggested that human society must be seen as in a constant tension and interplay between processes of regularization and rule building and deregularization and rule violation. She views the process of de-regularization as the result of a striving for personal or group advantage within the framework of rules. I would suggest adding another dimension: sheer pleasure at the beauty of having walked on the edge and got away with it, whether vicariously or personally.

If the issue of violence in Japanese society teaches anything, it is that people will try to break the rules, and try to walk as close to the edge as they can. This implies, among other things, that change, micro, macro, or in between, is inherently a psychological process, not merely a social one. Change is the consequence of people getting a kick out of watching the dominoes fall. No less it implies that we ought to take fun more seriously, at least as observers of the scene. Slipping into uncontrolled violence, for instance, would spoil the fun, among other things. Forcibly controlling it to an extreme degree would do the same, for other reasons.

It has not been argued here that fun is necessarily dependent on violence. I am arguing, however, that examining the modes and genesis of fun in a social context would be far more rewarding than has been previously supposed. It is highly likely that fun will emerge as a composite of many sources, each worth examination on its own merits.

Notes

1 I am grateful to two colleagues who contributed materially to this paper. The late Professor Hermann Conrad, of the Department of Anthropology, University of Calgary first sparked an interest in the subject of this paper. George Shand of Gyosei College helped complete this paper by suggesting a useful theoretical framework. All errors of fact and analysis are, of course, my own.

2 *Ōzumō* or grand *Sumō* refers to the system of national *sumō*, headquartered in Tokyo, which has an organized system of ranked professional champions from wrestling stables. Tournaments are held six times a year, and broadcast on national television.

3 It is true, however, that *manga* illustrators, along with the publishers of sex magazines in Japan have long played a cat-and-mouse game with the police on the issue of nudity and sexual portrayal (Bornoff 1992).

Bibliography

Ashkenazi, M. (unpublished) 'Ritual and the ideal of society in karate', paper presented at the Departmental Seminar, Department of Anthropology, University of Calgary.

Avedon, E.M. (1979) 'The structural elements of games', in E.M. Avedon and B. Sutton-Smith (eds) *The Study of Games*, Huntington, NY: Robert E. Krieger Publishing Co., pp. 419–26.

Blomberg, C. (1976) *Samurai Religion: Some Aspects of Warrior Manners and Customs in Feudal Japan*, Uppsala: University of Uppsala.

Bornoff, N. (1992) *Pink Samurai: The Pursuit and Politics of Sex in Japanese Society*, London: Grafton.

Borton, H. (1976) 'Peasant uprisings in Japan of the Tokugawa period', in J. Livingston *et al.* (eds) *The Japan Reader*, vol. 1, Harmondsworth: Penguin, pp. 49–55.

Burnett, J.H. (1983) 'Ceremony, rites, and economy in the student system of an American high school', in J. Harris and R. Park (eds) *Play, Games and Sports in Cultural Contexts*, Champaign, IL: Human Kinetics Publishers, pp. 283–97.

Caillois, R. (1979) *Man, play and games*, New York: Schocken Books.

Chagnon, N.A. (1968) *Yanomamo: The Fierce People*, New York: Holt, Rinehart and Winston.

Cheska, A.T. (1978) 'Sports spectacular: the social ritual of power', *Quest* 30: 58–71.

Coser, L. (1967) *Continuities in the Study of Social Conflict*, New York: The Free Press.

Cuyler, P.L. (1985) *Sumo: From Rite to Sport*, Tokyo: Weatherhill.

Davis, W. 1977, 'The miyaza and the fisherman: ritual status in coastal villages of Wakayama prefecture', *Asian Folklore Studies* 26(2): 1–29.

Eisenstadt, S.N. and Ben–Ari, E. (eds) 1990, *Japanese Models of Conflict Resolution*, London: Kegan Paul International.

Freilich, M. (1977) 'Mohawk heroes and Trinidadian peasants', in M. Freilich (ed.) *Marginal Natives at Work: Anthropologists in the Field*, New York: John Wiley and Sons, pp. 151–72.

Gluckman, M. (1963) *Order and Rebellion in Tribal Africa*, New York: The Free Press.

Goodger, J.M. (1985) 'Collective representations and the sacred in sport', *International Review for the Sociology of Sport* 20(3): 179–88.

Hall, I.P. (1997) *Cartels of the Mind: Japan's Intellectual Closed Shop*, New York: W.W. Norton.

Harris, J.C. (1983) 'Sport and ritual: a macroscopic comparison of form', in J. Harris and R. Park (eds) *Play Games and Sports in Cultural Contexts*, Champaign, IL: Human Kinetics Publishers, pp. 177–89.

Huizinga, J. (1955) *Homo Ludens*, Boston: Beacon Press.

Kalland, A. (1995) 'A Japanese shinto parade: does it "say" anything, and if so, what?', in J. van Bremen and D.P. Martinez (eds) *Ceremony and Ritual in Japan*, London: Routledge.

Koyama, T. (1964) 'The changing social position of women in Japan', in W.J. Goode (ed.) *Readings on the Family and Society*, New York: Prentice-Hall, pp. 237–42.

Krauss, E.S., Rohlen, T.P. and Steinhoff, P.G. (eds) (1984) *Conflict in Japan*, Honolulu: University of Hawaii Press.

Lebra, T.S. (1981) 'Japanese women in male dominant careers: cultural barriers and accommodations for sex-role transcendence', *Ethnology* 20(4): 291–06.

Lunsing, W. (1999) 'Prostitution, dating, mating and marriage: love, sex and materialism in Japan', in M. Ashkenazi and J. Clammer (eds) *Material Culture in Japanese Society*, London: Kegan Paul International.

Moeran, B. (1986) 'The beauty of violence: "Jidaigeki", "Yakuza" and "eroduction" films in Japanese cinema', in D. Riches (ed.) *The Anthropology of Violence*. Oxford: Basil Blackwell, pp. 103–17.

Montague, S.P. and Morais, R. (1976) 'Football games and rock concerts: the ritual enactment of american success models', in W. Arens and S.P. Montague (eds) *The American Dimension: Cultural Myths and Social Realities*, Port Washington, NY: Alfred Publ.

Myerhoff, B. (1975) 'Introduction' in S. Moore and B. Myerhoff, *Symbol and Politics in Communal Ideology*, Ithaca, NY: Cornell University Press.

Riefenstahl, L. (1976) *People of Kau*, London: Collins.

Robertson, J. (1989) 'Gender bending in paradise: doing "female" and "male" in Japan', *Genders* 5: 50–69.

Rozin, P. (1987) 'Psychobiological perspectives on food preferences and avoidances', in M. Harris and E. Ross (eds) *Food and Evolution: Toward a Theory of Human Food Habits*, Philadelphia, PA: Temple University Press, pp. 181–205.

Schodt, F.L. (1983) *Manga! Manga! The World of Japanese Comics*, Tokyo: Kodansha.

Schodt, F.L. (1996) *Dreamland Japan: Writings on Modern Manga*, Berkeley, CA: Stone Bridge Press.

Sélincourt, A. de (trans) (1966) *Herodotus – The Histories*, Harmondsworth: Penguin.

Siegel, B. Jr. (1973) 'Violence', in T. Weaver (ed.) *To See Ourselves*, Glenview, IL: Scott, Foresman and Co., pp. 334–36.

Taylor, P.J. (ed.) (1993) *Violence in Society*, London: Royal College of Physicians of London.

Ueno, C. (1987) 'The position of Japanese women reconsidered', *Current Anthropoloty* 28(4): 75–84.

8 At the interstices

Drinking, management, and temporary groups in a local Japanese organization[1]

Eyal Ben-Ari

Introduction

This essay represents an analysis of a *bōnenkai* which took place in December of 1982. *Bōnenkai*, sometimes translated as 'forgetting-the-hardships-of-the-year parties', are year-end parties held, for example, in Japanese companies and workgroups, in student clubs or among the a faculty of university departments (for examples see Lebra 1976: 118–9; Matsumoto 1970: 26; Skinner 1978: 463). The *bōnenkai* which is to be analysed here was organized by the Joint 'Sports Promotion Committee' of two communities in the city of Otsu (population 250,000) which lies just east of Kyoto. Twenty people participated in this gathering which lasted for over four hours, and which – like many drinking occasions in Japan – included a rich array of activities: formal and informal toasting, merrymaking, joking and singing, as well as more 'practical' pursuits such as gossiping, exchanging information and politicking.

An analysis of this affair may illuminate some of the broad social and cultural issues which have to do with drinking occasions in Japan. Scholars writing about this society have often noted that opportunities for imbibing may be of great consequence for individuals and for groups. Thus one finds that in the literature such occasions are seen to be marked by a number of distinctive features. The most common trait of drinking occasions which has been highlighted is their potential for stress release. Matsumoto (1970: 21; see also Plath 1964: 184), for example, stresses the necessity of drinking parties as 'a relief from the often excessive tensions and obligations of interpersonal relations in Japan.' Linhart (1986: 208; 1988: 291–2) talks of the opportunities provided by such gatherings for the reduction of stress from work and of their function of refreshing the male labour force for the next working day.

A related set of themes has to do with the contribution of such occasions to the solidarity of the groups in which the drinkers participate. Vogel (1963: 105) thus emphasizes how going out together serves to maintain rapport and camaraderie within the workgroup. Rohlen (1974: chap. 4), for his part, shows how such situations are related to the solidification of group identity and internal relations.

Yet other scholars have focused on the more instrumental aspects of drinking episodes. Atsumi (1979: 66; see also Takada 1983), for instance, brings out how parties often serve to provide the employees of large companies with opportunities to exchange the information necessary for efficient job performance. Finally, people like Moeran (1986) highlight how bouts of imbibement figure in the political processes by which communal coalitions and decisions are constantly formed and re-formed.

Yet in most of this literature there seems to be a tendency to leave the internal dynamics of these occasions unexplored. People are seen to enter these situations in which something happens to them, and then they return to everyday life somehow changed: revitalized or refreshed, reinforced with a sense of solidarity, or more politically and organizationally aware. Barring few exceptions – like Moeran's (1986) or Rohlen's (1974) analyses – drinking occasions are treated as a sort of 'black-box' within which something happens. In other words, in much of the literature there is very little explication of the processes which unfold within such situations and which facilitate or limit what they can accomplish in regard to the participating individuals or groups.

Moreover, most of the literature contains quite strong functional assumptions about the relation between drinking occasions and the wider social contexts within which they appear. Drinking occasions are seen as directly contributing to the smooth operation of various aspects of the social order to which the drinkers belong. Along these lines, one finds almost no explication of the ways in which these occasions evolve and develop according to the strategies and active manipulation of individual participants. Nor can one find any systematic attempts to delineate the limitations of such episodes in contributing to the operation of their wider social contexts.

These remarks suggest three sets of questions which seem to be of importance for the understanding of drinking occasions in Japan. The first involves the internal dynamics of these occasions. The need here is to explore the complex interplay of group dynamics and individual experience, and the peculiar mix of performance and improvisation which contributes to the capacity of such episodes to transform individuals and groups. The second set of questions is related to the tie between drinking situations and the wider social context. In this regard the necessity is one of delineating those peculiarities of the gatherings which may promote or limit their potential contribution to the workings of the social order and relations in which the participants take part. The third set of questions – which is itself a derivative of the former two – entails a detailed exploration of the possible positive contribution of such occasions to the solution of a specific kind of social problem: the management of conflict. In this respect the need is to show how the localization of conflicts within such situations involves a special potential for the management of external tensions between groups.

One further point should be mentioned and that is that I am intentionally going beyond the confines of the case study towards more general, and perhaps more speculative issues that have to do with Japanese society. My general thesis is that in order to understand the kinds of things which can be accomplished through drinking occasions, for example, the release of stress, the strengthening of group solidarity and identity, the inculcation of trust, or politicking, it is crucial to take into account the complex group dynamics which unfold within them. Thus, I relate my discussion to some of the problems that have to do with the creation of groups, and with the interrelations between groups and organizations. I conclude with a few words about the character of drinking occasions as temporary entities which are created *between* existing organizations or collectivities, and which, thereby, provide a mechanism for inter-group negotiation and conflict management.

Clearly a study of a single case limits both the strength and range of general or comparative arguments (Kennedy 1979: 671). But such a study precludes neither a delineation of the relevant attributes of the case in relation to other instances nor an exploration of the theoretical problems it raises. Thus, throughout the analysis and in the conclusion, I stress both the limits and possible contributions of the argument.

The Sports Promotion Committee

Organizational context

The Sports Promotion Committee (*taiiku shinkōkai*), as it is officially known, that arranged the year-end party was comprised of an equal number of representatives from two local communities: a new housing estate constructed in the late 1960s which had a population of 2500 people, and a small commuter village whose population numbered 300.[2]

The twenty members who made up the committee were, on the whole, quite young. The head or chairman – an electrical subcontractor for a North Kyoto firm – was in his early 40s. His two assistants – an owner of a car agency, and a manager of a stationery store in Kyoto – were both in their late 30s. The occupations of the other members – most of whom were in their 20s and 30s – were varied and included the following: students, municipal employees, a carpenter, the local rice shop owner, a university lecturer, a kimono designer, a truck driver, a blue-collar technician for a national company, and a number of white-collar workers employed throughout the Osaka and Kyoto areas.

Most members served a term of two years, although about half continued for a longer period. They were recruited into the organization in a number of ways. A few are asked by the heads of the neighbourhood association to join. Others, whether by intermediary or through personal acquaintanceships, were approached by people already in the committee. The reasons cited for joining the committee included a desire to contribute something to the local neighbourhoods and the enjoyment of sports. More often than not, however, I found that combined with these was a desire related to the opportunities such an association offered for striking up new acquaintanceships.

The annual programme of the sports committee included a crowded array of activities such as softball tournaments, swimming meets, volleyball and table-tennis matches, and a yearly ski outing. The high point of the sports calendar was, however, the annual sports field day (*undōkai*) (for an example see Ben-Ari 1986), which involved hundreds of participants. In addition, the committee members took turns in opening the school gym every Saturday night for the benefit of the adults and middle-and high-school pupils who wanted to participate in the games held there. On the city level, the two communities invariably sent teams to participate in softball and volleyball tournaments and in the city-wide sports field day.

The year-end party

The party which forms the focus of this study took place on a Saturday evening towards the end of December 1982. Around seven o'clock, twenty of us began to arrive at a commercial establishment that is part hot spring and part restaurant in North Kyoto. As the end of the year is a time of heavy partying, the use of this establishment's facilities had been booked weeks in advance.

Upon entering the *tatamied* room where the party was to be held we found that the low tables were arranged in six separate groups. Someone said that this just would not do: the tables, he said, are all disjointed (*bara bara*). We thus began to rearrange the furniture so that what was formed was one large rectangle around which people seated themselves.

As the restaurant's staff began to prepare the drinking and cooking utensils, I took stock of who was present. Since the sports committee belonged to two communities, people naturally divided along this line. Fourteen of the twenty participants were from the housing estate, while the other six individuals were from the commuter village. Cross cutting community membership, occupation was another differentiating factor. There were eleven *sarariiman* (white-collar salaried employees), two merchants, a housewife (the only women present and granted honorary male status for the evening), a university professor, two students (including myself), a car dealer, an electrician, and a carpenter. The ages ranged from 19 to 47.

It turned out that in terms of organizational affiliation, the people present were not only from the sports committee. This is because the committee had invited representatives from other local associations (which collaborated with it in various communal activities): the head of the local PTA, the secretary of the two communities' joint neighbourhood association, and four coaches from the children's sports teams (these people brought with them large bottles of sake which were consumed during the evening).[3] All in all, this was a rather heterogeneous group, and by my estimate more than one-third of those present were unacquainted with most of the others.

The head of the sports committee and his two deputies sat at the head of the table, next to the representatives from the PTA and the neighbourhood association. To their side sat the children's coaches, while the rest of us arranged ourselves in the remaining places according to no special rank or order. People kept rather quiet during the preparations although, from the small talk that went on, it appeared that for many of the participants tonight was to be only one out of a series of *bōnenkai* during December. People, it seemed, went to various places to 'forget' the yearly hardships they had endured with their co-workers or fellow students, but also with hobby club members, fellow players on softball teams, officials of other community organizations or with neighbours.

At about 7.30 when things were ready, the head of the sports committee stood, and from his place at the head of the table, asked everyone in very formal terms to pay attention. Then, raising a glass of cold beer, he made his opening remarks. After mentioning that this was the annual *bōnenkai* of the two communities' sports promotion committee, he thanked everyone for braving the cold of late December and coming to the party. He stressed his gratitude to everyone for their help and efforts throughout the year and his hopes that these would continue in the future. Then, addressing individually the head of the PTA, the neighbourhood association secretary and the head coach of the children's teams, he remarked about the contribution of these organizations to the activities organized by the sports committee. He ended by stressing again the future growth and strengthening of the committee, and of the two communities to which it belongs.

Three other people – the two deputy heads of the committee and the head coach – made addresses stressing similar themes as well as the contribution of the sports committee to the functions organized by other communal associations. Beer was poured all around and, at the cue given by the committee's head, everyone said *kanpai* (cheers) and downed the drink. The party had now formally begun.

As is usual on such occasions, the food was prepared collectively. People placed the meat and various vegetables into central pots and then fished them out when ready. Throughout the evening this activity was constantly accompanied by the consumption of cold beer and warm sake. The restaurant's two waitresses confined themselves to bringing us the food and replenishing our supply of drinks. Apart from this they did not stay in the room.

At this time things began gradually, very gradually, to warm up. People took this opportunity to become better acquainted with each other. New members in the sports committee who did not know the others well, or people from outside of the committee, talked of such things as regional Japanese cooking styles, the quality of different intoxicants, clubs and hobbies, place and type of work, children and school, or other *bōnenkai* and parties.

Then, around 8.00 or so, two new types of activities were initiated. First, the committee head and the head coach of the children's teams each began systematically to move around the room and to exchange drinks with each and every one of the participants. They would approach an individual, talk for a minute or two, pour and be poured a drink, toast that person, and then move on. These little chit chats often involved the affairs of the sports committee: for instance the need to recruit new members (and especially women), the coming year's activities, or the construction of a new softball field for the two communities. Later other people – usually older and more senior like the head of the PTA and one of the deputies of the sports committee – also began to move around and to form twosomes in which they would drink to each other's health. In this way not only did the original seating arrangements change, but one got the impression of a sort of slow but continuing stream of movement around the table.

Another type of performance constantly punctuated these activities: the singing of *karaoke* songs. *Karaoke* – literally, 'empty orchestra' – essentially consists of singing to a background of pre-recorded music while the singer adds the vocals. But as this is done through an electronic echo chamber it is very difficult to distinguish the quality of the singing: thus one can sing extremely poorly without the lack of talent really coming through to the audience. The songs themselves are usually of a highly sentimental nature and include recurring references to loneliness, lost love and drinking. The titles of some of the pieces sung that evening include 'Abandoned by a Woman', 'Homesick at the bar', 'Alone facing Osaka bay', 'Third year of unfaithfulness', or 'I'd like to forget'.

While the people who sang at the beginning were usually the bolder ones (again, usually older and senior persons), within an hour everybody, reticent or not, sang at least once. Whenever someone sang for the first time there was usually relative quiet; people would stop their conversations and listen. The shaky voices, flushed faces or nervous hands fingering the songbooks which accompanied some debuts well attested to the nervousness or embarrassment of some performers. In these cases, other people helped them along by singing the chorus lines, by clapping, or even by mouthing the words of the songs. From my own experience, I can attest to the difficulty of getting up to sing in front of such a group of people. But, as with others, when I sang a Hebrew lullaby people cheered me on, clapped their hands to the beat of the song, and aided me in completing my performance.

People's debuts were invariably followed by general applause and often by complimentary comments about the quality of the singing. Second, third, and fourth performances, however, were usually relegated to being a sort of background music for the other activities. An exception to this were amusing songs such as an attempted impersonation of a young female 'star' or a male–female duet sung by two men. In this last performance, the man who took the female role 'hammed' it up considerably and elicited roars of laughter. Another man who was sitting next to me during this performance commented, with a mixture of envy and amusement, this female 'play-actor' always tends to 'lose his face easily'.

As things began to really warm up, people told jokes and funny, often lewd, stories. Conversation wove in and out of a variety of themes in rapid succession. It often consisted of series of quick wisecracks, one-liners, retorts and quips which produced much laughter. Little by little, the participants began to show greater and greater familiarity. The language used began to assume the direct and rather guttural masculine form. People sat shoulder to shoulder, they hugged each other and looked into each other's eyes. Some lay on the floor, while others shouted or laughed loudly. Finally, as the evening wore on some would open their slacks and scratch their groins.

From around nine o'clock – the party by then had been going on for about two hours – groups of four or five individuals would sometimes disengage themselves from the main attractions and form their own little circles. Although such groupings did not occupy a specific part of the room (such as a corner), they often huddled together as if to create a separately focused gathering. Three examples, two short and one extended, may illustrate this. One such circle comprised the coaches of the children's teams and the head of the PTA. They discussed the training methods that could be introduced to the boys' baseball teams. They seemed to be sounding out different ideas in this regard: for instance emphasising batting or pitching, how many hours to hold a practice session, or what kind of game strategy would utilize the boys' capabilities to the full.

A second small group that split off to the side of the room included two villagers and two people from the housing estate. One of the villagers took this opportunity to initiate a discussion about the unique character of 'country folks'. He stressed how the villagers were more open, more prone to express their feelings directly, and somehow less touched by the inhibiting forces of citification than the residents of the estate. His remarks provoked a number of reactions which had to do with the general state of villages in the country and with the problems of human relations in a society which is rapidly developing.

Around 10.00 p.m., a third little grouping split off into the corner of the room. This group included the committee head and one deputy, the PTA chief, the head coach of the children's teams and the secretary of the neighbourhood association. I joined after the discussion had begun, so that I do not really know how it was initiated. But as I sat next to the group, it soon became apparent that some of the difficulties that had been involved in organizing the annual sports day (*undōkai*) were being aired. Conversation centred around who had come – and who had not – to aid in the preparations for this event which is the climax of the sports committee's annual calendar of activities.

Turning alternately to each of those present, the committee head spoke of the problems of communication between the committee and the neighbourhood association, that is, between the two organizations. In a sort of half chant, half ordered rendition, and with his voice slightly strained and rising, he counted out these difficulties: problems with the officials of the neighbourhood association not putting enough effort into recruiting people for the sports day; troubles in making sure that enough of these people come to help with the preparation of the grounds and equipment; and special difficulties with the heads of the association. These people were in charge of the recruitment of locals in order to help the sports committee.

What really riled him, stressed the committee's head, was that the head of the neighbourhood association had not even come to the sports day, and had sent in his stead one of his deputies. He concluded that in a community with some kind of tradition, the leaders of the neighbourhood association always put in an appearance on such occasions; it goes with their function, with their role.

This mild tirade went on for about five minutes during which the listeners nodded their heads and looked at the committee head with apparent sympathy. Then they delicately began to take apart what he had said. They would agree with some of his assertions and then would add something else. Thus, for example, the deputy head of the sports committee agreed that there were difficulties in recruiting people to the sports day, but that these were problems that could be found in any newly constructed neighbourhood in the country. Moreover, he pointed out, all in all the number of people coming to participate in this day-long event was growing yearly.

Another example was the reply of the head coach of the children's teams. This man, who was politically close to the head of the neighbourhood association, began to state that one must always look at both sides of a story. One has to understand, he continued, that the neighbourhood association has many demands on it, and so its leaders are very busy. Moreover, the head of this association is an executive in one of the giant department stores in Kyoto and so has to work on Sundays. With so many difficulties, he ended, it is not easy for this man to be at all of the activities held by the two communities.

For all of this, there was little feeling that these deliberations were intended to lead to any kind of systematic uncovering of the 'problematic' issues involved or to their solution. Rather, each claim was raised as though its actual declaration, its becoming part of public knowledge, would be sufficient in itself. The atmosphere was one in which not only could each person air his grievances more or less freely but, more importantly, be quite certain that they were noted by the others. Once this interchange had been concluded people rejoined the larger gathering and began again to participate in the larger group's activities.

At about 10.45 p.m. the last *karaoke* song, 'Osaka nightclub', was sung and one of the deputies of the committee went to stand at the head of the table beside the committee head (these were the only two people who went back to their original seats). Everyone stopped talking and attention focused on the deputy. In a strong and steady voice he led the singing, without accompanying music, of a traditional fishermen's song which used to be sung as groups of fishermen pulled in their nets in unison. Next, the head of the sports committee, again in formal terms, said that he hoped tonight's party had given everyone strength for the next year. Finally three *banzai* ('hurrahs') were given. The party was formally closed. People bowed to one another and thanked each other for coming. Eight of us continued onto a small tavern for more drinks and conversation before returning home.

Creating a frame

If the *bōnenkai* is an occasion that somehow operates on the participants and on the social order to which they belong, then an examination of how it is put together is crucial to understanding what it is able to accomplish. The logic by which the party is put together is related to the creation of a special reality which holds for the duration of what will be termed the drinking frame. The concept of frame derives from the work of Gregory Bateson (1972) and refers to the meta-communicative messages which provide information about how the activities and messages found within social events are to be interpreted. Goffman (1974: 45; Gusfield 1987: 79ff) defines these meta-communications as rules which define how the resources and actions within the frame are to be understood. In abstract terms, the contextual markers of the frame provide instructions about how the 'special reality' of the event is to be constructed. On a more concrete level the reality of the drinking frame is established through the following: a communication of messages about the formation of a special frame which is separated from everyday reality; a heavy stress within the frame on certain central messages; and a predication of behaviour on rules which differ from those governing everyday mundane activities.

The separation of the frame from external activities is effected, for example, through the use of space and time. The party occurs away from both work and home, in a specially designated drinking place.

Within the inn, it takes place in a separate room and the staff, even if they do have other rooms to serve, always maintain an appearance of monopolized service for the partyers (Befu 1974). Next, the party is scheduled for a Saturday evening, part of the weekend, as opposed to the working week. Finally, the highly structured formalities which open and close the event itself serve to clearly bind it from other social activities.

Within the frame one finds a heavy stress on messages which have to do with the unity and integrity of the assembled gathering. On a discursive level, all of the opening speeches focus on the contribution of the participating individuals, and of the organizations they represent, to a collective or communal effort. The first toast and the last *banzai* which are carried out *en masse* again underline in explicit terms the participation in a common endeavour.

Other means reinforce these messages on a non-discursive level. Take for example the seating – as in other Japanese drinking occasions – of the participants around one table to include everyone in the party (Befu 1971: 164).[4] Next, note the choice of participants to include people from organizations other than the sports committee which represents the associational unity of the two communities. Observe the dyadic exchanges of toasts which encompass the whole gathering. As Befu (1971: 165; see also Moeran 1985: 91) notes, this custom is a ritualized means for expressing a sense of solidarity between party members. Not only is the pouring done for each other, but it is done in public in front of the other guests.

In this regard it is important to note that mutual toasting as a means for creating or confirming a social tie may have similar meaning across contexts. Thus for example the importance of exchanging drinks in the *bōnenkai* is echoed in other kinds of formal opportunities: the mutual toasting that takes place between wedding partners (Hendry 1981; Edwards 1987), between *yakuza* initiants and their patrons (DeVos and Wadgatsuma 1967: 295), or between older and younger 'sisters' in the *geisha* world (Dalby 1985: 41).

Finally, take the singing in unison of the fishermen's song at the end of the evening, which restates the messages found in the speeches at the party's beginning. This restatement, however, differs from these earlier remarks in that it works simultaneously on a number of levels: through the actual words of the song which emphasize a joint task; through the form of the singing which expresses in performative terms (as a speech act) this joint task; and by its occurrence at the end of the evening when all of the other means of creating unity and solidarity have already been put into operation. One may expand this even further. Note that in contrast to the division of labour (within the sports committee and between it and other local organizations) that characterizes the everyday activities of these people, the fishermen's song evokes an image of a joint venture in which everyone participates as an equal unit in a common task.

These kinds of arrangements all work to make sure that no one is forgotten and that support and attention for all revolve within the group. What happens, in other words, is not only the creation of a collective entity towards which attention is directed. What is formed is a dense network of dyads which embraces all of the participants and which provides another base for the creation of the collective entity.

Being a separate frame also implies, however, the switching of behavioural codes. The most important of these codes seems to be the levelling of statuses (Lebra 1976: 118).[5] This is because for the duration of the frame the social distinctions of everyday life are apparently disregarded and a relative equality is temporarily established. The appearance of a sameness is achieved through the consumption of the same kind of food and the wearing of similar clothes, not unlike the wearing of uniform kimonos at hot springs. It is further accomplished through the blurring of any formal or fixed seating arrangements throughout the evening. Under these circumstances a university lecturer and a carpenter, a villager and a person from the new neighbourhood, can relate to one another with relatively little regard to their external attributes.

It is through these three elements then, that the special character of the drinking frame is established: the marking of the party as a special frame, the communications about the identity and solidarity of the assembled gathering, and the levelling of statuses. These form the setting, the preconditions for a further process that unfolds within the frame.

Group dynamics and individual experience

By this process people very gradually break down the distance and barriers which keep them apart in everyday life and evince increasingly intimate behaviour. On a rather self-evident level, this goes for the gentle negotiations, the chit chats and the small talk, by which people who are unfamiliar with each other can get to know one another. On what is perhaps a less obvious level, this goes for the attempts of some people to explore aspects of their public identity: witness the interchanges about the unique character of the village community. But these all belong to the first tiers, the first layers of intimacy. What happens during drinking occasions is that people can reveal more about themselves than pieces of information of limited facets of their identity.

This is because when the intimacy within the drinking frame is taken further, it results in what Lebra (1976: 110; see also Benedict 1967: 132) has termed social nudity, or what Hendry (1989) in different terms has called the process of 'unwrapping'. Here, the individual reveals aspects of the self as they are stripped of all face and social masks. Social nudity is exhibited in what are often deliberate violations of conventional manners and etiquette: in bragging, infantility, stupidity, boisterousness, highly emotional expressions, lying on the floor, or in female–male impersonations.

All of this is reinforced by the cultural definitions of manliness. In contrast to America, where the tendency is to assume that a man should be able to drink large amounts, in Japan there are positive valuations of both a man who can drink like a 'tiger', and one who can easily become drunk, but not drunken (Befu 1971: 164). There are almost no barriers, in other words, in the way of a descent into social nudity. Indeed, within such situations both stupidity and the show of human sympathy are actually signs of manliness (Lebra 1976: 118–9).

Yet social nudity entails more than a violation of norms or the expression of tenderness and affection. It works towards the expression of something else. Let us get at this by way of the *karaoke* performances although similar things can be said for the joking, playing, or dancing presentations that go on during many Japanese parties. In a word, *karaoke* provides a chance for many people to stand out: to become for a few minutes a film or singing star, or a fantasy character. In a society which provides relatively few opportunities for adult individuals to stand in the limelight, taking the microphone turns an individual into the centre of the group's attention, regardless of their singing skills (Stroman 1983: 43–9).

But what of those for whom singing is not easy? Remember the stress many suffer at the moment of selection to sing. But note also that the group reacts with sympathetic clapping, singing, and the occasional mouthing of the words. Here I would posit, following Rohlen (1974: 191), that when the ordeal is over, it is not unusual for the performer to feel a rush of relief and of gratitude to the others for their help. The singer is then 'deep into the group emotionally; for he has revealed his humanity and been accepted by the others' (Rohlen 1974: 191). Moreover, each person also acts as part of the assembled gathering in helping the other soloists and in receiving them into the fellowship. The constant alternation between performers and audience thus guarantees that each of the participants goes through the dual experience of performing and being performed to.

I am not, of course, denying the commercial impetus which lies behind the promotion of *karaoke* (Linhart 1986: 207). But to overemphasize this aspect is to lose sight of two things. The first is that singing and performing were a major part of Japanese drinking occasions long before this technological innovation. The second, and perhaps more important point, is that such performances engender a certain experience: the experience of exposing oneself before and performing within an intimate group. To continue the imagery of nudity, this process does not, of course, imply a total disrobement in front of the assembled gathering. To be sure, certain layers of propriety are left on. What it does imply, however, is that at least some kind of partial disrobement does take place.

What one finds in such situations, then, is a subtle interplay between group dynamics and individual experiences. On the individual level, this interplay is manifested in the fact that at some stage in the evening many, if not all, of the participants are caught up in an experience that somehow transcends them. But this is not only an individual experience – say the solitary engrossment found in painting or writing – but one that is also very much a collective one. Individual expression, to put this differently, is to a great extent coupled with an immersion within a larger body.

Along these lines the relative levelling of status during the drinking occasion should not be seen as the creation of some kind egalitarian set-up. It should not be seen as the creation of a frame within which each individual as individual is given pride of place or within which status or position are of prime import. Rather what is created is a frame where a dominant principle is that of a group that transcends individuals, and is more than the sum of its parts (in an additive sense). On a collective level, then, what is achieved is the creation of a temporary group. For what is created for the duration of the frame is an entity that is marked by boundaries from the outside and which is characterized by a certain identity, intimate behaviour and a sense of fellowship within it.

This is not to argue that this is a linear process by which people inevitably proceed from one stage to the next, or in which the group is irresistibly created. It is rather a process that at times progresses and at others regresses, and in which individuals may vary in terms of being caught up in the collective experience. Nevertheless, in many drinking occasions – like the committee's *bōnenkai* – there appears to be a strong force which works towards the creation of a temporary group: a strong force for the construction of an experience that transcends individuals.

Instrumental dimensions and the creation of trust

There is still a need, however, to explain how the occasional practical or political disinvolvements of four or five people during the party fit in with the general 'nonpolitical' logic of the drinking frame. During these relatively short periods of disengagement from the main group – and engagement in their own particular affairs – people have opportunities seriously to communicate about matters that are important to them. Two types of explanation have been put forward in order to explain the potential of these interludes for such communication.

The first explanation focuses on the process within which people break down the distance between them and tolerate, even encourage, intimate behaviour. This explanation runs along the following lines: during such disengaged interludes men, like the head of the sports committee, who are slow to speak out because of cultural (or personal) inhibitions, can sound out ideas, or discuss the problems which trouble them. The relaxation of normal behavioural codes is thus taken to be the prime element which facilitates communication. Nakane (1973: 129) introduces such an interpretation when she links the relaxation of associates during drinking episodes to the conversations they have about strategies and intrigues at the workplace. Skinner (1978: 473) brings in such an explanation in observing how the gossip which is allowed in drinking situations is used in order to gain knowledge about organizational decisions. Yet this kind of interpretation, while it well underlines the different normative conventions which govern behaviour during these occasions, does not suffice. This is because it fails to elucidate the process by which the bases, the common grounds, upon which the instrumental or political issues which concern the participants are established.

A more sophisticated explanation has to do with the establishment of these common grounds. In Japan, as indeed in most societies, there seem to be serious differences in the way people within or outside the group are treated. Often termed the *uchi* (in-group) – *soto* (out-of-group) distinction, these differences have to do with the assumptions made about people's behaviour within and outside of a group. To simplify somewhat, these assumptions include an emphasis on trust, direct discussion and a sharing of common goals inside the group, and an emphasis on a basic opposition or antagonism outside of it. But what is crucial in this regard is that the *uchi–soto* boundary, the in-group and out-of-group dividing line, is flexible (Ishida

1984: 23). That is, in different situations the boundary encompassing a group may be enlarged so that individuals or groupings which were previously defined as distinct become then defined as being merged with a larger body.

Communication between the participants, along these lines, is facilitated because the enlargement or expansion of the in-group allows the absorption of the parties into a larger, albeit, temporary group, within which difficulties and problems may be aired. While such an interpretation well highlights the crucial bases of trust and common goals in making it possible for the participants to engage in discussions between themselves, it is still lacking. This is because the very mechanisms for the creation of temporary groups are left unanalysed within it. This is also because the emergence of trust is treated as a 'given', as unproblematic in these situations. A more complete explanation then involves elucidating the ways in which trust – the very basis for any serious discussion about common concern – is built up in such situations.

In brief, my argument is for a focus on how the exchanges and negotiations which go on during the party may contribute to the emergence of a certain sense of trust between the participants. What one finds is a gradual and graduated progression of acts of exchange which can serve as bases for the creation or demonstration of trust: the dyadic toasts at the evening's beginning, the interchange of increasingly personal information, the mutual lowering of defences and, finally, the reciprocation of singing and social nudity through which rarely revealed aspects of the self are exposed. Here we have in miniature a process that stands at the heart of any relationship: a process 'in which each previous act of exchange serves as a building block upon which a relationship affording exchange of resources of higher value and requiring greater trust' (Befu 1987: 21) is built. Through these exchanges, then, the participants demonstrate that they have achieved sufficient interpersonal trust to form the basis for discussion about more practical issues. Once this trust has been demonstrated the participants can turn from mutual concern to mutual concerns (Bailey 1983: 47).

It is in this light that the similarity between the committee's *bōnenkai* and examples which abound in the literature should be seen. Vogel (1963: 105), for instance, relates how the drinking occasions of company men are used openly to air and correct problems within the workplace. Rohlen (1974: 126) talks of the special atmosphere created between co-workers during drinking in which it becomes particularly easy for people freely to discuss difficulties, offer criticisms, and exchange opinions. To reiterate, in these kinds of situations it is only once a modicum of trust has been demonstrated or established that the relatively unrestricted expression of issues can go on. By trust is meant a sense or belief that one can forward an argument or disclose a personal difficulty without fear that these would be used to someone else's immediate advantage.[6]

In these examples, however, the disclosures and displays go on between people who are tied by common pursuits and by relatively long acquaintanceship outside the drinking occasions. In these instances, then, the building of trust within the drinking frame is related more to an allusion to prior relations of mutual faith and confidence than to a building anew of such relations. In other words, it is related more to the actualization of a sense of trust which is already implicit in relations between people than a negotiation about its very existence.

The necessity of negotiating a sense of trust between participants from a much weaker starting point is more obvious in the case of the displays and expressions which are found in the *bōnenkai*. This is because the very heterogeneity of the assembled guests – in terms of local organizational affiliation as well as place of residence, age and occupation – and the relative weakness among many of prior ties are factors that make the expression of difficult issues problematic. Yet, as I have shown, especially in regard to the heated discussion about the sports committee and the neighbourhood association, the potential for such expression is indeed related to the process of negotiating – and one might well add re-negotiating – trust between the participants.[7] The *bōnenkai* thus works towards helping people to come to terms with the hardships of the year by allowing them to re-experience some of these very hardships within the special conditions of the party.

Drinking occasions and the wider social backdrop

How is the present analysis related to the ongoing debate about conflict management in Japan (Eisenstadt and Ben-Ari 1989)? I would argue that it represents an explanation of the workings of one mechanism of conflict management on which attention has recently become focused. In brief, this is the process by which an inter-organizational disaccord – in our case between the sports committee and the neighbourhood association – is transposed onto an interpersonal level. As Krauss, Rohlen and Steinhoff (1984: 13) note, this mechanism – one of the most effective and legitimate means used in Japan – keeps the conflict localized. Conflict, in other words, is handled by personalizing it, and by invoking the norms of interpersonal relations between the parties.

But as Krauss *et al.* well realize, there is more to these situations than a mere personalization of a conflict situation or a simple localization of wider tensions and struggle. This is because, as the conflict is expanded up or down between different levels, it is transformed: 'its character change in turn introduces new limits and avenues for resolution' (Krauss *et al.* 1984: 13). To put this by way of our case, the inter-organizational conflict is transformed because it is personalized within the context of a drinking occasion. That is, it is localized within a social frame that facilitates the expression of certain problematic issues on the basis of a temporarily created group within which trust is gradually demonstrated. It is precisely the different quality of relations between individuals which can unfold during drinking occasions which may be utilized in order to manage conflict.

This may become even clearer in regard to the way in which uncontrolled behaviour can be handled within such occasions. Thus one may well enquire as to what happens when things get out of hand in these situations? Here, reference must again be made to the ongoing group dynamics and the special conditions that they create. For what one must realize is that if any of the re-experiencing of difficulties within the small groupings becomes ungovernable, there is always a possibility of moving back into the larger group and having the uncontrolled behaviour of the participants absorbed there. Indeed, this can only be understood against the background, which is not always present in similar Western gatherings, in which tremendous care is taken to show that a group has been created and that everyone has a connection to someone else as well as (via the *karaoke*, for instance) that everyone has a connection to the group. This cushioning effect of the wider gathering within which the smaller group is embedded is again another of the special conditions of the drinking party.

These realizations, in turn, suggest the need to view the use of such occasions as part of people's strategies. For given the very predictability of such events one may well realize how they may be consciously and intentionally utilized in order to achieve practical goals: solidifying group morale, furthering personal gain, gossiping, politicking, and managing struggles.[8] In this sense I am suggesting a certain similarity between drinking occasions like the *bōnenkai* and other social practices often found in Japan: *tsukiai* (the obligatory socializing of white-collar employees), outings and contests, tours and excursions,[9] or communal bathing. All of these are social devices for the creation of temporary groups and may be used in order to further people's strategic ends. They should be seen, in other words, as techniques which are often created purposely for interpersonal communication which is 'warm', 'empathic', and which allows the exploration of problematic issues.

One must be wary, however, of too easy an assumption about the functional links between drinking episodes and the wider social context. This is because the unity or identity of the created group, the forming of ties between the guests, or the management of tensions between them, are all potential states that are somehow created within the *bōnenkai*. Whether in fact unity or divisiveness, intimacy or isolation, political co-operation or a continuation of conflict will come about is dependent on other things such as the political and economic relations between the participants or the opening of other social arenas for mutual contact. In other words, the relationship between participation in drinking occasions and the larger social backdrop is neither direct nor certain. As Sutton-Smith (1981: 474) puts it, 'play potentiates; it does not itself actualize'.[10] What situations like the *bōnenkai* constitute, however, are collective experiences that can be understood by many of the participants who were formerly just strangers or who were previously tied by relations marked by tension or outright conflict. Thus it is precisely because people do not forget what is expressed in such episodes[11] that they may be changed by the experience, and that upon a return to everyday life they may make use of or be influenced by what they have undergone.

Groups and temporary groups

The contribution of this analysis goes beyond an illumination of the intricate dynamics of drinking occasions in Japan. Its contribution also lies in highlighting a theoretical point of some importance for the understanding of this society. In brief, this point involves the operation of a number of mechanisms which seem to be crucial, in the Japanese context, for creating ties within heterogeneous gatherings, or between existing collectivities or organizations whose relations may be marked by tension or opposition. Drinking occasions, like the *bōnenkai* described here, are far from being the only kind of mechanism with such potential. Despite popular and academic stereotypes to the contrary, Japan offers a range of cases where *ad hoc* groups made up of people previously unknown to each other, or marked by ties full of tension, are created. Witness the very widespread, but as yet little analysed, phenomena of special task forces (Vogel 1975: xxi), study or advisory bodies (Harari 1982), tour groups, or inter-ministerial bodies (Campbell 1984). All of these temporary entities are established to mediate between different public and private organizations.

Almost all of the data about these *ad hoc* groups tend to focus on their formal aspects: allocation of responsibility, legal status, or influence on decision making. Nevertheless, a careful reading of these studies reveals that in all of the instances of impermanent groups, middle-class Japanese seem to have a number of mechanisms – like drinking, recreation activities, or rituals – which facilitate the relatively smooth creation of solidarity and a climate suited for close interaction. To reiterate, these mechanisms which operate in the interstitial spaces between different permanent organizations or collectivities make possible the creation of this solidarity and climate among people with different backgrounds, diverging allegiances and diverse external ties.

It is, for example, along this line that gatherings in many of Japan's old *geisha* establishments should be seen. For during these gatherings – which offer their own blend of entertainment and drinking – many of the country's behind-the-scenes political manoeuvres and big business transactions take place (Dalby 1985: 166). Indeed, one may well suppose that it is part of the *geisha*'s role to facilitate the creation of a special atmosphere at these gatherings and, through that, to actively participate in the complex dynamics which allow the participants to engage in more 'practical' discussions.

These social-interactional mechanisms point, I would argue, to a culturally constituted facility among many middle-class Japanese to move rather smoothly from one collective entity to another. A brief excursion into the social-psychological roots of such mechanisms may bring this out. Very few middle-class Japanese have a primary group, with the exception perhaps of the family, to which they remain affiliated for their entire lives (Befu 1980: 39). What does seem to be the case is that most of these people acquire through their socialization a learnt capacity to move from and relate to a succession of groups throughout their lives (Keifer 1970; Hendry 1986). This capacity is related to the complex processes of (direct, anticipatory and vicarious) socialization and an individual's procession, from childhood to old age, through a whole range of groups: play and neighbourhood groups, kindergarten and school classes, sports teams, student clubs, coteries of friends, and task and work groups.

In more abstract terms, middle-class Japanese acquire – through a process Bateson (1972: 167) terms deutero – or meta-learning – a capacity to move from one frame (Nakane 1973: 34), *waku* (Plath 1964), or *so* (Kumon 1982) to another. They learn to relate to groups on a meta level. This means that throughout their socialization, throughout a long series of interactive settings, these individuals learn the rules, principles, and interactional patternings that have to do with the creation of groups (Lennard and Bernstein 1970). As they grow older then, when interacting in new contexts and social collectivities, these rules and principles help them to engage in the patterns of interaction which create the novel settings.

Put somewhat differently, this implies that middle-class people in Japan learn to relate to a constant 'idea' or 'construct' of a group although they move *successively* and *concurrently* through many actual groups. Thus, in any specific gathering within which these individuals may find themselves, there are often found mechanisms which facilitate the creation of impermanent entities within which co-operation, solidarity and intimacy, and the management of tension, are made possible.

This point appears to be particularly important in the context of Japanese society. For what should be stressed is the operation of these mechanisms not only within the context of permanent, relatively long-lasting groups, but precisely in those situations where they are used to create a group among aggregates of strangers or among people or collectivities which are marked by ties of tension. The noted Japanese 'inclination' or 'preference' for operating in groups, to put this rather strongly, should not imply an inclination to operate in one specific group to the exclusion of others (although many academic portrayals of Japan seem to imply this). Rather this 'preference', a learnt capacity with which many individuals feel comfortable, works on a distinct level but which at the same time can be contextualized in any number of actual groups, temporary or permanent.

Conclusions and implications

Drinking occasions like the sports committee's *bōnenkai* are not only congregations of people, but also intricate congregations of processes: they are complex compositions of developments and operations. When seen in this light it may be clearer how the present analysis goes beyond the often penetrating insights into isolated aspects of drinking situations which are found in much of the literature on Japan. For only an appreciation of the full complexity of such frames can contribute to an understanding of the wide range of things they are able to accomplish: stress release and the revitalization of the individual, entertainment and excitement, the integration and solidification of groups, the exploration of identities and the establishment of trust, conflict management and politicking, or a commentary on the social order within which the frames are embedded.

At the same time, however, these situations are more than random agglomerations of processes and operations. This is because there is an internal logic, or to use another metaphor, an underlying order, to the way these processes unfold and the manner by which they condition each other. Thus it is not just a matter of launching into a preoccupation with instrumental matters or the management of tensions at the appropriate' stage in the sequence of events. It is no less a matter of the way this appropriateness is constructed: by the way each stage establishes facilitating or limiting conditions for the next.[12] To reiterate an earlier point, all of this is not to imply a definite and inevitable movement from one stage to the next, for people differ in their ability to use or their inclination to enter these complex frames.[13]

A recognition of these points leads us to deal with the nature of such mechanisms as the *bōnenkai* as social situations which are enacted on the basis of cultural 'outlines' or 'loose associative chains' (Rosaldo 1980). On one level the existence of an outline for the *bōnenkai* – an outline that in its general contours is found in many sectors of society – implies that there is a framework towards which the participants can orient themselves and within which they can interact with little of the fumbling around one finds in less structured social situations. In this sense, the familiarity with the programme and the feeling that one is 'in the know' seems to contribute a measure of freedom in the social exploration and interaction that go on.[14]

Yet conceptualizing the *bōnenkai* as being based on an outline suggests two further sets of issues which have to do with the wider implications of this study.[15] These issues have to do with how one may link the ongoing event to the concrete strategies people employ in order to further their aims and to the abstract level of cultural assumptions about the world.

First, these outlines are more than allusions to abstract principles, for they carry prescriptions as to the concrete actions and techniques which individuals may utilize. They are, following Rosaldo (1980), templates of ways in which perceptions, feelings and thoughts are fused into patterns for action. What is fascinating about the outlines of such events as the *bōnenkai* is that they are codified and formalized compositions, but allow, within general limits, much variation in terms of timing, tempo, accent and improvization. And it is this flexibility in turn which makes these techniques suitable to fit the peculiarities of different situations and contexts.

Yet these realizations directly raise a comparative question: In what way does the sports committee's *bōnenkai* differ from other Japanese drinking occasions? On the basis of a comparison with other cases reported in the literature (and unfortunately there are very few of these) I would suggest two main factors that differentiate between types of drinking occasions: their 'geographical' location, where they are held, and their social situatedness, that is, what kind of groups participate in them.

Group drinking in Japan tends to take place either within the context of commercial establishments like bars (Hendry 1987: 160ff; Takada 1983) or guesthouses (Martinez 1989) or in people's homes (cf. Bernstein 1983: chap. 4; Moeran 1985: 91ff.) and communities (Kelly 1985). While roughly similar types of social dynamics appear to take place in both types of places the crucial differences between them lie in the role such professionals as *mama-san*, hostesses, *geisha* or bar people can play. These professionals can facilitate the unfolding of such processes as social nudity or the creation of temporary groups.

The other differentiating factor is related to the degree to which the participants within parties are part of fixed, ongoing groups or organizations outside these special frameworks. Thus, the only really detailed ethnographies of such engagements (Moeran 1986; Rohlen 1974) deal with people who have had a relatively long acquaintance and a continuing membership in relations which exist outside of parties. In this sense the case of the *bōnenkai* documents and analyses an example of how a party facilitates a growing together of people marked by a weakness of prior ties. To put this on a more abstract level, drinking occasions differ in the ways in which they contribute to the reproduction or production of social groups and relations (Giddens 1976).

The second set of issues is related to how drinking occasions as 'outlines' reveal certain messages about constructing a miniature model of a cultural ideal: the *uchi* or in-group and its peculiarities, or the idea that one can, in principle, set up a temporary group among any gathering of individuals. As Bruner (1986: 69) notes, these outlines, or stories, images or associative chains, are the cultural means by which people's experience is given coherence and relevance.

In this respect, however, the present analysis has tended to stress such points as unity, solidarity or integrity. The underlying ideal, as it were, is one of 'sharing' and one that can be found at the basis of a variety of formal events in Japan (weddings, Shinto ceremonies, or children's festivals, for example). Surely, one may well object, these kinds of themes correspond both to the dominant ideology propagated mostly by the world of business and Japanese companies, and to the 'group model' of Japanese society (Dale 1986; Mouer and Sugimoto 1986).

Indeed, to use Mary Douglas's (1987: 11) words, occasions like the *bōnenkai* do 'construct ideal worlds'. What the analysis does not imply, however, is the validity of the ideals projected during such events within the social reality of Japanese society (which at times is, of course, marked by high levels of tension, conflict and divisiveness). It does attest, however, to the power of such occasions to convey these cultural ideals and to facilitate through the use of these ideals such 'practical' aims as conflict management or politicking.

Like other such opportunities around the world (Bott 1987:1 96) these are essentially conserving and conservative institutions. In this respect my analysis raises two further questions for research. On the one hand, there is a need to explore further the specific mechanisms by which such events contribute to the continuity of social structures where they occur, and to the maintenance of the social constructions of reality of their participants. On the other hand, there is a necessity to analyse how other 'special' social occasions such as theatre productions, students' demonstrations, labour strikes, or *manzai* (comic) performances (Tsurumi 1987), relate to the social order and to conceptions of this order, from what is basically a questioning or subversive stance.

Notes

1   Thanks are due to Don Handelman, Reuven Kahane, Brian Moeran, Judy Posner, Tamar Rapoport, Maidie Rosenblatt, Batia Siebzehner, and two anonymous reviewers for helpful comments on earlier versions of this paper, and to the Harry S. Truman Research Institute for helping me to complete it. Fieldwork on which this research is based was carried out within the framework of an Otsuki Peace Fellowship. This piece of research is part of a larger community study of the two localities mentioned in the text. Fieldwork was carried out from July 1981 to August 1983 during which time I participated in the sports promotion committee as a full member.

2   The estate and the village lie a few kilometres to the east of Kyoto's northern suburbs. Most of the local workforce – which includes a variety of middle-class occupations – commute daily to jobs outside the two communities in the nearby cities. With the

construction of a joint school in the late 1970s the two localities were amalgamated into one school or administrative district. This amalgamation led, among other things, to the establishment of joint village-estate organizations such as a PTA, a neighbourhood association and the sports promotion committee.

3   During 1982, the sports committee – with the encouragement of the local neighbourhood association and the city office – established teams for elementary school-age boys (baseball and soccer) and girls (volleyball). These teams were coached by people recruited by the committee from the two communities.

4   This kind of behaviour may well be contrasted to the American 'cocktail hour' (Gusfield 1987: 80) where different (much more individualized) strategies are used in order to ensure people's participation in the gathering.

5   In this sense the *bōnenkai* can be seen as a liminal episode (Turner 1969) in which a sense of *communitas* is effected.

6   A parallel process that goes on, it may be hypothesized, is a movement from the expression of stereotypic problems through the *karaoke* songs to the expression of real problems which are part of people's lives.

7   A related point is that drinking occasions such as the *bōnenkai* aid people in coming to terms not only with the facts of their situation but also with the emotions that accompany them: anger, frustration or ambivalence, for example (Lebra 1984b: 41).

8   Examples of the practical uses to which drinking episodes are put outside of Japan can be found in Lithman (1979), Wilhelm (1984), Kupferer (1979), Hunt and Satterlee (1986), and Mars (1987).

9   For a fascinating, if brief, description of a women's tour group, see Lebra (1984a: 271–3).

10   'Thus the Olympic Games make theoretically potential a universal world of co-operating nations . . . They create a fantasy of unity. The relationship of that fantasy to what may actually happen is however determined, even overwhelmed by many other variables. But at least play is a communicative form that can be understood by many who were formally completely entrapped within their more parochial boundaries' (Sutton-Smith 1981: 474).

11   Thus I am in full agreement with Moeran (1986: 227) when he stresses that despite what people say, they invariably remember, and make future use of, what is said during drinking occasions.

12   I would further hypothesize that the different processes within the frame are interlinked by complex ties of feedback. Thus, for example, 'side involvements' with practical issues or the management of conflict may amplify the general process of creating a group identity and solidarity. When seen against the wider backdrop of the frame, involvement with instrumental matters may involve not a depletion of group dynamics but an amplification of them.

13   Rosaldo (1986: 16) brings this point out when he talks of the possible heterogeneity of ritual, in which 'Multiple processes can occur together (but may follow) different pathways. Their coming together within a specific setting can be motivated (due to underlying coherence), accidental (more coincidental than not), or somewhere in between'.

14   As Sutton-Smith observes, there 'is a considerable consensus that the person who plays is at some ease with his environment and his fellows' (Sutton-Smith 1981: 455).

15   I am greatly indebted to two anonymous reviewers for aiding me in formulating these issues.

Bibliography

Atsumi, R. (1979) '*Tsukiai* – obligatory personal relationships of Japanese white-collar Employees', *Human Organization* 38: 63–70.

Bailey, F.G. (1983) *The Tactical Uses of Passion: An Essay on Power, Reason and Reality*, Ithaca: Cornell University Press.

Bateson, G. (1972) *Steps to an Ecology of Mind*, New York: Ballantine

Befu, H. (1971) *Japan: An Anthropological Introduction*. San Francisco, CA: Chandler.

—— (1974) 'An ethnography of dinner entertainment in Japan', *Artic Anthropology* 11 (supp.): 196–203.

—— (1980) 'A critique of the group model of Japanese society', *Social Analysis*, 5/6: 29–43.

—— (1987) 'Four models of Japanese society and their relevance to conflict', paper presented at a workshop on Japanese Models of Conflict Resolution, Jerusalem.

Ben-Ari, E. (1986) 'A sports day in suburban Japan: leisure, artificial communities and the creation of local sentiments', in J. Hendry and J. Webber (eds) *Interpreting Japanese Society*, Oxford: JASO Occasional Papers no. 5, pp. 211–25.

Benedict, R. (1967) *The Chrysanthemum and the Sword*, New York: New American Library.

—— (1934) *Patterns of Culture*, Boston: Houghton Mifflin and Co.

Bernstein, G.L. (1983) *Haruko's World: A Japanese Farm Woman and Her Community*, Stanford: Stanford University Press.

Bott, E. (1987) 'The Kava ceremonial as a dream structure', in M. Douglas (ed.) *Constructive Drinking*. Cambridge: Cambridge University Press, pp. 182–204.

Campbell, J.C. (1984) 'Policy conflict and its resolution within the governmental system', in E.S. Krauss *et al.* (eds) *Conflict in Japan*, Honolulu: University of Hawaii Press, 284–334.

Dalby, L.C. (1985) *Geisha*, New York: Vintage.

Dale, P.N. (1986) *The Myth of Japanese Uniqueness*, London: Croom Helm.

De Vos, G. and H. Wagatsuma (1967) 'Organization and social function of Japanese gangs: historical developments and modern parallels', in R. Dore (ed.) *Aspects of Social Change in Modern Japan*, Princeton, MD: Princeton University Press, NJ, pp. 289–325.

Douglas, M. (1966) *Purity and Danger*, London: Routledge and Kegan Paul.

—— 'A distinctive anthropological perspective', in M. Douglas (ed.) *Constructive Drinking: Perspectives on Drink from Anthropology*. Cambridge: Cambridge University Press., pp. 3–15.

Edwards, W. (1987) 'The commercialized wedding as ritual: a window on social values', *Journal of Japanese Studies* 13(1): 51–78.

Eisenstadt, S.N. and Ben-Ari, E. (eds) (1989) *Japanese Models of Conflict Resolution*. London: Kegan Paul International.

Goffman, E. (1974) *Frame Analysis*, New York: Basic.

Gusfield, J. (1987) 'Passage to play: rituals of drinking time in American society', in M. Douglas (ed.) *Constructive Drinking*, Cambridge: Cambridge University Press, pp. 73–90.

Harari, E. (1982) 'Turnover and autonomy in Japanese permanent public advisory bodies, *Journal of Asian and African Studies*, 17: 235–50.

Hendry, J. (1981) *Marriage in Changing Japan*, London: Croom Helm.

—— (1986) *Becoming Japanese: The World of the Pre-School Child*, Manchester: Manchester University Press.

—— (1987) *Understanding Japanese Society*, London: Croom Helm.

—— (1989) 'Humidity, hygiene or ritual care: some thoughts on wrapping as a social phenomenon', in E. Ben-Ari, B. Moeran and J. Valentine (eds) *Unwrapping Japan*, Manchester: Manchester University Press.

Hunt, G. and Satterlee, S. (1986) 'Cohesion and division: drinking in a English village', *Man*, 21: 521–37.

Ishida, T. (1984) 'Conflict and its accommodation: omote ura and uchi–soto relations', in E.S. Krauss *et al.* (eds) *Conflict in Japan*, Honolulu: University of Hawaii Press, pp. 16–38.

Jefferson, T. (ed.) (1975) *Resistance Through Rituals*, Birmingham: F.H. Wakelin Ltd.

Keifer, C. (1970) 'The psychological interdependence of family, school, and bureaucracy in Japan', *American Anthropologist* 72: 66–75.

Kelly, W.W. (1985) 'Rationalization and nostalgia: cultural dynamics of new middle-class Japan', *American Ethnologist* 12(4): 603–18.

Kennedy, M.M. (1979) 'Generalizing from single class studies', *Evaluation Quarterly* 3: 661–78.

Krauss, E.S., Rohlen, T.P. and Steinhoff, P.G. (1984) 'Conflict: an approach to the study of Japan', in E.S. Krauss *et al.* (eds) *Conflict in Japan*. Honolulu: University of Hawaii Press, pp. 3–15.

Kumon, S. (1982) 'Some principles governing the thought and behaviour of Japanists (contextualists)', *Journal of Japanese Studies* 8: 5–29.

Kupferer, H.J. (1979) 'A case study of sanctioned drinking: the Rupert's House cree', *Anthropological Quarterly* 52: 198–203.

Lebra, T.S. (1976) *Japanese Patterns of Behaviour*, Honolulu: University of Hawaii Press.

—— (1984) 'Nonconfrontational strategies for management of interpersonal conflict', in E.S. Krauss *et al.* (eds) *Conflict in Japan*, Honolulu: University of Hawaii Press, 41–60.

Lennard, H.L. and Bernstein, A. (1970) *Patterns in Human Interaction*, San Francisco: Jossey-Bass.

Linhart, S. (1986) '*Sakariba:* zone of "evaporation" between work and home?', in J. Hendry and J. Webber (eds) *Interpreting Japanese Society*, Oxford: JASO Occasion Papers, no. 5, pp. 198–210.

—— (1988) 'From industrial to postindustrial society: changes in Japanese leisure-related values and behaviour, *Journal of Japanese Studies* 14(2): 271–307.

Lithman, Y.G. (1979) 'Feeling good and getting smashed: on the symbolism of alcohol and drunkenness among Canadian indians', *Ethnos* 44: 119–33.

Mars, G. (1987) 'Longshore drinking, economic security and union politics in Newfoundland', in M. Douglas (ed.) *Constructive Drinking*, Cambridge: CUP, pp. 91–101.

Martinez, D.P. (1989) 'Tourism and the Ama: the search for a real Japan', in E. Ben-Ari, B. Moeran, and J. Valentine (eds) *Unwrapping Japan*, Manchester: Manchester University Press.

Matsumoto, Y.S. (1970) 'Social stress and coronary heart disease in Japan: a hypothesis', *Millbank Memorial Fund Quarterly* 63: 9–36.

McLuhan, M. and Fiore, Q. (1967) *The Medium is the Message*, New York: Bantam.

McMurrin, S. (ed.) *The Tauner Lectures on Human Values*, vol. 7, Cambridge, Salt Lake City: University of Utah Press.

Modjeska, N. (1982) 'Production and inequality: perspectives from central New Guinea', in A.J. Strathern (ed.) *Inequality in New Guinea Highland Societies*, Cambridge: Cambridge University Press, pp. 50–108.

Moeran, B. (1985) *Okubo Diary: Portrait of a Japanese Village*, Stanford, CA: Stanford University Press.

—— (1986) 'One over the seven: sake drinking in a Japanese pottery community', in J. Hendry and J. Webber (eds) *Interpreting Japanese Society*, Oxford: JASO Occasional Papers, no. 5, pp. 226–42.

Moore, S.F. (1975) 'Epilogue: uncertainties in situations, indeterminacies in culture', in S.F. Moore and B.G. Myerhoff (eds) *Symbol and Politics in Communal Ideology*, Ithaca and London: Cornell University Press.

Mouer, R. and Sugimoto, Y. (1986) *Images of Japanese Society*, London: Kegan Paul International.

Plath, D.W. (1964) *The After Hours: Modern Japan and the Search for Enjoyment*, Berkeley: University of California Press.

Rohlen, T.P. (1974) *For Harmony and Strength: Japanese White-Collar Organization in Anthropological Perspective*, Berkeley, CA: University of California Press.

Skinner, K.A. (1978) 'The Japanese salaryman in a government bureaucracy: a participant observation study of a public corporation'. University of Minnesota, unpublished PhD thesis.

Stroman, J. (1983) 'Boom with a beat', *PHP* 14: 43–9.

Sutton-Smith, B. (1981) 'The social psychology and anthropology of play and games', in G.R.R. Luschen and G.H. Sage (eds) *Handbook of Social Science of Sport*, Champaign, IL: Stripes, pp. 452–78.

Takada, M. (1983) *Sakariba no Shakaigaku*, Tokyo: *PHP*.

Tsurumi, S. (1987) A cultural history of postwar Japan 1945–1980. London: Kegan Paul International.

Vogel, E.F. (1963) *Japan's New Middle Class*, Berkeley, CA: University of California Press.

Vogel, E.F. (1975) 'Introduction: toward more accurate concepts', in E.F. Vogel (ed.) *Modern Japanese Organization and Decision-Making*, Tokyo: Tuttle, pp. xiii–xxv.

Wilheim, D.Z. (1984) 'A cross-cultural analysis of drinking behaviour within the context of international business', *Studies in Third World Societies* 28: 73–88.

9 Training for leisure

Karaoke and the seriousness of play in Japan

William H. Kelly

Order . . . brings security and stability, and a person has only to adjust to the models and principles that regulate life; he can express himself without resorting to the perpetual inventiveness demanded by a free society.

(Octavio Paz, *The Labyrinth of Solitude*)

. . . seriousness seeks to exclude play, whereas play can very well include seriousness

(Huizinga, *Homo Ludens*)

Forms, training and *karaokedō*[1]

The *kata* (form) and the concept of a way or path (*dō*) for mastering such form figure prominently in the practice and ideology of the fine arts and the martial arts in Japan. This emphasis on form and on disciplined training under the guidance of a teacher and usually within the rubric of a recognized school, is a distinctive feature of Japan's cultural pastimes (O'Neill 1984). An aesthetic rooted in Daoism and formalized over a seven-hundred-year period, this emphasis on *kata* persists as a generalized feature in what Befu terms the behavioural ideology (Moeran 1984: 254) of Japanese society, shaping not only the practice of so-called traditional Japanese arts – tea, flower arrangement, and music, for example, which have become the chariots of the nation's aesthetics and culture – but also contemporary forms of popular/mass culture (Yano 1995; Kelly 1998; Robertson 1998). It is also manifested in the reinvention and incorporation into Japanese society of activities imported from abroad such as baseball (Moeran 1984; Whiting 1990) tennis, and other sports, the teaching and practice of Western music and the appreciation of art forms such as painting and even cinema.

This emphasis on *kata* and the role of training and practice in its mastery has permeated the world of Japanese *karaoke*, spawning a major subsidiary industry of *karaoke* education, as well as a massive popular discourse providing guidance and advice for improving one's performance techniques and mastering the 'way of *karaoke*'. Much of this vast body of *karaoke* instruction is disseminated via the mass media – through television programmes, on radio, or in popular weekly and monthly publications and trade journals – but is also provided through formal instruction in the form of individual tuition, privately run *karaoke kyōshitsu* (karaoke classrooms), institutionally based classes, and via correspondence courses advertised regularly in trade journals and even in the national press. Instruction encompasses both technical and social aspects of performance and is dispensed by acknowledged experts – usually well-known professional singers in the case of television pro- grammes and correspondence courses – and semi-professional singers, or trained music and singing teachers in the case of more local forums. The range of instruction and 'how to' advice available is extremely broad, covering vocal technique, timing, and enunciation of sounds, stage posture, performance style, even microphone position, and advice on nearly every other imaginable aspect of self-presentation within the context of singing *karaoke*. The attention to detail and earnestness with which instruction is both sought and given suggests a seriousness to this form of 'play' which is much more pronounced in Japan than in other societies (for example, Britain). Although *karaoke* may be pursued for fun in Japan, it is also pursued seriously for fun, as several examples illustrate.

Television

This emphasis on education in the context of *karaoke* is reflected in several television programmes on the theme of amateur singing and is the primary focus of at least one or two. The most famous of these is *Nodo jiman* (literally 'proud voice'), a weekly amateur singing contest broadcast by the Japanese broadcasting corporation, NHK (radio and television) since the early postwar period. Throughout the programme, selected amateur performances are assessed by a panel consisting of two professional singers who provide commentary and advice on how to improve. This is always delivered gently – often diluted with praise for other aspects of the performance – and is gratefully received by the performer. An amateur singing contest, consisting of both serious and ludic performances and with a prevailing atmosphere of fun, *Nodo jiman* nevertheless incorporates this educational element adding a dimension of earnestness to the idea of amateur singing, reflecting the assumption that many amateur singers will want to work to improve their singing.

This is certainly the assumption of *Karaoke corner*, a programme broadcast weekly on Saturday evenings, which provides professional instruction on the singing of songs in English to an amateur guest singer. One episode for example featured a middle-aged housewife who wanted to master the song, 'Fly me to the moon'. After singing the song once to the accompaniment of the show's slightly rotund and bespectacled pianist, the guest singer was assisted by a panel of experts which included several professional singers, one a specialist in English-language songs and an Englishman with fluent Japanese who explained the meaning of the song's lyrics. Following her first performance of the song, guest singers provide advice for improving different aspects of the performance, sometimes demonstrating for the amateur guest singer who then practices repeatedly the problematic verses to the pianist's accompaniment. Equipped with pointer and lyrics chart, the Englishman then takes the singer through the lyrics, explaining particularly difficult passages. He addresses pronunciation problems and makes his own suggestions as to how to sing certain parts with reference to the song's meaning. The amateur once again sings the entire song, incorporating as many of the expert suggestions as she can remember, after which the song is sung by the group of four professional singers. At the end of the show, a *karaoke* version of the song is played so the programme's viewers can practise the song themselves at home. The entire programme is devoted to helping a single amateur singer, and the tens of thousands of television viewers whom she represents, to improve their song performances through professional assistance.

In addition to these regularly broadcast programmes, there are also a number of special features on *karaoke* and related subjects which touch on the theme of *karaoke* instruction. A particularly memorable segment of one of these featured a retired man who loved to sing, but whose timing was consistently much faster than the recorded version of the song. The programme followed this man's efforts to correct his performance flaw through personal tuition, practice, and a strict regime of breathing exercises and other techniques for pacing his performance. This gruelling struggle concluded with the protagonist's re-evaluation, which reveals his timing to be almost perfect, much to his relief. A vignette which might elicit little more than a 'so what' from a cynical viewer, it seems to serve as a poignant parable for the power of perseverance, discipline, determination and hard work in conquering even the most mundane of life's challenges.

Courses

Karaoke instruction is offered through a wide variety of courses, classes and do-it-yourself seminars. These are widely advertised nationally in *karaoke* trade journals, such as the Osaka-based *Karaoke Fan*, as well as in the mainstream popular press, such as popular magazines and daily broadsheets. At the local level, *karaoke kyōshitsu* (literally '*karaoke* classrooms') are organized privately or through a variety of community organizations. Heavily promoted by the *karaoke* and music recording industries, *karaoke* education constitutes an additional market for their products and a new sphere of employment for the professional singers who serve as the industry's pool of expert instructors. Now, instead of simply entertaining music consumers, they are occupied in training them in the mastery of techniques that will equip them to entertain themselves and their various circles of friends, cohorts and colleagues.

The extent to which a concern with training has permeated the overall *karaoke* phenomenon is reflected in the format of a magazine like *Karaoke Fan* which, as the name implies, is targeted specifically to *karaoke* enthusiasts. Sponsored by the *karaoke* and music industries, the journal provides its readers with information on anything pertaining to *karaoke* singing. It includes new trends and products, listings of the top ten songs, both *enka* and pop, reviews of selected *karaoke* venues, lyrics and music for dozens of songs, announcements of *karaoke*-related events and pages of practical advice for aspiring amateurs. Regular features such as *shitsumonhen* (literally, 'question-answer'), a question page and *jigoeuragoe* (literally, 'natural voice', 'falsetto voice') provide advice on topics ranging from singing duets, pronunciation exercises and proper enunciation, development of vocal range, and tips for scoring well in *karaoke* competitions. Each issue also contains the lyrics and music to at least a dozen popular songs, along with suggestions for how each should be sung. These include a brief, one paragraph introduction to the song, reminding the prospective performer of one or two important points to keep in mind when singing, as well as notations in the musical score itself, indicating features such as soft, loud, quick or slow for each part of the song. Finally, instruction is available through various mail-order *karaoke* seminars, also regularly advertised, and promising complete mastery of selected popular songs for the price of a cassette or videotape and a minimal investment of time.

Another form of *karaoke* training by post is *karaoke* correspondence courses. One of the largest of these, operated by *MC Ongaku Sentā* (MC Music Centre) in Tokyo provides cassette tapes of a wide selection of popular songs, most of which are *enka*, perhaps reflecting the age of the clientele to whom they primarily cater. According to one of their full-page advertisements in the national press (*Asahi shinbun*, 22 November 1994), each cassette includes three recordings of the song – one in a male voice, one in a female voice and a professional version – a 'lesson' by either one or several professional singers/instructors accompanied by either piano or guitar and a recorded *karaoke* version of the song for practising. A striking aspect in the format of these tapes is the degree of repetition of the various versions of the song which seems to be consistent with Christine Yano's observations of repetitiveness in professional *enka* performances during which a singer's current hit or flagship song might be repeated several times, seemingly to the continued approval of the audience (1995: 70). In the specific context of training, this emphasis on repetition is also consistent with an educational ethos which permeates many areas of endeavour in Japanese society, including aesthetic pursuits such as the tea ceremony and the martial arts – *sumō*, *judō*, *kendō* – and others.

The role of the professional singer as *sensei* (teacher) is an important element in both correspondence courses and mail order seminars as the legitimacy of the course depends in part on the reputation of the teacher. Most advertisements include photographs of the teaching staff of professional singers and many include either a profile of the master's career and credentials or a few words from the teacher, thanking students for their interest in and valuable feedback about the course and assuring them of his continued intention to help them as best he can to become better singers. One advertisement (*Asahi shinbun*, 9 January 1991) included photographs of the ten singer/instructors, above whom were printed the words *subarashii sensei, subarashii ressun* (wonderful teachers, wonderful lessons).

Classes

Karaoke kyōshitsu (karaoke classrooms) are usually small-scale classes operated privately or through neighbourhood and community organizations. Especially popular among middle-aged women (see Hasegawa 1994; Oku 1998 for example), *karaoke kyōshitsu* provide a social forum for meeting to share a common pursuit, and, in this sense, *karaoke kyōshitsu* are socially analogous with classes for *okeikogoto*, such as tea ceremony and flower arrangement, also popular among this sector of the population. One article which appeared in the monthly magazine, *Hōseki* (February 1992), classified *karaoke kyōshitsu* as one of the three most popular arts among housewives which not only confirms that their popularity among these women derives from their compatibility with a style of socialising already well-established among this group, but also suggests a conceptual link between a popular leisure activity and activities perceived to embody Japanese culture and tradition or between popular/ mass culture and 'high' culture.

Case study: *karaoke* education at a *rōjin daigaku*

Rōjin daigaku (lit. 'old person's university') is an institution that provides retired people with the opportunity to pursue coursework and extracurricular activities through participation in social clubs. Administered and operated by the regional government authority of *Osaka* prefecture, enrolment is competitive – with many more applicants than places – and limited for one year in order to provide as many aspiring students as possible with the opportunity to enrol. Successful applicants choose a major or special subject from a list which includes ceramics/pottery (*tōgei*), handicrafts (*shugei*), English conversation, health and exercise (*hoken taisho*), and welfare/wellbeing (*fukushi*), and also club activities such as calligraphy (*shodō*), magic, dance, painting, hiking, chorus singing and *karaoke*. Classes meet just once a week – on either a Tuesday or a Friday – and club activities run from two o'clock to five o'clock in the afternoon on the same days.

There is great variation in the popularity of different clubs among the students and this is reflected in membership. Whereas the hiking club for example had more than a hundred members, clubs such as photography (*kamera* as it was called), English, and the Japanese board game, *go* were cancelled due to lack of interest. Mr Ono, the student co-ordinator for the *karaoke* club explained that a hundred members was far too many and that as a result, the hiking club had been divided into four sections, each meeting bi-monthly. He suggested that the ideal club size is fifteen to twenty members, noting that if there are too many people, communication is not possible, as things become chaotic and disorganized – *bara bara ni naru* – as Mr Ono put it.

The *karaoke* club had between fifteen and twenty members with roughly equal numbers of men and women. On one of the days I visited, there were sixteen members in attendance – eight men and eight women – with the men seated on one side of a class which was divided by an aisle running front to back through the middle and the women on the other. The teacher was Mrs Kanesaki, a woman probably in her mid-fifties, who teaches such classes at a number of venues in the Ibaraki area of Osaka, which is also where she lives. The tools of Mrs Kanesaki's trade included a portable, double cassette player, a cassette recording of two versions of the song being taught – one with vocals and one without – and enough photocopies of the song lyrics for each student. Students were also provided with a cassette recording of the song for a small fee to cover its cost.

The format of the class was roughly the same from one meeting to the next. At each class, a new song – normally an *enka* song – was introduced. On one visit, the song was *Nagasaki usei* (literally 'the sound of Nagasaki rain'), which was played once as an introduction, a second time for a closer listening and then a third time with students singing along. This was followed by a few minutes of introductory remarks and explanation by the teacher, after which the song was sung two more times. The teacher then discussed the proper pronunciation of two sounds recurrent in the song, 'o' and 'n', explaining that when singing 'o', the mouth should be nicely rounded and that 'n' should be pronounced with the lips closed together, as if it were 'm', noting that in a singing contest or *karaoke taikai* (karaoke competition), one point would be deducted for each infraction. The song was then sung two more times and, although I then left to visit other clubs, I expect that it is probably played several more times thereafter. Although the class format was much the same from one club meeting to the next, there was some variability in both this sequence and in the content of explanations.

The photocopied sheets of song lyrics included not only the name of the song, its composer, lyricist, the name of the singer who popularized it and the lyrics, but also a complicated array of symbols and markings in the margins, cueing the singer on how to sing a particular line – quickly, slowly, in a high or low pitched voice, with intonation rising or sinking, tapering off. Explaining and demonstrating the significance of these cues was an important focus of the teacher's lesson.

From this brief sketch, several general points emerge. First, although the *karaoke* club is an extracurricular social activity, there is a degree of sobriety, even seriousness to the tone of the lesson. Students are instructed as if they were potential competitors in *karaoke* competitions (which they were not), as is evidenced by the teacher's repeated reference to the points docked for various infractions of *karaoke* form, technique and protocol. Second, the teaching and learning of the 'way of *karaoke*' involves a great deal of repetition. In the course of a single lesson, students may listen to and/or sing the same song as many as ten times. Although it is difficult to know how representative this particular example of *karaoke* education is, the emphasis on repetition as a means of mastery is central to the learning of the martial arts or the *okeikogoto* as well. Regardless of whether the activity is indigenous (*shodō*, *kendō*, *sumō*, or tea) or imported (baseball, tennis, golf), the aesthetics of repetition in learning remains the same:

> What matters most . . . is the realization of a quasi-somnambulist degree of unconsciousness; only if the performer can rely on a pattern of senso-motoric coordination so deeply ingrained that no phase of the performance requires cerebral intervention, is true mastery attained.
>
> (Singer 1973: 67)[2]

Although these principles are reflected in, if not the basis for, *karaoke* education at the *rōjin daigaku*, it is important to note that one of the primary functions of club activities in this context is social – they provide both a structured forum and a pretext for interaction – and it is this, more than the mastery of the particular activity which seems to be the major motivation for participation.

Discourse

Another avenue for *karaoke* education is the popular discourse articulated through articles published in a wide variety of weekly and monthly magazines which cater to every sector of the Japanese population. Whereas some of these publications, such as *SPA*, enjoy large circulation and broad readership, others are more defined in both the scope of their content – for example the women's gossip magazines *Bishō, Josei Seven, Shūkan, Josei* – and the specific group in Japanese society to which they are targeted, such as young men (*Popeye, Men's Non-no*), young women (*JJ, MORE*), housewives (*Shufu no Tomo, Shufu to Seikatsu, Orange Page*) or businessmen (*AERA, President*). There is a broad range of articles on *karaoke* contained within the pages of these publications, including reports on the business and economic aspects of the phenomenon, news on recent technological developments, essays and editorials pontificating on the musical and sociological implications of *karaoke*, and special features or retrospectives on *karaoke*, tracing the phenomenon's evolution and development and analysing its implications for Japanese society (*SPA* 16 June 1993). In addition to articles of general interest, there is also an extensive sub-genre of articles providing instruction for mastering the 'way of *karaoke*' which provide advice on virtually every aspect of performance, including when, what and how often to sing, vocal technique, stage gesturing, microphone position and general conduct as both performer and audience to the performances of friends, family members or company colleagues.

Advice is concerned with self-presentation, the development of an individual *karaoke* style and, related to this, proper *karaoke* deportment and etiquette vis-à-vis the others with whom one sings. Often presented as a list of 'how to' *karaoke* tips, the actual content of the advice varies, depending on the intended readership of the particular magazine. Thus, whereas advice in a magazine for young women employed as OLs or 'office ladies' tends to reflect a consciousness of their relative position within the workplace and the expectations of their status and role within the context of company-sponsored, 'after hours' leisure, that in magazines targeted towards their bosses reflects a very different perspective on an identical situation (that is, after hours socializing).

For example, one article which appeared in *Josei Seven* (22 April 1993), a gossip magazine targeted primarily to middle-aged housewives, but casually read by other groups of women as well,[3] suggests ten peices of advice for new *shakaijin*.[4] Potentially directed at women who might have just entered the workforce and published to coincide with the commencement of the fiscal year on 1 April, the tone of the article is instructional.[5] Drawing a clear distinction between *karaoke* for fun and *karaoke* in the context of 'after five' leisure (or *tsukiai*), the article opens with the following admonition regarding *karaoke* singing in a work related context, 'The singing-with-a-friend-on-a-Saturday frame of mind is not appropriate! From basic manners to what not to sing and fashion, teaching you all the keys to avoiding blunders'. Specific pieces of advice include the following:

1   Listen respectfully to the singing of the *sempai*[6] or boss.
2   Practise and be able to sing at least three duet songs so that you are able to accompany your boss on request.
3   Take care not to sing the boss's favourite song as he is likely not to be able to sing too many different songs.
4   Take care to avoid songs which are likely to have a depressing effect, such as those which are nostalgic or about separation and lost love.
5   Take care to avoid songs which are unfamiliar to others since they are more likely to chat during your performance if they do not know the song.
6   Avoid sexy songs which are likely to offend senior office ladies.
7   Choose a song which the boss has heard at least once before.
8   Wear a suit rather than a sexy dress out of respect for senior office ladies.
9   When not singing, be sure to maintain an awareness of and to express an interest in those around you.

The article concludes with a list of the ten best and worst song choices for 'after five' *karaoke* singing, each of which includes a detailed explanation for why the song is or is not appropriate. One song, by the popular group Dreams Come True (*dori kamu*) is recommended on the basis that it is an example of a modern pop song which is well known to middle-aged men (*ojisama*) due to its television exposure. Another song, 'Piece of my wish', is discouraged as being bad for the establishment of good chemistry between people. Although the precise relationship between this kind of article and the behaviour and attitudes of its intended readership, whose concerns and points of view it purports to represent, is difficult to discern, the article is representative of those targeted to this particular sector of the Japanese population.

According to a young Japanese woman with whom I discussed dozens of articles from the popular mass media, the tone underlying many advice articles targeted towards OLs is slightly dismissive towards the office superiors that its content purports to accommodate. They articulate a simplistic formula for manoeuvring through hierarchical relationships within the workplace, while assuming that young office ladies know much more about *karaoke* singing and popular music than do their seniors who must be humoured and placated. Thus, although such articles purport to instruct a younger generation of Japanese women entering the 'real world' (the workplace) for the first time on the etiquette and deportment appropriate to after hours socialising with senior colleagues, there is, according to this informant, an implicit suggestion that learning a few simple rules is all that is required to pay lip service to and effectively navigate one's way through authority structures in the workplace. Such articles are thus empowering to their readers, suggesting that despite their temporary and in most cases transient association with their place of work they are potentially able to exercise considerable control within the context of office leisure or *tsukiai*.

The concept of *tsukiai* with respect to *karaoke*-singing is much less resonant among housewives and this difference is reflected in the advice dispensed to this sector of the population. In one article, entitled *Shufu no tame no karaoke jōzu kōza* (Karaoke improvement course for housewives) popular (*enka*) composer Nakamura Yasushi, dispenses the following seven pieces of advice:

1   Sing a song that all present can sing. If you sing together, you feel less self-conscious and shy.
2   Sing loudly.
3   Sing songs that are not too difficult.
4   Avoid singing *chanson*.
5   Balance songs.
6   Be sure to praise your husband's singing.
7   Don't be discouraged if you are an *onchi* (a tone-deaf singer).

Noting that housewives are serious (*majimena*) and honest, Nakamura-*sensei* suggests that they are always concerned with doing the right thing, even when at play. As is typical of this popular instruction, the article also contains the lyrics to half a dozen songs, along with a paragraph of introductory commentary for each song, providing background and useful tips for performing the song. A significant sociological difference reflected in the advice and general tone of commentary between articles in publications for housewives versus those directed at younger, working women, is that articles directed towards the former tend to treat *karaoke* as a leisure activity pursued in the company of other housewives (and perhaps their young children) or as an activity analogous to other 'cultural pursuits' (tea ceremony, flower arrangement) which provide a means for self-improvement, a hobby and perhaps most importantly, a structured forum for being together with friends for a few hours each week under the guise of a shared pursuit. Although socialising in this context lacks much of the formality, instrumentality and sense of obligation which characterized *tsukiai* activities, the emphasis on self-improvement and self-development which is reflected in much of the *karaoke* advice for housewives and which is characteristic of the pursuit of the *okeikogoto* is, at least in the case of *karaoke*, linked with the importance of self-presentation within a collective context. This in turn is not a wholly individualistic aim, but one which is associated with the mastery of a manner and deportment which both shape and facilitate social interaction in any context.

Karaoke discourse and body techniques

In addition to the abundance of popular articles concerned with the sociology of *karaoke* and advice aimed at negotiating the social aspects of every conceivable *karaoke* situation, considerable attention is also devoted to what might be categorized as the sociology of the body within the context of *karaoke*. Like the job interview manuals circulated amongst university employment offices which advise prospective company recruits on even the most minute details of proper deportment in job interviews – posture, elevation of the head and chin when facing interviewers, distance between feet and direction/angle at which toes should be pointed when seated – such articles address similar concerns with respect to the *karaoke* stage. As is the case in the job interview manuals, much of this advice is gender-specific.[7] One article (*Shūkan josei*, 17 March 1997), entitled *Utai jōzu, kiki jōzu: kotsu to manā* (singing well, listening well: tips and manner), includes suggestions, all generously illustrated with sketches demonstrating the do's and don'ts of *karaoke* deportment. Men for example are advised to stand on stage square with feet apart at shoulder width, holding the microphone at the mouth with one hand and the microphone cord in the other hand, which should be placed in front of the navel. It is suggested that women stand with one foot placed slightly in front of the other and pointed at an outward angle, one hand holding the microphone at their mouth and the other at their side and that they avoid blinking too much. Leaning against a wall, turning and twisting excessively, putting a hand in the pocket or a hand on the hip (belt) are described as taboo. Even the proper way of holding the microphone is illustrated and described – in one hand, about one cigarette's length from the mouth. Holding the microphone in two hands or in one with the smallest finger up as a woman might hold a teacup are described as unacceptable or *dame* in Japanese.

This concern with performance style and the formalization of body movement on the *karaoke* stage is also manifested in articles which provide instruction on performance choreography. One issue of a popular weekly magazine for young women (*Shūkan josei*, 19 December 1995) included a special multi-paged section which provided detailed instruction on dance routines accompanying a selection of popular hit songs. Following the name of the song, the singer or group which popularized it, and a three-star difficulty rating in which either one, two or all three stars were shaded, indicating the difficulty of the routine, a sequence of illustrations, each with detailed instructions and one or two of the song's lyrics to provide a cue as to exactly where in the song the movement depicted should be performed. Below this, the full text of the song is printed, along with a few sentences in a shaded box labelled as 'one point advice'.[8]

As these few examples illustrate, a concern with form, etiquette, practice, training and self-improvement is pervasive in much of the *karaoke*-related discourse in popular weekly and monthly magazines. The content of such articles is tailored to their specific readership and although it is not clear what the precise connection is between the advice and commentary published in popular magazines and the behaviour of the magazine's readers is, it can be at least assumed that this discourse reflects and to some degree embodies issues relevant to actual practice. To put it in colloquial terms, it 'speaks' to its readers.

According to several Japanese acquaintances with whom this material was discussed at length, a major source of appeal of many popular articles on *karaoke* is the fact that they discuss openly aspects of the *karaoke* experience which are implicitly understood by readers, but seldom discussed among them. For example, several of these acquaintances explained that articles suggesting performance rules present scenarios which are very familiar to the experiences of most readers and the consciousness which underlies the prescribed behaviours mirrors the consciousness of readers who have invariably found themselves in similar situations. Thus, although there is an element of seriousness in a discourse which defines *karaoke* as leisure which, at least in certain circumstances, is 'rule bound', such articles are not necessarily read as serious guides for behaviour, but rather in a humorous light. Like the stand-up comic who makes explicit the unconscious habits and motivations of daily life, inviting the audience to laugh at themselves, so too these articles serve as somewhat light-hearted and humorous guides for navigating one's way through the web of human relationships which constitute any social situation, including a *karaoke*-singing session. As one young Japanese woman put it, readers recognize the concerns underlying the performance rules prescribed in many articles on *karaoke* as relevant to their own situations and find it funny.

Analysis

As I hope this sketch has illustrated, an emphasis on the patterning of performance through practice and training of the voice and body and by means of an adherence to performance 'rules' is a widespread and generalized feature of *karaoke* in Japan, although one which is manifested and emphasized differently in different contexts and among different sectors of the Japanese population. As regards the significance of this concern with the *kata* of form of *karaoke*, I would like to suggest the following speculative interpretations:

1 Form and performance dynamics

In his essay on sociability ('The sociology of sociability'), Georg Simmel suggests that one of the fundamental features of sociability, which he defines as 'the play form' of human interaction, is an emphasis on form

> Even the most primitive sociability, if it is of any significance and duration at all, places so much emphasis on form, on 'good form'. For form is the mutual determination and interaction of the elements of the association. It is form by means of which they create a unit. The actual, life-conditioned motivations of sociation are of no significance to sociability. It is, therefore, understandable that the pure form, the individuals' suspended, interacting interrelatedness (we might say), is emphasized the more strongly and effectively (1950: 44).

Noting that sociability has as its aim ' . . . nothing but the success of the sociable moment and, at most, a memory of it' (*ibid.*),[9] Simmel suggests that its character is determined by the personal qualities of the individuals interacting with one another. However, it is 'precisely because everything depends on their personalities, that participants are not permitted to stress them too conspicuously' (*ibid.*). As Simmel puts it, 'the personalities must not emphasize themselves too individually. Where real interests . . . determine the social form . . . the individual shall not present his peculiarities and individuality with too much abandon and aggressiveness'. Simmel continues, 'The most personal things – character, mood, fate – have thus no place in it (sociability). It is tactless to bring in personal humour, good or ill, excitement and depression, the light and shadow of one's inner life' (*ibid*: 291), concluding that, 'Without the reduction of personal poignancy and autonomy brought about by this form, the gathering itself would not be possible' (*ibid*.).

Within the context of *karaoke*-singing, the emphasis on the solo performance as expressed through the convention of the *ohako* or *jūhachiban* (lit. number eighteen)[10] serve as a kind of social mask behind which the individual can safely present themselves before the group, expressing something of themselves through the vehicle of a popular song which is at once an aspect of collective, perhaps even national culture, and at the same time an expression of personal taste. The emphasis on form and aversion to spontaneity and improvisation also serve to depersonalize performance by providing a framework of expected behaviour and implicit rules which structure action.

Simmel states the 'principle of sociability' as 'the axiom that each individual should offer the maximum of sociable values (of joy, relief, liveliness, and so on) which is compatible with the maximum of values he himself *receives*' (*ibid*.: 47), suggesting that the veiling of content behind the facade of form serves to nourish a climate in which this aim can be realized. This aspect of sociability is reflected in the concept of *nori* in Japanese and in the emphasis on maintaining a good atmosphere or *ii nori* which can be stated as the fundamental principles of *karaoke* singing and other forms of socializing in Japan. Thus, on the question of whether or not ability and talent are important, the answer must be informed by the fact that the aim of *karaoke* singing is, in most contexts, first and foremost sociable so that a successful performance is one which contributes to a happy lively atmosphere, regardless of its quality. The importance of contributing to the maintenance of a good atmosphere in the context of *karaoke* singing is the basis for much of the *karaoke* advice propagated in the popular press. Whether singing amongst friends, office colleagues or university club members, sensitivity to the likes, dislikes, and expectations of others and to the overall atmosphere is essential.

Finally, Simmel suggests that sociability is democratic in nature, noting that,

> . . . sociability . . . calls for the purest, most transparent, and most casually appealing kind of interaction, *that among equals*. Because of its very nature, it must create human beings who give up so much of their objective contents and who so modify their external and internal significance as to become sociable equals. Each of them must gain for himself sociability values only if the others with whom he interacts also gain them. Sociability is the game in which one 'does as if' all were equal, and at the same time, as if one honored each of them in particular. (*ibid*.: 49)

The emphasis on the solo performance and expectation within a *karaoke* gathering that everyone will take their turn at the microphone ensures that each person, regardless of their status outside the context of group socializing, participates in more or less equal measure with all others. Furthermore, the emphasis on form, as expressed in the expectation that an individual will have at least one song that they have mastered sufficiently to perform from beginning to end, ensure that individuals participate in the same way, that is to say with a degree of sincerity. As Allison (1994) suggests, there may even be a degree of intolerance expressed at the individual who sings a song with which they are not sufficiently familiar to avoid mistakes. Perhaps it is this fact which lies behind Kunihiro's otherwise peculiar claim that one should practise in order to get the most out of *karaoke*. The suggestion that one would approach *karaoke* singing with such purposefulness is in itself telling.

To conclude, it seems reasonable to suggest that an emphasis on practice, training and form – as explicitly manifested in various forums for *karaoke* instruction or implicitly understood by *karaoke* participants – serves to mediate social interaction by creating a 'safe' forum in which individuals' presentation of themselves is safely masked in the guise of a popular song. Ideally, this is adequately rehearsed to avoid embarrassment and circumscribed by rules and conventions which serve to establish and maintain a festive, enjoyable and, most importantly, a comfortable atmosphere in which to socialize.

2 Form and the legitimization of karaoke as national culture

The popularization of *karaoke* singing in Japan has involved not only the successful development, packaging and marketing of a form of popular culture to diverse sectors of the Japanese population, but more profoundly, the subtle and gradual transformation of *karaoke* from an activity perceived as 'popular' to one which is increasingly perceived as 'cultural' – that is, as representative of the nation's 'culture'.

This gradual shift from the periphery to the mainstream of Japanese life is by no means unique to *karaoke* among forms of Japanese popular culture. Commenting on a similar process with respect to the historical development of *manga* (comics), Sharon Kinsella notes that 'As *manga* was promoted within Japanese society, then *manga* editors responded by attempting to produce respectable and "cultural" *manga*' (1996: 389). In summarizing a similar process with respect to a dialectic between *enka* producers and listeners, Christine Yano notes, 'As *enka* becomes squeezed into the platform of official Japanese popular culture, so too, are its listeners somehow affirmed as official Japanese citizens' (1995: 156). Finally, in his recent discussion of the historical development of the multi-faceted *ken* game which survives today as the children's game, *janken* (paper-rock-scissors), Sepp Linhart notes that although 'born in the amusement districts', *ken* 'developed . . . into a way. This transformation included the publication of *ken* instruction manuals, the development of *sumō*–like rankings and ranking tables and, as in the case of *karaoke*, the rise of *iemoto* organizations' (1998: 332). These examples represent forms of popular culture which have undergone a process of cultural legitimization somewhat akin to Weber's notion of the routinization of charisma, in as much as charismatic popular forms originating on the margins of society become gradually adapted and incorporated into the mainstream.

3 What, if any, are the ramifications of this emphasis on form, practice and training for the notion of fun, and what, if any, might be the cross cultural implications?

In his early twentieth-century work, *Japanese Things* (notes on various subjects connected with Japan), Basil Chamberlain begins his entry on 'Fun', claiming that 'Serious ideas do for export. A nation's fun is for home consumption only – it would evaporate before it could be conveyed across the border' (1992: 195). Although Chamberlain might find the globalization of *karaoke* singing and its successful, if fleeting, transplantation into the UK surprising, it is clear that although the *karaoke* machine has been exported on a global scale, its uses within a particular society may reflect a high degree of specificity. Whereas karaoke is certainly a form of 'play' in Japan, it is play which can be and, as this chapter suggests, often is taken seriously in the sense that it is practised with some degree of earnestness. This is rooted in the widespread, albeit implicit expectation that the individual *karaoke* participant should pay some attention to the quality of their *karaoke* performance. This was expressed by the mama-san in Anne Allison's account of a Ginza hostess bar who advises a customer following a failed attempt to sing a new song, 'to buy a cassette of the song and practise it repeatedly for at least two weeks' (1994: 55). One university student suggested that this anxiety regarding one's performance is a matter of 'self–pride', meaning that one naturally wants to present themselves in front of others in the best possible light, even within the context of *karaoke* singing. Thus, *karaoke*'s seriousness in Japan may not so much imply a lack of fun, but may instead confirm Hosokawa's recent observation that, 'Discipline, ranking and objective ranking are indispensable in order that the Japanese derive maximum excitement from their leisure activities' (1995: 152).

By contrast, in the UK, the idea of taking *karaoke* seriously, either through practice and training or by performing earnestly seems to be completely antithetical to the enjoyment of it, which depends on the posture of treating it without the least bit of *gravitas*. *Karaoke* is and must be (if it is to be enjoyable) performed simply 'for a laugh' and it follows that performances are often embellished by stage theatrics and 'hamming it up' in front of an audience. To approach *karaoke* seriously is to extinguish that which makes it enjoyable. Whereas the spontaneous and improvised performance is likely to enhance its potential mirth in the UK, Hosokawa observes that 'spontaneity and improvisation are not highly esteemed in Japanese tradition' (*ibid.*: 151). This does not preclude the possibility of stage theatrics in *karaoke* in Japan, but rather implies that the limits of acceptability are defined differently. Although the emphasis on practice, training and form which is so widely manifested in Japanese *karaoke* implies, at least to the outside observer, a degree of seriousness to the activity, it does not necessarily follow that this implies a diminishment of a sense of fun by the majority of *karaoke* participants. As Huizinga has observed, 'There is nothing to prevent us from interpreting a cultural phenomenon that takes itself with marked seriousness . . . as play' (1955: 191).

166   *William H. Kelly*

Notes

1   Derived from the Chinese *Dao*, the suffix, *dō*, meaning literally 'path' or 'way' appears in the names of the *okeikogoto – chadō* (the way of tea), *shodo* (calligraphy) – and martial arts such as *judō, kendō* and *aikidō*. Characterized by the long and arduous training required to master them, such pursuits serve as a path to *Zen* understanding. As Suzuki explains with reference to the practice of swordsmanship, 'The point is . . . to utilize the art as a means to advance in the study of the way *(dao)*. When it is properly handled, it helps us in an efficient way to contribute to the cultivation of the mind and spirit' (1993: 132). The suffix has been applied in relation to *karaoke* to highlight the widespread emphasis on training by Hosokawa (1995); Kelly (1998) and in the popular press (for example, *SPA*, 16 June 1993, p. 21).

2   Miyanaga Kuniko has linked this emphasis on precise and flawless execution of action or movement embodied in the practice of *okeikogoto* and martial arts with the relatively favourable image of robots in Japan. Arguing that the 'major reason why the cultural image of a robot is not negative in Japan will be found in the basic notion of the human being in . . . Japanese tradition', Miyanaga explains that 'Moral conditioning in Japan is highly behavioural rather than psychological. As in flower arrangement, the tea ceremony, and karate . . . , learning begins with the assimilation of patterns, basically by copying the actions of the master . . . Real mastery is indicated by spontaneity of action; one responds to the situation spontaneously and correctly, without further reflection on the rightness of the action. The ideal is that one acts out of one's personality, with no errors. This is the height of moral perfection' (1985: 112).

3   One Japanese acquaintance described the typical reader of this genre of magazine as a bored, middle-aged housewife, explaining that both readers and magazines are likely to be found in the waiting area of a clinic or bank and at hairdressers or cafés which are not very stylish.

4   Becoming a *shakaijin*, a term which literally means 'social person', is synonymous with becoming a full and productive member of society. Marked by two principal events, marriage and entrance into the working world, the transition to *shakaijin* represents not only a 'coming of age', but more profoundly, the fulfilment of life's most important roles and the duties inherent in those roles. Rohlen's account of the entrance ceremony for new employees of a Japanese bank (Rohlen 1974) and Edwards' description of modern wedding ceremonies (Edwards 1989) provide detailed examples of the kinds of rites which mark the passage to *shakaijin*. Of particular interest is the content of the speeches delivered on such occasions, which reflect the nature and the gravity of the transition to *shakaijin*.

5   This is consistent with Tanaka Keiko's recent observation that a 'strong unifying theme that runs through Japanese women's magazines is the prescriptive approach which they adopt towards their readers' (1998: 110).

6   Literally 'before companion' and 'after campanion', *sempai/kohai* relationships permeate every realm of Japanese society and are generally associated with the expectation of certain duties and obligations on the part of one with respect to the others.

7   Thus confirming Mauss's observation (essays on 'body technique') that body techniques are divided and vary by sex (and also by age).

8   This is reminiscent of the 'one point' English lessons that have been broadcast daily on NHK radio for many years. Although it is not known whether or not the expression originated with these broadcasts, it has become widely associated with them and has entered common parlance as a reference to the 'quick tip' or 'tip for the day' style of advice or instruction in many different contexts.

9   In this connection, it is interesting to note the emphasis placed on the recording of social gatherings on film as a means of preserving their memory in material form. To this end, disposable cameras were on sale at the front counters of both of the *karaoke* boxes with which I was affiliated and as the manager of one of these venues explained, they were

purchased by customers for 'making memories' (*omoide o tsukurimasu*). See Ben–Ari (1991) for an analysis of the role of photography in a Japanese commuter village.

10 Both are composed of three Chinese characters, meaning 'ten', 'eight' and 'number' respectively, which can be pronounced in combination as either *jū* (ten), *hachi* (eight) and *ban* (number) or *o* (ten), *ha* (eight) and *ko* (number). Originally derived from Kabuki theatre, *ohako* or *jūhachiban* has been appropriated into the world of *karaoke* where it refers to a song which an individual regularly chooses to sing. Conceptually, it might be translated as 'a favourite', 'an old standby', a 'standard number' or one's 'forte'.

Bibiliography

Allison, A. (1994) *Nightwork*, Chicago, IL: University of Chicago Press.

Asahi shinbun, 22 November 1994, advertisement: *MC ongaku sentō*.

—— 9 January 1991, advertisement: *MC ongaku sentō*.

Ben–Ari, Eyal (1991) 'Posing, posturing and photographic presences: a rite of passage in a Japanese commuter village', *Man* 26: 87–104.

Chamberlain, B.H. (1992) (1905), *Japanese Things: Being Notes on Various Subjects Connected with Japan*, Tokyo: Charles E. Tuttle Company.

Edwards, W. (1989) *Modern Japan Through its Weddings: Gender, Person, and Society in Ritual Portrayal*, Stanford, CA: Stanford University Press.

Hasegawa, H. (1994) *Kyōfu! Obasan karaoke kyōshitsu* (Danger! Karaoke classrooms for middle–aged women). *Chisō no kagaku* 18 (July 1994): 63–5.

Hōseki (February 1992) *Ahh, tosui no mitsushitsu karaoke kyōsōkyoku* (Ahh, secret room of intoxication: karaoke rhapsody).

Hosokawa, S. (1995) 'Singing not together: *karaoke* in São Paolo', in W. Straw (ed.) *Popular Music – Style and Identity* (Proceedings of the 7th Conference of the International Association for the Study of Popular Music). Montreal: Dufferin Press.

Huizinga, J. (1950) *Homo Ludens*, Boston: The Beacon Press.

Josei Seben (Woman seven) (22 April 1993) *Jōshi, sempai, okyokusama ni kirawarenai: karaoke jū jō* (Don't be disliked by the boss, your seniors or the senior office lady: *karaoke* ten commandments), pp. 64–7.

Kelly, W.H. (1998) 'Empty orchestras: an anthropological analysis of karaoke in Japan', unpublished DPhil Thesis, University of Oxford.

Kunihiro, N. (1994) 'The electric geisha', in A. Ueda (ed.) *The Electric Geisha: Exploring Japan's Popular Culture*, Tokyo, New York, London: Kodansha.

Kinsella, S. (1996) 'Editors, artists and the changing status of *manga* in Japanese society 1986–1995', unpublished D.Phil. thesis, University of Oxford.

Linhart, S. and Frühstück, S. (eds) (1998) *The Culture of Japan as Seen Through its Leisure*, Albany, NY: SUNY Press.

Mauss, M. (1979) *Sociology and Psychology: Essays*, London: Routledge and Kegan Paul.

Miyanaga, K. (1985) 'Popularity of robots in Japan: tradition in modernization', *International Christian University Journal of Social Science* 24(1): 111–23.

Moeran, B. (1984) 'Individual, Group and "Seishin"', *Man* (NS) 19: 252–66.

Oku, S. (1998) '*Karaoke* and middle–aged and older women', in Tōru Mitsui and S. Hosokawa (eds) *Karaoke Around the World: Global Technology, Local Singing*, London and New York: Routledge: 55–80.

O'Neill, P.G. (1984) 'Organization and authority in the traditional arts', *Modern Asian Studies* 18(4): 631–45.

168   *William H. Kelly*

Paz, O. (1967) *The Labyrinth of Solitude*, London: Allen Lane.

Robertson, J. (1998) *Takarazuka: Sexual Politics and Popular Culture in Modern Japan*, Berkeley and Los Angeles, CA: University of California Press.

Rohlen, T. (1974) *For Harmony and Strength: Japanese White-Collar Organization in Anthropological Perspective*, Berkeley, CA: University of California Press.

Shūkan Josei (Woman's Weekly) (17 March 1997) *Utai jōzu, kiki jōzu: kotsu to manā* (Singing well, listening well: tips and manner), pp. 146–7.

Simmel, G. (1950) *The Sociology of Georg Simmel*, Glencoe, IL: The Free Press.

Singer, K. (1973) *Mirror, Sword, and Jewel*, London: Croom Helm.

Spa (16 June 1993) *Karaoke teikoku nippon no osorobeki kenjitsu tanjō 20 nen nippon shijō saidai saikyō no koraku dai kenkyō* (The formidable reality of karaoke empire Japan: the largest and most far reaching research ever conducted), p. 21.

Suzuki, D.T. (1993) (1959), *Zen and Japanese Culture*, Tokyo: Charles E. Tuttle.

Tanaka, K. (1998) 'Japanese women's magazines: the language of aspiration', in D.P. Martinez (ed.) *The Worlds of Japanese Popular Culture*, Cambridge: Cambridge University Press.

Whiting, R. (1990) *You Gotta Have Wa*, New York: Vintage Departures.

Yano, C. (1995) 'Shaping tears of a nation: an ethnography of emotion in Japanese popular song', unpublished Ph.D. thesis, University of Hawaii.

10 Is there a Japanese way of playing?

Rupert Cox

The Indian poet and linguist Ramanujan (1990) once posed the question: Is there an Indian way of thinking? He went on to show how, depending where the stress is placed, this question contained many questions. If approached in the same way, my question, *Is there a Japanese way of playing?* reveals many of the issues and complexities lying behind the topic 'Japan at Play'. The different emphases are as follows:

1   *Is* there a Japanese way of playing?
2   Is there *a* Japanese way of playing?
3   Is there a *Japanese* way of playing?
4   Is there a Japanese *way* of playing?
5   Is there a Japanese way of *playing*?

Attempts to address these questions have taken the following forms. To the first question it has been said that there is a Japanese way of playing, based on behaviour that is set apart (from the ordinary) by the availability and division of time. In pre-industrial Japan, time was defined for 'ordinary' people in three ways: *ke* – normal working time, *hare* – special, sacred time (festivals) and *kegare* – time of pollution (childbirth, death and menstruation). Play was a category of behaviour particular to special, sacred occasions (*hare*), typically the communal, ritual play (*kagura*) that took place at local shrines. Among the aristocracy and priestly classes play was also a function of time, but in this case, the excess of time and the desire for diversionary pastimes. With the advent of the modern era, leisure time and play become in many accounts almost synonymous. The argument is that increased industrial productivity and efficiency lead gradually but inevitably to the creation of surplus and hence 'longer working time constitutes the frame for leisure activities' (Linhart 1988). The question, which these studies raise is whether the existence of particular divisions of time are a prerequisite for play or rather a function of it.

To the second question: is there *a* Japanese way of playing? There is no single Japanese way of playing, although it is possible to identify a predominant Japanese word for play – *asobi*. Underneath this apparent linguistic unity there are different traditions and related terms, ancient and modern, rural and urban, classical and folk. A famous attempt at accounting for and reducing this diversity was made by the Japanese folklorist, Yanagita Kunio, in the 1930s. He suggested a distinction between two types of leisure: *ikoi* and *yasumi*. The former was an active (*de suru*) and the latter a passive (*de aru*) type of leisure; both were based on a model of premodern agrarian society. Yanagita Kunio argued that activities like *pachinko, pasukon* (personal computer), watching television and sleep, popular since the 1950s and 1960s, were representative of a passive way of playing, and that sports today, and the *okeikogoto* (aesthetic pursuits), popular since the Genroku period, demonstrate an active attitude to play (Yanagita 1989).

Related to this search for a Japanese way of playing is the third question, which asks if there is anything unique to Japanese forms of play. Yoshida Mitsukuni (1985) has suggested that, following the play model of the French sociologist Roger Caillois, what we see in Japan is special to Japan in only one respect. Caillois makes a very broad definition of human play identifying just four different types: *agon* (competition), *alea* (chance), mimicry (simulation), *ilinx* (vertigo). To this categorization Mitskuni added one further Japanese category: play of seasons, which refers to activities like the tea ceremony, flower arranging and moon viewing, which express elements of nature in refined and highly cultivated forms.

The fourth question in this list draws attention to the particular aspect of Japanese play that this chapter will address, namely the existence of a particular 'way' of playing in Japan. This is to talk of play as a classifying term – like *dō/michi* in the arts – within the life of particular forms of behaviour. The implication is that there may be a logical structure to play in Japan, a model of learning and practising play, which also makes sense of the experience of play. Such a concept is contrary to common-sense perceptions of play in the West which emphasize its unstructured and spontaneous nature. I shall suggest that play in Japan is based on the absence of a distinction between creativity and order and that even in structured, disciplined pursuits, such as those indicated by the term *shugyō* (religious austerities), play is a fundamental aspect. What the various *shugyō* do is manifest in tangible forms a Japanese cosmology, expressing as ludic and logical a particular relationship between nature and culture.

Finally there is the fifth question, which asks whether the Japanese play at all, or are they, as popular imagery often suggests so diligent and industrious that they are disinclined to spend precious time and energy engaged in non-productive activities. In fieldwork, carried out between 1992 and 1995, which focused on leisure activities in the urban areas of Kansai, it was found that most respondents identified 'play' (*pureei/asobi/rejā*) as a luxury activity, often involving a serious attitude and hard work. The most commonly agreed 'hobby' (*shumi*) in non-working hours was completely passive, sleep. Another example of Japanese industriousness are school children, who are often portrayed as having little or no capacity for play, because of the overwhelming emphasis in their lives on exam success. It is noteworthy that the official education ministry response to this problem has been a policy begun in 1992 to introduce not less, but more structured activities, including a 'self-learning' (*utori*) period and a greater emphasis on sports, into the primary school week. These initiatives which might appear counter intuitive to a Western educationalist are based, as I shall argue, on an understanding of play as an ordered activity, with a logic particular to its history and origins in Japanese folklore.

One of the earliest literary references to *asobi* occurs with relation to religious rites in the *Kojiki*, 'Record of Ancient Matters' (712 BC), one of two ancient compilations recording Japan's national myths. (Note the other is *Nihonshoki* or *Nihongi* – 'The chronicle of Japan') In the *Kojiki*, the term *asobi* is used to describe the shamanic dance performed by the goddess Ame no Uzume which entices the sun goddess Amaterasu out of the heavenly cave where, upset by the misdemeanours of her brother Susanō, she has hidden herself. According to a recent study (Averbuch 1995) of the origins and development of this shamanic dance into a form of theatre (*kagura*), *asobi* refers to 'songs and dances in the performance of *chinkon*-spirit pacification rites' (*ibid.*: 11).

We can identify two aspects of *asobi* from the *Kojiki* account, one is festive, humorous, even frivolous and the other is serious, disciplined and, at its most extreme, a form of asceticism. These two aspects reflect the extremes of temperament that the gods (*kami*) and *bodhisattva* are prone to display as forces of nature. The coexistence and mingling of these two elements also indicates the absence in Japanese religious thought and practice (*matsuri*) of a clear distinction between the realms of the sacred and the profane. Averbuch explains this as follows:

> A merry celebration, complete with song, dance and music is at work in both solemn and joyful rites. This essential characteristic of all Japanese festivals can be illustrated by the word *asobi* . . . It is often used to refer to worshipping or serving i.e. pleasing the *kami*. Thus, in Japan, the sacred often means great fun.
>
> (*ibid.*: 7)

This is an idea quite opposed to the classical philosophical tradition of the West, which from Plato and Socrates to the time of Rousseau and the Enlightenment, always displayed an 'anti-theatrical prejudice' (Denning 1996: 113). Cultural and social forms must mirror and confirm the sacred order of nature and any suggestion of unstructured playfulness should be seen as a diversion and a deception. This attitude was based on the assumption of a fixed causal relationship between the external cultural sign and the hidden order of nature, which admitted no room for dramatic elaboration. We shall see later that this Protestant disdain for the theatrical has its counterpart in Japan with the professed rational certainties of Confucian philosophy.

The kinds of rites, songs and dances which, in early usages, the term *asobi* has been used to describe, do not attempt a rigid imitation of the realm of nature because the 'nature' they are representing is a collection of wayward and unpredictable forces that cannot be formulated so unambiguously. *Asobi* imitates nature through active, theatrical performance. The more successfully that rites like *kagura*, identify, refine and express the unconstrained, playful temperament of the realm of the *kami/Buddha*, which is nature, the more 'cultured' they are held to be. Simply put, the temperament of Japanese nature is playful and the representation of this playful nature in the activities covered by the term *asobi* is 'culture' (Berque 1997).

There is a causative relationship between the realm of the *kami/Buddha* and the realm of human behaviour (culture) such that effort in one realm directly affects the other. The 'play' of the *kami/Buddha* affects man through natural forces, and through playing with or reconstructing the forms of nature, man may also affect the world of the spirits. Shamanic possession, shrine and temple ritual, popular theatre, all 'play' with nature, cultivating, reconstructing and refining nature as culture. These different forms are similar in that they all attempt to express the temperament of nature, by giving it shape and form. Some of these forms select and refine their expression of elements of nature to such a degree that the aspect of playfulness may appear not to be represented at all. The important point here is that the idea of 'play' is not separable from the forms that represent it. The idea of play, or the playful aspect of nature – the 'nature of nature' – is at the very heart of even the most ascetic disciplines, but is not so easily recognizable to outsiders, because its expression is usually so measured and controlled and structured (Berque 1997).

The austere religious practices of the *Shugendō* group of mountain ascetics known as *shugyō* for example, do not appear to involve any element of play. The term *shugyō* originally refers to the methods of 'self-cultivation' particular to two forms of esoteric Buddhism, *Shingon* and *Tendai* in the Heian period (794–1181). *Shingon* and *Tendai* Buddhism employed a variety of practices including prolonged spells of meditation and fasting as well as exercises like *kaihyōgyō*, 'endurance walking over mountains'. These practices constitute two methods: one demanding 'continual sitting' (*jōza zanmai*) and the other 'continual walking' (*jōgyō zanmai*) (Yuasa 1993: 11). It is out of the latter, active connotation of *shugyō* that a theory of the arts begins to emerge. The theory is that through continual and repetitive performance of systematically organized actions or tasks, the adept undergoes a psychological change. Privations also include standing under waterfalls, fire walking, fasting, meditation, isolation and sleep deprivation. All of these activities take place in the mountains, among those places where the forces of nature are at their most primal and unrestrained. To enter this terrain and to carry out these practices is to experience and ultimately establish some kind of lasting relationship with the temperaments of nature and therefore ultimately with one's own nature. Practitioners are said not merely to represent the elemental forces of nature, but physically to merge with and become part of them (Averbuch 1995).

Yuasa Yasuo describes it as follows: 'the connotations embraced by the word *gyō* carries the sense of strengthening the mind (spirit) and enhancing the personality; as a human being, by training the body' (1993: 10).[1] The goal of undertaking the active practice of *shugyō* was what the priest Kūkai, founder of *Shingon* Buddhism, called *sokushin jōbutsu*, 'enlightenment with this very body'. This state of being was based on the *Mahāyāna* Buddhist philosophy of the non-duality of body and mind. The physical form of the body and the state of mind as it repeatedly practises the same movements become one. It is also described as 'meditation in motion' (*undōteki meisu*) and as Yuasa points out: 'the philosophy behind it soon greatly influenced the artistry and martial arts of Japan' (1993: 14).

If these states are the goals of *shugyō* practices, then it is misleading to translate the term as 'self-cultivation';[2] rather 'there is an existential transformation and the self of everyday experience is discarded and transformed' (*ibid.*:196) as they require the practitioner to push their body to its physical limits.

The connection between *shugendō* austerities and play becomes clearer when viewed within a historical perspective. From the twelfth century some of the mountain paths of the *shugendō* practitioners (known as *yamabushi*) located between the religious centres of Yoshino and Kumano in the Kii Peninsula, became pilgrimage trails, popular among the aristocracy as an excursion away from the city of Kyoto and the concerns of court life (Averbuch 1995: 18). The popular pilgrimages which arose out of these mountain austerities also created a special relationship with nature which allowed the pilgrim to claim they were doing *gyō*. Pilgrims could and still do claim to be doing *gyō*, because the activity they undertake and the landscape they move through has form and bears similarity with *shugendō*. Like the 'mountain priests' (*yamabushi*) of *shugendō* they are literally and metaphorically following a path, making offerings and prayers as they go. The difference is that, unlike the monk, the strictures placed upon the pilgrim are not so disciplined and constraining. The structure of pilgrimage, the route, season, duration and accessibility of places to stay are designed to enhance an appreciation of the ludic elements of nature. As Nelson Graburn has pointed out in a seminal article on play in Japan, 'To pray and to play' are not mutually exclusive or contradictory practices (Graburn 1983). In this respect, *kagura* theatre and *shugyō* austerities are both 'ways' of playing which combine ascetic devotion and aesthetic pleasure. The magical rites of *kagura* have been transformed today into forms of mass entertainment and *shugyō* is difficult to separate out from popular pilgrimage. *Kagura* and *shugyō* are part of a cultural history of play in Japan which remains to be written and would require the description of activities as diverse as pilgrimage, gambling, the martial arts, tea ceremony and *karaoke*. One method of reducing this empirical diversity to a Japanese theory or way of play may be to focus on the concepts used to describe these kinds of activities.

Towards the end of the Heian period, the theory of Buddhist self-cultivation (*shugyō*) was incorporated into the practice and appreciation of the arts. One area where this continuity is clear, as Konishi Jin'ichi has pointed out, is the changing use and value of the quality of *yūgen* (cited in La Fleur 1983: 82,174). The origins of *yūgen* are in *Tendai* Buddhism where it means 'difficult' in the sense of profound, distant or obscure' (Thornhill 1997: 36), but as an aesthetic value in *Waka* poetry and *Nō/Nōgaku* theatre around the end of the twelfth century, its meaning changed. The poet Fujiwara Shunzei (1114–1204) was the first to treat it as an aesthetic effect, 'derived from a sense of longing for an unseen world, or sometimes a sense of wonder at the innate mystery of things' (*ibid.*: 39), and he drew directly on sources from *Tendai* Buddhism to do so. This was a merging of the methods and goals of self-cultivation and of the literary arts. It was tremendously important, for as Yuasa says: 'Accordingly, the ultimate, ideal condition of aesthetic appreciation has been sought in an analogy or comparison with the experience of *satori* (enlightenment) . . . through the 'practice' (*keiko*) of poetic composition, that is, through training the mind in attempting to compose better poems, just as the monk attempts to achieve *satori* through self-cultivation, 'a poet pursues beauty, expressed by the word *yūgen*' (1993: 24). The literary aesthetic *yūgen* was later changed again and applied, along with other terms from Zen like *keiko* (practice) to *Nō* theatre and its repertoire of bodily movement by the *Nō* playwright and theoretician Zeami (1363–1443).

For Zeami the relationship between the 'practice' (*keiko*) of *Nō* and its actual theatrical performance was similar to a monk's practice and realization of enlightenment (*satori*) (La Fleur 1983: 127). At the base of this merging of methods of Buddhist self-cultivation with different artistic genres was a view of 'skill' (*myōyo/waza*) not simply as a technique but as a spiritual phenomenon. The result of this, according to Okada Takehiko, was that 'skill was even thought identical to study (*gaku*) as something' . . . which leads 'to a self awareness penetrating the very core of one's life in the world' (Bloom and Vogel 1997: 298). In other words, to study any art form like poetry or *Nō* is also to practise a skill with spiritual ends. It is described metaphorically as *dō* or 'the way'. The idea of *dō* in the arts is positioned in time and space as a 'path' (*dō/michi*). On this 'path'/'way', through the skilful performance of prescribed actions, one undergoes physical and ideally spiritual change. But it is not possible to progress along this way through trying to possess skill as a form of knowledge. 'Skill' or 'art' is acquired through experience and as such is known as *jissenteki kufu*, or 'doctrines realized through practice'.

Principles of knowledge based on practical experience are 'rules without rules' (*mukiteiteki kitei*), which when they are embodied by the master in performance are called *junsui keiken*, or unconditioned 'pure experience' (*ibid.*: 299, 300). According to this theory, one can only 'know' about any of the arts through the experience of doing them and becoming skilled. It should not be possible to articulate that experience in anything other than the artistic 'forms' (*katachi*) of that skill, which in the case of the way of tea for example, is characterized by the physical properties of the expert body and the objects used in performance. Connecting the arts to Buddhist concepts suggests they can only be understood as 'religious' in intent and meaning. About this Toyo Izutsu has written that:

> The *dō* (way) in the field of art is a way of leading to spiritual enlightenment through art . . . In the artistic *dō* . . . particular emphasis is laid on the process, the way, by which one goes toward the goal. To every stage of the way a certain spiritual state corresponds, and at every stage the artist tries to get into communion with the quintessence of art through the corresponding spiritual state, and make himself bloom in the art.
>
> (Izutsu 1973: 531, quoted in Pilgrim 1993: 56)

The concept *dō* expresses the relationship between ascetic methods of spiritual germination and maturation and aesthetic practices as a 'religio-aesthetic awareness' (Pilgrim 1993). This is a useful expression because it emphasizes the simultaneous development and mutual borrowings of the arts and certain Buddhist concepts. The development of the arts was strongly influenced by the concepts of other religious traditions, which did not conflict with Buddhist doctrine and could be expressed in an aesthetic form. Even before Zen Buddhism was established in Japan, there was a powerful connection between religious practice and aesthetic sensibility whose origins were in Shintō. As Richard Pilgrim has noted, the idealization of the beauty of nature and an emphasis on ritual forms as orthopraxis in Shintō aimed at a 'poetic transformation' of the ordinary world (1993: 8). These ritual and aesthetic aspects of Shintō were adapted and absorbed within the arts during the ninth to twelfth centuries.[3] The primary philosophical source and inspiration of the Zen arts is Buddhism but as Sanford, Lafleur and Nagatomi (1992) point out in their use of the term 'flowing traces', there were many other influences which left their mark and continually blurred the distinction between the aesthetic and the ascetic (1992: 5). When treated historically the arts do not simply express Buddhist ideas in an aesthetic form, rather, certain Buddhist concepts were developed with the arts. Without the arts these concepts would have had little substance and perhaps no widespread appeal. Buddhism was the primary but not the only religious phenomenon in the arts for it was entirely compatible with other religious traditions like Shintō, Daoism and Confucianism. This notion of compatibility was supported by a doctrine called *honji suijaku*: 'its main premise was that the multiple deities or *kami* usually identified with Shintō are, in fact, the 'manifest traces' (*suijaku*) of primordial Buddhas and *bodhisattvas* who are their 'original ground' (*honji*), (Sanford, La Fleur and Nagatomi 1992: 3).

There are multiple religious influences in the early development of the Zen arts and as we shall see in their subsequent history to the present day many secular ones as well. In this syncretic history not only is the distinction between ascetic forms of self-cultivation and aesthetic pursuits blurred, but also the distinction between sacred and secular and elite and popular. What appears to remain consistent through all these changes is 'the assumption that the path of the Buddha and that of the artist could with very little difficulty be seen as one' (*ibid*.: 6).

The establishment of a register of aesthetic criteria through which participatory experience in the Zen arts could be made 'spiritually' meaningful appears to have taken several centuries. Artistic pursuits and aesthetic taste had developed under the patronage of elite and courtly circles prior to the arrival of Zen Buddhism, but it is not until the twelfth century, approximately six centuries after the introduction of Buddhism into Japan, that it is possible to describe artistic pursuits like the 'way of tea' (*Chadō*), as the means to religious transformation. The earliest concrete expression of the merging of Buddhist concepts with Japanese artistic and aesthetic interests took place in the literary arts. After three centuries of secluded development within courtly circles and monastic institutions, it was at this point that Buddhism and the arts reached out to a popular audience. The 'way of poetry' (*Kadō*) signalled this shift and heralded an increasing awareness of artistic pursuits as religious and spiritual *dō*. Many other arts followed soon after including the martial way *kyudō* or 'way of archery'.

Two points are clear about the early history of artistic pursuits in Japan. First that Japanese artistic interest and aesthetic expression always enjoyed a close connection with religion. Second, that the development of these arts as religio–aesthetic pursuits cannot be separated from their patronage by elite social groups like the imperial court.

The enthusiasm for the arts by these elite groups in the Heian period is well documented in the 'Tale of Genji' (*Genji monogatari*) and was not very much concerned with their spiritual dimensions. They approached the arts as a form of 'connoisseurship' and in doing so point towards their secular, social and playful dimensions. Central to the development of the 'social aspect' of the arts in this period as a 'communal cultural activity, a setting within which to engage in a culture of social intercourse' was the 'tea ceremony' (*chanoyu*) (Varley and Elison 1981: 189). Tea drinking had been imported from China in the early part of the Heian period by Buddhist monks who valued its medicinal properties. At the same time it enjoyed some early popularity at the court of the Heian emperor Saga (809–823). It only began to be appreciated as an exceptionally aesthetic pursuit much later in the fourteenth century as part of the passion for 'Chinese things' (*karamono*).[4] Within aristocratic circles, *chanoyu* became a particularly specialized form of aesthetic expression with particular places (*kaisho*, 'banqueting chamber') and people (*dōbōshu*, literally 'companions' or connoisseurs) for practice. So closely was the tea ceremony identified with these aesthetic developments that the term *chanoyu* became synonymous with 'connoisseurship' (*ibid.*: 188). But the aestheticization of tea was not simply the result of a desire for prestige, a form of 'conspicuous consumption', but the result of a change in social relations. The relaxation of the differences between classes, particularly that between the 'court' and 'military aristocrats' (*kuge* and *buke*) led to an increase in the kinds of formal social events which *chanoyu* was suited to meet: 'the most elegant social gatherings during the fourteenth century were increasingly abandoned, at least by the upper classes, in favour of more ceremonially precise behaviour on formal occasions of social intercourse. Such precision was most clearly observable in the serving of tea.' (*ibid.*: 202–3)

The values of these elitist social gatherings were particularly ostentatious and defined by such aesthetic terms as *yūgen*, which we have come across before, *miyabi* ('refinement') and *yūga enrei* ('elegant and sensuously beautiful'), all 'based on a sense of refinement or decorum and a visuality of resplendent colours' (*ibid.*: 203). The aesthetic quality of *miyabi* was used in different ways (like *yūgen*) which it is worth briefly describing because they illustrate once again the lack of a clear distinction between the realms of the religious and the artistic, the sacred and the secular, the serious and the playful. *Myogisho*, a dictionary of the Heian period defines the word *miyabi* with the characters *kan* ('leisure') and *ga* ('refinement'), evoking the courtly refinement idealized in the hero of the 'Tale of Genji'. But as Michelle Marra has indicated, this definition is restrictive and overlooks the meaning and use of the second character (*ga*) with its reference to a 'secluded life' indicative of 'spiritual freedom' (1991: 49). The ambiguity in the word *miyabi* meant it could refer both to a spiritual withdrawal from the world as well as to an idealization of the aesthetic values of the Heian Court. The term could also be used as an affirmation of Confucian social values, which is evident in the writings of Yoshida Kenkō (1283–1352) a Zen scholar of the period. Contradictions in the use and meaning of the same aesthetic value are also apparent in their actual application to artistic practices, like *chanoyu*.

At the same time as *chanoyu*, known in its elegant form as '*kaisho* tea', was being enjoyed in aristocratic social gatherings, another form of tea, *wabi-cha* or 'poverty tea' was gradually developing.[5] *Wabi-cha* was influenced by its gaudier cousin but claimed to be a version of the tea ceremony directly inspired by and expressive of the concepts of Zen Buddhism. It is from Murata Shuko, the Zen abbot who is credited with the creation of *wabi-cha* that we get the famous principle *Zen cha ichimi* or 'Zen and tea are one'. Nevertheless, as Varley and Elison (1981) have pointed out, the aesthetic ideals of *kaisho*-tea were extant in *wabi-cha*:

> the late medieval *wabi-cha* ceremony was based on a close association between a yearning, on the one hand, for the multihued and dreamlike world of the Tale of Genji and, on the other hand, the more recently cultivated liking for the earthly, monochromatic perhaps Zen-inspired values of the spiritual microcosm of the tea hut.
>
> (*ibid.*: 209)

These 'Zen-inspired-values' were the values of the *wabi* aesthetic of 'poverty' and 'simplicity' but they did not immediately preclude earlier aesthetic associations. There was a shift in tastes and this is clear in the transition from the use of refined *karamono* ('Chinese things') to reliance upon *wamono* which had an unassuming, rough and 'withered' texture. The person who finally replaced earlier aesthetic ideals like *miyabi* with *wabi* and *sabi* ('poverty' and 'rusticity') and established a new orthodoxy for the practice of tea is Sen no Rikyū (1522–1591). In the so-called 'Rikyū revival' the teamaster Sen no Rikyū and his method were established as the yardstick by which accomplishment in the tea ceremony could be measured. Rikyū studied under a disciple of Shuko and continued to develop tea as a form of Zen practice. But it would be a mistake to regard him as a spiritual recluse, for throughout his life he had strong connections with the merchant community in Sakai, which was his birthplace and also the most important centre for the practice and patronage of tea.

Both Zeami Motokiyo (1363–1443) in the field of *Nō* theatre and Sen no Rikyū in *wabi-cha* achieved their positions of importance partly because they codified in detail the standards for practice and progress in their respective forms. This process was repeated in the reorganization of the martial arts as *budō* and *bushidō*, which also reflects the influence of state power on the operation of the arts. The systems for ordering the martial ways, tea and *Nō* theatre were arranged hierarchically, according to neo-Confucian principles. As William Lafleur has indicated, there was a 'coalescence' between the cosmic order of medieval Buddhism upon which the arts were originally modelled to the social order of Edo period Confucianism (1983: 143–4). It was a shift from a hierarchy of value to the value of hierarchy.

The increasing rationalization of the arts was not only the consequence of different philosophical models but also of changing social conditions. During the Edo period there was a huge expansion in the numbers and classes of people practising the arts. This was the outcome of urbanization, the creation of surplus wealth, high rates of literacy, a transportation and communication network and an 'attitude of conspicuous cultural liberality' (Nosco 1990: 18). Enthusiasm for the arts was at its height in the Genroku era (1688–1704) and centred on the city of Edo where there was the highest concentration of people and wealth. As Peter Nosco indicated, with the expression 'conspicuous cultural liberality', the arts were not the preserve of any one particular group. The 'arts' included activities for entertainment (*yūgei*) and for self-cultivation (*būgei* – martial arts). But during this period the distinction was eroded to the point where all these activities were known as *geidō* (artistic ways). There is one further classification of artistic activity: the *taishū geinō* or 'popular performing arts' which it is important to mention because they were the most numerous and widely participated in.

Taishū geinō are forms of 'popular culture' and different from the arts mentioned above because they are 'self-supporting and sustaining, that is those forms that require neither the financial patronage nor independent wealth of the producer of the culture' (*ibid.*: 16). The social and economic circumstances, which gave rise to these forms of popular culture had an impact on the classification of all of the arts. An inventory published in 1775 lists seventy-four types of 'leisure' activity including everything from martial arts and the tea ceremony to types of street music and performance (Nishiyama 1997: 48). There were associations (*bunka shakai* – cultural communities) which formed around the participants of these activities. Some were relatively unstructured and self-supporting and others were highly organized and patronized. The structured activities were those like the Zen arts, considered to be of a 'cultured' nature (*kyōyō*) and not purely for 'entertainment and amusement' (*goraku*). New cultural forms in this period like the *geidō* ('artistic ways') are indicative of what Nishiyama has called a 'social world of play' (*ibid.*: 54). In this world, new aesthetic terms were created to structure and identify the feelings and emotions being expressed. These were terms like *hari*, 'strength of character', *bitai*, 'allure', *akanuke*, 'urbanity', and best known of all, *iki* and *tsu*, which Nishiyama describes as follows: 'the aesthetic consciousness of *iki*, is part of a refined consciousness of sensation, *tsu* is the aesthetic consciousness put into practice, a mode of behaviour' (*ibid.*: 58). The aesthetic consciousness of *iki* was typified by courtesans and female *geisha*, while *tsu* was a model of cultivation for men.

The expansion in popular forms of entertainment and creation of new aesthetic terms in the Genroku era made the elite arts less exclusive and weakened their spiritual claims. The elite arts came to be distinguished through their institutional forms (as an ordered system), rather than by their aesthetic and spiritual philosophies. They were closely associated with the rise of private academies during the middle decades of the seventeenth century. These academies began as centres for the 'civilization' of the samurai but by the end of the eighteenth century were centres of education 'marketing scholarship to willing consumers who derived personal enrichment or professional advancement through their training' (Nosco 1990: 33, 279). But the formal establishment of a system for organizing and marketing the 'traditional cultural forms' (*igei*) of the arts had taken place before the rise of the private academy. This was the *iemoto* (patriarchal) system, which in functional terms is a hierarchically organized patron/client system of instruction, usually run along family lines.

The *iemoto* system began in the fifteenth century as a means of organizing the arts practised by the aristocratic and warrior communities. However, the system that has survived until today emerged after the Genroku era when there were large numbers of people taking up artistic pastimes. The *iemoto* replaced the *dō* metaphor, reinventing its religio-aesthetic tradition by treating the transmission of the 'way' as 'filiation'. Through the metaphor of kinship (*iemoto*), the practice of the arts became constrained within an institutional matrix of power and authority. As Paul

Varley has written: 'Establishment of the Iemoto system as Yūgei during the eighteenth century was clearly an effort to fix the traditions of these acts and prevent heresies from arising among their followers'. It also 'represented an attempt to harness and profit from the large clientele for these elegant pastimes' (Varley in Varley and Kamakura 1989: 173).

Practice and progress in the arts was now more than a question of aesthetic taste and spiritual cultivation and linked to a hierarchical ranking system. It was within and through this system rather than the religio-aesthetic dimensions of practice evoked by the metaphor *dō* that practitioners took part in the Zen arts. The *iemoto* had an overt politico-economic dimension as the student registered on entry and continuously qualified their relationship with the school and its members by the regular payment of fees. Identification with a particular individual as a repository of aesthetic sensibilities and spiritual wisdom was superseded by the exigencies of their rank as 'senior' (*senpai*), or 'master' (*sensei*), and role as the communicator of forms of 'knowledge'.

The emergence of the *dō* metaphor in the medieval era and the *iemoto* system in the eighteenth century are attempts to establish a structured tradition for the arts; efforts which continue today in the 'culture centre' (*karucha sentā*). Like the *iemoto* system, the culture centre has explicit social, political and economic dimensions. Arising out of the 'leisure boom' in the 1970s and 1980s, the culture centre is organized and maintained by large media organizations like NHK and Asahi and department stores like Hankyu and Mitsukoshi. As such, they are administered as part of the 'culture industry' (Adorno 1984), and are now the most popular and convenient means for Japanese urbanites to engage in 'traditional pastimes' (*dentōtekina mono*), as well as modern and foreign diversions (Moriya 1984). With the formation of the *iemoto* system and more recently the culture centre we can detect a significant paradigm shift from the personal to the organizational. Within institutional formations of power and authority, the rules and idioms that serve to enhance and legitimate that authority tend to be the most highly valued.

These institutional changes coincided with a growing awareness of, and demand for, the arts and entertainment among the urban populace, generated by a vigorous economy and the development of the modern market system in the Taishō era (1912–26). The emergence of mass cultural institutions such as department stores brought significant changes in the organization and support for the arts. The arts began to be regarded as an item of mass culture, something that may be possessed by achievement and certification within a hierarchical system, rather than a matter of skill. 'People began to regard a work of art as an object and separate from the act of creating it, something to be bought, valued and displayed' (Havens 1982: 30).

These changes in the organization of the arts came together in the postwar period after a period of extraordinary economic growth (1970s and 1980s). 'Culture' (*bunka*), became a keyword in political, intellectual and even popular circles (*ibid.*: 25). Two organizations were set up to promote these interests, the Cultural Agency of the Education Ministry in 1968 and the Japan Foundation in 1972. These systems of state support and commercial patronage aimed to preserve and promote a sense of national identity through defining and organizing all forms of play as 'cultural' pursuits. As Moriya has indicated, these modern policies are a continuation of neo-Confucian philosophies in the Edo period and the educational policies of the Meiji period which sought to impose some form of control over the public enthusiasm for playful diversions in the 'entertainment zones' (*sakariba*) by establishing an 'entertainment system' (*kogyo seidō*) (Moriya 1984: 109). In the Edo period the realm of 'culture/general education' (*kyōyō/keikogoto*) had overlapped with 'play'/ 'entertainment' (*asobi/yūgei*), 'for the notion of play presupposed the learning of an art' (*ibid.*: 113). Reports from foreigners visiting Japan at this time indicated a 'very positive attitude' towards entertaining pastimes (Linhart 1988: 272). By the Meiji period it was considered immoral to study the arts as a form of play (*asobi*) and the term *yūgei* took on a vulgar sense (*ibid.*: 113). Since the Taisho era (1912–26) the terms *yūgei* and *asobi* had been replaced by terms like 'culture' (*bunka*) and 'civilization' (*kyōyō*) which are officially sanctioned and supported by state and commercial institutions (*ibid.*: 114).

In the 1960s and 1970s, with both state and private patronage, there was a huge growth in the construction of the 'culture' (*karucha/bunka*) industries; using the term loosely to include, for example, the building of new theatres and concert halls. At the local level, the number of prefectures with cultural programmes rose from eight in 1968, to be all-inclusive in 1976. In 1977, an official comment spoke of 'an unprecedented rise in public expectations of the arts' (*ibid.*: 25). Large sums of money were now being invested in the arts, and although in 1980 the Agency for Cultural Affairs devoted 40 per cent of its total budget of two hundred million dollars to the arts, the bulk of funding came from the private sector.

The arts have always been overwhelmingly dependent on private and commercial support. Before and after the Meiji Restoration, artists relied on the patronage of wealthy merchants and samurai as benefactors. The emergence of culture centres about twenty years ago, while encouraged and partly funded by state institutions, could not have been sustained without commercial backing. Large commercial institutions such as department stores, railway companies, and particularly media corporations like NHK and Yomiuri, recognized and responded to a burgeoning middle class with time and money to spend on what was being called 'leisure' (*rejā*). We have to be careful how we understand a term like 'leisure' (*rejā*) which in the Japanese context is fundamentally not opposed to work. It came into use in the 1960s and has a 'sense of luxury' and an aspect of 'active use' (Linhart in Daniels 1984: 210–11).

The so-called *rejā* (as 'leisure') boom was so important that there was official recognition for it as a major goal in life by the establishment in 1972 of the Office for the Development of the Leisure Industry. The development of culture centres during the period of the leisure boom in the 1970s and early 1980s brought unprecedented levels of involvement in the arts. Culture centres so fundamentally changed the way instruction was organized in the arts that the *iemoto* could now be defined institutionally, as part of a commercial enterprise (Moriya 1984: 108). Postwar, middle-class engagement with the arts had already converted the *iemoto* into a national institution. As a concern of the Education Ministry, the *iemoto* system had become much more respectable (even being described in quasi-spiritual terms as part of *shugyō*) than it had ever been in the pleasure quarters of nobles and merchants in the Edo period. Now under the auspices of commercial enterprises, the ethos, operation and ethics of the *iemoto* system changed. The rigid hierarchical social structure and exclusivity of the *iemoto* system relaxed. Schools of the arts became less restrictive and more popular and available. Convenience, cost, and the ease of access to those sections of the population who had the time and money to attend, were important criteria for their operation. Today, the *iemoto* is located in environments like schools and culture centres.

In fact, the notion of training in the arts being part of a commercial enterprise has a longer history than culture centres, and goes back to the introduction of *depāto*, (department stores) in the late Edo period and their subsequent popularity in the Meiji and Taisho periods (Creighton 1995). Department stores were and still are centrally important institutions in urban centres for the selection and preservation of 'culture' (*bunka*) for the general populace. They promote the exhibition, demonstration and learning of the arts. Although in terms of active public involvement they have been replaced by culture centres today, there remains a link in popular perceptions between commercial institutions and the display and performance of high cultural pursuits like the Zen arts.

The question which this brief cultural history of play presents is how it may be possible to connect *rejā* activities in a contemporary culture centre with the concept of *asobi* in medieval era performances of *kagura* theatre. I have proposed that there are common themes underlying all the historical shifts in the meaning of play. We have seen how there is always a tension between the structure of play and the sensations which participation in any form of play may evoke. All Japanese ways of playing are subject to constraints: of ritual form (orthopraxis), of institutional, ideological, and commercial forces. This suggests that to describe the Japanese way of playing we need to identify the structural forces, which construct 'play'. The risks in this approach are that play is reduced to a discourse, where the power of ritual, institutional, ideological and commercial structures at particular points in time and space determine the form and process of play.

The other theme which emerges from this cultural history is the ambiguity of Japanese ways of playing which always seems to be a mixture of opposing categories: the sacred and the secular, the aesthetic and the ascetic, the serious and the frivolous. This is not an uncommon way to try and define play, by contrasting it to what appears to be its opposite (Mergen 1984: 61). The problem with this approach is that it reduces play to a structure of binary oppositions: sacred–profane, work–play, nature–culture, and we end identifying play by asking the classical anthropological, 'Do they have a word for X?' kind of question. As with all structuralist theories, this approach cannot account for the historical changes in conceptions of play (Campbell 1989).

There may be no need to force a choice between play as a function of linguistic or historical structure because what we have in Japanese play is the absence of distinctions, in other words our distinctions between 'work' and 'play' are inappropriate here. It may be necessary to locate first the linguistic structures of play in Japan, but then to look at how these structures are not secure, but flexible and changing, they are a system of representations, not equivalent to experience.

Play is not a substantive, an object, but a quality of experience arising out of something that people do. However, while certain kinds of distinctions that we might make are absent or deconstructed, there are certain conditions necessary for Japanese play. There is a necessary relationship between play in Japan and changes in the context, in the material conditions of life, although interpretations of this relationship are too varied to sustain an explanation purely in terms of the changing conditions of production.

Many sociological studies are based on this kind of functional approach, examining play in its institutional setting (Sutton-Smith 1974: 27). They focus almost exclusively on the socio-historical context of play. In contrast, theorists like Groos (1901), suggest that in play the context is not the context of real life and that it is the content of human behaviour, which ought to be stressed. Play, for Groos, is distinguished by the absence of concern for goals. It is divorced from reality, a type of human experience which is totally non-productive, except as an experimental practice for life, or what Alice Cheska calls 'buffeted learning' (Cheska 1981: 14). This type of theory which idealizes play as a function of a universal human experience, or natural stage in human development, is often created by professionals, working in nursery schools and therapy clinics and, as Sutton-Smith has pointed out, tends to ignore the ways in which play can be distinctly un-ideal (Mergen 1984: 61).

Perhaps the strongest versions of the idealized play theory are those formulated by Huizinga (1949) and Caillois (1961), who have proposed that play is the origin from which social and cultural institutions have emerged. More usefully perhaps, Huizinga and Caillois both emphasized that play is not defined by form or content (text), but by the experience of participants. The emphasis on play as experience is useful because it demonstrates how participants' characteristics can shape the nature of the activity and restore the sense of human agency. Perhaps the way forward when we try to identify a Japanese way of playing is to recognize that we are talking simultaneously of the creative experience of participants and also of the structural logic of certain activities. Japanese concepts of play all refer to a different relationship in time and space between the participant and the act.

A Japanese way of playing, like any way of playing is both the symbolic expression of the relationship between the act and the participants' self and also of the structural logic of the activity in question. The play element seems to arise out of the logical de-structuring, the ludic logic at the heart of the concepts which identify certain activities and the contextual structuring of these activities in time and space. This ludic logic makes play an affirmation of certain cultural ideals and the social order; it is also a playful subversion of them. Playful activities are not 'play' because they suspend the rules of reality, but because those who participate accept the context which constrains their action and the ludic structure which frees it. If there is a Japanese way of playing it is to be located in the relationship between the ludic logic at the heart of Japanese concepts of play and individual experience in particular contexts.

Notes

1 Corresponding to *shugyō* in Sanskrit is *tapas*, a word whose etymology gives the sense of forging the spirit through the disciplining of the body and awakening a new self (Yuasa 1993: 8).
2 The term *shugyō* is made up of two Chinese characters, one meaning 'to master', the other, 'a practice' (Yuasa 1993: 196).
3 The view that Shintō and Buddhism reflected a common reality was contested by scholars in the late eighteenth and nineteenth centuries.
4 Zen priests were an important part of this development, for they travelled to China and brought back these 'Chinese things' (*karamono*), also described as *basara*: 'a term that implies both exoticism and ostentation' (Varley and Elison 1987: 197).
5 *Wabi-cha*, 'poverty tea' was part of a new criteria of taste for things that were *kasuo kotan* or 'plainness and refined simplicity' (Elison and Smith 1981: 203).

Bibliography

Adorno, T. (1984) *Aesthetic Theory*, trans. C. Lenhardt, London: Routledge and Kegan Paul.

Ames, R.T., Dissanayake, W. and Kasulis, T.P. (1994) *Self as Person in Asian Theory and Practice*, Albany, NY: State University of New York Press.

Andersen, J.L. (1987) 'Japanese tea ritual: religion in practice', *Man* 22: 475–98.

Andersen, J.L. (1991) *An Introduction to Japanese Tea Ritual*, Albany, NY: SU NewYork Press.

Asquith, P.J. and Kalland, A. (eds) (1997) *Japanese Images of Nature: Cultural Perspectives*, Nordic Institute of Asian Studies: Curzon Press.

Averbuch, I. (1995) *The Gods Come Dancing*, Cornell: Cornell East Asian Series.

Barthes, R. [1970] (1982) *L'Empire des signes* (Empire of Signs), translated by Richard Howard, New York: Hill and Wang.

Ben-Ari, E., Moeran, B. and Valentine, J. (eds) (1990) *Unwrapping Japan*, Manchester: Manchester University Press.

Berque, A. (1997) *Japan, Nature, Artifice and Japanese Culture*, Northamptonshire: Pilkington Press.

Bloom, I. and Vogel, J. (eds) (1997) *Meeting of Minds: Intellectual and Religious Interactions in East Asian Traditions of Thought*, New York: Columbia University Press.

Bourdieu, P. (1984) *Distinction: A Social Critique of the Judgement of Taste*, trans. R. Nice, London: Routledge and Kegan Paul.

Brandon, J.R. (ed.) (1997) *Nō and Kyōgen in the Contemporary World*, Honolulu: University of Hawaii Press.

Brown, K.H. (1997) *The Politics of Reclusion: Painting and Power in Momoyama Japan*, Honolulu: University of Hawaii Press.

Caillois, R. (1961) *Man, Play and Games*, New York: Free Press.

Campbell, A.T. (1989) *To Square with Genesis: Causal Statements and Shamanic Ideas in Wayapi*, Edinburgh: Edinburgh University Press.

Cheska, A.T. (ed.) (1981) *Play as Context*, West Point: Leisure Press.

Creighton, M.R. (1995) 'Imaging the other in Japanese advertizing campaigns', in J.G. Carrier (ed.) *Occidentalism: Images of the West*, Oxford: Oxford University Press, pp. 135–61.

Daniels, G. (ed.) (1984) *Europe Interprets Japan*, Kent: Paul Norbery Publications.

Denning, G. (1996) *Performances*, Chicago: University of Chicago Press.

Elison, G. and Smith, B.L. (ed.) (1981) *Warlords, Artists and Commoners: Japan in the Sixteenth Century*, Honolulu: University of Hawaii Press.

Fu, C.W. and Heine, S. (eds) (1995) *Japan in Traditional and Post-modern Perspectives*, Albany, NY: State University of New York Press.

Goff, J. (1991) *Nō Drama and the Tale of Genji*, Princeton, NJ: Princeton University Press.

Graburn, N. (1975) *Ethnic and Tourist Arts: Cultural Expressions from the Fourth World*, Berkeley, CA: University of California Press.

Graburn, N. (1983) *To Pray, Pay and Play: The Cultural Structure of Japanese Domestic Tourism*, Centre des Haute Etudes Touristiques, Serte B no. 3.

Groos, K. (1901) *The Play of Man*, New York: D. Appeton and Company.

Havens, T.R.H. (1982) *Artist and Patron in Post-war Japan: Dance, Music, Theatre and the Visual Arts 1955–1980*, Princeton, NJ: Princeton University Press.

Hendry, J. (ed.) (1998) *Interpreting Japanese society*, London: Routledge

Hendry, J. [1987] (1995) *Understanding Japanese Society*, London and New York: Routledge.

Hendry, J. (1993) *Wrapping Culture: Politeness, Presentation and Power in Japan and Other Societies*, Oxford: Oxford University Press.

Hsu, F.L.K. (1975) *Iemoto: The Heart of Japan*, New York, London, Sydney, Toronto: Schenkman Publishing Company.

Huizinga, J. (1949) *Homo Ludens: A Study of the Play Element in Culture*, London: Routledge and Kegan Paul.

Hume, N.G. (1995) *Japanese Aesthetics and Culture*, Albany, NY: State University of New York Press.

Ivy, M. (1995) *Discourses of the Vanishing: Modernity, Phantasm, Japan*, Chicago: University of Chicago Press.

Kasulis, T.P., Ames, R.T. and Dissanayake, W. (eds) (1993) *Self as Body in Asian Theory and Practice*, Albany, NY: State University of New York Press.

Kiyota, M. and Kinoshita, H. (eds) (1990) *Japanese Martial Arts and American Sports.: Cross Cultural Perspectives on Means to Personal Growth*, Proceedings of the 1989 United States–Japan Conference, Tokyo: Nihon University.

Kondo, D.K. (1985) 'The way of tea: a symbolic analysis', *Man* 20: 287–306.

Koren, L. (1994) *Wabi Sabi for Artists, Designers, Poets and Philosophers*, Berkeley, CA: Stone Bridge Press.

La Fleur, W.R. (1983) *The Karma of Words: Buddhism and the Literary Arts in Medieval Japan*, Berkeley, CA: University of California Press.

Linhart, S. (1988) 'From industrial to post industrial society: changes in Japanese leisure-related values and behaviour', *Journal of Japanese Studies* 14(2): 271–307.

Marra, M. (1991) *The Aesthetics of Discontent: Politics and Reclusion in Medieval Japanese Literature*, Honolulu: University of Hawaii Press.

Marra, M. (1993) *Representations of Power: The Literary Politics of Medieval Japan*, Honolulu: University of Hawaii Press.

Mergen, B. (ed.) (1986) *Cultural Dimensions of Play, Games and Sport*, Champaign, IL: Human Kinetics Publishers.

Moriya, T. (1984) 'The history of Japanese civilization through aesthetic pursuits', in T. Umesao, H. Befu and J. Kreiner (eds) *Japanese Civilization in the Modern World*, Senri Ethnological Studies no.16. National Museum of Ethnology, Japan, p. 105–17.

Nagatomi, S. (1992) *Attunement through the Body*, Albany, NY: State University of New York.

Nishiyama, M. (1997) *Edo Culture: Daily Life and Diversions in Urban Japan, 1600–1868*, Honolulu: University of Hawaii Press.

Nosco, P. (1990) *Remembering Paradise: Nativism and Nostalgia in Eighteenth Century Japan*, Council on East Asian Studies: Harvard University Press.

O'Neill, P.G. (1984) 'Organization and authority in the traditional arts', *Modern Asian Studies* 128(4): 631–45.

Ooms, H. (1985) *Tokugawa Ideology: Early Constructs 1570–1680*, Princeton, NJ: Princeton University Press.

Pilgrim, R.B. (1993) *Buddhism and the Arts of Japan*, Chambersburg, PA: Anima Books.

Pincus, L. (1996) *Authenticating Culture in Imperial Japan: Kuki Shuzo and the Rise of National Aesthetics*, Berkeley, CA: University of California Press.

Plutschow, H.E. (1986) *Historical Chanoyu*, Tokyo: The Japan Times Ltd.

Pollack, D. (1992) *Reading against Culture: Ideology and Narrative in the Japanese Novel*, Ithaca, NY: Cornell University Press.

Ramanujan, A.K. (1990) 'Is there an Indian way of thinking? An informal essay', in M. Mckim (ed.) *India through Hindu Categories*, Delhi: Sage Publications, pp. 41–58.

Reader, I. (1991) *Religion in Contemporary Japan*, Basingstoke, Hampshire and London: Macmillan Press.

Sadler, A.L. (1962) *Cha-no-yo: The Japanese Tea Ceremony*, Tokyo: Charles E. Tuttle Company.

Salter, M.A. (1977) *Play, Anthropological Perspectives*, West Point, NY: Leisure Press.

Sanford, J.H., La Fleur, W.R. and Nagatomi, M. (eds) (1992) *Flowing Traces: Buddhism in the Literary and Visual Arts of Japan*, Princeton, NJ: Princeton University Press.

Sutton-Smith, B. (1976) 'Current research and theory on play, games and sports', in T. T. Crais (ed.) *The Humanistic and Mental Health Aspect of Sports, Exercise and Recreation*, Chicago, IL: American Medical Association.

Thornhill, A.H. (1993) *Six Circles, One Dewdrop: The Religio-Aesthetic World of Komparu Zenchiku*, Princeton, NJ: Princeton University Press.

Varley, P. and Elison, G. (1981) 'The culture of tea?', in G. Elison and B.L. Smith (eds) *Warlords, Artists, and Commoners: Japan in the Sixteenth Century*, Honolulu: Hawaii University Press.

Varley, P. and Kumakura, I. (1989) *Tea in Japan: Essays on the History of Chanoyu*, Honolulu: University of Hawaii Press.

Veblen, T. [1899] (1994) *The Theory of the Leisure Class*, Harmondsworth: Penguin Books.

Yuasa, Y. (1993) *The Body, Self-Cultivation and Ki-Energy*, trans. S. Nagatomo and M.S. Hull, Albany, NY: State University of New York Press.

Yanagita, K. (1989) *Yanagita Kunio Zenshu*, vol. 29, Tokyo: Chikuma Shobo.

Yoshida, M. (1985) *Asobi: The Sensibilities at Play*, occasional publication found as offprint in National Museum of Ethnology in Osaka, Japan.

11 When the goal is not a goal

Japanese school football players working hard at their game

Simone Dalla Chiesa

Sports clubs

University sports are practised in two distinct categories: the *kurabu*, or *bu* or *bukai*, and the *dōkōkai* or *aikōkai*. The *bu* is used for competition and there is only one *bu* for each type of sport. In 1986, at the University of Tsukuba, where I carried out fieldwork from 1983 to 1987, there were thirty-seven. *Bu* depend on the physical education department: they offer facilities for meetings and nominate a teacher in charge of each team. *Dōkōkai* or *aikōkai* operate at a more recreational level and are placed among the cultural associations of the university (there were fourteen sport *dōkōkai* and sixty-seven cultural associations in 1986), with headquarters and a lecturer in charge. The activities of each *dōkōkai* are structured so that one student can be a member of several *dōkōkai* at the same time; while the *bu* train more often and more intensively, and thus require a total psychological and physical commitment to the team. However, the two organizations are very similar, and are closely related to high school teams as well. In this chapter I want to analyse Japanese youth football – university *dōkōkai* and *bu*, and high school clubs – in order to explain the purpose to which the Japanese school system promotes and organizes such sporting activities.[1]

Structure

Anyone can enter the *dōkōkai*, no matter what his physical or technical skills, and he may leave whenever he wishes. But once he is a member, the youngster is required to participate in all the team activities. Members are classified in several hierarchical levels, each characterized by its own roles, duties and degree of integration within the team.

At the bottom level are the first graders or *ichinensei*. At the beginning of the academic year, in April, they often start to attend several *dōkōkai* and choose one to follow after the first few months of school. The members' list, or *meibo*, is only arranged after the summer vacation, so at this stage they are not full members of the team and are not required to attend all practices. The *ichinensei* have the special duty of preparing and rearranging the playing field before and after training.

The second and third graders (*ninensei* and *sannensei*) are at an intermediate hierarchical level. They are the core members of the team, and as such have no hard duties, but are required to attend all practices regularly and to organize the extra sporting activities and retreats. Yearly, the captain in charge appoints a new captain among the *sannensei*. The role of the captain is to decide the programme and exercises of each practice, to choose players for the team that will play in the championship matches, and to hold official team meetings.

The fourth year students (*yonensei*) and the graduate students (*daigakuinsei*) are at a level of integration similar to that of the *ichinensei*. Due to their skills and experience they enjoy a very high status within the team; however having to study for the final exams, they have the implicit authorization to attend practices only occasionally.

Foreigners and women are considered to be outsiders. Foreign graduate students are often the oldest players of the *dōkōkai*, but are also among the newest members, having just joined the team like the *ichinensei*. They are treated with great deference, except from the seniors who joke around and use informal language. Women represent a very particular case. In the *dōkōkai* of Tsukuba, there was an attempt to organize a female team. The girls were practising along with the men, playing together in the mini games (even if never receiving a pass from a male player), but they were excluded from the exercises. This attempt to include them was aborted after a year. The female presence remained as assistants, or *manējā* (manager). In male teams, female *manējā* fulfil organizational duties, such as collecting for the *konpa*, the social club fees, and for extraordinary purchases such as tracksuits, balls, and so on, filling out the *meibo* (members' list), and so on.

The figures for 1985 were fifty-nine male members, with an average of 50 per cent *ichinensei*, and seven girls. The *dōkōkai* had no appointed coach. The teacher in charge carried out the duty for few months, and then disappeared. This absence is not common in young amateur teams (but the role of the coach will be described later).

The activities of the *dōkōkai* can be divided into three types: non-competitive sports, competitive sports, and non-sports. In the first type, practices, retreats and non-competitive matches are involved.

Practice

Practices take place on the main pitch, three times a week, twice in the evening (one for about ninety minutes and the other two hours) and one during the day (two-and-a-half hours). It does not occur in rainy weather or snow, but is regularly held under any other conditions. If the field is not playable, practice is shorter and takes place at a nearby field, or it consists of jogging through the campus. There are no training sessions in the gym, which would be impractical due to the number of members. The *kurabu* members workout with machines at the main gym. Each player exercises in whatever way he feels is best for him.

All members, all sixty players, may attend field practices at the same time. Even injured players must attend. If the injury allows it, an injured player will force himself to do what all the others are doing. If the injury is too serious, he will just sit on the edge of the pitch during the whole practice. Officially, the *manējā*'s presence is mandatory too. However, it is often the case that the girls arrive towards the end of practice in order to attend the concluding meeting. Exemption to practice is granted in case of colds (*kaze*) or before school tests.

Practice takes place in several distinct phases:

1   A preparation phase. Players arrive on the field a few at a time, usually wearing the playing uniform and the team tracksuit. When this is not possible they change at the sidelines; they never use the dressing room. Then the *ichinensei* go to get the balls from the storage room and inflate them, bring the team vests, and put out goals and markers on the field. Once they have received the balls, the others use them freely, usually warming-up with dribbling exercises (two against one), three against one, and so on.

2   The official beginning of practice. The captain calls a meeting (*shūgō*), getting all the members in a circle, informs them about the progress of the last championship match, and announces the daily programme of practice. From this moment, the division *senpai/kōhai* (senior/junior) disappears and all players do the same things.

3   Warming up. No jogging, but repetition of dribbling in various formations/exercises.

4   The main phase of practice: drills or game schemes. Sometimes, three different drills are carried out (wings and midfield) at the same time in front of the same goal. Each drill can be only made up of passes or of short plays in various formations, and so on, and it is completed with a shot at the goal. After having taken part in a drill playing in a certain role, each player goes back to the centre of the field and starts to line up to play the same drill again in a different role. This happens until he has participated in at least in one drill for each position, not just in his usual position or with his strongest foot. So, this causes multiple errors, which are neither criticized (by disapproval of fellow players) nor corrected (by the captain). This phase can last more than one hour. Depending on the number of players attending practices, three to five different sets of drills are completed.

5   Minigames. Sometimes five-a-side minigames are played without a goalkeeper or with a rotating one. The captain takes care of the timing but there is no referee.

6   The final *shūgō*. The captain makes a final overview of practice and *manējā* gives official team notices and the other members give various announcements.

7   At times, the captain orders the players to run ten or twenty laps of the length or the width of the field. It is mandatory to do this, but no one enforces it. At the end the *ichinensei* rake the ground and take the goals and markers back to the storeroom. Having worn their tracksuit and changed again, the players leave the field. I have never seen any player take a shower in the dressing rooms after a practice.

The retreat, or *gasshuku*, is an intensive practice period of seven to ten days, held during the summer holiday at the university's hostel on the shores of Lake Yamanaka. The practices are identical, only longer and held daily.

Competitive and scrimmage matches

Once a week, part of a practice session is dedicated to a ninety-minute match against the *dōkōkai* from the School of Medicine. The players divide themselves according to their roles (defence, midfield and forward) and a senior from each group decides the rotation. Each one has to play for the same amount of time as each of his teammates. A referee is present, but in spite of hard tackles, fouls are completely absent. During my playing period with the *dōkōkai* of Tsukuba, only one non-competitive match against an external team (that of the high school of Takezono) was scheduled, which however did not ever take place.

The *dōkōkai* participates in a regional championship along with the *dōkōkai* of the other universities. The season begins around June and continues until the following January. Games are played every Sunday, with a long rest period for holidays and quarterly exams. There are only around twenty matches a season. One team for the *dōkōkai* is registered for the championship. Each member of the *dōkōkai* has the right to play in the championship, regardless of his technical capabilities. However, due to the number of *ichinensei*, this right is limited to the senior members. The composition of the team is decided by the captain just before each match. The players reach the playing field already wearing their playing uniform, and no one takes a shower or changes after the match. Very few friends attend the game.

Leisure and non-sporting activities

10 October is *Kyōiku no hi*, or sports day, a festival part of the official *hare/ke* (sacred and profane) rhythm of school life. On this day, tournaments and competitions of all sports are organized in every school. Teams are freely formed by classmates and friends, sometimes mixing men and women. Club and *dōkōkai* members participate too, but in different sports from those they usually play. In order to highlight the non-serious content of sport's day, the teams sign up to the tournaments with funny names, as opposed to the official, 'heroic' names or of the *bu* and *dōkōkai*. The most important leisure activities for each single club are the 'social drinking' parties called *konpa*. A *konpa* is organized at the end of each period of exams, and again to initiate the *ichinensei* at the end of April and again at the end of each *gasshuku*. These gatherings are the only opportunity to socialize between male and female, as on the field they are hardly allowed to speak to each other.

Another group activity is the International Cup in Tokyo in December. The university players attend the match in ordinary clothes, generally – but not necessarily – all together. The junior and senior high school team players, on the contrary, watch the game sitting next to each other, wearing their school sporting suits and cheering on the teams with klaxons.

Junior and senior high school football

In the high school, football is practised at two different levels as well. The recreational level is formed by the *kurabu* that meets once or twice a week. All the cultural associations have the status of *kurabu* too. There is also the competitive level of *bu*, whose full name is *bukatsu*. In the schools that I visited a ratio of 5 to 1 exists between the cultural clubs and the sports clubs, and the vast majority of sports may be practised through the *bu* only.

The *bu* is open to everybody. The youngsters are strongly urged to participate in these activities, both from scholastic authorities (especially in areas where there is juvenile delinquency) and from peers. When the *bu* sets itself a specific competitive objective, it happens sometimes that the players are divided into three different teams, based on their strength, theoretically, but actually according to their age (as reported by Furunuma, 1990: 69). The psychophysical commitment is very stressful, and the teachers of the schools that I visited reported a strong decrease in attendance during the second and third year of school, with the approach of entrance exams. The periodical press gives contradictory data about attendance. It is shown that there is often an increase in participation in the second and third years (for example, Zenkoku chūgaku sakkā, 1987: 76, 80; 1990: 147).

From the point of view of the technical efficiency and the physical integrity of an athlete, the rhythm of the *bukatsu* is insane. Of the students that I interviewed (Junior High Schools Yatabe and Meikei), 72 per cent of those that are in a *bu* are committed for an average of 6.2 afternoons a week, with practice times during the week for one-and-a-half to two hours and, on the weekends, for four hours. The average time commitment for all participants in a *bukatsu* is four afternoons per week. These figures refer to all sports, not only to football. In Tsukuba, the football *bu* practices six days a week, sometimes at 7 a.m., before classes. The single practice sessions have absurdly intense rhythms. Sixty players participate in a typical football practice *bu* of the Shimizu Shiritsu Shōgyō Kōtōgakkō (description in Furunuma 1987). The programme sees thirty minutes of 'warm up' with the ball, one hour ten minutes of collective drills, thirty-minute drills for each field position, then finally forty minutes of laps and head shots, totalling about three-and-a-half hours. A 'free practice' usually follows all the above, during which, after having worked out in the gym, the players repeat on their own initiative the already completed field exercises. In conclusion, the required commitment of a young athlete is similar to, if not more demanding than, that of an adult professional. Once arrived home, after practices, the youngster neither studies nor watches television but simply sleeps.

At the *bu*'s practices one or two coaches (a coach *kōchi* and a technical manager *kantoku*) are present, even as many as three in the more competitive high schools. These coaches are physical education teachers that specialize in the sport, or teachers of curricular subjects that practised it at a high level in their youth, sometimes even ex-baseball coaches (Zenkoku Chūgaku sakkā, 1990: 147). There is great pressure from the body of teachers towards these teachers to direct a *bu* or a *kurabu*. So the school often puts its young athletes in the hands of persons coincidentally available, without taking into consideration their real knowledge or willingness to practise. Besides these coaches, the Japanese youth teams are not followed by any other staff. The figure of the masseur is absent, as well that of a team physician. Injured players are taken to the school health centre.

Competitive activity consists of participating in the national championships of junior and senior high schools. With regard to the regional championships, the final tournament follows with forty-eight champions of each *ken* that get great interest from the public and the media. I have no detailed figures of non-competitive matches, but in reference to some journalistic sources (Ōnuki 1986: 114, 117), I have deduced that their scarcity constitutes a problem at high-school level football too.

Frames

The Japanese football society is an everlasting society. A *bu* or a *dōkōkai* can start from an explicit request from the students, or perhaps a lecturer may propose himself as the coach for a certain sport. But then, after it has been created, the club becomes an institution completely independent of its players. It exists before their arrival and will still be running after the three or four years after they have left school and the team. Joining such an institution is officially voluntary. However, since the pressure on the youngsters to practise a sport is very strong and sports are played only in the *bu*, joining a *bu* is actually mandatory. Here, freewill is limited to the type of the sport practised.

Once a team is joined, the youngster is involved in a series of activities where the development pattern is already decided and the roles remain relatively unchanged. The injured players and the *manējā* organize at the field's borders, the secondary activities for bad weather or an impracticable field, and the daily practices at fixed hours of certain *bu*s, all reveal that to be a member of a team is first of all a matter of dedicating a large amount of time to it, no matter what activity is performed. The *bu* and *dōkōkai* are similar in this respect, the difference being the amount of commitment on the part of the players. In both cases, the timing of these activities expands to fill the day as the youngster assumes his role as player much earlier than the practice (or the championship match) begins when he goes towards the field already wearing his tracksuit, and and leaves that role when he is back home and wears ordinary clothes again. By not washing themselves at the end of each practice players avoid the way strong symbolic acts such as a shower or the *ofuro* (bath) separate practise time from the rest of the day. They will take a bath only late in the afternoon, so practice time extends itself symbolically until it swallows up the entire public life of a club member, whose membership then becomes, in essence, a 'full-time' matter. This is why junior and high school players all attend the Toyota Cup match in their teams' tracksuits.

Because the only reasons for being temporarily excused from a club's activities are studying or catching a cold, this shows that around the team there is a wider and dominant social environment, namely the school, whose duties should take absolute precedence over the team.

Team life may be structured in four symbolic frames. Arranged on a scale of decreasing importance, they are:

a   school: being a student (of a certain institution);
b   club: being member of a team;

c   practice: field training with the team;
d   drill: playing with the ball.

The smallest frames are entirely encased within the larger ones. The same principle of compulsion applies when one moves from a larger frame to a smaller one. Choosing a certain school may be a free act (albeit in the case of public schools conditioned by the place of residence), but, after that, youngsters are often forced to became members of a sports club. This memberships requires practising with the team, and this, in turn, requires them to play with the ball. A player cannot refuse to attend the practices just as he cannot refuse to give in a report. The same happens at university level where, however, the choice to join a team is free. Each frame has its own set of rules and roles, which must never contradict those of the larger frames. So, for instance, a player must always fulfil his duties as a student. Problems arise only when the sets of rules and duties of a club's life override those of ordinary, non-school life. Many mothers that I interviewed complained about the fact that their daughters were obliged to bow to the *senpai* (seniors) of their team including, for example, if they met by chance at the big stores on a Sunday. Forgetting to bow would result in punishment and humiliation at the next practice. In the martial arts clubs, infringing this rule may result in very harsh body punishments.

At a deeper level of analysis, however, frame d stands apart from the others. Clearly set within the limits of the two *shūgō*, this is the core activity of a team's life. On this occasion only the team members leave behind their roles of *senpai/kōhai* in order to assume their field roles, playing goalkeeper, defender, forward, and so on. A different set of duties comes into effect that consists in, for example, not suddenly leaving the field (cf. Huizinga 1949 on these implicit obligations in the games) but mostly in respecting the rules of play. There is no judgement on the performance.

Work, leisure, play and flow

In order to classify the activities of the four frames according to their content, I derived from Blanchard and Cheska (1985: 46–52) a graph with two variables on its orthogonal axis. The first vertical axis represents the continuum between leisure, on the one side, and work, constraint, purposefulness on the other. The classification of an activity on this axis does not depend on its type and structure, but on social considerations and how an individual perceives its compulsion. This continuum reflects the 'classic' opposition between these two categories that is also seen by Huizinga (1949), De Grazia (1962), and Norbeck (1974), and between the categories of intrinsic and extrinsic motivations of Csikszentmihalyi (1975: 2–5).

The second horizontal axis, represents the continuum between pleasurability (Blanchard and Cheska 1985: 46–52), autotelic enjoyment or flow, 'a psychological state based on concrete feedback, which acts as a reward in that it produces continuing behaviour in absence of other rewards' (Csikszentmihalyi 1975: 23–48) on the one hand, and non-flow on the other. Also, in this case, classifying an activity in this dimension does not depend on its structure, but on the mental status in which it is lived. The content of play, or playfulness, of an activity, may be said to be proportional to the vicinity of the crossing of the two axes, an ideal point of 'total play'. Generally, activities are located at different points on the two continuums (see the known example of flow experienced by surgeons during operations, Csikszentmihalyi, Holcomb and Csikszentmihalyi 1975). Nevertheless, it is true that the system of reward and punishment that conditions the 'work' activities makes it more difficult to find autotelic enjoyment in them, and therefore the position on the first axis influences that on the second.

If we try to classify the activities within the frames (b) 'being a member of the team' and (c) 'going to a practice' along the two axes, their shared principle of compulsion obliges us to put them, on the horizontal axis, both in a 'work' position exactly like the activities of the first frame (a) 'being a student'. In a similar way, the classification of the team activities on the field (different from attending the Toyota Cup match and participating in a *konpa*) of these two frames is one of non–flow on the horizontal axis. As a matter of fact, to play a sport as 'leisure', the youngsters have sports day.

The fourth frame (d) 'playing with the ball' requires different considerations. Actual field practice only consists of drills, and therefore, apparently, its purpose lies in staging a sequence of integrated ball and human movements that, after a series of perfect exchanges and rebounds, ends with a final shot at the goal. It is like a splendid pinball game with moving parts. This fact, along with the peculiar social interaction between players, different from that of the major frames, allow us to put ball playing among the leisure activities on the vertical axis of the classificatory scheme.

A drill is a structured activity that seems to coincide with one definition of a game, namely an activity of uncertain result 'characterized by (1) organized play, (2) competition, (3) two or more sides, (4) criteria for determining the winner, and (5) agreed upon rules' (Roberts, Arth and Bush 1959: 597, quoted in Blanchard and Cheska 1985: 22). By setting time frames, space and rules, and so defining the purposes and the uncertainty of the result, games limit the incognita thanks to a reduction of the informationally meaningful area. With a clear feedback of the action, the flow experience comes easier, and this makes of games and sports the top autotelic activities (Csikszentmihalyi 1975: Chapters 3 and 4). Therefore, potentially, ball play is a flow activity, autotelically enjoyable. The problem is that there is little competition in drills, and no winner. Drills may be considered as a kind of solitary game, in which a player plays against himself in order to improve his technique and performance. However, they are practised over and over again for hours, so that practising with the ball often turns out to be boring and tiring. This increases the loneliness and the psychological strain on a single player, and makes it more difficult for him to see drills as a flow/play experience. At this point, the various obligations that brought the player to participate overrun the leisure aspects, and drills end up being both total work and a non-flow activity.

Team practice lacks competitiveness in facing new situations whose conclusion may be uncertain (Blanchard and Cheska 1985: 52–3, Csikszentmihalyi 1975: 30). The drills do not offer this, due to their repetitiveness, and the Wednesday friendly game is just a variation on the drills. Only during the weekend official match are all the parameters applied, but the match involves only fifteen players out of the sixty, and always the same ones. Again, no flow is experienced by the ordinary player.

Ethics of effort

The amount of time dedicated to the drills and the absence of any athletic preparation and pre-practice suggests that the purpose of the training of a Japanese football team is not scoring goals against an opponent, but the building of a kind of perfect machine with mechanics based on the integrated movements of its individual parts, namely the gestures of the players. But this is a utopian objective that is never reached, for the number of players is excessive, the long wait between play lowers technical performance, and football is subject to too many environmental variables for a perfectly automated ball action to occur.

The small company supporting the football team is well aware of such failure. Thus, we arrive at a new level of explanation: the purpose of the activity carried out on the field could actually be just to bring together a group of people who want to try for an impossible goal, that of becoming one collective, selfless, moving body. What is important is to take part in the challenge with all one's energies and efforts and final results do not really matter. What is realized here in a concrete form is the abstract principle of *makoto*, 'sincerity of purpose' and 'concentration of the mind'. All this is even more true for those with an injured leg: their participation is of greater value because it requires strong physical endurance, and reveals a greater commitment to the team. It is the same kind of sacrifice noticed by Whiting (1977, 1989) in his famous books on Japanese baseball, where this kind of ethics may require an athlete to give away his professional career, even his own life, for the team (Whiting 1977: 15, 22, 26, 37; 1989: 37–8, 54). In the Tsukuba football *dōkōkai*, this limit was symbolically reached by the dash running at the end of a practice session, a last aerobic strain that is of no use athletically and actually tires the athlete even more. In American and Japanese baseball teams, players run laps after practice as punishment for not having fully engaged in the activities. In the *dōkōkai*, all players must run, and the seniors were the ones starting off and setting an example. In my opinion, the experiment made at Tsukuba of involving women in actual play could be read as an attempt to draw to the team their physical commitment as well as their psychological support.

It could be said that players only play to show their devotion to the team. If this is the goal, the type of sport practised – football rather than baseball or table tennis – looks rather secondary. Since the value of the athlete is measured on effort and not on final achievement, someone who shows enough commitment can become a 'good player' in any sport. Actually, such values may be pursued by any type of activity – not only sport, but also jazz dancing or singing in a choir.

If we assume that a sports team finds its *raison d'être* and its identity in facing other similar entities through competition, we must say that these Japanese clubs are not real teams. They very seldom face any opponent. During the drills, the team works alone, and, when an opponent is necessary, the players of the same team take on this role. Action and reaction always occur within the closed group of 'friends'. No actual gaming occurs. The players seem, instead, to stage a representation of the game for their own interest. This lack of *agon* is betrayed by the lack of fouls during practices and is the cause of the poor, confused performance of the *dōkōkai* during the weekly championship matches.

The only form of inside/outside interaction seems to be a non-competitive, non-sporting event like watching the Toyota Cup, climax of the annual ritual cycle – *nenchūgyōji* – of a team. During this occurrence, all the young football players of Greater Tokyo celebrate together their own identity of values, their reciprocal non-opposition and their substantial interchangeability. Unable to express their disapproval of what occurs on the field and thus, according to a Japanese journalist, 'stupid' (Hosokawa 1989: 46–7), they equally support both competing teams by blowing their horns. School sports teams emerge from this analysis as entirely oriented towards themselves, only engaged in the self-celebration of their sacred and profane activities. As such, they do not seem to have any motivation other than merely existing as a group.

Juvenile sport in context

In the Japan of the 1980s, the school totally dominated a youngster's life, having obliterated from the scene all other agencies traditionally engaged in the socialization and enculturation of the young. Along with offering a complete educational package, based on both a formal curricular education and an informal socialization, Japanese schools, albeit with great local variation, were apparently trying to realize a disciplinarian project aimed to control the mind and social attitudes of the young through the control of their bodies. This project was carried out by the enforcement of various rules concerning hairstyles, uniforms (see Sakamoto 1986, 1987, 1993), daily behaviour outside school, places of residence (like in the *zenryōsei* system of certain private schools, in which the students were obliged to reside on campus), and sporting activities.

It is within this frame of reference that an explanation of the function of club sports may be attempted. By organizing afternoon activities through the clubs, schools attain several goals:

a   To build a social environment dominated by vertical relationships. In clubs, members have the same status before society at large, but are differentiated among themselves by those very same criteria based on age and relative seniority that regulate vertical relations within the wider society. It is the same function that used to be carried, in the village, by the traditional peer associations such as the *kodmogumi* (children's group), *musumegumi* (daughters' group) and *wakamonogumi* (young people's group). At school, the ideal environment for horizontal interpersonal relationships is already set by classroom life.

b   To increase the length of the presence of the youngsters at school, and so reduce their free time.

c   To consume the youngster's physical energy – even if it affects their study – and, by mechanically doing so to avoid distractions among the students (Kojima 1983: 170).

d   To control directly the activities of the peer group, so that the students could be exposed only to those ideas defined as culturally or pedagogically useful.

So protected from harmful behavioural models, and constantly enlightened by adult ideals, the youngsters should absorb only proper norms and values, and would not develop any deviant tendencies. Sports clubs provide the ideal environment for this physical and mental disciplining of the young. This seems to be confirmed by the principle of self-management, another element of continuity between village and school associations. In the closed and protected world of the school, the transmission of knowledge occurs by example as well as by imposition. In the Confucian tradition, however, example and imposition must find a balance in which the former plays a dominating role. The students are supposed to observe the adults and then spontaneously behave in a proper way (like in the Reitaku *Kōtōgakkō*, founded on the 'moralogy' of Hiroike Sentarō 1978: 32–5). For this to happen, however, youngsters have to be left alone in self-managed social groups – just like they are in a village. And indeed, at school, a teacher is put in charge of the school associations with the role of setting a permanent example for the students, and at the same time to prevent distracting behaviour. He or she will monitor situations without taking any action, unless problems arise and direct intervention is needed. In the same way, a club's coach does not act as a technical adviser (indeed he is not required to have such capability), but as a kind of 'ethical' guide – like a *daisenpai*. The ideal football team does not need him to intervene at all: once he has decided the contents of the practice, the coach is there only to observe the players from the edge of the field (as noted in Furunuma 1987: 50 and in Zenkoku kōkōsakkā, 1990: 146–7). When the enculturation of the young is almost complete, as in the case of university students, adult control is no longer necessary and the figure of the coach disappears. University *dōkōkai* do not have any coaches.

Conclusions

The sporting activity of the *bu* or *dōkōkai* is indeed a form of physical education, even if it is never considered as such. But it is not in the end deigned to preserve or improve the youngsters' health or body usage. Instead, it serves to shape their *seishin* (the mind, the moral) and their social skills utilizing the body (*karada*) as a physical or physiological tool, without reaching the extremes of body discipline described by Foucault (1975). In a *bu* of high-school level, sport is set in an institutional frame that describes itself as free and recreational, when in fact it is not. The physical education activities of the *bu* are excessive, as they must be in order to prevent distraction. As social skills are learnt, adult control and physical strain gradually disappear. In university *bu* and *dōkōkai* sports teams, physical activity remains strong – at a different degree – but now it is valued as an instrument to show devotion towards the team. In any case, it is not fundamental for the functioning of the association. So, at the university, other cultural *dōkōkai* arise that allow practising activities more freely and recreationally. The young football player grows up in these sports societies feeling his relationship with the team with a strong sense of compulsion. Through the team's closed world rituals, he learns to respect a sharing of duties and a ladder of authority both based on seniority. So, he knows that, through the years, he too will go up the ladder, no matter what his merits or individual capabilities are. These very same principles apply up to the university and then to the *kaisha* (company), with no discontinuity, so that one can always count on being in a world of stable structure and invariant values. It may be said that the factor that substitutes for the pleasure of playing and the experience of flow is this sense of stability. In exchange for this sporting adventure, led by the strong arm of the school, the youngster must offer to the team total dedication and all the energies that study leaves him. This is the only requirement for a team member to be successful in football society. As athletes, the young learn quite soon that they are valued certainly more for their efforts then for their goals.

Note

1   Besides my own personal experience as a member of Tsukuba University's *sakkā* and table tennis *dōkōkai*, this analysis is based on: (a) a study of daily life and society, and the educational and socializing role of student associations, that I conducted in several schools around the University of Tsukuba (Ibaraki-ken), especially the *Meikei Gakuen* (junior and senior high school) and the junior high school of Yatabe, between 1984 to 1987; (b) magazine articles on younger Japanese football leagues, and (c) the theory of the psychology of play developed by Mihalyi Czikszentmihalyi (1975), founded itself on the classic text of Caillois (1958), and the more recent classification of play in Blanchard and Cheska (1985).

Bibliography

Blanchard, K. and Taylor Cheska, A. (1985) *The Anthropology of Sport*, South Hadley, MA: Bergin and Garvey Publishers.

Caillois, R. (1979) (1958) *Man, Play and Games*, New York: Shocken Books.

Csikszentmihalyi, M. (1975) *Beyond Boredom and Anxiety: The Experience of Play in Work and Games*, San Francisco, CA: Jossey-Bass.

Csikszentmihalyi, M. and Graef, R. (1975) 'Flow patterns in everyday life', in M. Csikszentmihalyi, *Beyond Boredom and Anxiety: The Experience of Play in Work and Games*, San Francisco, CA: Jossey-Bass, pp. 140–60.

Csikszentmihalyi, M., Hamilton Holcomb, J. and Csikszentmihaly, I. (1975) 'Enjoying work: surgery', in M. Csikszentmihalyi, *Beyond Boredom and Anxiety: The Experience of Play in Work and Games*, San Francisco, CA: Jossey-Bass, pp. 123–39.

De Grazia, S. (1962) *Of Time, Work and Leisure*, New York: The Twentieth Century Fund.

Foucault, M. (1975) *Surveiller et punir. Naissance de la prison* (Discipline and punish: the birth of the prison), Paris: Gallimard.

Furunuma, S. (1987) 'Furunuma Sadao 'Teikyō Kōkō kantoku' no zenkoku kōkō no jitsuryoku shindan – Shimizushō' (The strength of Japanese high school football teams according to Furunuma Sadao, coach of Teikyō High – Shimizu Commercial High School) *Sutoraikā* 7: 49–51.

Furunuma, S. (1990) 'Furunuma Sadao (Teikyō Kōkō kantoku) no zenkoku kōkō no jitsuryoku shindan – Furitsu Takatsuki Minami Kōkō' (The strength of Japanese high school football teams according to Furunuma Sadao, coach of Teikyō High: Takatsuki Minami Municipal High School), *Sutoraikā* 12: 68–9.

Hiroike, S. (1978) *Morarojii kyōiku* (The education of moralogy), Kashiwa: Morarojii kenkyūjo.

Hosokawa, S. (1989) *Sakkā gurui (Fool for Soccer)*, Tokyo: Tetsugaku shobō.

Huizinga, J. (1955) (1949), *Homo Ludens. A Study of the Play Element in Culture*, Boston: Beacon.

Kneller, G.F. (1965) *Educational Anthropology: An Introduction*, New York: John Wiley and Sons.

Kojima, K. (1983) *Gakkō no bunka o tsukuru. Chisei to shakaisei o motomete* (Building school culture: for intelligence and social skill), Tokyo: Kyōiku shuppan.

Mauss, M. (1950) (1934) 'Les techniques du corps' (Body techniques), *Sociologie et anthropologie*, Paris: Presses Universitaires de France, pp. 363–86.

Monbushō (1978) *Chūgakkō shidōsho Hoken taiiku hen* (Advising in junior high school, health and physical education).

Norbeck, E. (ed.) (1974) 'The anthropological study of human play', *Rice University Studies* 60 (3).

Onuki, T. (1986) 'Jiyū ni torai shitai bokutachi no sentaku' (Our choice to give it a free try), *Sakkā daijesuto* 7: 112–8.

Roberts, J.M., Arth, M.J. and Bush, R.R. (1959) 'Games in culture', *American Anthropologist* 61: 597–605.

Sakamoto, H. (1987) *Seito kisoku manyuaru* (A databook of school rules), Tokyo: Gyōsei.

Sakamoto, H. (1992) (1986) *Kōsoku no kenkyū* (Research on school rules), Tokyo: San'ichi shobō.

Sakamoto, H. (1993) *Kōsoku saiban* (Trials related to school rules), Tokyo: San'ichi shobō.

Shimizu, K. (ed.) (1993) *Kyōiku dēta rando '93–'94* (A databook of educational statistics), Tokyo: Jiji tsūshinsha.

Shimizu, K. (ed.) (1999) *Kyōiku dēta rando 1999–2000* (A databook of educational statistics, Tokyo: Jiji tsūshinsha.

Vigarello, G. (1988) *Une histoire culturelle du sport* (A cultural history of sport), Paris: Editions Robert Laffont.

Whiting, R. (1977) *The Chrysanthemum and the Bat. The Game Japanese Play*, Tokyo: The Permanent Press.

Whiting, R. (1989) *You Gotta Have Wa*, New York: Vintage.

'Zenkoku chūgaku sakkā ichibu shōkai – Akeno chūgaku (Oita-ken)' (1987) (Introducing one high school football club: Akeno Junior High, Oita prefecture), *Sutoraikā* 7: 80–1.

'Zenkoku chūgaku sakkā ichibu shōkai – Nirasaki kōkō (Yamanashi-ken)' (1987) (Introducing one high school football club: Nirasaki Senior High, Yamanashi prefecture), *Sutoraikā* 7: 76–7.

'Zenkoku chūgakusakkā ichibu shōkai – Kenritsu-Iwaki kōkō (Fukushima-ken)' (1990) (Introducing one high school football club: Iwaki prefectural High, Fukushima prefecture), *Sutoraikā* 12: 146–7.

12 Professional soccer in Japan

John Horne

Introduction

The globalization of football has begun to attract attention from academics from different disciplines, although initially it was British-based, and mainly English, sociologists who predominated. Studies have moved away from an almost exclusive focus on fan violence (Williams *et al.* 1984; Murphy *et al.* 1990; Giulianotti, Bonney and Hepworth 1994) to ethnicity and nationalism (Duke and Crolley 1996), labour migration (Bale and Maguire 1995), the World Cup (Tomlinson and Whannel 1986; Sugden and Tomlinson 1994; Sugden and Tomlinson 1998) and the impact of modernity (Giulianotti and Williams 1994). More recently MacClancy (1996), Armstrong and Giulianotti (1997) and Armstrong (1998) have produced volumes reflecting the interest of anthropologists and ethnographically inclined sociologists in football in different parts of the world.

One feature of these most recent contributions to the study of the globalization of the sport has been the recognition of the need to examine the cultural meanings attached to social changes involving sport and leisure activities in particular places. These meanings attached to sports may differ from one place to the next and without detailed research – 'ethnosociologies' as John MacAloon (1992) refers to them – little progress can be made in unravelling cultural diversity in the meanings of sport. Alongside global processes social scientists of sport also have to study specific places, situated in particular historical and cultural contexts. In contrast to many of the other contributions to this collection however, this chapter primarily relies upon desk-based research. Whilst it must therefore be regarded as more speculative, it is based upon six years of monitoring and reviewing contemporary and historical data, popular magazine and newspaper articles (in Japanese and in English) and academic writings on sport in Japan. The author is also deeply indebted to the many Japanese colleagues and students who have helped collect information, in some cases translated it, and also discussed his impressions of *sakka* over the years.

If good sociological practice can be defined as the combination of the sociological imagination with historical and comparative analysis, the new sociological interest in place, space and localities, amidst contemporary debates about globalization, should help us make better sense of both the 'orient' and the 'occident'. It should also help to make some form of rapprochement between sociological and anthropological approaches to sport. The subtle but significant ways that anthropologists can contribute both to anthropology and to the interdisciplinary sphere of sports studies has recently been outlined by Noel Dyck (1998). In addition to those studies noted above on football by anthropologists, he mentions Alter (1992), Archetti (1996), Brownell (1995), Klein (1991), Blanchard (1995), and his own collection of essays (Dyck 2000).

Thus, both anthropologists and sociologists have begun to emphasize the importance of sport and the ludic for understanding deeper structures and meanings pervading all areas of wider society. In studying the ludic one can acknowledge its importance in social life, offering utopian moments when process temporarily triumphs over product (Whannel 1993), but also one must recognize its interdependence with economic, political and ideological relations and interests. The role of sport and the ludic is not just one of 'reflecting' society but also 'reproducing' it; that is, it has a constitutive role as well (Gruneau 1983).

In this light it is possible to consider how in the 1990s football has truly become the 'world game'. Following the 1994 World Cup Finals in the US it became clear just how much global interest had been generated by the tournament. There was an estimated audience of two billion watching the final match alone between Brazil and Italy. Forty multinational corporations paid US$400 million in total to gain 'official product' status and guaranteed global advertising. It was attended by over 3.5 million football supporters. Four years later the World Cup phenomenon took another leap forward at France 1998. 190 countries competed in the qualifying stages to reach the thirty–two finalist positions – the largest number ever. Ian Taylor (1998) has described it as the largest 'mass marketing of happiness' ever. Lodged between these two massive football spectacles in 1996 came the unprecedented decision taken by FIFA – the Federation International of Football Associations, football's world governing body – to allow Japan and South Korea to co-host the first Asian-based World Cup Finals in 2002. The rest of the chapter will examine the recent growth of professional soccer in Japan in the light of this. The structure of the Japan Professional Football League (J League) and its first six seasons of operation (1993–8) are analysed. Attention focuses on the commercial interests involved: the sports workers, the soccer players and managers, and the consumers, spectators and fans of the J League teams. A number of issues and areas for further research are identified.

The rise of the Japan professional football league (J League)

The Japanese national soccer team had often been beaten by their near neighbours South Korea in World Cup qualifying matches before 1993, the year of the J League launch. Ijiri Kazuo (1994: 77) suggests that many Japanese felt that this was acceptable: 'We beat them at baseball; they beat us at soccer'. For South Koreans, soccer had enjoyed a special position as a sport at which they could regularly defeat the Japanese, and thus sustain some national prestige. In the 1993 World Cup Asian Zone qualifying tournament they lost to Japan and some called the defeat 'the worst humiliation since the 1910 annexation' (by Japan) (Ijiri 1994: 77). In fact it has been suggested that it was as a result of this defeat that the South Korean Football Association put forward its bid to host the 2002 World Cup Finals in competition with that of Japan. The reaction of the Japanese audience also demonstrated a new level of intensity of involvement in the game. According to one commentator, the fans regularly sang *Kimigayo*, the (*de facto*) national anthem before each game of the tournament (Ijiri 1994: 77). What this comment also suggests is that football had become a symbolic battleground for a 'new Japan', in which some of the old arguments about the singing of the national anthem had been silenced.

On Thursday 28 October 1993 the final matches of the Asian Football Confederation qualifying tournament for the 1994 World Cup were played in Doha, Qatar. With thirty seconds remaining Japan was leading Iraq by two goals to one and seemed to have secured a place at the 1994 finals. Then, from a corner kick, the captain of the Iraqi team headed an equalizing goal, which sent Saudi Arabia and South Korea, despite their earlier defeat at Japan's hands, through to the US finals instead. For the Japanese team, and over 1000 of their supporters who had accompanied them to the Gulf, there was a sense of disbelief. For those millions of Japanese watching what has become known as 'the tragedy of Doha' at home – in what amounted to the fifth-largest television sport audience ever in Japan – the feeling of anti-climax was profound. Yet in May 1995 the Japanese Football Association (JFA) officially applied to host the 2002 World Cup Finals. After Mexico dropped out of the bidding, the only other contender was South Korea. So whatever decision was made the 2002 FIFA World Cup finals would be the first to be based in Asia. The Japanese 2002 bid, which was inaugurated in 1989, can be seen alongside the launch of the Japan Professional Football League (J League) in 1993, as part of a strategy to raise both the level of public interest in, and quality of, Japanese football.

In 1991 soccer ranked twenty second in terms of sports participation by the total population, and, significantly, was second in popularity to baseball amongst the 15–19 year olds (*Asahi Shinbun* 1992: 65, 66). Soccer enjoyed greater involvement and more popularity than baseball in high schools at the end of the 1980s and beginning of the 1990s. A survey conducted in December 1992 found 31.4 per cent of respondents wanting to attend a J League game at a stadium, compared with 33.5 per cent for baseball. Soccer had most appeal for children and young adults. The seeds of Japanese interest in soccer had clearly become greater in the 1980s and early 1990s. They had been encouraged by the corporate sponsorship and staging of international football competitions such as the World Football Club Championship (otherwise known as the Toyota Cup) from 1980, the FIFA World Youth Championships, and the Asian Cup in 1992.

In 1992, whilst the Japanese national soccer team won the Asian Cup, semi-professional/amateur teams like Mitsubishi Motor, Furukawa Electric and Toyota Jidōsha were lucky to attract 2000 spectators. In 1993, however, full-time professional soccer – in the shape of the J League – was launched with a massive injection of capital – estimated to be £20 billion – and a large marketing campaign. Reborn as Urawa Red Diamonds, JEF United Ichiwara and Nagoya Grampus Eight respectively, each with a mascot, team song and colours, these three teams, along with seven others, were initially expected to attract between 15,000 and 30,000 fans twice a week. This they did in the first half of the 1993 competition, and they continued to play to sell-out crowds into the third J League season in 1995.

From the outset it was planned to expand the J League and eventually to allow relegation and promotion between the J League and the semi-professional/amateur Japan Soccer League (now renamed Japan Football League or JFL) to happen in 1999. Since 1993 the teams in the JFL that wished to be considered for J League status had not only to finish in the top two places of the JFL but also to pass basic stadium requirements, and other criteria, such as potential level of spectator interest and local community support. Table 12.1 shows how the J League line up evolved from May 1993 to the start of the sixth season in March 1998.[1]

From 1999 two divisions were created out of the existing 18 J League teams and the semi–professional company teams in the Japan Football League. There were sixteen teams in the J League First Division and ten teams in the Second Division. It was envisaged that gradually most of the semi-professional company teams in the JFL would be able to meet the criteria for promotion into the J League should they finish in one of the top two positions. Teams in the JFL in 1997 that still retained a clear corporate identity – such as Honda, NTT Kanto and Sagan Tosu, similar to Japanese baseball teams – also had to alter their names in order to compete in the new expanded J League.[2]

Table 12.1 The Japan Professional Football League (J League) line-up 1998

Club	Main sponsors	city
Verdy	Yomiuri Nippon (press, TV)	Kawasaki
Marinos	Nissan (motors)	Yokohama
Antlers	Sumimoto Metal, Kashima	Kashima
JEF United	JR East (rail) Furukawa Electric	Ichihara
Urawa Reds	Mitsubishi (motors)	Urawa
Sanfrecce	Mazda (motors), Hiroshima	Hiroshima
Gamba	Matsushita Electric (Panasonic)	Suita, Osaka
AS Flugels	All Nippon Airways (ANA) and Sato Kogyō	Yokohama Fukuoka
Shimizu S-Pulse	Shizuoka (TV)	Shimizu
Grampus Eight	Toyota, Tokai Bank	Nagoya
Bellmare Hiratsuka (1)	Fujita	Hiratsuka
Jubilo Iwata (1)	Yamaha	Iwata
Cerezo Osaka (2)	Yanmar, Capcom, Nippon Ham	Nagai, Osaka
Kashiwa Reysol (2)	Hitachi	Kashiwa
Kyoto Purple Sanga (3)	Kyocera	Kyoto
Avispa Fukuoka (3)	Fukuoka City, Sanyo Shinpan	Fukuoka
Vissel Kobe (4)	Not available	Kobe
Consadole Sapporo (5)	Not available	Sapporo

Sources: *World Soccer* May 1993: 4–5; January 1994: 54; December 1994: 51; January 1996: 44; October 1998: 59; *Japan Almanac 1993, Asahi Shinbun*: 36; *Nippon* 1993/94, *Yano-Tsuneta Kinenkai*: 30; *J League Official Guide*, 1997: 151; *Sportsworld Japan*, March–April 1998: 24–27.

Notes: (1) from 1994; (2) from 1995; (3) from 1996; (4) from 1997; (5) from 1998

Another change introduced from 1999 was the dropping of the penalty shoot out as a way of deciding tied matches. For the first time since its creation the J League permitted drawn games. These have been technically allowed in JML baseball for some time, although the vast majority of baseball matches do not result in a tie (Horowitz 1995). From 1999 three points were awarded for a win in the ordinary ninety minutes of play; two points for a win in extra time through the scoring of a 'golden goal' (the first goal scored in the thirty minutes extra time period); and one point awarded to each team for a draw after 120 minutes' play. In a commitment to consistency the J League announced that this points system would apply for at least three years (*World Soccer*, October 1998: 46).

As Yomiuri and Nissan respectively, *Verdy* Kawasaki and Yokohama *Marinos* were the cream of the old semi-professional/corporate football league in Japan. The two teams played the opening game of the J League on 15 May 1993. Hence it may not be so surprising to see that they accomplished championship successes in the first three seasons. *Verdy* Kawasaki – reportedly playing in a 'Brazilian' style, with zonal rather than man-to-man marking and a strong midfield – won the first and second Suntory championships in 1993 and 1994. The following year Yokohama *Marinos* won the first stage and, although *Verdy* won the second stage for the third time, it was the Yokohama based team that became overall J League champions in 1995. Subsequently Kashima *Antlers* – sponsored by both the town's local authority and local employer Sumimoto Metal – and *Jubilo* Iwata – based on the old Yamaha side – became pre-eminent, winning consecutive J League stages in 1996 and 1997 respectively.

After an initial boom in the first three years average crowd sizes in the J League have been in decline. As can be seen in Table 12.2, in the 1997 season average attendance dropped close to 10,000. It was hoped by the J League authorities that the creation of playoffs, plus the added incentive for all J League teams to play for maximum points, would create more excitement, and attract supporters for those teams not in contention for the championship. With qualification for the FIFA World Cup (France 1998) by the national team and the prospect of co-hosting the 2002 World Cup with South Korea, it was clearly considered possible that football would be back in fashion if the changes for the 1998 season created an exciting spectacle. At the time of writing however (October 1998) J League attendance since the World Cup finals have not been increasing and the greater attraction of professional baseball continues to be a talking point in the Japanese media (*Nikkei Weekly*, 19 October 1998: 10).

Table 12.2 also shows average attendance figures by stage and the number of games played compared with Japanese Major League (JML) professional baseball. Whilst some questions about the accuracy of attendance figures may be asked, baseball clearly remains the most popular live spectator sport in Japan. In baseball the Central League figures are swollen by the presence of the ever-popular Yomiuri Giants whose average attendance per home game was 53,864 in 1995 and 53,800 in 1996. Leaving aside the Giants the lowest average gate in the Central League was still a very respectable 19,900 enjoyed by Hiroshima Toyo-Carp. Whilst the J League has started to develop its 'star' teams – *Verdy*, *Marinos*, *Kashima*, *Jubilo*, etc. – they have not yet got such audience 'pulling' power as the Giants.[3]

Table 12.2 J League and professional baseball attendance 1993–7

Season	J League			Professional baseball	
1993	1st stage	16876		Central League	n/a
	2nd stage	19077		Pacific League	n/a
	Total average (180 games)	17976		Average (260 games)	n/a
1994	1st stage	19679		Central League	n/a
	2nd stage	19517		Pacific League	n/a
	Total average (264 games)	19598		Average (260 games)	n/a
1995	1st stage	16724		Central League	31573
	2nd stage	17120		Pacific League	24733
	Total average (364 games)	16922		Average (260 games)	28153
1996	(two-stage system dropped			Central League	31300
	due to Olympic Games)			Pacific League	22800
	Total average (240 games)	13353		Average (260 games)	27050
1997	1st stage	10611		Central League	n/a
	2nd stage	n/a		Pacific League	n/a
	Total average (364 games)	10131		Average (260 games)	n/a

Sources: *J League Guide* 1997: 86; *Asahi Shinbun* 1996: 268; *Asahi Shinbun*, 1997: 276; *World Soccer*, October, 1997: 67; *World Soccer*, February 1998: 41.

Sakka and internationalization

Symbolizing the internationalism of football, J League team names are a mixture of European languages – especially English, Spanish, Italian, German – and Japanese. Some teams are named after the city/place where they are located, others after chief sponsors and some a combination of both. Some teams have a playing name and a club name. Of the original ten J League clubs, for example, *Verdy Kawasaki* has 'Yomiuri Nippon FC' and 'Verdy' on the team badge. *Kashima Antlers'* name derives from the deer that inhabit the area around a shrine in Kashima. *Urawa Reds* have 'Mitsubishi Urawa' on their badge and were known as 'red diamonds' after the company symbol. In an apparent bid to gain authenticity *Gamba Osaka*'s badge features the motto 'Gamba Osaka Since 1991'. Similarly Shimizu's team badge has 'EST. 1992' on it, whilst the 'S' in *Shimizu S-Pulse* can stand for 'soccer', 'speedy' or alternatively the original media company sponsor 'Shizuoka'. Nagoya's *Grampus Eight* gained its name from the legend that killer whales (*grampus* in Latin) saved Nagoya from fire by spouting water from the sea. The team's badge features a cartoon killer whale, while eight is considered to be a lucky number (*World Soccer*, December 1995: 11).

All the teams that have joined the J League since 1994 have also got composite names such as *Bellmare Hiratsuka*, *Cerezo Osaka*, *Kashiwa Reysol* and *Consadole Sapporo*. *Kyoto Purple Sanga* apparently derives its name from the colour associated with the Japanese royal family (for many centuries resident in Kyoto) and *sanga* being a

Buddhist term in Sanskrit for 'friends united'. *Avispa Fukuoka* were known as *Fukuoka Blux* before their elevation to the J League, when the name was altered because 'Blux' – which stood for 'Brave Lads with Ultimate X' – sounded too much like 'Brooks' when pronounced in Japanese, an athletic wear company with no relationship to the team. *Vissel Kobe* (so named after 'the Vi(ctory Ve)ssel') bear the legend 'Vissel Kobe 1995' on the team badge. Unlike previously promoted teams neither *Kyoto Purple Sanga* nor *Avispa Fukuoka* were based on a former corporate club with an illustrious past.

A further aspect of the 'international' status of soccer is the fact that different J League teams have reflected playing styles from around the world in their game. The football played by the teams has usually depended on their managers and players. Hence *Kyoto* was hailed as a 'Brazilian' team in their first season (although this did not prevent them from establishing the record for losing the most consecutive J League matches!). *Fukuoka* and *Marinos* have been seen as 'Argentinean', and *JEF United Ichihara* and *Sanfrecce Hiroshima* played a 'European' style game in the early seasons. In the J League there were five Brazilian and three Dutch managers during the first stage of the 1995 season. Brazil has been the main source of imported players, although other South American and European countries are involved. In 1995 there were over 30 Brazilians registered in the J League, although regulations prohibit more than three foreign players per side from being on the pitch at any one time. Dunga, the Brazil team captain in 1994 and 1998, heads the list of Brazilian national team players in the J League. When he joined *Jubilo Iwata* in 1995 there were seven Brazilian national team players in the J League (*World Soccer*, October 1995:50). This attempt to mould a team into a particular national style of play has not always worked. On appointment to *Jubilo Iwata* in 1997 new manager Felipe announced 'I am converting this team from European to Brazilian football' (quoted in *World Soccer*, April 1997: 48). A few months later he resigned, complaining that the Japanese players did not 'take the game seriously enough' (quoted in *World Soccer*, August 1997: 48).

Arsene Wenger, manager of Arsenal in the English Premier League, was another successful import to Japan from France. He managed Nagoya in 1995 and 1996, and has been retained as a technical adviser to the Japan Football Association (JFA). His own success with Arsenal, and the triumph of the French team at the 1998 World Cup finals, has enhanced his reputation even further in Japan. It was on his recommendation that another Frenchman, Philippe Troussier, the manager of South Africa's national team at the 1998 World Cup finals, was appointed as manager of the Japanese national team in August 1998 (*World Soccer*, October 1998: 46). In each of these ways football in Japan has been tied symbolically to the world outside of Japan.

Migrant sport workers

One of the aims of the launch of the J League was to broaden the pool of Japanese soccer players. In the 1960s and 1970s there was a handful of good players, but a large supporting cast was lacking. In the 1980s, however, more young Japanese began to play soccer than baseball at school and in university. Rather than send players abroad it was hoped that by attracting leading players from Europe and South America to Japan that Japanese players could learn from their example. Japan's roll call of some of the greats of soccer history has grown, but at a slower rate after 1995 and the downturn in attendance. The flow of talent has been slow in going the other way. In 1996 Miura Kazuyoshi, a leading forward in Japan's national side at the time, returned to *Verdy* in the J League after a year's loan with *Genoa* in Serie A in Italy. As a young player he spent five years in Brazil (with *Santos*) and regularly trained in Brazil to maintain a permanent residence permit there. His performance in Italy was not very impressive. At the time of writing the latest Japanese star to leave the J League was Nakata Hidetoshi, a young midfield player formerly with *Bellmare Hiratsuka* who made the biggest impact on the British media in the Japan national team at the 1998 World Cup finals. Nakata joined *Perugia* in Italy's Serie A after the World Cup and made an instant impression by scoring twice on his debut in September. According to newspaper reports 500,000 Perugia shirts bearing his name and his No. 7 were being shipped to Japan for fans following his progress (*Guardian*, 16 September 1998: 31). Nakata was also voted Asian Football Confederation player of the year in 1998 and became the subject of a documentary focusing entirely on himself when NHK had cameras tracking every move during a J League game before the World Cup. As in other 'star systems' however, after the rise the fall has started to occur, with the Japanese media beginning to discuss why Nakata did not sing the national anthem before games in France, and questioning his nationality. He is thought to be of Korean parentage (*Guardian*, 16 September 1998: 31; Ogasawara Hiroki, personal communication, 1998).

In the case of baseball Japan has come to be a source of economic opportunity – albeit on a small scale – for North American players, and those who would normally have looked to North America (for example, baseball players in the Dominican Republic). In 1995 this development was highlighted by the signing of the North Americans Shane Mack and Julio Franco to Japanese baseball teams for two years on salaries of US$8 million and US$7 million respectively (*Guardian*, 4 February 1995). The motivations of the foreign soccer players in Japan are not solely dictated by financial rewards, but the salaries of some foreign players have been several times that of a minister of state in the Japanese government. At the time of the launch of the J League in May 1993 most of the coverage in Britain was related to Gary Lineker's £1.8 million annual salary. Hampered by injury, Lineker's record for the first J League season was twelve appearances and four goals: his four goals thus costing Nagoya approximately $1.75m each! He remained at the top of the J League salary rankings until his decision to retire from the game through injury in November 1994, at the end of the second stage. Lineker was one of six J League players to receive an annual salary in excess of £1 million in the first two seasons. Only two of these – Miura Kazuyoshi and Ruy Ramos – were Japanese or naturalized Japanese (*World Soccer*, April 1994: 56). Former world footballer of the year, and Brazilian minister of sport, Zico (real name Arthur Antunes Coimbra), Lineker and Pierre Littbarski of Germany, had, or had virtually, finished their active playing careers in their own countries and came abroad to round off their career. The problem for Japanese players is that the relative financial return for playing abroad is small compared to staying in Japan (*Sports World Japan*, August 1998: 23).

Comparing professional soccer and baseball

It has been argued that 'exotic Japan' has often been the favourite image for Western observers of Japanese culture and society. In sports literature, too, the emphasis has been upon the exotic and the un-western – *sumō*, the martial arts and 'samurai baseball' (Whiting 1976, 1989). In conclusion we will briefly outline Whiting's 'samurai baseball' perspective – which has become the dominant frame through which sport in Japan written about in English has been understood – and highlight similarities and differences between professional baseball and soccer.[4]

The key features of baseball 'samurai style' can be summarized as:

1   the inculcation of *bushidō* spirit (or the 'way of the warrior' or samurai) through a strict training regime which promotes endurance, *gutsu* and *seishinshugi* (spirit-ism) – sometimes referred to as 'death training';
2   anti-individualism and a stress on the importance of group/team harmony or *wa* through adherence to beliefs such as 'the tall tree catches the wind' and 'the nail that sticks out will be hammered down';
3   hierarchical manager–coach–player relations, which elevates the position of manager and subordinates players within a system of control similar to a 'total institution' covering not just the regular season but also close season and life outside baseball;
4   a style of play – sometimes referred to as 'mechanical baseball' – in which the distinctive tactics are safety plays and the use of the 'sacrificial bunt';
5   the importance of media coverage, for example the extensive coverage of not just professional baseball, but also the national high school championships and the highlighting of the importance of the psychological confrontation between *pitchā* and *battā*, similar to that in *sumō* bouts in match commentaries; a
6   the distinctive baseball 'star system', including the differential treatment of foreign (especially American) or *gaijin* stars, foreign-Asian (especially Korean or Chinese) stars, and Japanese stars in the Major League.

Roden (1980: 532) argues that Whiting's 1976 essay is merely a contemporary example of the patronizing cultural relativist approach to Japanese involvement in baseball which has been utilized in order to maintain 'the national integrity of the sport' in the US. Whilst it is possible to read Whiting in this way, it is also instructive to use his framework for comparative purposes.

How far can elements of the '*samurai* style' of sport be seen in Japanese soccer? With respect to the attempt to inculcate the *bushidō* spirit through a strict training regime there is some evidence that from the very beginning of the J League players' capacity for endurance was a key requirement. As we have noted the original ten–member teams faced each other four times in a season divided into two stages.

The winners of each stage then played each other for the title. The Yamazaki-Nabisco (League) Cup competition meant that the season comprised two games a week, with the Emperor's Cup – between J League teams and company teams in the JFL – to follow the end of the normal season (*World Soccer*, May 1993: 5). The decision that no drawn games would be permitted, and that sudden death extra time and a penalty shoot out when scores were still level would be used to decide the winner, undoubtedly added to the players' burden compared to other leagues. This is probably what prompted Gary Lineker to observe in an interview prior to the start of the J League in 1993: 'I have to undergo three months of pre-season training, which is probably the longest period in the history of football' (*World Soccer*, May 1993: 2).

The apparent stress on anti-individualism and the importance of group/team harmony or *wa* in Japanese baseball was actually utilized by the J League as it attempted to establish a distinctive position for itself *vis-à-vis* professional baseball. Baseball played a key role as a negative discourse in debates about the relative merits of the two sports in the Japanese media although in fact baseball presents many situations for the pitcher, the team captain, the number 4 player and players in other positions to demonstrate their individuality, skill and personality (Ogasawara 1997: personal communication). The existence of hierarchical manager–coach–player relations, which elevates the manager to the role of a deity and subordinates players within a system of control covering all their life, is not too dissimilar a picture from that which obtains in some teams in European football. As the J League developed, fewer Japanese managers were left in charge. As noted most managers come from Europe or South America. Arsene Wenger described one of the advantages for him in working in Japan was that he could concentrate single mindedly on football as he could not understand the language and hence media criticism or other sources of distraction! (*World Soccer*, September 1996: 21).

The style of play – sometimes referred to as 'mechanical baseball' – in which the distinctive tactics are safety plays and the use of the 'sacrificial bunt' – was related to the criticism that the Japanese play baseball in a passive way. One of Whiting's informants told him: 'There is very little anticipation on the part of the players during games. They just wait to be told what to do. They don't predict what the pitcher will throw or what direction the ball will be hit' (Reggie Smith quoted in Whiting 1989: 320).

Prior to the 1998 Football World Cup a former head coach of Yomiuri (now *Verdy Kawasaki*) made a similar comment about the national team's style of play: 'Nakata is the key man . . . the rest aren't world class . . . Japan is an economic power, so Japan's qualification is good for football as a whole, as a package. But Japanese football itself isn't so attractive. They can only play systematically' (Yuasa Kenji, quoted in *World Soccer*, July 1998: 93).

The importance of media coverage has already been discussed, including the extensive coverage of the national high school championships as well as professional baseball. On the face of it soccer would not appear to offer the same opportunities for the highlighting of the psychological confrontation between *pitchā* and *battā* in baseball, an emphasis that is also a feature of *sumō* match commentaries. The fact that a penalty shoot out was used as the final deciding factor in drawn J League matches may have partly been introduced to stimulate such 'one-on-one' situations.

The baseball 'star system', and especially the differential treatment of foreign (especially American) and foreign-Asian (especially Korean or Chinese) stars, occupies much of Whiting's writing (Whiting 1989: 201ff). Whiting's analysis of sporting culture in Japan suggests that there has been little room for players who stand out for their individuality – the sort of player needed to help out in a crisis on the football pitch. Hence it can be suggested that the role of *gaijin* players as 'Anti-Christs' would not be such a dominant feature of Japanese football. On the face of it, because of the influence of South America and Europe in the game, more freedom and self-expression might be allowed. Foreign managers have been able to dictate play and shape team playing style according to their background and experience of football in Europe or South America. Part of the distinctive appearance of Japanese football players has their been their long or dyed hair and earrings.

Yet Japanese as well as *gaijin* rebels have existed in baseball. Ochiai Hiromitsu, the leading baseball player in the 1980s, or 'the *gaijin* who speaks Japanese', provided a good example for Whiting (1989: 203–4) when he told him:

> The history of Japanese baseball is the history of pitchers throwing until their arms fall off for the team. It's crazy. Like dying for your country – doing a *banzai* (yelling 'long live the Emperor!') with your last breath. That mentality is why Japan lost the war . . . Spirit, effort, these are words that I absolutely cannot stand.

Buruma (1996) suggests that the heart of the dilemma for Japanese officialdom is how to build up national strength without damaging the spirit of *wa* and how to separate Western techniques from Western ideas that might upset the Eastern order? From China the formula *wakon yosai* (Japanese spirit, Western skill) was introduced into Japan during the Meiji era. But whether this is enough to compete adequately in a Western sport is the question. In baseball, he suggests, this thinking has been preserved. Buruma (1996: 244) states that 'the world of baseball, or any sports, is more conservative than other parts of Japanese life' and there was little sign of change to the rest of the Japanese social order. But maybe this is where professional soccer, in constituting a deliberate effort to reshape this relationship, has in turn started to influence changes in baseball in the 1990s. Tom Verducci quotes Robert Whiting as follows:

> When I came here, every kid was wearing a Giants cap . . . Now the J League has all these longhaired players and crazy Brazilians running around, and it's more in tune with the younger generation. In America people say baseball is a game for 50-year-old males. It's true to a certain extent'.
>
> (Verducci 1994: 31)

Japanese baseball has been responding to the challenge of the J League in a number of ways. The 1994 baseball championship decider (the 45th Japan Series) was between *Seibu Lions* and *Yomiuri Giants*. For the first time in the forty–five–year history of the series it featured some night games – starting at 6.15 p.m. – since the midweek day games had only been attracting single figure television ratings. Proof that baseball still had audience pulling power was confirmed earlier during the 1994 season when a match between the Giants and the Chunichi Dragons attracted a 48.8 per cent television share – the highest for a baseball match in Japan since the ratings system began in 1963.[5] Interest in baseball – the National High School Championship and both the professional Japanese Major League and the Major League in the US – has been maintained. The ML has gained more exposure in Japan through the success of Nomo Hideo and this has created further opportunities for commercial exploitation through the advertising and marketing of ML goods. In 1998 interest in the JML has been further enlivened through the success of Yokohama Baystars (formerly Taiyo Whales), who have reached the championship play offs for the first time in thirty–eight years by winning the Central League.

Another change that has occurred in Japanese baseball that may be seen as related to the emergence of soccer as a serious competitor was the adoption of 'free agency' for players.[6] The JML finally permitted it in 1993. The JML was not overwhelmed by the players' response. Players needed to have a minimum of ten years' service to be eligible but only five out of the sixty eligible players filed for free agency in 1993. There was however a 25 per cent jump in average player salaries in 1994 – to the equivalent of US$422,000. Perhaps this helps to explain why the whole *Yakult Swallows* team dropped out of the players union in 1993. 1993 was also the year that the number of foreign players in a team was increased from two to three (Verducci 1994: 32). It would appear from the attendance ratings in baseball, which have remained buoyant in the mid-1990s while those in the J League have plummeted, that the longstanding attraction of the game, in addition to the adjustments that have taken place to make it more attractive to spectators and to potential players, have worked.

Conclusion

Spectators may have been experiencing the J League as a consumer event, rather than a sports match. As we have seen after the first three seasons the level of enthusiasm has died down quite considerably. Alternatively, perhaps we should view the J League experience in the same light as Joy Hendry (1997: 84) uses with respect to gardens in Japan. It can be seen as one way of turning the 'unpredictable and dangerous world into a manageable, cultural context'. The experience of professional soccer enabled a balance to be struck between nostalgia and internationalization, a way of managing change and the potential for change in Japanese society. There are still similarities in the J League crowd behaviour with the orchestrated cheerleading apparent at baseball fixtures. In gardens, and the numerous theme parks that have developed in the past two decades, the West is 'tamed'; in soccer stadiums the West is manifested, but not in ways that fundamentally challenge the basic principles of Japanese society. Such sites of leisure can be seen as 'de-compression' chambers from the shrinking world of time–space compression brought about by the globalizing 'condition of post-modernity' (Harvey 1989). At the same time the growth of soccer is also related to attempts to manage economic, demographic and urban change in Japan. Soccer is being manipulated by different interest groups to accommodate new demands and initiate new ways of thinking. It may be a 'funny old game', but it is never just a game.

Notes

1   In the first three seasons of the J League all clubs played each other four times on a home and away basis, in two stages. Unlike British and most other European leagues, if scores were level after full time, a period of thirty minutes' extra time was played. If the game was still tied results were resolved on the basis of a penalty kick shoot out. Teams losing a penalty shoot out were awarded one point from the 1995 season (*World Soccer*, April 1995: 45). With the gradual expansion of numbers of teams, and hence the potential number of competitive games per season increasing, the J League was reorganized for the 1996 season. The two-stage system was abandoned in favour of a single format with two (home and away) meetings each season. A break in the summer of the 1996 season was also introduced to enable the national under–23 team to compete at the Atlanta Olympics and a League Cup competition to take place for those not eligible. In 1997 and 1998 the two stage format of the J League was resumed and the league expanded from sixteen to seventeen and then eighteen teams.

2   This chapter was originally drafted in October 1998. For observations on the 1999 J League season see Birchall (2000) and Horne (2000).

3   The Yomiuri Giants have a special place in the annals of Japanese baseball and are considered to be 'Japan's Team'. In 1974 their record nine straight series wins came to an end but subsequently they were known as the 'V9 Giants'. A demonstration of the wider influence of the performance of the Giants on Japanese society is the statistic that the economy grew 4.25 per cent on average during each of the eight years that the Giants won the Central League in the period 1973 to 1990. Sponsored by the proprietors of the largest circulation newspaper in the world they celebrated their sixtieth year in 1994 with the 'gift' of a league title for the first time in three barren seasons (Verducci 1994: 30).

4   In a highly informative historical survey of the initial encounters between Japanese and American baseball teams, Roden (1980) outlines the development of *besuboru* (baseball) in Japan and reminds us that the sport is normally referred to as *yakyū* in Japanese, a word meaning 'field ball' derived from the combination of Chinese characters.

5   All 130 *Giants* games were on television in 1994 compared to the coverage of teams like the *Seibu Lions* who only appeared five times in the 1994 season (Verducci 1994: 30).

6   Until the mid–1970s professional athletes in team sports in North America were subject to a set of employee restrictions known as the 'reserve system' which actually began in baseball in 1879. It virtually bound a player to one team in perpetuity and professional athletes in team sports were the property of who ever owned the team. It enabled owners to set salaries relatively low and prevented players from being able to sell their abilities to the team that would give them the best deal in terms of money and playing/working conditions. Until the mid–1970s, baseball players in the US were tied to their clubs even when out of contract. Players had often objected to the reserve system, but in the 1970s organizations were established to challenge the system through the courts. In 1976 they ruled that players had the right to become free agents – to accept contracts from other teams when their contracts expired.

Bibliography

Alter, J. (1992) *The Wrestler's Body: Identity and Ideology in North India*, Berkeley, CA: University of California Press.

Archetti, E. (1996) 'The moralities of Argentinian football', in S. Howell (ed.) *The Ethnography of Moralities*, London: Routledge, pp. 98–123.

Armstrong, G. (1998) *Football Hooligans: Knowing the Score*, Oxford/New York: Berg.

Armstrong, G. and Giulianotti, R. (eds) (1997) *Entering the Field: New Perspectives on World Football*, Oxford/New York: Berg.

Asahi Shinbun (1992) *Japan Almanac 1993*, Tokyo: Asahi Shinbun Publishing.

Asahi Shinbun (1996) *Japan Almanac 1997*, Tokyo: Asahi Shinbun Publishing.

Asahi Shinbun (1997) *Japan Almanac 1998*, Tokyo: Asahi Shinbun Publishing.

Bale, J. and Maguire, J. (eds) (1995) *The Global Sports Arena*, London: Frank Cass.

Birchall, J. (2000) *Ultra Nippon: How Japan Reinvented Football*, London: Headline.

Blanchard, K. (ed.) (1995) *The Anthropology of Sport: An Introduction*, Westport, CT: Bergin and Garvey.

Brownell, S. (1995) *Training the Body for China: Sports in the Moral Order of the People's Republic*, Chicago, IL: The University of Chicago Press.

Buruma, I. (1996) *The Missionary and the Libertine: Love and War in East and West*, London: Faber and Faber.

Cromartie, W. with Whiting R. (1991) *Slugging it out in Japan*, Tokyo: Kodansha.

Duke, V. and Crolley, L. (1996) *Football, Nationality and the State*, London: Longman.

Dyck, N. (1998) 'Sociology, anthropology, and sport studies: surveying the boundaries', paper presented at the XIV World Congress of Sociology, Montreal, Canada, July 1998.

Dyck, N. (ed.) (2000) *Games, Sports and Cultures: Anthropological Perspectives on Sport*, Oxford/New York: Berg.

Giulianotti, R., Bonney, N. and Hepworth, M. (eds) (1994) *Football, Violence and Social Identity*, London: Routledge.

Giulianotti, R. and Williams, J. (eds) (1994) *Game without Frontiers: Football, Identity and Modernity*, Aldershot: Arena Books.

Gruneau, R. (1983) *Class, Sports and Social Development*, Amherst, MA: University of Massachusetts Press.

The *Guardian*, various issues

Harvey, D. (1989) *The Condition of Postmodernity: An Enquiry into the Origins of Cultural Change*, Oxford: Basil Blackwell.

Hendry, J. (1997) 'Nature tamed: gardens as a microcosm of Japan's view of the world', in P. Asquith and A. Kalland (eds), *Japanese Images of Nature: Cultural Perspectives*, Richmond: Curzon Press, pp. 83–105.

Horne, J. (1996) '"Sakka" in Japan', *Media, Culture and Society* 18(4): 527–47.

——, (2000) 'Soccer in Japan: is "*wa*" all you need?' in G. Finn and R. Giulianotti (eds) *Football Culture: Local Contests, Global Visions*, London: Frank Cass.

Horowitz, I. (1995) 'Betto–san and the white rat: evaluating Japanese major league baseball managers vis-à-vis their American Counterparts', *International Review for the Sociology of Sport* 30(2): 165–78.

Ijiri, K. (1993) 'Soccer fever', *Japan Echo* 20(4): 77.

J League Official Guide (1997) Tokyo: Shogakkan.

Klein, A. (1991) *Sugarball: the American Game, the Dominican Dream*, New Haven, CT London: Yale University Press.

MacAloon, J. (1992) 'The ethnographic imperative in comparative olympic research', *Sociology of Sport Journal* 9(2): 104–30.

MacClancy, J. (ed.) (1996) *Sport, Identity and Ethnicity*, Oxford/New York: Berg.

Murphy, P., Williams, J. and Dunning, E. (1990) *Football on Trial*, London: Routledge.

The Nikkei Weekly, various issues.

Ogasawara H. (1997, 1998) personal communication.

Roden, D. (1980) 'Baseball and the quest for national dignity in Meiji Japan', *American Historical Review* 85(3): 511–34.

Sports World Japan, various issues.

Sugden, J. and Tomlinson, A. (eds) (1994) *Hosts and Champions: Soccer Culture, National Identities and the USA World Cup*, Aldershot: Arena Books.

Sugden, J. and Tomlinson, A. (1998) *FIFA and the Contest for World Football: Who Rules the Peoples' Game?* Cambridge: Polity Press.

Taylor, I. (1998) 'Contradictory aspects of contemporary football', paper given at the FIFA Conference The New Economics of World Football, CIM (International Media Centre), Paris, July.

Tomlinson, A. and Whannel, G. (1986) *Off the Ball: The Football World Cup*, London: Pluto Press.

Verducci, T. (1994) 'Away games', *Sports Illustrated*, 31, October, pp. 30–7.

Whannel, G. (1993) 'Sport and popular culture: the temporary triumph of process over Product', *Innovation* 6(3): 341–9.

Whiting, R. (1976) *The Chrysanthemum and the Bat*, New York: Dodd, Mead and Company.

——, (1989) *You Gotta Have 'wa'*, New York: Vintage Books.

Williams, J., Dunning, E. and Murphy, P. (1984) *Hooligans Abroad: The Behaviour and Control of English Fans in Continental Europe*, London: Routledge and Kegan Paul.

World Soccer, various issues, London: IPC Magazines.

Yano–Tsuneta Kinenkai (1993) *Nippon 1993/94: A Charted Survey of Japan*, Tokyo: Kokuseisha.

13 Japan in the world of Johan Huizinga[1]

Jan van Bremen

[N]o humane discipline, however rigorous, should fail to evoke from the student some sharper sense of the quandary of human existence; and if it does not do this it is trivial scholarship and morally insignificant.

Rodney Needham (1978: 3)

Histrionism and society

Play is truly universal. Adults and children play, in times of peace and war (Ben-Ari 1989; Feige & Ben-Ari 1991), in leisure and pain, in hospitals and churches (La Barre 1969 [orig. 1962]), even in extermination camps.[2] The Frenchman Jean-Gabriel de Tarde (1843–1904) made play coterminous with social efferves-cence, declaring: 'Social evolution begins and ends in games and fêtes'. This puts the ludic in the centre, albeit in a nineteenth century, evolutionary way. In this contribution, I should like to examine ludic phenomena in Japan, guided by the work of a more recent scholar, the Dutch historian Johan Huizinga (1872–1945). It may seem surprising. Huizinga's contributions to Japanese studies are negligi-ble, as shown below. His links to anthropology are more important. They are briefly sketched to illustrate his influence in the humanities. His studies of the ludic are the main subject of this chapter. My examples of ludic manifestations in Japan are based on reports and studies by folklorists and anthropologists and on personal observation.

Games and feasts are ludic by nature and abound in Japan where there are many contests, festivals, celebrations, and rites. A fair amount is known about such practices, both in the past and the present. The ludic is embodied in roles people play, or are made to play, and in guises, masks, foods, tools, events, and settings. Some feasts and games entail danger besides entertainment and labour. One instance is riding big tree-trunks down steep slopes in the *Mihashirasai* or *Onbashira* festival in the city of Suwa in Nagano (Moriya and Nakamaki 1991: 16–19). Life and limb may be lost and ludic injuries and deaths incurred. More often banquets and parties, both formal and informal, are the setting for ludic events (Itō 1984; Moeran 1986). Everyday games and leisure pursuits may be reckoned to the ludic domains open to all (Linhart 1984, 1995; Hendry 1990).

Johan Huizinga was intrigued by the ludic – the very word is his – and driven to explore the realms and boundaries of seriousness and play in human cultures and societies. One can see why his work had appeal and some reasons are given in passing. The main exercise is to appraise ludic manifestations in Japan in the light of Huizinga's work.

Huizinga set down his thoughts on the ludic four times between 1919 and 1938. In *Herfsttij der middeleeuwen* (Waning of the Middle Ages) of 1919 and *Erasmus* of 1924 he shows a keen interest in the ludic. The ludic is the sole topic of an address of 1933, and its enlargement, published in 1938, the book *Homo ludens*. These works became widely known only after the author's death in 1945. He wrote mostly in Dutch, his native tongue. He had to be translated into languages more in international use in order to be read abroad. Before I turn to the contents, a brief look at the English, German and Japanese editions sheds light on translations in the spread of ideas.

The *Waning of the Middle Ages* and *Homo Ludens* have been translated into nearly twenty languages (Lem 1993: 254). An examination shows that not every translation is based on the original edition, and that the translations and the originals are not always completely the same. Thus R.F.C. Hull wrote in the Translator's Notes in the English edition of *Homo Ludens*, published in 1949

> This edition is prepared from the German edition published in Switzerland, 1944, and also from the author's own English translation of the text, which he made shortly before his death. Comparison of the two texts shows a number of discrepancies and a marked difference in style; the translator hopes that the following version has achieved a reasonable synthesis.

Nonetheless, and there are other differences (see note 21), an important passage in the Dutch text is not found in the English edition of *Homo Ludens*. It is a key passage, to be cited further down, where Huizinga explains why he introduced the word 'ludic'. Does the English translation made by Huizinga contain this passage? Does the German edition have it too?

On appearance *Homo Ludens* was sent to the publishing house of Diederichs in Jena for a possible German translation. The authorities demanded that a passage, about the puerile nature of National Socialist meetings, be deleted from the German edition. Huizinga refused and withdrew the book. The German edition was published in Switzerland in 1944 (Lem 1993: 254). It is the edition translator Hull mentions in his notes.

There are two editions in Japanese. The first edition was published in 1963 and is based on the German translation. For the second edition, published in 1973, the translator also consulted R.F.C. Hull's English translation (in the American edition published in Boston in 1955), Corinna von Schendel's Italian translation of 1949, Cecile Seresia's French edition of 1951 and the Dutch edition (Takahashi 1973: 476).

In sum, the diffusion of Huizinga's works is wide. In the rendering of his ideas in so many different languages the aporias in the discourse are obvious, but perhaps inescapable in translations.

The world of play

Ceremonies and celebrations are frequently held in Japan. Besides, there is a wide variety of ludic spheres, such as fun parks and amusement quarters (*sakariba*), and a rich assortment of ludic spectacles and events, such as sports and festivals. Ludic manifestations met my eye when first in Japan, early in the 1970s. A Chinese anthropologist there at the time seemed also struck by the ludic elements in celebrations and feasts. He wrote with a keen sociological insight about the religious festivals, and the recreational activities of office workers, company personnel and other members of face-to-face groups:

> [A] Japanese phenomenon that impressed me was the ubiquitous song and dance processions in temples and streets during big festivals such as Obon, the ancestor festival. Young ladies and often little girls are very much a part of the song and dance routine during Obon. Their activities continue from early evening through the small hours of the morning. Processions during many other festivals feature men and mature ladies, four abreast, dressed almost uniformly in blue and white kimonos, joyfully singing, clapping, and dancing in unison through the streets thronged with gay [sic] spectators.
>
> However, these are temporary groups. Of even more interest are the recreational activities of those who work in the same department, bureau, or even the same clinic.
>
> (Hsu 1975: 14–15)

The recreational activities of the members of such corporate groups have since been studied in more detail, for example, in the case of a central Tokyo bakery given on p. 223.

Television offers games, sports and entertainment to society on a large scale. In the 1970s, sets were found in nearly every house, shop and office, usually switched on. Some histrionic presentations seen in the 1970s are still broadcast today, for instance, the 'Eight O'Clock Show' (*Hachiji da yo!*), a weekly programme popular with children. In a humorous and ludicrous fashion, actors play in scenes, taken from daily life, familiar to the audience of schoolchildren and members of their families. 'Bizarre' is a daily show for adults called the 'Eleven p.m. show'. Among the different tests of the show are masters of extraordinary lore, who will read a person's character, fate or other business from parts of the body, not so much the face or the palm but sooner the buttocks and breasts. One ludic performance, seen fresh in the field, was a merry programme broadcast on New Year's morning. Among a string of performers was a fart artist. He was asked about his art and to demonstrate his skills before the camera and microphone. He moved objects and piped tunes to the delight of his hosts, the studio audience and the family where I was.

In the 1980s, television appeared in shopping malls, stations, buses, ferries, taxis, airports and aeroplanes. New ludic devices were invented. A variety of portable and machine-bound games, videos, compact disks and virtual realities have appeared. They have serious and recreational uses and are worked in laboratories, offices, game arcades, waiting rooms, play tables and seats, homes and public spaces. Digital cities, the Internet, and cyberspace add yet other ludic spheres. Truly, from Heian times to the present, Japan has been an energetic play culture.

Folklorists distinguish several kinds of ludic figures in present and former times. One group is called *hayarigami*, short-lived gods who suddenly appear, gain fame, and after a brief spell, disappear again. There were many such *kami* in the Edo period (Miyata 1989), and there are many today (Miyata 1990). In the early summer of 1979, for example, the figure of a woman with a terrifyingly wide mouth (*kuchisake onna*) surfaced in the popular press. Sightings were first reported in central and west Japan, then spread to the east and the south. She would reveal herself to girls who had just entered secondary school. In the course of a few years, the solitary figure had developed into a group of three sisters. The story was that the oldest sister obtained her gaping mouth in a traffic accident. The second sister acquired her deformity through a mistake in plastic surgery. The youngest sister received her scar at the hands of her two elder sisters (Miyata 1990: 19–33).

Recently, a number of studies were made of ludic images in pre-industrial times (Komatsu 1992; Kondō 1990). A forerunner appeared in the 1960s, a pioneering study of the so-called earthquake prints (*namazue*) that circulated shortly after the Edo earthquake disaster of 1855. Some prints show the angered earthquake deity in the guise of a catfish or catfish-man. Others show eschatological (*yonaoshi*) scenes, where the catfish forces the rich to give up their hoarded wealth through the orifices of their bodies, and bestow it on the poor. The deity is a trickster, a character ludic by nature, who brings disaster and riches all at once (Ouwehand 1964; 1979).[3]

The earthquake god, in its guise as a huge catfish or catfish-man, is a ludic figure. Other traditional forms of extra-humans beings (*ijin*) are foxes and badgers, *tengu*, *oni*, and *kappa*. The offspring of sexual unions between *ijin* and humans may also be included (Komatsu 1985). A comparable view was taken of the arriving Westerners (*ijin*) and their streets (*ijingai*) and houses (*ijinkan*) in the foreign enclaves in the nineteenth century.

Representations of a one-sided, thus ludic figure are found the world over (Needham 1981). The shape is encountered in Japan in the form of one-sided carp, said to live in certain old temple or shrine ponds, and in the figure of the 'half man', a one-legged creature, thought to be a mountain god (Yanagita 1929: 52, 57, 59).

In rites and festivals of a calendrical nature, ancestors and visiting gods are the main guests in Japan. They often appear in ludic guises. At shrines and temples vendors make a ludic world with their persons, stalls and wares. The ludic is part of the self-presentation and performance of the members of ordinary Japanese groups. It is manifest in their language, costumes, signboards, business cards, and rites (Raz 1992). Some groups are particularly flamboyant in this respect, notably mobsters, members of motorized gangs, *takenoko*, and entertainers. Their lives are bound up with the theatres, amusement quarters, playgrounds, parks, game centres, sports arenas, bars, and resorts that dot the urban and rural landscape in Japan.

It is common to impose burdens on newcomers and trainees. Ludic burdens were a conspicious part of a six-day training programme conducted by an institute called the Ethics Retreat (*Rinri Gakuen*), founded in 1975, and situated at the foot of Mt Fuji at the time of research, which was between 1978 and 1981. The course included a contest, the marathon. On the evening before their departure, the trainees were made to put on plays. Only on this occasion were they allowed to poke fun openly at the institute, the course and the instructors (Kondo 1990: 76–115).

The appreciation of the play element in culture can give new insights to social behaviour. In Japan, established opinion sees the young drivers of customized motorcycles and cars, the members of 'violent driving tribes' (*bōsōzoku*) that emerged in the mid-1970s and 1980s, only as juvenile delinquents. But their lifestyles may be better understood as a social game, and their mischief as a form of fun and play to its practitioners (Sato 1991).[4]

At the time, the 1970s and 1980s, in different parts of the world, a revitalization of public celebrations and rituals was noted. New rites were created and old ones revived in places with a prospering economy. It has been argued for Europe, that the driving force behind the recovery or reappearance of many rites was an increase in the ludic element, at the expense of liturgy. It infused old rites with new life (Boissevain 1992). In other words, the fireworks became more important than the saints in religious festivals in rural Malta (Boissevain 1965).[5]

What about Asia? Has play come to prevail over liturgy in its industrial societies, too? In Japan, most nuptial rites are conducted in commercial wedding parlours, where one may see the patrons acting in ludic scenes, stage-mastered by the enterprise (Edwards 1989). Such parlours are widely found in Asia, in Korea, Taiwan, Singapore, Hong Kong. There is a corresponding increase in decorative expenditures in mortuary rites in Asian countries with a prosperous economy (Stefánsson 1991; Honda 1993).

One study explicitly suggested that ludic elements gained the upper hand over liturgical ones in the course of Japanese history. It argues that the transformation is seen in changes in the performance of the monkey rite. Until about the middle of the thirteenth century it was a magic rite, performed for the protection of horses. The monkey acted as mediator between animals and deities. 'Special status' people (read: outcastes) acted as their trainers. The transformation of the monkey rite, from sacred to secular performance, occurred in early-modern society, and the monkey had become a scapegoat by the end of the sixteenth century. The performance disappeared in the twentieth century, but was revived by special status people, who continue to be the monkey trainers, now as a clowning act for the amusement of passers-by and holiday-makers. The show may be likened to a mirror, where audiences look and laugh at a succession of ludic images, modelled after themselves (Ohnuki-Tierney 1987). Nevertheless, one wonders why the transformation took place at a time when horses were such a major concern, and remained so three more centuries? Was the magic protection offered by monkey rites no longer needed?

Ludic happenings were observed, early in the 1980s, in everyday life in a small family-owned bakery in central Tokyo. The employees' trip, and company outings, were ludic escapades. Another was the annual beer garden party, held by the owner on the roof of his factory. Here, the company's suppliers were ostensibly the guests. In reality, they were pressed into the role of performers, to amuse the owner and his staff (Kondo 1990).

Ritual clowning has been part of seasonal rites for visitor-gods, like those of the traditional *Namahage* type, where young men dress and behave like demons. A ludic facet of folklore studies is caught in a vignette, printed in a book about this festival, where the ethnographer writes:

> A high school teacher I met who prohibited his students from joining the festival because it involved drinking stated that there were quite a few students who showed an interest in joining the festival as a significant experience of their youth, something they would always remember. The same teacher, who is a local folklorist, showed his own interest in the festival by tape recording its varied sounds.
>
> (Yamamoto 1978: 127)

The fact is, that nearly every practice can be ridiculed. Daily activities, such as polishing and sweeping, are part of the cleaning operations habitually performed in Japanese schools, youth hostels, old people's homes, temples, and neighbourhoods. The wholehearted participation in these rituals of cleaning, and there is often little to clean, and the freely giving of one's time is required, if the worker is to maintain relationships with others, and clean soul and mind as well (Reader 1995). A grotesque of the belief, that the right attitude will bring the right result, unfolded in the Japanese Alps in the winter of 1972. In ritual punishment, twelve members of the radical United Red Army Faction (*Rengō sekigun*), nearly half the group, were beaten, stabbed and tortured to death by their comrades, for insufficient efforts to discard their bourgeois ways (Steinhoff 1992).

In the face of continuous shift and change, where possible the claims to tradition and the history of a rite should be studied. The question: how many times something has to be done for it to be a tradition, was playfully answered that judging by imperial wedding and funeral rites in twentieth century Japan, with a deadpan, 'at least once, possibly twice' (Smith 1995: 31).

Huizinga's sense of the ludic

Huizinga's explorations of the play element in culture were welcomed in the humane disciplines, though not without retort. An anthropologist judged that games and plays were not distinguished clearly enough by Huizinga. One could not differentiate well enough between a game and a ritual, a match and a war, between playing and gambling (van Baal 1981: 291). The critic himself did not hesitate to name the earliest forms of rites as he saw them: taboo, prayer, offering, sacrifice, divination, singing, dance, trance, and the dramatic presentation of myth are, with magic, the forms to consider (van Baal 1981: 169). One notes that about half of these forms are ludic in nature.[6]

Huizinga was not blind to conceptual problems. He reminded anthropologists of the fact that: 'We must always be on our guard against the deficiencies and differences of our means of expression. In order to form any idea at all of the mental habits of the savage [read: the other] we are forced to give them in our terminology'

(Huizinga 1949: 25). But if there are ludic elements and forms, is there a ludic emotion common to the participants? Does the term 'ludic' denote a universal inner state? Some ethnographers think that human nature is basically the same and presume that inner states have been adequately discriminated by the psychological vocabularies of their own languages. Yet research finds no universal inner states corresponding to a particular word or phrase (Needham 1972, 1981). That is why it is difficult, if not impossible, to translate sentiments or meanings from one language into others.

Wisely, Huizinga concentrated on play in its social forms: 'Play can only be a factor in culture in so far as it contains a social element: games, contests, displays, performances, dance and music, pastorales and masquerade are the materials that concern us.'[7] In the 1933 address, he distinguished play by some six features. A major characteristic is that play is not serious, in principle at least. Play has its times and places, moments of tension and release, display and drama. Play can be competitive, even turn into a fight. Play entails wagers and has winners and losers, honest players and cheats.[8]

Huizinga appears astonished over the fact that ethnologists and students of comparative religion paid so little attention to play. They even lacked an adequate vocabulary. That is why he introduced the word 'ludic' (Huizinga 1950 [1940]: 27):

> If I were to summarize my argument in theses, one would be that ethnology and related disciplines give too little place to the notion of play. For me, at any rate, the commonly used terminology with respect to play was not sufficient. I constantly felt the need for an adjective to *play*, that simply expresses 'what belongs to play or playing'. 'Playful' would not do, as it has too special a nuance of meaning. I should like to be permitted, therefore, to introduce the word *ludic*. Although the presumed basic form is unknown in Latin, in French the word is found as *ludique* in psychological tracts.[9]

Huizinga saw a serious shortcoming in the explanation of a game that ignored the players:

> Most of these explanations do not ask the question, or only secondary, what and how play itself is, what it means to the players themselves.[10]

This advice is echoed in the behest heard above to consider perpetrators and their deeds not only in terms of crimes or misdemeanours but also in terms of games and play. Huizinga recognized play as 'an absolute primary category of life, a totality'[11] and 'in its many concrete forms itself, as social structure'[12] (Huizinga 1950 [1940]: 32).

Huizinga pointed out formal identities of ritual play. One of the 'considerable correspondences between ritual and ludic forms'[13] is the drawing of boundaries around the place where the action is:

> Formally speaking, there is no distinction whatever between marking out a space for a sacred purpose and marking it out for purposes of sheer play.

The turf, the tennis-court, the chessboard, even pavement-hopscotch cannot formally be distinguished from the temple or the magic circle.

(Huizinga 1949: 20)[14]

There are further resemblances. Both proclaim a standstill to ordinary life. Both are limited as to time and place and combine rules with freedom.[15] Rites and plays have more features in common (Huizinga 1949: 21–22), for instance, they may be repeated (1950 [1940]: 39–40: 71).

The historian did not think much of the theories in his time, calling them contradictory and partial. He was fascinated by real games and play:

> Theory doesn't help us much in reaching a satisfactory determination of the concept of play. The whole category is strangely intangible. It is difficult to delimit it well, one can hardly demarcate it from myth and cult, for instance. The most essential properties of play can be ascertained at best, not explained . . . [16]

The first task in Huizinga's view was to describe the formal properties of the social and cultural forms of the ludic. Doing so in a comparative way, he found that 'As different as all these forms may be, so similar are they the world over.'[17] Huizinga's identification of play, and his analysis of social forms, is insightful and meaningful to students of humankind.

Today the play element in culture is still insufficiently understood. It was said, for instance, that '[t]he failure to find in one's theoretical models of humankind a place for fantasies is one of the factors responsible for the failure to link theories of culture, and thus also of religion, to theories of other aspects of human beings and their various manifestations' (Elias 1991: 77).[18] A new vocabulary is being made to better grasp these matters. It speaks of cerebral memory images, synthetic images, and levels of symbolic integration, and about the relationships among reality adequate symbols, fantasy symbols, wish and fear symbols, and others (Kilminster 1991: xv).

The Japanese illustrations in *Homo ludens*

Huizinga took his material from world history and his examples from a wide range of cultures, including Japan. In *Homo ludens*, Huizinga refers eight times to that country. His remarks are based on sources in Western languages. The first reference is in the chapter, 'The play-concept as expressed in language'. Having asked Johannes Radher, then the professor of Japanese in Leiden, Huizinga states that play is expressed in Japanese by the verb *asobu* (to play), and seriousness by the noun *majime* (earnestness).[19] Radher also pointed out to Huizinga the use of play-language (*asobasekotoba*) by women, and the existence of notions of life as play, such as the masking of aristocratic life behind play (Huizinga 1949: 34–5; 1950 [orig. 1940] 62–3).

The second reference is brief, a mere mentioning of Japan as a related case. In the chapter 'Play and contest as civilizing functions', the reference is to seasonal contests, tournaments of songs and games between the young men and girls of a group at the spring or autumn festivals, found in Tonkin, Tibet and Japan (1949: 55–6, 1950: 84).

The third reference, in the same chapter, is the first of three references to Japanese chivalry:

> In every archaic community that is healthy, being based on the tribal life of warriors and nobles, there will blossom an ideal of chivalry and chivalrous conduct, whether it be in Greece, Arabia, Japan or medieval Christendom.
>
> (1949: 64)[20]

The fourth reference to Japan, in the chapter 'Play and war', is also to chivalry, but now in the writer's own day:

> It was reported by the Domei agency that after the capture of Canton in December, 1938, the Japanese commander proposed to Chiang Kai-shek that the latter should fight an engagement, which would be decisive, in the plains of Southern China for the purpose of saving his military honour, and then acknowledge the decision as terminating the 'incident'.
>
> (1949: 99)[21]

The fifth reference, in the same chapter, is again to chivalry in medieval times in Japan, Europe and the Muslim world (1949: 102).[22]

The sixth reference is to poetry in Japan. The chapter 'Play and poetry' says that, 'Originally the haikai must have been a game of chain-rhymes begun by one player and continued by the next' (1949: 124).[23] The seventh reference, in the same chapter, is also to poetry and has it that 'Right up to 1868 the Japanese used to compose the weightiest part of a State document in poetic form' (1949: 127).[24]

The eighth reference is to the arts. In the chapter 'Western civilization *sub specie ludi*', it says: 'Style and fashion, however, and hence art and play, have seldom blended so intimately as in Rococo, except perhaps in Japanese culture' (1949: 186).[25]

As *Homo ludens* saw the light in 1938, a reference is made to Japan, albeit indirect, as a breaker of treaties. Take Japanese Micronesia, for instance. The Caroline, Marshall and Mariana Islands were taken from Germany in 1914 by the Japanese Navy. The League of Nations placed the territory under Japanese mandate in 1920. When the Japanese government withdrew from the League of Nations over Manchuria in 1933 it annexed the mandated islands. In the chapter, 'The play-element in contemporary civilization', Huizinga states of modern nations:

> Now this is our difficulty: modern warfare has, on the face of it, lost all contact with play. States of the highest cultural pretensions withdraw from the comity of nations and shamelessly announce that '*pacta non sunt servanda*'
>
> (1949: 210)[26]

Maskers and spoilsports

Erasmus taught the ground rule of seriousness and play in one phrase, found in the 'Praise of Folly' (*Encomium moriae*) of 1509. It was repeated by Huizinga in the biography: 'Whoever tears off the masks from the game of life, is thrown out' (1950 [orig. 1924]: 67).[27] It tells that false play and hypocrisy are not the worst crimes; the true miscreant is the one who quits or changes the rules of the game. Huizinga said more about this fact in *Homo ludens*:

> The player who trespasses against the rules or ignores them is a 'spoil-sport'. The spoil-sport is not the same as the false player, the cheat; for the latter pretends to be playing the game and, on the face of it, still acknowledges the magic circle. It is curious to note how much more lenient society is to the cheat than to the spoil-sport. This is because the spoil-sport shatters the play-world itself. By withdrawing from the game he reveals the relativity and fragility of the play-world in which he had temporarily shut himself with others. He robs the play of its *illusion* a pregnant word which means literally 'in-play' (from *ilusio, illuder* or *inludere*). Therefore he must be cast out, for he threatens the existence of the play-community . . . In the world of seriousness, too, the cheat and the hypocrite have always had an easier time of it than the spoil-sports, here called apostates, heretics, innovators, prophets, conscientious objectors, etc. It sometimes happens, however, that the spoil-sports in their turn make a new community with rules of its own. The outlaw, the revolutionary, the cabbalist or member of a secret society, indeed heretics of all kinds are of a highly associative if not sociable disposition, and a certain element of play is prominent in all their doings.
>
> (1949: 11–12)

Huizinga's studies of the play element in culture and society have been widely translated and published in a number of editions that are not completely the same. How much it matters, in the transmission of ideas on the ludic, is hard to say. The fact remains that Huizinga's work has been widely received as a guide in histrionic worlds. Ludic manifestations become clearer in the light of his notion of play. If social life is bound by games and feasts, it is also bound by ludic forces more horrendous, such as forms of ritual suicide and self-mummification. Japan, as a ludic culture in a high degree, makes up a fertile testing ground in both directions.

Notes

1 This chapter issues from papers read at the Sixth Triennial Conference of the European Association for Japanese Studies, Sixth Session of the Japan Anthropology Workshop, in September 1991 in Berlin, and the symposium, 'The Ludic - forces of generation and fracture', in the Universität Heidelberg, Seminar für Ethnologie, in October 1993.
2 George Eisen, 'The game of death and the dynamics of atrocity', paper read in the

symposium: 'The ludic – forces of generation and fracture' Universität Heidelberg, Seminar für Ethnologie, 25–31 October 1993.

3 The 1964 edition is illustrated. More reproductions are found in the 1979 edition, some in colour.

4 Some scholars come to advocate a 'ludic methodology', for instance Droogers (1994).

5 The analysis itself, and the sweeping conclusion for the whole of Europe, has been challenged (Roelofs 1995).

6 Van Baal (1966) made a monumental study of the ludic in his almost 1000-page ethnography of the Marind-Anim culture of South New Guinea, of which some 300 pages are about myth and some 500 about rites.

7 Factor van cultuur kan het spel slechts zijn, voorzover het een sociaal element bevat: wedstrijden, kampspelen, vertooningen, opvoeringen, dans en muziek, herdersspel en maskerade vormen de stof die ons aangaat' (Huizinga 1950 [orig 1933]: 5).

8 het is in beginsel *niet-ernst*; meer specifieke kenmerken in zeer veel gevallen aanwezig: (1) van bijna alle spel, zoodra het collectief is, een wisselwerking inhoudt van mensch of mensch, kan gezegd worden, dat het een element bevat van *binding* en *ontknooping*. Het spel schept, tijdelijk en plaatselijk, een eigen, uitzonderlijke, omheinde wereld binnen de gewone, waarin de spelers zich naar eigen, dwingende wet bewegen, totdat die wet zelf hen verlost. Het spel *bant*, dat wil zeggen, het spreekt een tooverwoord, dat dwingt. Het spel *boeit*. (2) het spel *vertoont* iets. Vertoonen is verwezenlijken, verwezenlijken binnen die eigen, tijdelijk geldige wereld, door het spel zelf geschapen. Het spel is een *handeling, dromenon, drama*. Hier liggen de gewichtigste verbindingen van spel en cultus. (v. bremen: merk op dat cultus voor Huizinga met het goddelijke, met het heilige verbonden is). Huizinga wijst op de reeks en overgangen van: cultus, spel en feest. (3) niet doorlopend aanwezig, maar wel van gewicht: het spel is *strijd*. Zich meten, wedijveren, om het mooist pronken. (4) aan het spel als strijd is een bijzonder element verbonden, namelijk de inzet, de wedde. Men speelt òm iets: om het intreden van een kosmisch gevolg, als het spel cultus is; waar het dit niet is, om een bruid, om een koninkrijk, om zijn hals of om geld. Het spel moet ernst zijn. (5) het spel schept *stijl*. Rhythme, herhaling, cadans, refrein, gesloten vorm, akkoord en harmonie, alles attributen van het spel, ze zijn ook alle constituenten van den stijl. (6) wat *stijl* heet in het aesthetische, heet in het ethische *order* en *trouw*. Spel veronderstelt *associatie*, in den besten zin van het woord (Huizinga 1950 [orig. 1933]: 5–7, italics JvB).

9 Indien ik mijn betoog in stellingen samenvatte, zou een er luiden, dat de ethnologie en de haar verwante wetenschappen aan het begrip spel te weinig plaats inruimen. Mij was althans de algemeen gebruikelijke terminologie ten opzichte van het spel niet voldoende. Ik had voortdurend behoefte aan een adjectief bij *spel*, dat eenvoudig uitdrukt 'wat tot spel of spelen behoort'. '*Speelsch*' kon daartoe niet dienen, het heeft een te speciale nuance van beteekenis. Men veroolove mij daarom het woord *ludiek* in te voeren. Al is de veronderstelde grondvorm in het Latijn onbekend, in het Fransch komt het woord als *ludique* in psychologische geschriften voor' (Huizinga 1950: 27).

10 De meeste verklaringen houden zich met de vraag, wat en hoe het spel op zich zelf is, wat het voor de spelers zelf beteekent, slechts in tweede instantie bezig (Huizinga 1950 [1940]: 29).

11 een volstrekt primaire categorie van het leven, een totaliteit (Huizinga 1950 [orig 1940]: 30).

12 in zijn menigvuldige concrete vormen zelf, als sociale structuur (Huizinga 1950 [1940]: 31).

13 De verregaande gelijksoortigheid tusschen ritueele en ludieke vormen (Huizinga 1950 [1940]: 47).

14 Formeel is de functie van deze afbakening tot gewijd doel of tot louter spel volkomen dezelfde. De renbaan, het tenniscourt, de hinkelbaan, het schaakbord verschillen flinctioneel niet van den tempel of den toovercirkel (1950 [1940]: 48).

15 De uitschakeling van het gewone leven, . . . , de tijdelijke en plaatselijke begrensdheid, het samengaan van strenge bepaaldheid en echte vrijheid, dat zijn de voornaamste gemeenschappelijke trekken van spel en feest (1950 [1940]: 50).

16 Tot een bevredigende bepaling van het begrip spel brengt ons de theorie weining nader. De geheele categorie spel blijft merkwaardig onvast. Zij laat zich niet goed afgrenzen, men kan haar bijvoorbeeld uit die van mythus en cultus nauwelijks afscheiden. De essentieelste eigenschappen van het spel laten zich hoogsten constateren, niet verklaren (Huizinga [orig 1933]: 7–8).

17 Zoo verscheiden al die vormen zijn mogen, zoo gelijksoortig vindt men ze over de geheele wereld terug (Huizinga 1950 [1940]: 161).

18 Elias saw Mozart as a man midway between a bounded artisan and a free artist, a ludic role new to the society at the time (1993; orig. 1991).

19 Linhart (1984: 209) remarked: 'Had Huizinga been able to read Japanese, he would have discovered that in Japan, as in many other cultures, play was something sacred'.

20 In iedere conceptie van archaïsche levensvorming op den grondslag van krijgshaftig en adellijk stamleven groeit een ideaal van ridderschap en ridderlijkheid, hetzij bij Grieken, Arabieren, Japanners of middeleeuwsche Christenen. (1950: 92).

21 This anecdote is found in the text of the English edition, but no source is given. In the Dutch edition, the text is in a footnote. The Japanese news agency Domei is cited in a Dutch newspaper (1950: 127, note 3) as the source: 'Volgens de Japansche persagentuur Domeik [sic] zond de Japansche opperbevelhebber na de inneming van Kanton aan Tsjang Kai Sjek een uitdaging, om in de Zuid-Chineesche vlakte een beslissende slag te leveren, daarmee zijn krijgsmanseer te redden, en zich bij de uitspraak van het zwaard neer te leggen (N.R.C. 13. XII 1938).

22 1950: 130, 131, 132.

23 1950: 152–3.

24 1950: 156 In Japan bleef nog tot de omwenteling van 1868 de kern van ernstige staatsstukken in dichtvorm opgesteld.

25 1950: 217.

26 1950: 243 Juist echter de moderne oorlog heeft schijnbaar elke aanraking met het spel verloren. Hoog gecultiveerde staten trekken zich uit de gemeenschap van het volkenrecht geheel terug, en belijden zonder schaamte een *pacta non sunt servanda*.

27 Wie het spel des levens de maskers afrukt, wordt eruit gesmeten.

Bibliography

Ben-Ari, E. (1989) 'Masks and soldiering: the Israeli army and the Palestinian uprising', *Cultural Anthropology* 4(4): 372–89.

Bergsma, W. (1981) *Johan Huizinga en de culturele antropologie*, Groningen: Rijksuniversiteit Groningen, Instituut voor Culturele Antropologie.

Boissevain, F. (1965) *Saints and Fireworks: Religion and Politics in Rural Malta*, London: The Athlone Press.

Boissevain, J.F. (ed.) (1992) *Revitalizing European Rituals*. London: Routledge.

Droogers, A. (1994) 'Turner, spel, en de verklaring van religie', *Antropologische Verkenningen*, 13/4: 31–45.

Edwards, Walter (1989) *Modern Japan through its Weddings. Gender, Person and Society in Ritual Portrayal*, Stanford, California: California University Press.

Elias, N. (1991) *The Symbol Theory*, London: Sage Publications.

Elias, N. (1993) (orig. 1991) *Mozart. Zur Soziologie eines Genies. Herausgegeben von Michael Schröter*, Frankfurt: Suhrkamp.

Feige, M. and E. Ben-Ari (1991) 'Card Games and an Israeli Army Unit: an interpretive case study', *Armed Forces and Society* 17(3): 429–48.

Hendry, J. (1990) 'Children's contests in Japan', in: A. Duff-Cooper (ed.) *Contests, Cosmos, The Yearbook of Traditional Cosmology Society*, vol. 6, Edinburgh: Edinburgh University Press, pp. 81–93.

Honda, H. (1993) '*Haka wo baikai to shita sosen no "tsuibo" Kankoku nanseibu ichi nôson ni okeru san-il no jitsurei kara*' (Commemorating ancestors: Remaking graves in a mountain village in Southwest Korea), in *Minzokugaku Kenkyū* 58/2: 142–69.

Hsu, L.K. (1975) *Iemoto: The Heart of Japan*, New York: Schenkman Publishing Company.

Huizinga, J. (1950) (orig. 1924) 'Erasmus', in J. Huizinga, *Verzamelde werken, Deel 6*, Haarlem: Tjeenk Willink, pp. 3–194.

Huizinga, J. (1950) (orig. 1933) *Over de grenzen van spel en ernst in de cultuur. Rede door Huizinga als Rector Magnificus gehouden op de 358e Dies Natalis der Leidsche Universiteit*, 8 Februari 1933, H.D. Tjeenk Willink and Zoon NN, Haarlem 1933, reprinted in J. Huizinga, *Verzamelde werken, Deel 5*, Haarlem: Tjeen Willink, pp. 3–25.

Huizinga, J. (1950) (orig. 1938) *Homo ludens. Proeve eener bepaling van het spelelement der cultuur.* Haarlem: H.D. Tjeenk Willink and Zoon, 1940 (orig. 1938), reprinted in: J. Huizinga, *Verzamelde werken*. Deel 5. Haarlem: H.D. Tjeenk Willink and Zoon.

Huizinga, J. (1949) *Homo ludens: A study of the play-element in culture*, trans. by R.F.C. Hull, London: Routledge and Kegan Paul.

Huizinga, J. (1973) *Homo ludens*, trans. H. Takahashi, Tokyo: Chûô bunko.

Itō, M. (1984) *Utage to Nihon bunka. Hikaku minzokugakuteki approach* (Feasts and Japanese Culture in a comparative anthropological approach), Tokyo: Chûô kôronsha.

Komatsu, K. (1985) '*Nihon mukashibanashi ni okeru irui konin*' (Inter-species marriages in old Japanese tales), *Nihongo/Nihon bunka kenkyū ronshú*, no. 3, pp. 163–88.

Komatsu, K. (1992) *Nihon yōkai ibunroku* (A collection of unusual stories about Japanese monsters), Tokyo: Shogakukan.

Komatsu, K. (1992) *Ikai junrei* (Pilgrimage to the other world), Tokyo: Seigensha.

Kondo, D.K. (1990) *Crafting Selves. Power, Gender and Discourses of Identity in a Japanese workplace*, Chicago University of Chicago Press.

Kondō, M. (ed.) (1990) *Niho no yōkai* (Monsters of Japan), Tokyo: Kawada shobō shinsha.

La Barre, W. (1969) (orig. 1962). *They Shall take up Serpents. Psychology of the Southern Snake-Handling Cult*, New York: Schocken.

Lem, A. van der (1993), *Johan Huizinga. Leven en werk in beelden en documenten*. Amsterdam: Wereldbibliotheek.

Linhart, S. (1984)) 'Some observations on the development of the "typical" Japanese attitudes towards working hours and leisure', in Daniels, Gordan (ed.), *Europe Interprets Japan*, Tenderden: Paul Norbury Publications, pp. 207–14; 269–70.

Linhart, S. (1995) 'Rituality in the *ken* game', in van Bremen, J. and Martinez, D.P. (eds) *Ceremony and Ritual in Japan*, London: Routledge, pp. 38–66.

Locher, G.W. (1958) '*Huizinga en de culturele antropologie*' in *Bijdragen tot de Taal-, Land- en Volkenkunde*, deel 114: 170–91.

Miyata, N. (1989) *Edo no chiisana kamigami* (Edo's little gods), Tokyo: Seidosha.

——, (1990) *Yōkai no minzokugaka* (The folklore studies of monsters), Tokyo: Iwanami Shoten.

Moeran, B. (1986) 'One over the seven: sake drinking in a Japanese pottery community', in Hendry, J. and Webber, J. (eds) *Interpreting Japanese Society. Anthropological Perspectives* Oxford: JASO Occasional Papers, no. 5, pp. 226–42.

Moriya, T. and Nakamaki, H. (1991) *Nihon no matsuri. Matsuri no saundosukeepu* (Japanese festivals. The sound scape of festivals), Tokyo: Maruzen.

Needham, R. (1972) *Belief, Language, and Experience*, Oxford: Basil Blackwell.

—— (1980) 'Unilateral figures', in *Reconnaissances*, Toronto: University of Toronto Press.

Needham, R. (1981) 'Inner states as universals', in *Circumstantial Deliveries*, Berkeley, CA: University of California Press, pp. 53–71.

Ouwehand, C. (1964) *Namazu-e and Their Themes. An Interpretative Approach to Some Aspects of Japanese Folk Religion* Leiden: E.J. Brill.

Ouwehand, C. (1979) *Namazue. Minzokuteki sōzōryoku no sekai* (Earthquake prints). The world and the power of folk imagination, trans. K. Komatsu, S. Nakazawa, Y. Iijima and S. Furuie, Tokyo: Serika shobō.

Raz, J. (1992) 'Self-presentation and performance in the yakuza way of life. Fieldwork with a Japanese underworld group', in *Ideology and practice in modern Japan.* (eds) R. Goodman and K. Refsing, London: Routledge, pp. 210–34.

Reader, R. (1995) 'Cleaning floors and sweeping the mind: cleaning as a ritual process', in *Ceremony and Ritual in Japan*, London: Routledge, pp. 227–45.

Roelofs, G. (1995) 'Rituele veranderingen in Europa. Een kritiek op Boissevains opvattingen over rituele revitalisatie', *Etnofoor*, VIII (1): 83–101.

Sata, I. (1991) *Kamikaze biker. Parody and Anomy in Affluent Japan*, Chicago: The University of Chicago Press.

Smith, R.J. (1995) 'Wedding and funeral ritual: analysing a moving target', in *Ceremony and ritual in Japan*, London: Routledge, pp. 25–37.

Stefánsson, H. (1991) 'The art of moving house to heaven and absolving spirits from defilement: on Taiwanese forms of funerary accessories' *Bulletin of the Cultural and Natural Sciences in in Osaka Gakuin University*, 23–4: 91–114.

Steinhoff, P.G. (1992) 'Death by defeatism and other fables: the social dynamics of the Rengō Sekigun purge', in Sugiyama Lebra, Takie (ed.) *Japanese Social Organisation*, Honolulu: University Hawaii Press, pp. 195–224.

van Baal, J. (1966) *Dema. Description and analysis of Marind-Anim culture (South New Guinea)*, The Hague: Martinus Nijhoff.

van Baal, J. (1981) *Man's Quest for partnership. The Anthropological Foundation of Ethics and Religion*, Assen: Van Gorcum.

van Bremen, J. and Martinez, D.P. (eds) (1995) *Ceremony and Ritual in Japan: Religious Practices in an Industrialized Society*, London: Routledge.

Yamamoto, Y. (1978) *The Namahage. A festival in the Northeast of Japan*, Philadelphia, PA: Institute for the Study of Human Issues.

Yanagita K. (1929) *Daishikō no yûrai* (The origins of Kôbô Daishi legends), in *Nihon Densetsushū* A collection of Japanese legends, Tokyo: Arusu.

14 The countryside reinvented for urban tourists

Rural transformation in the Japanese *muraokoshi* movement

Okpyo Moon

Introduction

Rural deterioration is a global phenomenon faced by almost all industrializing and urbanizing societies in the world. In Japan, it is indicated by the fact that the rural population that occupied well over 70 per cent of the total population in the 1920s has decreased to just over 20 per cent in the early 1990s. Similarly, the proportion of those engaged in the primary industries (agriculture, fishery and forestry) has decreased from 19.9 per cent of the total population in 1955 to 2.1 per cent in 1993. The problem of the rural population drain and the consequent economic decline was so seriously felt that the Japanese government issued a special law concerning underpopulated areas in 1970. This introduced various measures to improve rural conditions, such as a redistribution of industrial centres, the introduction of special tax concessions and other financial subsidies. Through these measures, it was hoped to create more job opportunities, to raise the overall welfare level and thereby to reverse, or at least to slow down, population flow from rural to urban areas. Despite these efforts, however, the population flow from rural to urban areas has continued and the number of villages and towns (*machi/mura*) officially designated as 'underpopulated areas' (*kasochiiki*) and therefore believed to need special protection, reached 1151 in 1980, nearly 40 per cent of the number of all such units in Japan (Kawamata 1985: 21). Moreover, the fact that most emigrants from rural areas were young and economically active aggravated the problem of population ageing. For instance, while the national average of the proportion of those aged 65 or over was about 12 per cent in 1990, in rural areas, it is often over one third of the whole population.

These decaying rural conditions constituted the main reason for the rise of the *muraokoshi*, or the village revitalization movement, in Japan. These movements, that began to be observed from the late 1970s, are various forms of self-help efforts initiated by those living in the countryside to revitalize their economy and society. As I have noted elsewhere (Moon 1997a), the development of the tourist industry has been one of the most widely adopted strategies toward this end and numerous ski resorts, golf courses or multi-purpose complexes were constructed to provide rural households with supplementary income. In villages that are thought to be unsuited for these facilities, people have resorted to 'regional character' to attract tourists, emphasizing qualities such as lifestyle, speciality products, industry, nature, culture, history, folklore, and so forth. In short, everything that is considered unique to the locality, and that might attract the attention of urban tourists, has been turned into a commodity and exploited.

What concerns us here is the fact that, whatever form it takes, the developmental process of this new type of rural tourism involves a re-definition of the countryside and of those who live there *vis-à-vis* the cities and urban folks. While the dominant image of rural areas used to be as a place for hardworking farmers and cultivated paddy fields, now, as a tourist destination, it has been turned into a place for leisure, play and consumption. The rural landscape and its local character and identity has been reconstructed and represented in a way to satisfy the tastes of the urban tourists, whether it be for nostalgia, a concern for nature, historic flavour, exoticism, traditionalism or authenticity. The countryside is therefore no longer represented as a place for farming, dirty hard work, poverty, backwardness, oppressive 'feudal' values, ignorance and irrationality, as found in the discourses of modernization, but as an ultimate source of Japanese identity that preserves its unique history, culture and unpolluted nature.

In contrast to previous revitalizing efforts initiated by the national and local authorities that were largely focused upon economic revitalization, *muraokoshi* movements of the 1980s have rather adopted the character of an identity movement. Local people are attempting to re-define the meaning of their existence in a postindustrialized setting in which their position as producers and suppliers of food is being constantly undermined. Those who live in the Japanese countryside nowadays can no longer be considered as an occupational group engaged primarily in agriculture (or in forestry and fishing). More than 90 per cent of Japanese farm households are the so-called *kenkyo nōka*, or part-time farmers, in that they have significant sources of income outside agriculture. There are also among the rural residents many who are not engaged in agriculture at all.

For many of them, the major reason for having remained in or having returned to their villages is to inherit their rural households, and to take care of their parents, and most of *muraokoshi* movements have been initiated by these people. It seems, therefore, that economic motivation only partly accounts for their activities. Equally important is the motivation of constructing a new identity that would help them to overcome not only the material disadvantages of rural decline but also their self-conception as losers in industrialized and urbanized modern Japan. The *muraokoshi* movement is often defined as one that enables rural residents to take pride in (*hokori to suru*) what they are and what they have. As rural ways have always been described as backward compared to urban ways in the modernization discourses of the 1960s and 1970s, what is intended in the *muraokoshi* movement may be considered as a move in the opposite direction. As one of the oft-cited *muraokoshi* catch phrases expresses it, this is an act of 'taking a reverse grip on depopulation (*kaso o sakate ni toru*)'.

The question of how views of urban and rural life are changing, and in what ways such changes can be seen as reflecting overall changes in the value orientation and lifestyles of Japanese people at large, are what the present chapter seeks to examine through a consideration of the *muraokoshi* movement. In particular, it will focus on how Japanese rural society has been transformed in the process of constructing and presenting a new concept of countryside in the development of the rural tourism that has constituted a major part of most village revitalization attempts.

Changes in the patterns of Japanese domestic tourism

Tourism has a very long history in Japan (Ishimori 1989). Since ancient times, travelling has offered spiritual and aesthetic resources for many well-known literary works, and travelling in the form of religious pilgrimage to famous Shintō shrines and Buddhist temples had developed among the aristocrats as early as the tenth century AD. During the Tokugawa (or Edo) period (1603–1868), the pilgrimage tradition became popular among the lower classes, and religious associations known as *kō*, with the specific purpose of supporting pilgrimage to a shrine or a temple, were formed throughout the country, including remote villages. With the abolition in the Meiji period (1868–1912) of the post station (*sekishō*) and transit permit (*tsukō tegata*) system that controlled people's movements during the early modern period, the amount of travelling increased greatly. The development of a modern railway system no doubt contributed further to this increase.

During this period, one may also note considerable diversification in the form of recreational travel (Ashiba 1994: 31–2). For instance, while pilgrimage, sightseeing and relaxing in hot springs had been the major purposes of recreational travel until that time, around the beginning of the last century seaside and mountain resorts began to appear, and areas like Karuizawa were developed as summer homes for the upper classes. Under the influence of the foreigners, mountains that had mostly been objects of religious belief and pilgrimage emerged as places for enjoying natural beauty and for mountaineering.

Despite this diversification, the pattern of travelling in groups has remained dominant for most Japanese tourists, both in domestic and overseas journeys (Shirahata 1996). The practice of group tourism in Japan has its origin in the Middle Ages in the tradition of pilgrimage that continued and was popularized in the Edo period. Later, during the early Meiji period, regular trips were institutionalized in such modern organizations as schools, firms, and other workplaces for the purposes of learning, spiritual training or the fostering of group solidarity. This has effectively contributed to a continuation of this dominant travelling pattern as a universal 'rite of passage' and established it as an essential part of national culture. The sight of a large group of people travelling in rented buses, visiting well-known scenic spots, and relaxing in hot springs has been known until recently as the most prevalent pattern of Japanese domestic tourism. Hence, one observer writes,

> For Japanese, travelling is a collective activity. It does not mean that there have been no individual trips. There were also people who travelled alone and such journeys were often charged with heavy sentimentalism. But, one may say that the very fact that special sentiments accompanied an act of travelling alone means that such an act is unusual [in Japanese culture]. Travelling alone

without specific destination is a form of journey that can be traced back to
Bashō and Shaigyō in the past. It may be a pattern that is perhaps envied by
many Japanese but that is still considered odd when it comes to oneself
practising it. Most of us travel in groups or with groups at the back of our minds.
An act of getting away from one's own community is very difficult [for the
Japanese], but we cannot but notice that even travelling that appears to be an
opportunity of getting away functions as an element that strengthens the groups'
solidarity. This is indeed an important starting point to think about Japanese
culture.

(Kato 1976: 181)

There have nevertheless been certain changes in the form of Japanese group
tourism. Japanese domestic tourism has greatly increased in quantity since the early
1960s along with the rapid economic growth of the country. But the increases were
mostly comprised of those travelling in family groups and in small groups of close
acquaintances instead of in large coach tours. Consequently, the big tour groups that
consisted of more than 50 per cent of all travellers in 1966 decreased to 34.7 per
cent in 1976 while those travelling in family groups increased from 24.7 per cent to
34.1 per cent and those travelling in small groups from 24.7 per cent to 26.3 per cent
during the same period (Shirahata 1996: 208–9).

Data like these are indicative of a change in the pattern of Japanese domestic tourism and leisure style. In the past, the commonest pattern had been that
individual members of a family went out on a recreational journey separately,
with the members of a community or organization that each of them respectively belonged to. Therefore, the father might travel with his workmates in
the company, mother with members of a housewives' association, and the son/
daughter with his/her school. However, family holidays apparently emerged as
a new form of leisure around the 1970s.[1] A tendency has also been noted, especially among younger members of society, that a growing number of people
prefer individual or small group tours to that of a large party in which they have
to follow a pre-arranged schedule and individual action is limited (Moeran
1983: 104–5).

The emergence of rural tourism in Japan is closely related to these changes in the
interests and behaviour of Japanese domestic tourism. As we have noted, since the
1960s, the hitherto predominant pattern of visiting well-known places in large
parties has decreased and small group tours for sports or other recreational purposes
have emerged as a new pattern. Along with this, one may also note a decrease in
the traditional *monomiryūsan* type of domestic tourism that usually comprised visiting
a sacred place, enjoying a scenic landscape and relaxing at recreational areas
(Kanzaki 1991). Instead, those who seek pure recreational activities such as skiing,
golf, mountaineering, walking, or simply encountering (*fureai*) nature and people
have increased. It was these new types of domestic tourists that became the main
targets of developers of rural tourism.

As we have seen, many villages became abandoned and forgotten in the process
of industrialization and urbanization, and this was especially so in remote mountain

areas. On the other hand, the demand for leisure and recreation has constantly expanded along with the rapid economic growth in the country since the mid-1950s. The need has been increasingly aggravated by problems of over-population, pollution of air and water, a shortage of water and green spaces, and so forth, in the metropolitan areas where more than three-quarters of the population is concentrated. This urbanized population began to view the countryside in a different light. Rural villages were no longer seen as suppliers of farm products, timber, silk cocoons and a never-ending supply of migratory labour force, but rather as a source of unpolluted water, abundant verdure, health and repose, spiritual recuperation for an urbanized population suffering from crowded and 'dehumanized' living conditions. The construction of motorways running through woodland areas (*supa-rindo*) throughout the country in the 1960s and 1970s has also considerably improved access to the hitherto remote mountain villages. The villages have therefore come to be sought after by urban residents as places of rest, repose, leisure, play and recreation, and those coming to villages for these purposes has begun to increase.

One of the earlier patterns of rural tourism development in Japan was to be found in sports resorts located in villages in mountain areas that were decreasing in population more rapidly than those in the plains (Moon 1989; Matsumura 1997). With the rapid decline of forestry and other mountain-related industries after the Second World War, much communal land was sold or leased out to supplement the declining economy (*Sanson Keizai Kenkyūsho* (ed.) 1994). Thus, ski resorts that began to appear in the 1960s greatly increased in the 1970s. The increase in the 1980s was more remarkable, however, as the government took resort development as the major strategy against the depopulation problem. For instance, the number of ski lifts in the country increased from 816 in 1970, to 1707 in 1980, and, again, to 2729 in 1990. The number of villages and towns that have ski resorts within their territory increased from twenty-four in 1969 to thirty-three in 1990. It is reported that more than twenty new ski slopes were being opened annually from 1985 until the early 1990s when the post-bubble economic depression began to be felt (Mizo 1994: 13–14).

This resort-type development is perhaps what most dramatically transformed the rural landscape. Also, resort development projects are usually carried out beyond the villagers' means, involving capital penetration and appropriation of village resources, such as land, by outsiders, thereby raising a dependency problem. They also raised the problem of environmental destruction (Matsumura 1997). Golf courses, for instance, were condemned for being the major source of water pollution in many rural areas. Moreover, with economic depression, many large-scale complexes have met with financial difficulties. So-called 'green tourism' (*gurin tsuarizumu*) or 'regional tourism' (*chiiki kankō*) have in some ways appeared as an alternative type of rural tourism in response to the failure of these large-scale resort developments. According to Ashiba (1994: 72), in the Japanese context, the term 'regional tourism' designates 'a form of tourism that has developed with specific local features including history, culture, lifestyle, industry, etc. as its resources and with the movements of people who seek these features as its background'. Similarly, 'green tourism' designates a type of tourism seeking an encounter between urban and rural residents. The 'rural resort' (*nōsanson rizoto*) type of development emphasizes rural/urban exchange instead of a one-sided development of rural areas as recreational places for urban people.

Types of *muraokoshi* and rural transformation

As indicated above, the development of tourism has been one of the chief strategies of village revitalization in Japan. Although 'agriculture and tourism' has long been a catch phrase in most rural developmental plans in Japan (Moon 1997a: 221), a majority of the areas that adopted this strategy are hinterland regions that have hitherto been regarded as lacking any resources that might attract tourists. In those areas, tourist attractions had to be invented and this invention of tourist attractions has constituted an important part of many village revitalization (*muraokoshi*) movements. It relies upon the newly emerging idea that hinterland cultures and histories can be utilized as tourists resources as well as upon the fact that there has emerged a class of people who seek them.

Muraokoshi *as an economic movement*

As revitalizing efforts initiated by those living in rural areas, the *muraokoshi* was first known as the 'one village, one product' (*isson ippin*) movement started in 1979 by Hiramatsu Morihiko in Oita, Kyushu. As it was initiated by a local government leader who was formerly a Trade and Finance Ministry (*Tsusanshō*) employee in the central government in Tokyo, it may be difficult to regard the movement as wholly civic-centred and voluntary. Nevertheless it was widely publicized as the first of its kind initiated locally. This fact was particularly emphasized since it started during the period of the Third National Development Plan (the *Sanzenshō*) (1977–1983) when the main slogan was 'from centre to provinces' and the aim to create an 'era for provinces' (*chihō no jidai*). The leader of the movement, Hiramatsu, particularly emphasized voluntary participation and the self-help spirit by putting forward such slogans as 'the prefecture helps those who help themselves' and by encouraging competition among the villages and towns within a prefecture (Hiramatsu 1982, 1987, 1989).

With the decline of agriculture in general, and in the face of steep decline in the younger population, the means of livelihood itself was seriously threatened in many remote villages and the 'one village, one product' type of economic revitalization movement through specialization of production had considerable appeal. Little more than a decade after it started, it is reported that more than 70 per cent of all Japanese villages have adopted the movement in one form or another, and with varying consequences (*Asahi shinbun*, 25 November 1988). According to Hiramatsu, who has since become internationally famous, the movement has been exported to mainland China where it has been adopted in the form of a 'one street, one product' movement in Shanghai, 'one village, one treasure' movement in Tenjin, and 'one person, one talent' movement in Uhan (Hiramatsu 1987: 87–91).

The 'one village, one product' type of *muraokoshi* movement is basically an economic movement in that it takes as a main reason for population decline inferior economic conditions in provincial areas, meaning fewer opportunities for education and employment. What it tries to do, therefore, is to raise the general income level of local people so that it approximates that of those working in metropolitan areas. Unlike efforts to create or attract industrial centres to rural areas, however, the success of the 'one village, one product' type of economic revitalization movements depends closely upon a dialogue between the urban consumers and rural producers. In other words, to be able to revitalize the rural economy to any meaningful degree by developing speciality products, the rural producers, or at least the movement leaders, have to be extremely well informed about current changes in urban tastes, especially those of the metropolitan population who are the major consumers.

Whether the product thus developed is to be economically viable depends further upon how effectively the marketing is organized. Well-known cases of such speciality products are invariably those that have been able to develop effective nationwide marketing (Kawamata 1985; Hiramatsu 1982; Inoue 1989; Kamechi 1984). For instance, to take the famous king prawn production of the island of Hime, in Oita prefecture, the prawns are sold mainly to big retailers of metropolitan areas such as Tokyo (30 per cent), Osaka, Kyoto and Nagoya (30 per cent), and other areas including Kyushu (25 per cent) while the rest (15 per cent) are sold through a nationwide telephone ordering system (Inoue 1989: 181). This means that *muraokoshi* involves a profound reorganization of production and marketing that totally integrates rural areas and urban needs.

At the local level, however, speciality products thus created are often advertised as a new *meibutsu* of the region, that is, products unique to the locality that can be used as a tourist attraction. As the act of buying presents (*omiyage*) constitutes an essential part of Japanese tourist behaviour (Graburn 1983), most domestic tourist destinations have their own *meibutsu*, or 'famous products', that range from edible items such as sweets, pickles, mushrooms and wine to non-perishable goods such as lacquer ware, china, textiles, and so forth. Such *meibutsu* are deeply connected with the history and identity of the region and decorate an important part of Japanese tour guide materials. Although the new speciality created in the 'one village, one product' movement do not normally share the historical flavour that the well-known traditional *meibutsu* have, by turning them into one, local people also create a new identity for the region and its people.

As an attempt to create local character for a product, and to attract more tourists, various events are organized in connection with them. For instance, in one village in Oita prefecture that has been extremely successful in the specialization of *ume* (Japanese plum) production, the farmers have invented as tourist attractions events like *ume* festivals, trips to *umeboshi* (where *ume* are pickled) factories, sightseeing of *ume* flowers, *ume* beauty contests, and so forth. Similarly, in Kanazawa, Ishikawa prefecture, which is famous for lacquer ware and special dyeing techniques known as *aozome*, the tourists are invited to visit the lacquer ware museum and participate in the making of lacquer ware or in the dyeing of the material as part of 'experience tourism', in addition to buying the *meibutsu* on the spot.

Muraokoshi *as a recreational movement*

The village specialities created by the 'one village, one product' movement are mostly farm products, but they have sometimes come to include cultural items as well, especially during the later development of the movement. For this reason, the leaders of the 'one village, one product' movement claim that it is not simply an economic movement but ought to be understood as a cultural movement in a wider sense. Despite these claims, it is apparent that the primary aim of the 'one village, one product' type of *muraokoshi* movement lies with economic revitalization by means of creating work and employment opportunities. Also, as we have noted, although the specialities of the 'one village, one product' movement are sold to tourists as *meibutsu*, economically more successful ones are those that are marketed nationally rather than those that are just marketed locally, or that rely on sporadic tourist visits.

There are on the other hand types of *muraokoshi* in which attempts have been made to revitalize village life by means of 'creating and staging an event' (*ibento-zukuri*). If the 'one village, one product' (*isson ippin*) movement is a revitalizing effort that is centred around work and productive activities, the emphasis is shifted here to recreative activities, such as play, leisure and learning. Unlike the 'one village, one product' type, where local people are only producers for the urbanites who are the major consumers, in an 'event type', local residents are considered an equally and at times more important audience than anyone coming in from outside, such as tourists. In other words, revitalizing efforts of this type focus upon creating opportunities not of work but of new experience and pleasure for local people, thereby raising the quality of everyday life rather than simply the economic standard of living as in industrial movements already mentioned.

The scale and nature of the events range from small-scale ones such as organizing a folk music concert, inviting a foreign theatre group or holding wine tasting parties, to extremely large scale ones such as hosting the Asian Games as in the case of Hiroshima for 1994.[2] As can be seen in some of these examples, one element of the revitalization movement is to introduce unfamiliar 'urban' experiences. For instance, drinking high-quality French wine in a small town in Hokkaido (Kamechi 1984: 3–18) or watching a Shakespeare play acted in English by an Oxford University drama group in a remote mountain village in Hiroshima (the case of *Shakugi-mura*, Hiroshima) are certainly novel occurrences. One effect of offering such an opportunity is to make the villagers feel that it is by no means culturally backward to live in villages. Such an event also provides the villagers with an opportunity of getting together and sharing out-of-the ordinary experiences and enjoyment. Since agriculture itself has become increasingly individualized and automated, along with commercialization and mechanization, such an opportunity seems to be valued especially by a village's young people, both male and female.

If the refreshing *mezurashiza*, or the rarity, is one aspect that is emphasized in planning an event, another aspect is genuineness. The element of *mezurashiza* may be sufficient to attract initial attention, but, as time goes by, people soon realize that the kind of experience offered is only a second- or third-rate imitation of the same kind of experience that can be enjoyed in any city. Simply rare but non-original experiences of this kind can therefore hardly attract the attention of urban tourists or potential returning migrants – another important group of audiences the event planners have in mind. It is for this reason that local character is always emphasized in any plans for an event. The event planners, whether they be amateur local leaders or professional planners (*kikaku kaisha*), are keenly aware that the success of an event largely depends upon the extent to which they have been able to create something unique. For this purpose, regional character, natural or cultural, provides an indispensable resource to be utilized.

Combined with special local customs, tradition, history or even with modes of livelihood such as whaling or deep-sea diving, an event becomes a unique and genuine experience.[3] The genuine quality of the events thus created serves as an important resource for tourist attraction as modern tourists tend to seek genuine and authentic experiences (MacCannell 1976). The events staged in remote rural areas as part of the *muraokoshi* movement are thus advertised through local papers or even on nationwide television networks to attract urban tourists. By resorting to the uniquely local resources, it also becomes easier to attract the attention of local residents and get them fully involved in the plans.

Muraokoshi *as an environmental movement*

Environmental issues may be considered another important theme of the contemporary regional movement. It is of course rarely the case that a revitalization movement of one region concentrates upon only one theme or another. Even when it started with a specific focus upon one particular theme, it gradually develops into a movement of a more syncretic nature, subsuming all the other current themes, whether they be economic revitalization, recreation, protection of nature or the reconstruction of tradition. Considering different themes separately, however, we can trace the major reasons for the development of different themes and the significance of the shifts of emphasis in each of those developments.

We have already noted a shift of emphasis between 'one village, one product' type and the event-making type, from 'work' (*shigoto*) to 'play' (*asobi*), from material prosperity to cultural richness and a better quality of life, and so forth. A similar shift can also be noted between industrial movement of a governmental type and the later developed environment-oriented movement initiated from below. In this case the shift is perhaps more clearly observable since the aims of the two are in sharp conflict, and hence more difficult to combine, compared to the cases of economic and recreational movements discussed. This is because economic development of any kind indispensably involves partial destruction or transformation of nature while the environmentalists pursue the reverse, that is, the protection and preservation of nature. Since the 1970s, when environmental consciousness was enhanced in Japan through incidents such as diseases caused by pollution, there have emerged many citizens' resistance movements against plans to build contaminating facilities such as industrial complexes or golf courses, despite the fact that such facilities may considerably benefit the local economy (Broadbent 1998).

Here again, one may note a clear shift from an emphasis on economic prosperity to that of the quality of life, from 'development' and transformation of nature to its protection. Whether the consequences of such movements really amount to environmental protection remains in doubt, however. Since what is pursued in the name of environmental *muraokoshi* is often the promotion of nature tourism, they more often lead to its transformation, overuse or even destruction than to its preservation and protection (Moon 1997a). Nevertheless, at the discursive level, it is strongly emphasized that the *muraokoshi* pursues development 'that is kind to nature' (*shizen ni yasashii*), 'that seeks a dialogue with nature' (*shizen to no kōryū*), or 'that is adapted to nature' (*shizen ni awaseru*). Such attitudes towards nature, it is further argued, reflect a return to traditional Japanese values where human beings are perceived as part of nature rather than as its one-sided utilizer.[4] What is implied in this argument is that the environmentalism in the *muraokoshi* movement is an attempt to move away from the hitherto dominant 'industrialization equals exploitation of nature equals economic development' model that originated in the West and has caused pollution in the country.

Another characteristic feature of an environmentally based revitalization movement is that it often proceeds with a strong appeal to the 'recovery' of communal spirit, i.e., a spirit of living together. A typical example can be seen in the case of the River Yahagi Recuperation Movement in Aichi prefecture. (Kamechi 1984: 290–9). It was basically a story of the residents of nineteen villages and towns located along the River Yahagi, who have, after years of fierce opposition, finally succeeded in reaching a point of mutual understanding and co-operation. The years of conflict and opposition existed between the residents of the upper and the lower ends of the river as the industrialization of the upper area during the 1960s and 1970s, and consequent pollution of the River Yahagi, seriously threatened the main means of livelihood in the lower region, which depended on the fishing and seaweed industry.

In the mood of growing environmental consciousness in Japan in the 1970s, there had emerged in this region a few voluntary citizens' groups who took the recuperation of the River Yahagi as their main target. Thanks to the efforts of these groups, the residents of both regions had come to an agreement that the recuperation of the River Yahagi is in the long run a concern not just for the lower region but for all. A practical consequence of the agreement was the establishment of a sisterly relationship between two towns located at the upper and lower end of the river that had been in most bitter conflict for the past few years. To carry out recuperating activities, a separate civil council was set up and all the development plans were subjected to the close scrutiny of the council.

The incident was publicized as a test case for the regional revitalization movement especially in that it displays a good example of the revival of community spirit (*kyōdōtai seishin*) that is rooted in the mutual co-operation, sacrifice and the ethics of living together. It is said that, with the advancement of industrialization and capitalism, these good values of traditional Japan have been overwhelmed by such values as efficiency, rationality and competition, and caused serious harm to the environment that can only be healed by returning to traditional Japanese values.

As it is believed that traditional values are preserved better in rural areas than in industrialized urban areas, the former must revitalize their lost virtues and take pride in them. Such virtues can become tourist resources as well since the urbanites will come and relax in the simple kindness (*sobokuna ninjo*) of the rural people. In the *muraokoshi*, therefore, the recuperation of unpolluted nature, reconstruction of the landscape (*keikan*) and revitalization of lost customs are all merged.[5]

Muraokoshi *and the reconstruction of tradition*

The rediscovery and revalorization of local cultural tradition is an essential part of the current regional movements in Japan. If modernization and industrialization have been a move towards cultural homogeneity at the global level, the emphasis upon regional character found in contemporary *muraokoshi* movements may be understood as a move in the opposite direction, namely towards rediscovering and re-affirming cultural difference. The widely discussed Japanese uniqueness debates can be considered as one such example at the national level. It is interesting that, as the uniqueness debates surfaced when one of the key state rhetorics was internationalization, the slogan 'era for provinces' (*chihō no jidai*) appeared as a political rhetoric when regional character was almost on the verge of extinction due to rapid urbanization and industrialization. The *muraokoshi* in this context may thus be interpreted as a cultural movement that attempts to create, whether on the basis of existing tradition or on completely new grounds, a unique local culture, which can be distinguished from internationalized and thus characterless metropolitan culture.

Efforts in this direction were first indicated by the interest shown in traditional folk cultures. Since the early 1970s, more than 200 folk museums have been opened throughout Japan (Kanzaki 1988: 46). In their effort to discover cultural roots, the urbanites turn to rural areas where traditions are believed to be more widely preserved than in the cities. Thanks to consistent official attempts to modernize and rationalize rural lifestyles, however, not much of the traditional way of life has remained today, even in rural areas. In many cases, therefore, it has to be reconstructed through careful study and investigation. Along with the renewed boom of national ethnology since the late 1960s, therefore, various volunteer groups have been formed to study forgotten local history, and to reconstruct now extinct local cultural traditions. Also, in the belief that a rediscovery of cultural uniqueness is an effective way of attracting tourists, much of the local government budget for regional revitalization has been assigned to such activities in many villages.[6]

The local cultural movement leaders engaged in these tasks have to re-educate local residents in their own cultural traditions, while the aim of their work, whether it be newly opened ethnology museums or reconstructed monkey show performances, is to satisfy the nostalgia of urban tourists in pursuit of their own forgotten past. What one has to note here is that the tradition thereby reconstructed does not necessarily mean a return to the past. As can be seen in the following examples, often specific images of the past are selectively reconstructed in modern settings and are subsequently endowed with meanings appropriate to the context.

Typically, contemporary *muraokoshi* or village revitalization movements are initiated and carried out by one individual, or a small group of volunteers. Unlike economic or event type movements, however, the immediate benefits of cultural revitalization movements are much more difficult to grasp. Such efforts, therefore, are often accompanied by stories of 'lonely struggle' at an initial stage until they can secure local as well as outside support. The revival of monkey shows (*saru mawashi*) in Koshu, Yamaguchi prefecture, was one such example (Kanzaki 1988: 71–81). The area was known to be the centre for a monkey show, a traditional Japanese folk art, which had been widely performed from the Edo (1603–1868) period until early Taisho (1912–25). It is said that, until early in the twentieth century, more than 150 monkeys were raised in this area for the purpose, and to become a monkey artist (*saru genin*) had been one of the major aspirations of the Koshu people. Yet, there was no heir to the tradition when the last artiste died in 1967, and it is only recently that the practice was revived thanks to the more than ten years of lonely effort on the part of one local young man. The initiator and team of a few supporters subsequently formed around him now stage the monkey show all over the country.

It started with two monkeys donated by the Monkey Centre of Aichi prefecture following an appeal by this enthusiastic young man. After the art was introduced by NHK (Japanese broadcasting corporation) through one of its *Shin nippon kikō* (Travel around New Japan) programmes, however, invitations came from all around the country, and many aspiring young men came to Koshu hoping to be trained as monkey dance artistes. The revival of the monkey dance has also served as a significant tourist attraction as many people come to the village to watch the show, as it has now become famous for the event. Not only tourists but also many ethnologists, primatologists, media people, writers and so forth now visit the area to learn more about the monkeys' physiology and related customs. Tourism based on the show has therefore contributed to the revitalization of the village economy. What is more significant, however, is the fact that the popularization of the monkey show has enabled people to re-evaluate and take pride in their hitherto neglected tradition.

Similar efforts to revive or reconstruct tradition have been noted in many parts of Japan as part of people's attempts to revitalize their local economy and society. At times, they comprise simply collecting old farm tools or other folk artifacts, which have long gone out of use and have hence been forgotten even by the local people themselves. Such collections, while they are the fruits of the conscientious study of many amateur local historians and ethnologists, and despite the fact that they constitute the main property of the widespread folk museums, are quite separate from people's everyday life and are exhibited mostly for tourists, schoolchildren or nostalgia-seeking urbanites. In other cases, however, the reconstruction has had a more immediate impact upon the lives of local people. In the case of the monkey show revival, for instance, local people play the role of showman, supporters of the reconstruction movement and audiences at the same time. We may see a similar impact upon the lives of the local people from the example of the Aizu Retro Society (*Aizu Fukkokai*) that has attempted a revival of Tokugawa merchant culture (Moon 1997:184–5; Kamechi 1984: 92–9; Inoue 1989:113–23).

In regional movements resorting to the reconstruction of local cultural tradition, therefore, the main emphasis is placed again upon creating difference and uniqueness. On the one hand, it serves as a means of attracting nostalgic tourists as the authenticity thereby created often has a great appeal to modern urbanites who have long left their home towns and have thus become rootless (MacCannel 1976). Such activities, however, are not simply geared towards the possible economic benefit thereby obtained. Or, to put in another way, it is difficult to interpret them as a simple act of commodification or fetishization of their own culture and life for tourist consumption. As mentioned above, in many of the cultural reconstruction activities, local residents are often as important an audience as those coming from outside. The reproduced past is often as alien an experience to the modernized localities themselves as it is to the urban tourists.

Rural tourism and changing concepts of rurality

The idea that an ordinary rural area without any specific attractions such as a spa, a mountain, a historical building or monument, or a famous shrine or temple, can become a tourist destination is relatively recent in Japan. In the case of international tourism, the common pattern has been that those who have wealth and power visit those who have not. The west visits the east; the north visits the south. In the case of domestic tourism, however, this pattern has not always been followed. In Japanese domestic tourism, especially since the eighteenth century when tourism in the form of pilgrimage began to be popular among the masses, the common historical pattern has been that people, both urban and rural, visited well-known and often sacrilized third places whether they be shrines, temples, scenic places, hot springs or whatever. Between the cities and the countryside, the tourist flow has been from the latter to the former, rather than *vice versa*. Therefore, Edo (Tokyo), Kyoto, and the cities on the way were among the popular tourist destinations in traditional Japan, about which numerous travel diaries exist.

Since around the 1980s, however, rural areas have emerged as new tourist destinations, and people began to travel to them simply to enjoy the landscape, nature, history or local character. The fact that there has emerged a class of people who consider 'rural features' as recreational resources themselves is a new phenomenon that indicates a significant change in the conceptualization of rurality in Japan. As William Kelly (1986: 606) once noted, there have always existed two different languages concerning the countryside (*nōson*) in Japan. First, there is a language derived from the modernization model, where country people are represented as backward, poor, illiterate, feudal, superstitious and irrational – a place that needs to be developed and changed. At the opposite end, there is the language of rural nostalgia in which villages are imagined to be places where everything that is lost in the industrialized modern world is preserved (see Table 14.1).

The two different views have interchangeably dominated policies and attitudes towards rural communities. While one may say that the modernization perspective dominated policy decisions and the local people's perception of themselves up until the early 1970s, in the *muraokoshi* rhetoric of the 1980s and the recent popularity of

Table 14.1 Changing views of urban and rural life

Modernization and urbanization (1950s, 1960s 1970s)	Idealization of the countryside (1970s, 1980s, 1990s)
Urban (rural)	Rural (urban)
developed (backward)	nature (culture)
prosperity (poverty)	Heart-*kokoro* (materialism)
sophisticated (rustic – *inaka*)	*furusato* (city, unfamiliar)
the succeeded (the failed)	humane living (crowded, polluted)
science (superstition)	sacred (secular)
rationality (irrationality)	communal spirit (individualism,
civilization (ignorance)	capitalism)
modernity (tradition)	authenticity (alien)
Western-ness (Japanese-ness)	tradition (modernity)
towards homogeneity of culture	Japanese-ness (Western-ness)
(urbanization, modernization)	Re-discovery of cultural and regional difference (idealization of the countryside)

rural tourism, we can note a clear shift in the reverse direction, reflecting an overall change in the value orientation of Japanese people living in a postindustrial era.

Both approaches, however, seem to have similar effects upon transforming the countryside. In the case of the modernization approach, the transformation of rural landscapes largely occurred as a result of the construction of roads, irrigation ditches, buildings and other kinds of welfare facilities. The various campaigns to 'rationalize' rural lifestyle implemented in the 1950s and 1960s also had a notable impact upon changing rural society. The *muraokoshi* movements of the 1980s, and various types of tourism development projects pursued as part of them, transform rural society in a different way. Although it appears that rural society and culture is idealized in the latter approach, the representation is often based upon certain selected images of rural life rather than its reality. What is attempted in many *muraokoshi* movements, therefore, basically amounts to a reconstruction of the countryside in a way that matches this imagery. Such activities as reconstruction and preservation of old thatched houses, unused fireplaces (*irori*), out-dated lifestyles and a re-invention of traditional local dishes and specialities are a few examples.

As we have seen, one of the main purposes of this reconstruction is to attract urban tourists. In the words of one tourism department official at Ise city, what attracts tourists nowadays is 'newly constructed old things' (*atarashiku tsukuraretta furui mono*). It is true that such attempts reflect part of the struggle of the local residents themselves to discover a new meaning for their existence in industrialized modern Japan. As cultural hegemony lies within the cities, and with the urban way of life, however, this search for a new identity can only be achieved through a dialogue with the urbanites. The influence of urban people is therefore constantly present at all levels of the village revitalization movements. In fact, though it may sound ironical, the degree of success of regional revitalization movements or any related tourism development efforts seems to depend upon how effectively their efforts are communicated to the urban folks who are the major consumers of rural features nowadays.

Notes

1 The turning point may have been the boom of the 1970 Osaka Expo tour, that was mostly taken by family units.
2 When I visited the prefectural office in the summer of 1993, for the purpose of research about regional revitalization (*chiikikatseika*), I realized that the main department in charge of the preparation of the Asian Games for the next year (1994) was the Department for the Revitalization of the Township (*Machiokoshika*).
3 See for example Sashida 1984; Kanzaki 1988, Kaso o shakade ni toru kai (Association for taking a reverse grip of the de-population problem) 1987; and so forth.
4 According to Professor Itoh Abito of Tokyo University, for instance, the environmental emphasis in the *muraokoshi* movement ought to be interpreted as a continuation of ideas originally developed by Ninomiya Sontoku (1789–1856), a government-designated agricultural reformer (*tokunōka*) of the late Tokugawa period, who emphasized the ethics in utilizing nature to human ends.
5 A group forming part of a *muraokoshi* movement in Gunma prefecture, for instance, attempts to reconstruct the traditional *yui* relationship. This is the non-monetary type of labour exchange relationship that was widely practised for such tasks as rice transplantation (Moon 1989). It almost completely disappeared in rural Japan with the introduction of wage labour. By reinstating it, it is hoped to recover the pre-capitalist patterns of human relationship based on the co-operative spirit of a community.
6 In the case of one village in Gunma prefecture, most of the local government regional revitalization (*chiikikatseika*) fund was spent on purchasing old thatched houses in the village and renovating them into museums.

Bibliography

Ashiba H. (ed.) (1994) *Shin kankōgaku kairon* (A new introduction to tourism studies), Tokyo: Minerva Shobō.
Broadbent J. (1998) *Environmental Politics in Japan: Networks of Power and Protest*, Cambridge and New York: Cambridge University Press.
Chiikikatseika senta (Regional revitalization centre) (ed.) 1985, *Machizukuri handobuku* (Town-making handbook), Tokyo: Regional Revitalization Centre.
DuPuis E.M. and Vandergeest, P. (eds) 1996, *Creating the Countryside: The Politics of Rural and Environmental Discourse*, Philadelphia, PA: Temple University Press.
Graburn, N. (1983) 'To pray, pay and play: the cultural structure of Japanese domestic tourism', Aix-en-Province: Centre des Hautes Etudes Touristiques, Cahiers du Tourisme.
Graburn, N. (1995) 'The past in the present in Japan: nostalgia and neo-traditionalism in contemporary Japanese domestic tourism', in R. Butler and D. Pearce (eds) *Change in Tourism: People, Places Processes*, London: Routledge.
Hinrichs, C.C. (1996) 'Consuming images: making and marketing Vermont as distinctive rural place', in E.M. DuPuis and P. Vandergeest (eds) *Creating the Countryside: The Politics of Rural and Environmental Discourse*, Philadelphia PA: Temple University Press, pp. 259–78.
Hiramatsu, M. (1982) *Isson ippin no susume* (The progress of the 'one village, one product' movement), Tokyo: Gyosei.
Hiramatsu, M. (1987) *Tokyo de dekinai koto o yatte miyo!* (Let's try something that is not possible in Tokyo!), Tokyo: Bunkeishunshu.
Inoue S. (1989) *Chiiki zukuri shindan* (A diagnosis of region making), Tokyo: Tōyukan.

Ishimori, Shuzo (1989) '*Tabi kara ryoko e*' *Kendai nihon bunkani okeru dentō to henyō 6, Nihonjin to asobi* (Play and the Japanese), Tokyo: Tomesu Shuppan, 92–112.

Kajiwara, K. (1997) 'Inward-bound, outward-bound: Japanese tourism reconsidered' in S. Yamashita, K. Din and J.S. Eades (eds) *Tourism and Cultural Development in Asia and Oceania*, Bangi: Kebangsan University Press, Malaysia.

Kakizaki, K. (1998) 'Gasshō zukuri shuraku hozon undō no kiseki' (The locus of the movement for the preservation of the *gassho zukuri* hamlet), *Shirakawa mura kyōiku iinkai*, Gifu Prefecture (ed.) *Shirakawa Sonshi* (A history of Shirakawa) vol I.

Kamechi, H. (1984) *Muraokoshi runetsansu* (A renaissance of village revitalization movement), Tokyo: Gyosei.

Kanzaki, N. (1988) *Chiikiokoshi no fuokuroa* (Folklore of regional revitalization), Tokyo: Gyosei.

Kanzaki, N. (1991) *Monomiryusan to nihonjin*, Tokyo: Kodansha.

Kaso o shakade ni toru Kai (ed.) (1987) *Machiga hiraku: sakaderyu machizukuri shakuho* (Towns are shining: methods of townmaking of the reversal strategy), Tokyo: Daiichi Hoki.

Kato, Hidetoshi (1976) 'Chapter 7: Ryoko (Travel)', in *Nihonjin no seikatsu* (Japanese life), Lecture series *Hikaku Bunka* (Cross-Cultural Comparison) 4, Tokyo: Kenkyusha.

Kawamata Y. (1985) *Henkyaku jidai no machizukuri* (Townmaking in a changing era), Tokyo: Gyosei.

Keizaiseizaku Hershūkai. (Editorial Board of Economic Policies) (ed.) (1989) *Furusato sosei: socho seizakushu* (Creation of old home town: collection of government policies), Tokyo: Daiichihoki

Kelly, W. (1986) 'Rationalization and nostalgia: cultural dynamics of new middle-class Japan', *American Ethnologist* 13(4): 603–17.

Kim, I. (1994) *Japanese Rural Society and Regional Revitalization Movement*, Seoul: Nanam (in Korean).

Kwon, S. (1997) 'Religion and the development of mass tourism in modern Japan', *Area Studies* 6(1), Area Studies Centre, Seoul National University, Korea (in Korean).

MacCannell, D. (1976) *The tourist: a new theory of the leisure class*, New York: Schocken Books.

Marcus, G.E. and Fisher M.M.J. (1986) *Anthropology as Cultural Critique*, Chicago and London: University of Chicago Press.

Martinez, D.P. (1990) 'Tourism and the ama: the search for real Japan' in E. Ben-Ari, B. Moeran and J. Valentine (eds) *Unwrapping Japan: Society and Culture in Anthropological Perspective*, Manchester: Manchester University Press.

Matsumura, K. (1997) *Sanson no kaihatsu to kankyōhōzon* (Development of mountain villages and environmental preservation) Tokyo: Nansosha.

Mizo, Y. (1994) *Kankō o yomu: Chiiki shinkō e no teigen* (Reading Tourism: suggestions towards regional revitalization) Tokyo: Kokon Shōin.

Moeran, B. (1983) 'The language of Japanese tourism', *Annals of Tourism Research* 10(1): 93–108.

Moon, O. (1989) *From Paddy Field to Ski Slope: The Revitalization of Tradition in Japanese Village Life*, Manchester: Manchester University Press.

Moon, O. (1997a) 'Marketing nature in rural Japan', in P.J. Asquith and A. Kalland (eds) *Japanese Images of Nature: Cultural Perspectives*, London: Curzon Press.

Moon, O. (1997b) 'Tourism and cultural development: Japanese and Korean contexts', in S. Yamashita, D. Kadir and J.S. Eades (eds) *Tourism and Cultural Development in Asia and Oceania*, Bangi: Kebangsan University Press, Malaysia.

Moon, O. (1997c) 'History and culture of Japanese group tourism', *Area Studies* 6(1), Area Studies Center, Seoul National University, Korea (in Korean).

Sanson Keizai Kenkyūkai (ed.) (1994) *Sanson ga kowareru sono maeni* (Before mountain villages are destroyed) Tokyo: Nihon Keizai Hyōronsha.

Sashida, S. (1984) *Kaso o sakade ni toru* (Attacking the problem of under-population by reverse grip), Tokyo: Akebi Shobō.

Shirahata, Y. (1996) *Ryokō no susume: showakara unda shomin no shin bunka* (Evolution of travelling: the new culture of the common people born in the showa period) Tokyo: Chūōkōronsha.

Smith, V. (ed.) (1989) *Hosts and Guests: The Anthropology of Tourism,* (second edition), Philadelphia, PA: University of Pennsylvania Press.

Somusho Tokekyoku (Statistics Bureau, Management and Coordination Agency (ed.)) 1997, *The 47th Japan Statistical Yearbook.*

Sonraku shakai kenkyūkai (ed.) (1991) *Tenkanki nōson no shutai keisei: nōson shakai hensei no ronri to tenkai III* (Subject formation in changing rural society: the logic and development of the formation of rural Society III), *Sonraku shakai kenkyū* (Studies in village society) 27, *Nōsangyoson bunka kyōkai.*

Yamazaki, M., Oyama, Y. and Oshima, J. (1993) *Gurin tsuarizumu* (Green tourism), Tokyo: Ie no Hikari Kyokai.

Yorimitsu R. and Kurisu, Y. (1996) *Gurin tsuarizumu no kanōsei* (Possibilities of green tourism), Tokyo: Nihon keizai hyōronsha.

15 From curing and playing, to leisure

Two Japanese hot springs: Arima and Kinosaki *onsen*

Sylvie Guichard-Anguis

Introduction

Most people living in Japan for some time have the experience of staying overnight in a Japanese hot spring resort or *onsen*. Bathing naked with unknown people of the same sex gives a feeling of strange intimacy. The opportunity of catching a glimpse of the board on which are written the different qualities of the water in which one bathes is offered, but generally it goes unnoticed, as most of the participants are not especially preoccupied with curing some part of their body. The banquet or the gourmet meal that follows the bath, with their assorted delicacies, are no doubt part of the experience of fun and relaxation, and come to be associated with the satisfaction and pleasure. Those who are used to indulging themselves in this kind of relaxation will certainly have noticed how different one *onsen* can be to another. Between the very rustic in remote places in the mountains, like *Nyūto onsengyō* in Tōhoku, for instance, to the huge hotel complexes on the seashore of Beppu or Atami, lies a wide range of opportunities.

This chapter will deal with two of them, both located in Hyōgo prefecture in the same kind of setting: a small valley in the mountains, a few kilometres from the sea. Situated at the opposite ends of the prefecture, Arima *onsen* and Kinosaki *onsen* differ widely in their location, however. The first is part of modern Kobe City, and the second is apparently isolated, near the Japanese seashore.

The guidebook *Spas in Japan*, in its English edition, gives for Arima the following description:

> Features: Japan's oldest hot spring resort lying at an elevation of 363m at the northern foot of Mt Rokko. . . . Well known for long as a hot spring resort with history and tradition, along with the Kusatsu and Dogo spas . . . The spa has become a leading pleasure resort in the Kansai area, with many *ryokan* having facilities such as restaurants providing entertainment.

It is needless to point out that this description insists only on the main features of this so-called pleasure resort, without taking notice of its curing abilities. The characteristics of thermal waters, their temperature, the number of wells and springs, and the indications for bathing and drinking are quoted at the end of the description, without any further details, as for every other hot spring that is listed in the book.

For Kinosaki the description goes as follows:

> Features: one of the leading spas in Hyōgo prefecture, the other being the Arima spa. The Otani river runs through the middle of the town; there are rows of willows and cherry trees on both banks extending one kilometre, and many bridges over the river produce a distinctive mood. The *ryokan* are built in this beautifully harmonious scenery with a characteristic atmosphere of a Japanese hot spring resort. . . .

In this so-called characteristic atmosphere of a Japanese hot spring resort lies much of my present concern. Other features give details of the surroundings and of its facilities for excursions and visits. Not a single remark is dedicated to the curing benefits of bathing in those waters.

These statements lead to several questions: why are those two hot spring resorts associated with pleasure, and why does the description of the willow and cherry trees have greater importance in attracting visitors than the percentage of sodium or calcium-chloride in the thermal waters? Yamamura Junji (1988), one of the leading experts in this field, gives the following definition for an *onsen*. According to the Law of the Hot Spring Resort, *onsenshō*, dating back to 1948, *onsen* is any spring of water gushing out from the underground as warm water, mineral water, vapour or gas with an average temperature of 25° or more. It has to possess at least one of the listed components (minerals, and so on) at a given percentage. In the gap between the legal definition of the hot spring resort and their descriptions in the book as spas lies part of the answer, that is to say the evolution of the purpose of staying at an *onsen*. It seems closer nowadays to the presence of the aforementioned willows and cherry trees than to the qualities of the hot water. Behind this evolution lie the notions of free time and leisure, rather than medicine.

My first interest stems from the evolution of urban landscapes and urban structures and the process of adaptation to their urban functions, through destruction, renewal or protection. The analysis of these two hot spring resorts will stress the activity of visiting. The evolution of the urban landscapes of Arima and Kinosaki reflect one of the purposes of those visits. Associated by law and by science to curing, Japanese hot spring resorts seem to exist nowadays mainly for indulging oneself in pleasure and activities related to leisure. Was the evolution the same in both places? Does it give rise to the same type of *onsen*, or does this evolution materialize in different ways in different places? How has curing come to be associated with leisure? How has this combination of two apparently contradictory worlds appeared? Those are the questions this chapter would like to address. The historic evolution of those two *onsen* will appear separately, before dealing with the problem of fun and leisure in those *onsen* in a contemporary perspective.

Arima *onsen*, the inner parlour (*okuzashiki*) of Kansai

Arima is often referred to as the inner parlour, *okuzashiki*, of Kansai. In this expression lies much of Arima's history and characteristics.

Figure 15.1 Arima Hot Spring Resort

From the tale of the three crows to the two visiting monks

Arima boasts of being one of the oldest *onsen* in Japan. A legend sets its origin during mythological times, as for many other hot spring resorts. According to it, three crows curing their wounds in a pool were discovered by the gods Onamuchi no mikoto and Sukuna Hikona no mikoto who were travelling through the country, looking for some curative herbs. The gods understood that this pool was a hot spring. They are both now enshrined in the *onsenjinja* (Shintō shrine of the hot spring) of Arima. Then the history of Arima claims to bear a strong connection with that of the country itself until the Meiji period. As far back as the sixth century, the empress Suiko (592–628), the thirty-third one, is credited with building a temple, the Jakuseizan Gokuraji. According to the *Nihonshoki* (720),[1] several emperors stayed at the present Arima. Among them, in 631, the emperor Jōmei stayed over for eighty days from September, and in 638, three months from October. In 647, the emperor Kōtoku (645–54) stayed eighty days from October. They came travelling in a basket (*kago*) and stayed in the *angū*, the temporary palace. Both of these emperors were lamenting the fact that they had no heirs and their stay is believed to be linked to this fertility problem. As the empress bore children some time later, the properties of the thermal waters became associated with fertility. This was one of the reasons why Toyotomi Hideyoshi (1536–98)[2] favoured this *onsen* later too. Even before antiquity, Arima *onsen* boasts of attracting renowned visitors and being a famous resort. But the main purpose of those visits was to cure a problem. Unhappily, no records remain of the ways those emperors entertained themselves while staying so long in the mountains. The only supposition which can be made, is that choosing autumn for their stay, they had long opportunities to enjoy the bright colours of this season, still favoured by visitors to the Kansai region (Kobe, Osaka and Kyoto).

Another characteristic of this *onsen* through its historic evolution lies in the succession of periods of prosperity, followed by the near disappearance of the *onsen* itself. Through the centuries inundations caused by mountain streams, earthquakes and fires took their toll regularly. The later visit of two monks had a great influence on the evolution of Arima. The first one, Gyōgi, in 724, is credited with being at the origin of the revival of Arima, which somehow had disappeared. He is supposed to have built the hot spring resort temple (*onsenji*). According to the legend he met a sick man, while travelling in the mountains, who turned out to be Yakushi Nyorai (healing Buddha) and who announced to him that he was going to hot springs. The *onsenji* still holds a festival (*matsuri*) in memory of Yakushi Nyorai. Part again of the known world of antiquity, Arima is quoted in the *Man'yōshū* (around 750),[3] and the name of the *jinja* of Arima appears in the *Engishiki*[4] among the gods' records. Although regularly visited by important dignitaries, it was wiped out by a *yamatsunami* (a mountain big wave) type of inundation in 1097, and the following day by an earthquake. Its second resurrection came with a second monk, Ninsai, coming from the Kogenji temple in Yoshino (in the Kii peninsula), who played a fundamental role in creating the present Arima. In 1191 he built the twelve lodgings, *shukubō*, (the origin of this number may come from the twelve guardian deities of Yakushi Nyorai), where sick people and travellers could stay.

At this stage of historical development the blending of religious ideas through Shintō and Buddhism, and more prosaic ones such as health problems have to be stressed. There seem to exist no precise limits between what is mundane and belongs to the secular world and what are spiritual, religious matters. This trend which appears from the beginning of the history of Arima seems fundamental. Here may lie some explanation of the connection of Japanese hot spring resort with entertainment and pleasure. Curing holds a spiritual aspect and, in turn, a long stay with plenty of free time involves a holiday aspect. So those three worlds came to be related in one way or another.

From Toyotomi Hideyoshi to the Kansai okuzashiki

Around the end of the Heian period (794–1185), the *onsen* became very popular among the courtiers. But it entered a third period of abandonment after two big fires in 1528 and 1576 which reduced it to ashes. The third big step in the history of

Arima is linked with the several visits of Hideyoshi. He came in 1583, in 1584, in 1585 with his wife, and then nearly every year until his death. He enjoyed the place so much that he built his own private palace. Making Arima a temporary palace resort was a custom which was begun already, as we noted, during antiquity with the long stays of the emperors. An important part of Arima cultural heritage comes from this period as Sen no Rikyū (1552–91) the great tea master came along with Hideyoshi. A record of one tea gathering, *chakai*, they had in Arima in 1590 remains.

A great part of the Arima of today dates back to the numerous works that Hideyoshi undertook. The river that used to cause flooding was straightened. After the entire destruction of Arima by an earthquake in 1596, he rebuilt the town. The number of temple lodgings grew to twenty. The common bath was at the centre of the *onsen* and two or three inns (*yadoya*) were attached to every lodging. Local lords (*daimyō*) had their own lodging (*gojobō*). Motonoyu, now enclosed in the *onsen* kaikan (hot spring resort centre) was the only place where people could bathe. In Motonoyu there were two baths to enter into the waters: Ichinoyu for the customers of the lodgings located in the southern part of Arima, facing the *onsen jinja*, and Nin'yu for those in the northern part. Ten lodgings depended on each. For instance the customers of Gojobō, Okunobō, Iseya and Amagasakinobō had to go to Ichinoyu.

Shops dealing with everyday needs could be found, as stays usually involved one week at least. According to the folklore historian Mori, quoted by Yamamura (1988), among the 623 donors who made a gift for the reconstruction of the main hall of a temple in 1725, sixty-seven were from inns, forty-seven from baskets makers, twenty-three from writing brush makers. Altogether, around 130 shops with local products (*bunsanhinten*) could be counted. Those local products, bought as souvenirs, were part of the recreational atmosphere of the *onsen*. They were also a leading part of the local economy as in most of the hot springs resorts in those days. The *onsen* itself stood around the present Kitanomachi and Hyotanmachi. According to the same source, 59 per cent of the donors for the reconstruction of the temple Rakushiji (a fire reduced it again to ashes in 1659) came from the Kinki region. Around half of the donors belonged to the *daimyō* or *bushi* warlords class. The Bunka (1804–18) and Bunsei (1818–30) eras were the period when the *onsen* reached its greatest prosperity.

Hitomawari, a stay of seven days, then *futamawari*, a two-week stay, then a three-week stay, *mitsumawari*, were recommended in the *Arima nyūyūki*, written in 1452 by a monk of the Shōkoku temple in Kyoto. During the first stay it was recommended to stay briefly in the water, the second time as long as one wishes and the third time briefly again. This way of taking a healing bath is still part of the curing method nowadays. On a noticeboard in the lodgings a few directions gave details of the best way of entering the waters. First, splashing water was recommended, then gargling, then chanting and pronouncing the name of Yakushi Nyorai. If the bather was in a hurry, pronouncing the name eight times was supposed to be enough.

The opening of the waters to the people who stayed in the lodgings, were announced by *yuna*, *onsen* prostitutes. Giving information and in charge of the tea service, they were classified into two groups. From 13 or 14 years old to 22 or 23 years old they belonged to the *shōyuna* (younger *yuna*). The oldest ones, around 40 years old, were called the *ōyuna* or usually *kakayuna*. They were the ones who practise the *geigoto*, the artistic accomplishments in poetry, *ikebana*, tea ceremony, and so on. One girl of each group was attached to every lodging and owned a specific name attached to it, for instance Tsune in the Naka no bō. *Yuna* existed until the beginning of Meiji period (1868–1912) and counted much for its fame and prosperity. The closeness between those several worlds may again catch our attention. In such a relaxed atmosphere, bathing in the water was just a part of a stay, which seems rather close to some long vacation. It involved curing, of course, but a lot of other activities, which did not belong to the realm of everyday life and had their importance for the attractive character of Arima. The location of Arima on the other side of a steep mountain, which meant for centuries great difficulty of access, fostered this feeling of remoteness to the realm of everyday life.

Arima nowadays, the north part of Kobe City

In 1874 a railway line was opened between Kobe and Osaka and this explains the increase in the number of customers to Arima. The *onsen* turned gradually into a recreational area for the inhabitants of those two big cities. Nowadays it takes around an hour from Umeda station in Osaka to reach Arima and half an hour from Sannomiya station in Kōbe. It became a town (*machi*) in 1897 and in 1947 Arima (2,949 inhabitants) was incorporated into Kobe City. In 1973 it became Kitaku Arimachō, an administrative part of the northern district, and began to experience a decrease in population (2,549 inhabitants in 1989) due to its location on the other side of the Rokko mountains which act as a barrier to communications. In 1988 the number of Japanese style inns (*ryokan*) amounted to thirty, and company housing to thirty-six. Today Arima offers stays in concrete buildings of several floors, which stretch along very narrow roads. Parking and traffic represent the biggest problems of the town, as the *ryokan* and hotels want to have their own bus stop in front their main entrance. The names of some of those *ryokan* still make reference to their historical origin, to name a few Kadonobō, Gojobō, Okunobō, and so on. Some of those hotels offer a large range of sports facilities. A few blocks of old wooden houses can be found around the *onsen kaikan*. Managed by the city of Kobe it remains as the only municipal public bath. People used to stay an average of one night, which is the common use in all the hot springs resorts in Japan nowadays. Arima has evolved from a long-stay type of hot spring resort, to a kind of recreational area composed of high rise, concrete *ryokan* close to Osaka and Kobe cities.

Kinosaki and the seven hot waters tour

A tale of birds and monks

The origins of the Kinosaki hot spring resort are told by legends rather close to the ones of Arima involving birds then monks, giving natural and religious powers to the curing waters. A big bird, curing its wounds in some water, is discovered by a peasant. According to the legend, the gushing water (*yu*) was called *Kō no yu*. In 717

Figure 15.2 Kinosaki Hot Spring Resort

a monk by the name of Dochi, after a thousand days of penance, is credited with having dug in eight different places which gave way later to the Mandarayu. As far back as antiquity this hot spring resort seems already to have been famous, as it is quoted in the *Kokinwakashū*.[5] Other hot springs appeared progressively during the Kamakura (1185–1333) and Edo (1603–1868) periods. The hot spring resorts became famous among courtiers, the priests of great temples and literati in the old capital of Kyoto because of its beautiful setting.

Kinosaki can be categorized, like Dogo *onsen* near Matsuyama (Ehime prefecture), as the public outdoor bath type, which differed from the private type as in Kusatsu or Ikaho, both located in Gunma prefecture and very popular. In 1808 a book by Shiba Noritsugizan (1736–1807) praised the curing ability and the quality of the surroundings of this hot spring resort, initiating an era of prosperity to this *onsen*. In those days visitors asked local inhabitants to provide food and lodging. This type of accommodation turned gradually into a *ryokan*. Around the middle of the Edo period those *ryokan* were given a number and some sixty-three had got a licence by the end of this period. The public outdoor baths (*sotoyu*) numbered six. Until the end of the Meiji period (1868–1912) the visitors first entering Kinosaki went to pray at the temple of the hot spring resort (*onsenji*) where they received a *yushaku* (a ladle). They had to use it while bathing. At the end of their stay they gave it back as a token of gratitude to the temple. So the same intimacy between curing and religious matters in the historic evolution of Kinosaki can be stressed, without forgetting a literary atmosphere which is specific to this hot spring resort.

All the *sotoyu* were public baths and were free at the beginning, then a small amount of money was requested. They were administered by an association of inns, founded around the end of the Edo period. In 1890 the village of Yushima was founded and the administration of the *sotoyu* entrusted to it. The number of *ryokan* dwindled from sixty-three to twenty-eight after the Sino-Japanese war (1894–5), but Kinosaki was designated as a recuperation centre for soldiers wounded in the Russo-Japanese war (1904–5), and its economic situation improved a little.

Prosperity and decay in Kinosaki during the first half of the twentieth century

In 1911 the San'in railway line was opened and the hot spring resort became very popular in the Hanshin (Kobe, Osaka) area. In 1923 Hyōgo ranked first among all Japanese prefectures thanks to the popularity of Kinosaki, which got 1,010,000 visitors for that year, according to a survey made by the Department of Health from the Home Office.

On 23 May 1926, an earthquake wiped out the town, leaving 272 dead and 198 wounded. The reconstruction began with the public outdoor baths (*sotoyu*) which fortunately were rather well spared by the earthquake. The entire hot spring resort was rebuilt centring around those public outdoor baths. The Kinosaki of today dates back to this period of reconstruction, which ended around 1935. Because of its literary background, its development was oriented according to the image of a popular and refined *onsen*, stressing the formula *kyōzon kyōei* ('living together and prosperity for every one'). Its special administration gave place to one of the most famous trials in the history of the Japanese hot spring resorts from 1927 to 1948. It was based on private rights to dig for waters. The agreement assessed the basic idea of the 'Living together and prosperity for everyone' administration in Kinosaki. Private baths in *ryokan* are now therefore extremely restricted. The creation of the present Kinosaki dates back to 1955 when its population numbered 5523 inhabitants on its merger with another village.

In 1989 the visitors to the hot spring resort numbered 1,150,000, among whom 838,000 stayed in *ryokan* and 248,000 made a day trip. In 1988 its population had decreased to 4970 inhabitants, facing the same trend as in Arima. Crossed by the Maruyama River, which flows into the Japan Sea just a few kilometres away, the town is bordered on three sides by mountains and extends along a small stream, the

Otanigawa, which flows into the Maruyama. Its development was hindered by its location, being rather remote from the Hanshin area. It still takes more then three hours to get to Kinosaki from Osaka by train. Blessed by beautiful natural landscapes the town has always adopted a protective attitude against modifications that could be involved in the modernization process.

The public baths are still the only places in Kinosaki where modification and adaptation to new trends are allowed. The entire town planning of Kinosaki focuses on the tour of the outside public baths (*sotoyu meguri*). They number seven and are the following: the Jizōyu, the Satonoyu, the Yanagiyu, the Ichinoyu, the Gōshonoyu, the Mandarayu, and the Kōnoyu. From 1959 to 1975 the *sotoyu* were again modified and enlarged. In order to maintain the unity of its landscapes, an ordinance to protect the environment of Kinosaki (*Kinosakicho kankyō hozon jōrei*) was established in 1974. An association for the protection of the hot spring of *Kinosaki* (*Kinosakionsen no machinami mamoru kai*) was founded in 1982. The case of Kinosaki offers a rather different evolution from the one in Arima. Denying modern trends, the hot spring resort has adopted a protective attitude, which may hinder further economic development based on bathing in hot waters. Those initiatives put Kinosaki at the forefront of protection movements by citizen inhabitants, and its case has become famous among several networks involved in the protection of old urban landscapes.

Arima and Kinosaki: from playing to leisure

Arima: Japanese style bath and modern leisure

Although high-rise and built in concrete, the *ryokan* still offers a Japanese style (*wafuku*) atmosphere inside, as bathing in a hot spring cannot be Westernized, as one of my informants told me. As regards this question, the only real exception which can be noticed in Japan are the Kuraus houses (*kuahausu*) of German origin built these last years, which include swimming pools, sauna, and so on as well as Japanese-style hot baths. As visitors stay only one night in the *onsen*, curing cannot be the main motive for coming any more. A quick glance at the several pamphlets enhancing their attractive features, issued by the town of Arima and the *ryokan*, gives a close idea of what visitors are looking for during their short stay.

Not a single reference to the quality of the water appears in those documents. On the contrary, the atmosphere of the bath and its decorations are emphasized in several booklets issued by the *ryokan*. For instance, the big inn Koyokaku which boasts 192 rooms, several meeting rooms and banquet halls from 70 *tatami* to 288 *tatami*, offers two baths. The Ichinoyu is Japanese style while the Ninoyu is antique roman, an exception to our previous statement, but both have an outside bath (*rotenburo*) which is highly favoured by modern Japanese visitors. This *ryokan* offers a wide range of facilities, from bowling alley to swimming pool, from Japanese garden to recreation room (*gorakushitsu*), snack bars with *karaoke*, and so on. The Arima Grand Hotel promotes its room for the tea ceremony (*chashitsu*) which incorporates the mountain landscape as a background *shakei*. Named 'Yukian' by the last grand tea master of the Urasenke school, Tantansai, this *chashitsu* of four *tatami* and a half is the centre on which focuses a large complex dedicated to the way of tea. There, people from Osaka, Kobe, and so on can devote themselves to large tea meetings (*chakai*) or a full tea presentation with a meal (*chaji*) or merely have their *kaiseki* tea meals, receptions, and so on.

The old Gojobo boasts a *furansu kafe dobo* (a French café) serving cakes, a handicraft *mingei* shop, and a tea room (*salon de cha rocio*). Needless to say, the main purpose of these so-called *ryokan* is to offer all the amenities inside their own enclosed space, from sportive to recreational and cultural ones. The customer checks in in the afternoon, and is supposed to check out the following morning without setting a foot outside the *ryokan*. The wide range of facilities inside is dedicated to keep him or her in, without giving the client the opportunity to know the rest of the town. Banquet rooms and meeting rooms are evidence of the large groups that come to use the numerous facilities.

'Parlour playing' (*zashiki asobi*) is still in practice. Singing, dancing and playing cards with the customers while the banquet is going on, is still the work of forty-four to five *geigi geisha* depending on ten *geisha* houses (*okiya*) in Arima. They range between 15 and 60 years old. An interview with a so-called Shizunesan in the 1990 spring issue of the town magazine, *Yukemuri*, gives some details of this type of entertainment nowadays, which includes some pieces of advice. It runs as follows: 'first, it is better to arrange the coming of the *geisha* when booking the *ryokan*, which will also provide for the payment at the end of the party. It costs around 16,500 yen to call one'. In consequence, for what a group of ten persons can afford, I quote her own words in Japanese '*wakate hitori, onēsan hitori, oshamisen hitori no sannin o yobu suru no ga jozuna yobikata desu*' ('one young, one older, one on the *shamisen*[6] calling three is the right thing').

Being opposed to the self-serving attitude of the big hotels and the *ryokan*, the municipality of Arima seems to be facing hard times in town planning (*machizukuri*). Those involved in the accommodation business are quite indifferent to the global vision of the hot spring resort. The location of the town in the Rokko range is emphasized in the pamphlets. But little is said about the town itself, as little homogeneity and harmony remain between the setting and its immediate natural environment. Its attractive characteristics seem to rely more on local products (*meisan*), famous seasonal spots (*kisetsu no midokoro*) and annual events (*nenkan gyōji*).

Arima bamboo ware is one of its most famous local products as it was exported at the turn of the last century to Western countries and has been in several world exhibitions as testified by large boards hanging in bamboo shops. This material comes from the Rokko mountains. The frequent visits of Hideyoshi and Sen no Rikyū greatly influenced the conception of these products, as a majority of them is still devoted to the practice of the tea ceremony. An exhibition of some of the finest of those works is held every year during the large tea meeting (*ochakai*) in November. As this bamboo ware, which is entirely hand made, is getting more and more expensive due to Japanese labour costs, some bamboo ware is imported from China or Taiwan to sell at a lower range of prices. The latter are regarded as cheap souvenirs in comparison with the continuing craft tradition (*dentō kōgei*).

Another famous local product of Arima is the *ningyō fude*, which is said to be unique in the whole of Japan. A small doll pops out of the writing brush, when using it. The brush itself is decorated with an intricate pattern of silk threads of different colours. Only one shop selling the product remains in Arima. Compared to the 500 places in the countryside where it was produced as a sideline during the Edo period, there remain no more than fifty.

Seasonal changes are favoured in the mountains and are listed among the famous historical spots (*meisho*) of old Arima. Pamphlets issued by the town give the list of shrines, temples and parks in the ancient ruins of a historical place like the *Zuihōji* (famous for its scarlet and golden maple trees in the Autumn, a municipal park since 1951), where the sights are the most appreciated.

The main events in the annual calendar are the Irizome and the Arima Ochakai, both associated with the history of Arima. Dedicated to the two Buddhist monks, Gyōgi and Ninsai, who helped to develop or reconstruct Arima, the Irizome festival takes place every 2 January. Blending two religious traditions, the ceremony involves the *onsenjinja* with the body of the Shintō deity (*shintai*) of Onamuchi no mikoto, and the *onsenji* with two images of the Buddhist monks carried on a *mikoshi* (palanquin of a Shintō god). The Shintō and the Buddhist priests, the *geigi* dressed in *yuna*, and the owners of the *ryokan*, all follow in a procession which by its composition gives valuable information on the close relationship between such different worlds. Spiritual values from two different origins, commercial ones related to the very mundane ones are all associated to ensure the prosperity of the town. In this ceremony, the healing and spiritual virtues of the water seem to support the commercial success of the hot spring resort.

The large tea meeting (*Ochakai*) takes place every 2 and 3 November. The two schools of *chanoyu* (tea ceremony), Urasenke and Omotesenke, take in turn its organization. A religious offering of tea (*kencha*) takes place in the Zenpukuji in memory of Sen no Rikyū. Powdered tea (*matcha*) is served in outdoor style *nodate* in the grounds of the Zuihōji, the other sites (*seki*) being scattered all over the town, especially in temples, compelling the amateurs to stroll from one place to the other. Several hundreds of practitioners participate in those two days, which count for one of the main events of the year in Arima, as the whole city is involved in this event.

Kinosaki between literature and kanisuki

The main attraction in Kinosaki is the quality of its urban landscape, blending with the Otanigawa and the willow trees, which border it. The rows of wooden *ryokan* of no more than two floors along the road, add to this very particular atmosphere. But it too seems to face some hard times, as it cannot adapt to the demands of mass tourism: the same phenomenon as the old bathhouse in Dogo *onsen*. Due to the type of development chosen by the town, little may be done as far as the buildings themselves are concerned. The ordinance dating back to 1974 gives little freedom as far as the height of the buildings, the choice of the material, and so on, are concerned. In order to respond to ever diversifying demand, modern facilities were added to some of the outdoor baths. According to the city officials those additions were made for the purpose of emphasizing the individualistic characteristic of the seven *sotoyu*. The Konoyu became an outdoor bath with a traditional Japanese garden *yu teien buro*, while a jacuzzi was added to the Ichinoyu and a sauna to the Jizoyu. This municipal policy focuses on the idea of considering the whole town as one big *ryokan*, inside which visitors can choose their rooms, stay overnight, go out to bathe in one or several outdoor baths, do some shopping, and have a drink at a café (*kissaten*) while strolling around the town. The sight of customers clad in the *yukata* (summer cotton *kimono*) of their *ryokan*, with *geta* (wooden clogs) on their feet and a basket filled with soap and a hand towel hanging from their arms, has nearly vanished from most of the Japanese hot spring resorts, as people stay inside the big *ryokan*. In the summer season, a lot of visitors staying in Kinosaki prefer going to the sea. Takeno beach is just a few kilometres from Kinosaki. Spending the day on the seashore, then going back to the hot spring to indulge oneself in a outdoor bath, seems to have become a new habit in Japan, closer to modern leisure.

Neither *geisha* nor important *matsuri* can be found in Kinosaki. The hot spring festival on 23 and 24 April, on a much more modest scale than in Arima, is dedicated to Dōchi, the Buddhist monk credited with the foundation of the hot spring resort. The policy of the town towards attracting visitors focuses on the literary atmosphere of Kinosaki, as the long-standing custom of writers and calligraphers visiting is documented in a small museum and in inscriptions on stone monuments scattered around the town. Shiga Naoya (1883–1971), whose stay in Kinosaki led to his famous work *Kinosaki nite*, published in 1918, is one of the most famous.

The traditional handicraft of Kinosaki, boxes, toys, and so on decorated with coloured straw (*mugiwara saiku*) reached its prosperity during the Taisho period (1912–26). As it is getting more and more expensive for the same reasons as the bamboo ware in Arima and with the shortage of people who want to follow this traditional craft, the town tries to find new ways of making this tradition part of its cultural identity. Teaching it in schools or to housewives' groups is part of this programme.

Gourmet food and seafood products bolster the attraction of Kinosaki, especially during the winter months. A great crab from the Japan Sea (*matsubagani*), cooked in several ways, is available from November to March. Going to Kinosaki in the winter for a lot of visitors who come from the Kansai region, means walking to one of the public baths while discovering the landscape of the small town covered with snow, and then back to the *ryokan* to enjoy a *kanisuki* (crab fondue) supper.

Conclusion

From their mythical and historical origins, an intimate relation with religious matters was involved in bathing and taking a cure in the hot waters of Japanese hot spring resorts. As curing involved a long stay, people had a lot of free time. This religious aspect has almost disappeared nowadays, but the idea of having some leisure time around the custom of having a hot bath remains. As taking a cure is no longer the main aim of those with a very short stay, entertaining oneself turns out to be the main purpose of all the leisure facilities, which spread around the hot springs resorts, inside and outside the *ryokan*. Bathing becomes reduced to a small part of the visitor's stay, which involves playing sports, enjoying gourmet food, buying local products, discovering unfamiliar aspects of a Japan removed from the great urban centres (autumnal colours in the mountains, snow-covered landscapes, and so on). It has a complementary role, and appears as one among several attractive characteristics that foster tourist competition among *onsen*.

The flexibility with which the resorts have evolved from one world to the other was due to the fact that there was no segregation between them. It is still difficult to distinguish work from play on a lot of social occasions in modern Japan. How should a golf tour on a weekday be classified for instance? Some fun is involved in spite of playing with colleagues or business associates. One of the most radical changes in modern Japan comes from the fact that the new types of occupation tend to involve segregation. *Rejā* (leisure) has its own world, which becomes more and more independent of other types of occupation: working, resting, and curing. One of the main reasons for the changes in those two *onsen* is that they have evolved from a play-oriented society, to a leisure-oriented one.

In Kinosaki, the choice of an original solution which relies on protection, compared to most Japanese hot springs resorts seems closer to behavioural habits rooted in the past and hinders modern economic development. Taking a cure and playing could go together, but *rejā* by definition has to stand alone. The influence of this evolution on urban landscapes has begun to show its impact, with the numerous plans for leisure parks scattered all over Japan. The Dutch city of Huis Ten Bosch, built on reclaimed lands between Sasebo and Nagasaki, opened during the spring of 1992, gives an illustration of an entirely new conception of a city built for leisure.

Notes

1 *Nihonshoki* (or *Nihongi*) is a collection of ancient chronicles of Japan, depicting its mythological origins to the end of the reign of the Emperor Jitō in 696.
2 Toyotomi Hideyoshi (1536–98), warlord of humble origin, rose to be one of the few men who unified Japan. He is one of the greatest figures of Japanese history.
3 *Man'yōshū* (Collection of the ten thousand leaves) is the earliest extant collection of Japanese poems. The most recent one dates from 759.
4 *Engishiki*, a collection of fifty books or fascicles of supplementary governmental regulations, was compiled between 905 and 927.
5 *Kokinwakashū*, or *Kokinshū* (Collection of Japanese poems from ancient and modern times), was compiled around 905.
6 *Shamisen* is a three-stringed plucked lute.

Bibliography

Guichard-Anguis, S. (1993) 'Stations balnéaires japonaises: de la pension de famille minshuku, au complexe hôtelier et au parc de loisirs', Talence, CESURB, *Recherches Urbaines* (8): 85–101.

Jarassé, D. (ed.) (1996) *2000 ans de thermalisme*, Clermont-Ferrand: Institut d'Etudes du Massif Central, Coll. *Thermalisme et civilization*, IV.

Koga, G. (1987) 'Onsen to keikan' (Hot springs and landscapes), *Onsen* 55(11).

Nihon, Onsen Kyōkai (Japanese Association of Hot Springs) (1983), *Spas in Japan*, Tokyo, Nihon Onsen Kyōkai.

Nishimura, T. (1990) '*Kinosaki onsen no keikan hōzon to seibi*' (Protection of landscapes and equipment in the hot spring of Kinosaki), *Onsen* 58(7).

Shiga, N. (1986) *Le séjour à Kinosaki (Kinosaki nite)*, Paris: Arfuyen.

Sōrifu (Prime Minister's Office) (1990) *Kankō hakusho* (White paper on tourism), Tokyo: Okurashō.

Yamamura, J. (1988) *Nihon no onsenchi: sono hattatsu. Gendai to arikata* (Japanese hot springs: development. The present and their way of being), Tokyo: Nihon Onsen Kyōkai.

Yoshida, M., Tanaka, I. and Sesoko, T. (1987) *Asobi: The Sensibility at Play*, Tokyo: Tokyo Cosmo Public Corporation.

Zadankai: Kinosaki onsen no kyōzon kyōei (Round-table talk: coexistence and mutual prosperity of the hot spring of Kinosaki) (1980) *Onsen* 48(8).

Zadankai: Kinosaki onsen no machizukuri (Round-table talk: urban making in the hot spring of Kinosaki) (1985) *Onsen*, vol. 53, 5.

16 Illegal fishing and power games

Ulrike Nennstiel

With the development of leisure time and tourism, as well as transport facilities easing access to remote areas of the country, illegal fishing has become a frequent phenomenon in Hokkaido as well as in other parts of Japan. In several areas, even the term 'illegal fishing season' has come into use. For some people, intentionally engaging in unlicensed fishing activities has become an exciting game, while others still try to ignore the legal restrictions imposed on amateur angling. Professional fishermen, on the other hand, doubtless regard it as a threat to their income. Obviously, the leisure and pleasure of some people is regarded as a serious problem by others.

From about ten to fifteen years ago, in Hokkaido, illegal fishing has grown into such a severe problem that fishing co-operatives have organized campaigns in Sapporo and other central cities in order to make people aware of the impact they might have by going out to the sea or to a lake to fish 'just for pleasure'. However, campaigns like these have not had much of a visible effect. There have also been lawsuits against illegal fishing, but even these have not been able to bring about an essential change to the situation. None the less, it seems reasonable now to expect anyone wanting to fish to know that there are legal restrictions imposed on the pleasure of going out to a lake and catching whatever one can.

In this chapter, one concrete case of seemingly casual small talk at the shore will be used as an example to reveal the power relations involved in the phenomenon of illegal fishing, as well as the legal and economic conditions these relations are based on. The research on illegal fishing was accomplished as a minor part of field studies done at lake Notoro in the spring and summer of 1990.

Lake Notoro, lying in the north east of Hokkaido, was opened to the Okhotsk Sea several years ago. Most of the surroundings of the lake are covered in grass and reed, but there are two fishing villages and an extended harbour with facilities for food processing and transport facilities as well. The harbour and the adjacent land, however, have never been used in accordance with their original aim. Instead, tourists and amateur anglers park their cars at the quay and enjoy sitting there for angling.

There are only thirty-two fishermen living by the lake. They engage mainly in joint cultivation and fishing of marine life such as scallop, lobster, plaice, sea urchin and others. However, illegal fishing has increased so much that the professionals have taken a variety of measures aimed at confining it. As a last resort, they have instituted a kind of 'guardsman system'. Every night, eight fishermen keep watch at the lake from 7 o'clock in the evening until 3 o'clock in the morning. For the fishermen this means that every one of them has to stay out every fourth night. Apart from that, they have one man employed almost exclusively to watch strangers strolling around the lake during the daytime. Even with this drastic measure, again and again they find nets or other devices for catching fish used by people without a fishing licence, and often they realize, for example, that lobsters they have caught and left outside to keep them alive, are being stolen. This is what angler *A* had been confronted with just before the following scenario occurred.

A was driving his car around the lake with the intention of watching for anglers and other strangers who might be engaged in unlicensed fishing. Reaching the quay of the huge disused harbour he stopped near a couple who were sitting behind their car angling. The fisherman got out of his car. Looking around, and seemingly without any particular purpose, he asked the people where they were from, and talked about the weather, the sea and about fish. He sauntered to the edge of the pier and, looking down into the water, he found what he was searching for – bait for catching lobsters put into a net, and bound with a rope to one of the concrete posts tying up boats. Shaking his head, the fisherman criticized as stupid the actions of people who cut mackerel[1] into pieces, put it into nets and put them in the lake.

'Everyone knows it's forbidden to engage in unlicenced lobster fishing'. Keeping his eyes on the strangers, who were apparently preparing to grill their catch for an outdoor dinner, he added: 'The people who cut this ought to eat the mackerel instead . . .' The tourist glanced at the big letters on the fisherman's car which showed the name and occupation of its owner. He seemed a bit bewildered, but hastily agreed with what the man was saying, while *A* continued to refer to the problem of illegal fishing, talking half to the stranger, half to himself. 'I don't understand why people still try to catch lobster though everybody knows it's forbidden.' 'Me neither', the other one nervously affirmed, outwardly devoting all his attention to his fishing rod. The fisherman knelt down at the edge of the quay and, politely ascertaining 'It's not yours, is it?', he loosened the knot and let the net with the mackerel sink down to the bottom of the lake. The tourist did not show any sign of emotion. Murmuring 'I came to warn you, but the police will patrol here within less than 30 minutes',[2] *A* got into his car and left.

The strangers are just two of the many tourists who come to the lake for a weekend or for a holiday. They enjoy fishing and eating their catch – as many people do. But this time their fun was suddenly brought to an end. They did not get the lobsters they were looking forward to. Their tools were lost, and their bait was lost too. Probably, at least for this evening, they could not even enjoy any more angling.

The fisherman, on the other hand, did not go out for fun. He is tired of having to stay awake every fourth night, and particularly of having to do so not in order to work and make money, but to prevent other people from breaking the law. Notwithstanding, in the end it was he who was enjoying the encounter – as far as it can be said that either one was enjoying it at all. It was he who was exercising power and achieving success in what he went out for – that is, in actively interfering with other people's attempts to take away what he considers his own. In this sense, there occurred a role reversal. The ones who set out to have fun lost their tools and their good mood as well, while the one who came out with a negative and rather passive goal, namely to 'prevent' others from getting what they went out for, in the end, took over the active and, comparatively, more enjoyable part.

None of the persons 'playing a role' during the encounter enjoyed 'pleasure' in the sense that Mercer (1983) describes, as being based on 'a whole-hearted and unselfconscious involvement' (Mercer 1983: 84), though both of them did have pleasure in a certain sense. The fisherman enjoyed destroying the bait, superiority in the dialogue, and, last but not least, taking revenge for the stolen lobsters – though, in all likelihood, the revenge did not hit 'the right' note. The stranger, on the other hand, enjoyed getting out of the situation without running into serious trouble. His pleasure had been converted from that of fishing and the intended lobster dinner to the mere relief of having avoided further unpleasantness.

Differing from the mechanism Thompson discovered by studying consumption and play, the joy of the tourist was not '[. . .] enhanced by the confrontation with the reality principle' (Thompson 1983: 136), but rather abruptly brought to end when he found himself confronted with the 'reality principle', because, almost simultaneously, he had to realize that he was the one to succumb in the controversy. He was not able to '[. . .] overcome [. . .] the "obstacle" of the reality principle within the field of pleasure', but the reality principle destroyed his pleasure entirely. The fisherman, on the other hand, started his actions from the base of the 'reality principle' and, finally, he experienced pleasure – although only within the framework of hardship. He initiated the confrontation, and he attained 'victory', while on the surface both sides were engaging in nothing more than conversational small talk.

The discrepancy between what was going on under the surface and what was actually brought up in words can be explained by Goffman: '[. . .] since each participant in an undertaking is concerned, albeit for differing reasons, with saving his own face and the face of others, then tacit cooperation will naturally arise so that the participants together can attain their shared but differently motivated objects' (Goffman 1967: 29). Indeed, there seemed to exist a tacit agreement between the fisherman and the stranger to continue to play the role each one had taken, as long as the other one would not violate the rules of the game.

The fisherman was ready to save the face of the tourist and not directly to accuse him, as long as he could prevent him and, maybe others, from illegal fishing activities. He was not interested in punishing the one he had caught red-handed as severely as possible, but rather he intended to use his time to prevent as many people as possible from fishing illegally. The tourist, on the other hand, could not blame the fisherman for the bait nor for his arrogant manner, and even an argument about the question of whether the legal regulation of fishing rights was appropriate or not, undoubtedly, would have unmasked him. Therefore, neither dared openly to mention what both of them actually were concerned about. The superficial small talk as such began in a way as described by Strauss: 'Opening gambits are made in which persons test each other and then move on to other conversational maneuvers [. . .] After certain interchanges, there is quite literally "no return"' (Strauss 1977: 62).

The phase of the conversation making it impossible to 'return', was initiated by the fisherman as he came 'to the topic'. Though the stranger was puzzled when he realized who it was he was talking to, he immediately decided not to take any risk, and managed to keep '[. . .] "composure", that is, self-control, self-possession, or poise [. . .] also, what is thought of as an affective side, the emotional self-control required in dealing with others' (Goffman 1967: 222). He tried to avoid any unpleasant incident and, after learning the identity of the fisherman, he pretended to share the viewpoint of his opponent. He demonstrated '[. . .] capacities for standing correct and steady in the face of sudden pressures [. . .]' (Goffman 1967: 217) – though this, like the small talk, was true only on the surface. In fact, the tourist completely lost his ground, while the fisherman, with increasing aggression, took the active part in the encounter.

The tourist's attempt at 'countering an assignment [. . .] while it is occuring' (Strauss 1977: 83) failed. He could not avoid taking the role of someone who condemns illegal fishing, while at the same time, he felt himself discovered doing exactly what he pretended to condemn. Once assumed, he could not help continuing to play the same role throughout the encounter. Hence he was forced to accept all further moves made by the fisherman, and to consider all possible consequences before any word he wanted to say himself. He had no chance to take a different stance like, for example, to assert that he had never heard anything about legal restrictions imposed on amateur angling. He could not blame the fisherman for destroying his bait, after, following the rules of the game, he had disclaimed that the bait was his own. He had to follow up this strategy, as '[. . .] strategies often require temporary acceptance of the other's claim and control over your own, in order not to break off interaction, and to succeed in establishing (your) long-range aims' (Strauss 1977: 87) – notwithstanding that the 'long-range aims' of the tourist at this stage had already been reduced merely to getting out of the encounter without being caught.

The fisherman, on the other hand, aimed not only to prevent *this* angler from lobster fishing, but to let as many people as possible know that they risk losing their bait and being seized by the police, if they engage in illegal fishing activities. Having his catch stolen, he felt he was treated unfairly as described by Goffman: 'Just as the individual owes others courtesies, so they owe courtesies to him, and should they fail to treat him properly he may find he must risk retaliatory acts in order to show that advantage cannot be taken of him' (Goffman 1967: 221). The fact that the tourist he was talking to, and the person who stole his catch probably differed, was insignificant to the fisherman at the moment he found the bait for the forbidden lobster fishing.

Summing up, the fisherman having to go out and 'defend' his income seemed to be vunerable, but analysing the scene described he clearly turned out to hold the stronger position during the encounter. Hence, it appears relevant to examine the structural context and legal framework lying behind it.

The fishing law was enacted in 1949, and has remained fundamentally the same since. Relevant to the case of Notoro, this law states (paragraph 2, article 9) that one needs special permission (*gyogyōken*) to engage in pisciculture, in the cultivation of mussels, and in fishing activities. Details concerning special rights for various fishing methods like, for example, employing a fixed net, and concerning the partition of a lake or a coastline into zones for diverse fishing activities are decided by the local cooperative (section 2, article 8). There is one paragraph (section 8, article 127–32) especially assigned to account for the particular conditions of inland fishing in lakes and rivers. The framework for responses to violations is laid down in section 10, allowing for imprisonment for up to three years, or a fine of 2 million yen, for severe cases of persons ignoring this law. Article 140 of the same paragraph explicitly calls for the confiscation of all fish and fishing tackle, including boats, from someone caught fishing illegally. Consequently, the fisherman destroying the bait of someone else stays within the framework of legal action. To formulate it from a different perspective, his position in the encounter is made strong by 'having the law on his side'. What does this mean in the context of the social and economic structure in which the encounter was embedded?

Generally speaking, fishermen hardly ever attain high social status within Japanese society, although the techniques they employ and the risks they are ready to take have influenced the Japanese diet and eating habits for many centuries. Actually, there are quite a few people called 'fishermen' (cf. Nennstiel 1991) who are rather rich people, but they seem to be held in lesser esteem because of the traditional image associated with the work of anglers that is characterized by the 'three Ks': *kiken* (dangerous), *kitanai* (dirty), and *kusai* (malodorous). The work of those going out on a fishing smack for net fishing, and of those walking in cold shallow waters or using a small motorboat to carry out inshore fishing corresponds to this image. One ought to know, however, that the large number of men hired to work on a fishing smack, or to help prepare tackle for small net fishing, catching octopus, crab, and so on are not counted as 'fishermen', because they do not belong to any fishing co-operative, nor do they own any fishing rights. In other words, being a member of a fishing co-operative is the precondition to acquire fishing rights and to be a 'fisherman' according to the legal regulations. Most of the wealthier fishermen, on the other hand, do not go out on a fishing smack, nor otherwise engage in fishing activities themselves (though this is required as one of the preconditions for being legally allowed to hold fishing rights), but rather they carry out managing or representative functions in and out of the fishing co-operative.

At Notoro lake, as in many other places in Japan, the fishermen cultivate and sell almost all of the marine life themselves. To borrow their own words, they view the lake as their 'field for cultivation', as the farmers view their land. Unlike the farmers, however, the angler cannot divide the lake into plots treated as personal property, but they have to 'cultivate their field' in common. The co-operative decides the quantity each one of them is allowed to bring in, and when. Knowing all that, it seems hardly surprizing that the fisherman view tourists fishing in the lake as people stealing their harvest.

According to information given to me by some of the anglers of Notoro lake,[3] they work a total of between 150 and 200 days a year. Unlike most fishermen all over the country they consider their work neither dangerous, dirty, nor even malodorous. The place where they work on the lake is very close to the shore, and, if it is windy, they do not go out at all, because otherwise they could risk damaging their tackle. Considering the aspect 'dirty', of course, neither the tools nor the mussels, and so on, are as clean as paper and pencil might be, but they are clean in comparison to, for example, fishing nets and the equipment for the cultivation of seaweed, to say nothing about the dirt farm workers or miners might have to face. Most of the time the anglers at Notoro lake do not even wear waterproof clothes for work, but just jeans; this can be seen as another indication that they consider their work as neither dirty nor malodorous. In comparison to other people labouring in the primary sector, the working conditions of the fishermen at Notoro lake seem extraordinarily attractive.

Talking about their income, the fishermen at Notoro lake, on the average, report sales of about 30 million yen a year.[4] Although exposed to the influences of nature their income is comparatively stable and reliable, since, actually, it depends more on cultivation than on risky fishing activities. The equipment required is quite expensive, amounting to 15 million yen for a good boat, and to about 6 million for the cultivation tools,[5] but of course, these are not bought annually, nor ever all at once. Certainly, there is the annual expenditure for repairing the equipment, for fuel and so forth. Nonetheless, without a doubt, on average they earn more than the 'average salaried worker' in a big city, not to mention those white-collar workers living in villages or working for smaller companies.[6]

It seems appropriate, therefore, to question the adequacy of the legal regulations, in the face of the importance of one or two lobsters for the fishermen compared to the recreation and joy that successful angling and an outdoor dinner would mean for the tourist. Admittedly, lobsters are expensive, their price being more than twice as high as for any other marine life the fishermen sell to the co-operative, and they make up about 9 per cent of their income. According to information given by one of the fishermen those who are good at lobster fishing could earn up to 3.5 million yen in ten days, and this figure is only for lobster catches. But still, one is inclined to think that two or three lobsters stolen for an outdoor dinner ought not to cause a really serious problem for the angler. Could one look, then, at the scene described as the angler making fun out of frightening people who come for amusement, and 'playing' with those who leave the cities in search for pleasure and recreation?

The fishermen observed played an invented role in seemingly helping the tourist not to be caught by the police, while in fact, it is not the 'police', but only the watchman employed by the fishermen who is about to pass by. Nevertheless, it is not just for amusement that the fisherman warns his adversary about the watchman he himself is paying for. The 'role' he chose is based on quite serious considerations. What matters to him is to prevent as many people as possible from fishing illegally, not the pleasure of seeing his 'enemies' being caught. He is not particularly enjoying his patrol job nor can he be said to be playing intentionally with the tourist. The 'power game' seems to be initiated on another level of the social structure, as '[. . .] persons present in a social situation can serve not only as witnesses but also as the very objects upon which the individual acts [. . .]' (Goffman 1986: 206). The question occuring then would be who are the 'players' and what are the rules of their game?

Let me once again cite Thomas who explained 'games' as '[. . .] conflicts of interests between people or groups of people such as political parties, governments and businesses [. . .]' (Thomas 1984: 15). In the example discussed in this chapter, it is clearly not 'political parties', nor 'governments', but rather 'businesses' which hold the strings in their hands. If it were only one or two holidaymakers fishing for lobsters for their outdoor supper they ought never to become a threat to the fishermen living under economic conditions such as those described above. Actually, the problem is caused by the number of tourists, since it is not just 'a few' people coming to the lake, but quite literally thousands.[7] Depending on the scale, it seems self-evident that with their number surpassing a certain limit, the tourists do become a threat to the fishermen, even if each person would be considering only his or her own supper, and about 30 per cent of the tourists would not even do that. But why has it become difficult to prevent the holidaymakers at the lake from engaging in illegal fishing?

According to research done by the the municipal association for the development of tourism, 96 per cent of the people coming to Abashiri do so for 'touristic leisure' (*kankōrejā*), to enjoy nature and stay outdoors to pursue sports and hobbies. Asked in a questionnaire with multiple answers, more than 50 per cent of the tourists chose 'looking at the scenery and the mountainous landscape around the lakes' as something they were enjoying particularly. The number of those stating that they came mainly for angling is comparatively low, amounting to about 600 people 'only', but those stating that they came looking forward to gathering mussels (*shiohigari*) accounted for 20 per cent of the tourists, corresponding to 400,000 persons a year! (Abashiri *kankō shindan hōkokusho* 1989:70)

Many of these people might be disappointed when they have to realize that their expectations might not hold true, since they are not allowed to enjoy the lake in every way they would like to. The expectations of most holidaymakers are based on images built upon what they can see in leaflets about Abashiri and Notoro lake. One of the photographs in these leaflets shows people gathering 'something' in the shallow waters at the shore of Notoro lake. These 'something' are probably short-necked clams which can be found there in huge numbers. Looking at the photographs, however, citizens in the metropolis might think of sea urchins, scallops or, at least, clams bigger than the ones mentioned. The text next to the picture refers to Notoro lake as, according to Ainu legend, 'home to the world's fishes', and characterizes the lake for its richness of plants and abundant fish during each of the four seasons. The tourists, consequently, might imagine themselves gathering their own 'natural food' from the lake to make an 'all-natural barbecue' in the middle of an 'all-embracing nature' (Abashirishi Abashiri *kankōkōsha* 1990: 9).

Tourists attracted by commercial advertisements of this sort might feel quite dissatisfied with being restricted only to look at nature so colourfully displayed in the prospectus. Municipal officers in the division of tourism and members of the association for the promotion of tourism being responsible for producing this expectation, do not, of course, intend to make the tourists feel discomfort, but, notwithstanding, they almost inevitably do so. They tend to ignore the problem they are creating, because they show interest only in the number of tourists coming to the city, how long these visitors stay, and where they will buy their souvenirs. The situation of peasants or fishermen never enters their minds, except to make use of these 'traditional sectors' for further attracting tourists by offering the chance to experience harvesting first-hand or to go out fishing under the leadership of an expert.

In almost unanimous agreement, members of the city council strive for a policy that pays primary attention to 'bringing outside money into the city'. This means that they offer special conditions to companies who might be interested in establishing a plant or a branch in Abashiri as well as to undertake any effort to attract as many tourists as possible. Fishing and agriculture are valued as those sectors that historically caused Japanese to settle down in this area and gave rise to the development of the city; therefore, according to the assembly, they should not be ignored. Considering the future, however, these traditional sectors seem to be devoted to decline, and councillors regard it as indispensible for the 'future of the city' to promote tourism, even if it should be at the expense of agriculture and fishing. The farmers and the fishermen in the assembly do not dissent from this 'general opinion', but they do not represent their colleagues. If there is anybody at all in the assembly dissenting from the 'general opinion', then it is the members of the communist party doubting whether 'bringing outside money into the city' really is the most suitable way to meet the needs of the citizens.

Summing up, the following conclusions may be drawn. First, what on the surface appears to be occasional small talk, turns out to be a dispute between a fisherman and a tourist about the lobsters the tourist was aiming to enjoy for his outdoor supper. Second, if the object of this fight were of concern exclusively to the two persons directly involved, it would not have been worthy of any further consideration. However, this particular dispute can be regarded as a substitute for a conflict representing the competing interests of the traditional sector fisheries on one hand, and those of tourism, which is regarded as 'the business of the future' on the other. Third, legally, the fisherman still holds the stronger position, and this becomes decisive in the example offered. The attitude of the city council, however, aligns with a more universal tendency which, in the future, might bring about a change in the legal regulation in favour of tourism *vis-à-vis* fishing. Fourth, economically the one or two lobsters the conversation was about should not be too important for either of the opponents, but they do become significant because of the huge number of tourists who would be happy if they could succeed in catching lobsters for their meal. The fishermen at Notoro lake enjoy extraordinarily good working conditions and a relatively stable and reliable income. Still, whether they and many other anglers engaging in fresh water or inshore fishing will be able to survive economically, in the long run, will probably depend on political issues, including the legal regulations.

Notes

1   Mackerel is used as bait for catching lobsters.
2   In fact, the police do not engage in preventing crimes, but only in their disclosure, and hence, they could not be expected to come and patrol the lake. The fisherman is actually referring to the watchman the fishing co-operative has employed to watch strangers at the lake during the day.

3   The figures given below were true for the year 1990, when the research at Notoro lake was done.
4   This data is based on interviews with several fishermen from Notoro lake, but it is almost congruent with the sales figures of 954 million for the year 1990 relating to the whole lake (Abashirishi 1994: 36).
5   This information, again, was given by the fishermen themselves.
6   In 1989 the average monthly income in Hokkaido was 76.750 yen per person, or 212.750 yen per household. In Abashiri, it was higher than the average in cities, the third highest for Hokkaido, after Sapporo and Chitose (Kyōikusha 1990).
7   The tourists travelling to Abashiri numbered more than two million persons in 1989 (Hokkaido Abashiri *kankōkyōkai* 1990), and, according to the figures given by the municipal section for commerce and industry, about 180,000 came to Notoro lake in 1989 (Abashirishi 1994:104).

Bibliography

Abashirishi (ed.) (1994) *Abashiri tōkeisho* (Statistics of Abashiri).

Abashirishi/Abashiri kankō shinkōkōsha (1990) *Ohotsku Abashiri.*

Goffman, E. (1967) *Interaction Ritual. Essays on Face-to-face Behavior*, New York: Anchor Books.

Hokkaido Abashiri kankōkyōkai (1990) *Heizei gannendo. Abashiri kankō shindan hōkokusho* (Report of a diagnosis of the tourism in Abashiri).

Kyōikusha (ed.) (1990) *Nihon Almanac 1990. Gendai Nihon o shiru sōgō dētā banku* (Japan Almanac. A comprehensive data bank for the knowledge of present-day Japan), Tokyo: Kyōikusha.

Mercer, C. (1983) 'A poverty of desire: pleasure and popular politics', in Carby, Curti King, Chambers (eds) *Formations of Pleasure*, London: Routledge and Kegan Paul, pp. 84–100.

Nennsteil, U. (1991) *'Wer gilt in A. als en "Fischer"?'* (Who is regarded as a fisherman in A.?), in *Tokyo Rikkyo daigaku keizaigaku-bu. Rikkyo keizaigaku kenkyu* (Tokyo Rikkyo University Economics Research), 44(3): 155–71.

Nōrin suizanshō (1949) *Gyogyōhō* (The fisheries law).

Strauss, A. (1977) *Mirrors and Masks. The Search for Identity*, London: Martin Robertson.

Thomas, L.C. (1984) *Games, Theories and Applications*, Chichester: Ellis Horwood Limited.

Thompson, G. (1983) 'Carnival and the calculable: consumption and play at Blackpool', in Carby, Curti/King, Chambers (eds) *Formations of Pleasure*, London: Routledge and Kegan Paul, pp. 124–36.

17 Hunters and hikers

Rival recreations in the Japanese forest

John Knight

Introduction

Some years ago the *Asahi shinbun* reported an incident in which a hiker encountered a hunter in the mountains. The hiker, frightened by the nearby blast of gunfire, went over and asked the hunter to be more careful with his gun. The hunter responded angrily. 'Aren't you the one who should be careful? We have permission to hunt, but did you get permission to hike?' (*Asahi shinbun* 7/12/1993). The same article catalogues a number of other incidents involving anti-social behaviour on the part of hunters towards passers-by, creating the impression that the aggression of the Japanese hunter is not exclusively directed to his animal prey.

These incidents, minor in themselves, crystallize a growing problem. Hiking and other forest leisure activities are becoming increasingly popular in Japan, but a rise in forest recreation among the national population is complicated by the fact that the Japanese forest is also the site of local activities. Japanese mountain villagers hunt during the winter and gather throughout the year. This territorial overlap between local and national recreations is a source of tension, friction and even at times violence. Every year reports of hunting accidents appear in the Japanese newspapers, including a growing number of confrontational incidents, like the one above, involving hikers from the cities.

This chapter examines the phenomenon of forest recreation in Japan. It focuses on the forest recreation of mountain villagers, the rise of forest recreation among the national population, and the relationship between the two. Data is drawn primarily from the municipality of Hongū-chō, lying on the southern Kii Peninsula, western Japan, where anthropological fieldwork has been carried out in a number of different spells since 1987, and also from secondary literature on forests and forest tourism in other regions of Japan.

Japanese forests

Two-thirds of the Japanese land area consists of mountain forest, known as *yama*. The Japanese archipelago can be divided into two main ecological zones corresponding to two kinds of indigenous forest – beech forest (*bunarin*) and warm temperate forest (*shōyōjurin* or lucidophyllous forest). However, in the 1990s around

45 per cent of the Japanese forest area consisted of coniferous timber plantations. The remainder of the forest area is usually characterized as 'natural forest' (*tennenrin* or *shizenrin*), but most of this forest is, in fact, secondary, anthropogenic forest – such as that felled in the past for fuel (charcoal or firewood) – and only around 5 per cent of Japan's forest area is primary forest.

Hongū-chō covers an upland area of steep hills and low mountains, along with a number of high mountain peaks (two of which exceed 1000 metres). Settlement in Hongū is generally on low altitude slopes of below 500 metres. Villages were originally surrounded by lucidophyllous forest which, over time, has been cut, gathered from, swidden-farmed, planted and generally anthropogenically altered.

The forest has contributed in important ways to upland livelihoods. It has supplied fuel in the form of firewood and charcoal, green fodder for farming and various foodstuffs for the upland population. Many forest animals and birds were hunted for their meat (and also for the medicinal or tonifying value of their body parts or substances). Nuts, berries, wild mushrooms and a wide range of *sansai* or edible plants (bracken, silvervine, fern, butterbur, and so on) were gathered. Forest plants were used for medicine, basket materials and fibres (textiles). Sakaki, pine, hemlock and maple were used as sacred offerings in the home or at festivals. Miscanthus grasses for thatching were also obtained from the *satoyama*.

In the modern period, the primary importance of the forest for livelihood has been in connection with forestry. Most of the upland population was employed in the forestry industry, producing charcoal or timber. In the timber plantations, forestry labour consists of planting saplings, cutting undergrowth, thinning and of branching. Until recently, men had to stay in the mountains for extended periods – 'mountain stays' (*yamadomari*) – but in the postwar period the expanding network of forest roads has gradually made forestry a commutable occupation.

The *yama*: danger and licence

Japanese folklorists and other scholars have argued that a dualistic worldview existed among rural, especially upland Japanese in which 'the village world' (*sato no sekai*) is imagined as starkly opposed to 'the mountain world' (*yama no sekai*) (Yukawa 1991; Katō 1993: 202–4).

> Conduct which would call into question one's sanity in the everyday world [of the village] becomes natural conduct in the mountains. It has come to be realized that this is possible because the mountains are a different world from the village. In other words, the mountains are a separate world [*ikai*] which can be seen to have its own separate way of thinking and ethics. This territory is symbolized by the existence of the mountain spirit.
>
> (Yukawa 1991: 50)

The mountain forest or *yama* is a mysterious, dangerous place inhabited by ghosts, demons, and a range of other assorted spirits. Foresters, hunters or gatherers experience sudden, unaccountable weariness in the *yama*. Or they hear somebody calling to them but get no response when shouting back, or see somebody who then disappears. Such incidents are often accounted for as 'tricks' of the raccoon-dog (or, more rarely, the fox) or by reference to the presence of old graves in the mountains. There are many ghost stories. In Hongū some years ago, a hiker from the city reported that when passing along the old pilgrim's forest trail (the *Kumano kodō*) through an old abandoned village, he was invited into a house by an old woman and her daughter who offered him tea. But while he was waiting inside, his two hosts disappeared! It turned out that an old woman and her daughter really had lived in that house long ago! This contemporary ghost story attracted considerable media attention, including a television crew which came to film the old abandoned house in question.

The *yama* is a place where untoward deaths occur, including suicide, infanticide, murder, and execution. For example, in Ibaraki prefecture an old woman starved to death in a tiny mountain hut, where she had gone a month before (Yukawa 1991: ii–iii). She had been living alone in the village since her three sons had outmigrated, and opted to die slowly living in the mountain hut, far from the village. Yukawa holds that the incident reveals a latent pattern of thought about mountains among the Japanese (*ibid.*). The *yama* are also associated with activities of the Japanese underworld, such as organized poaching (*Asahi shinbun* 29/1/1988, 10/3/1988), illicit cultivation of marijuana (Nozoe 1994: 212), or gangland punishments and disposal of bodies.

The *yama* has long been a space for fugitives. Many of Japan's remote settlements trace their origins to the Genpei Wars, and the refugees who, escaping from persecution by the victors, fled into the mountains. Many mountain villages on the Kii Peninsula claim *ochiudo* (literally, 'fallen people') origins. This fugitive theme is famously depicted in Japanese cinema, in films such as the 1958 Kurosawa classic *Kakushi toride no sanakunin* (English title, '*The Hidden Fortress*'), in which the remaining members of a defeated ruling family in the sixteenth-century civil wars first hide in the mountains and then, when pursued by the victors, attempt to flee to safety through the mountains. This fugitive tradition finds more recent expression in the many claimed forest sightings throughout Japan of Aum Shinrikyō followers wanted by police in connection with the 1995 sarin gas attacks on the Tokyo subway. Such rumours circulated in the interior of the Kii Peninsula – for example, in the winter of 1995–6 such a rumour went round in Hongū upon the sighting of a tent in the forest.

Gambling is said to have taken place in the mountains, where it was safe from detection by the authorities. Long viewed in rural areas with moral opprobrium, gambling, where it did take place, was shrouded in secrecy. Gamblers congregated in certain places in the mountains, out of sight of fellow villagers. In some cases, these places are associated with frightening legends, such as the appearance of wolves, which, some suspect, were made up by gamblers to keep villagers away at night. The *yama* is also a place of sexual liaisons. This is shown in the 1985 film *Himatsuri* directed by Yanagimachi Mitsuo (screenplay by Nakagami Kenji), where the *yama* features prominently as the site of adultery and other illicit relationships among villagers. In present-day Hongū, there are certain spots in the mountains where courting couples go in their cars.

Hunting

The *yama* has also long been a site of recreation for the upland population. The *yama* was the 'playground' or *asobiba* of village children where a wide variety of games were played.[1] Hunting and trapping of small birds and animals was a popular form of play for boys. The writer and former forester Ue Toshikatsu recalls that when he was a boy, throughout the year he would set hare traps in the forest on the long journey to school each day, and then inspect them on his return (Ue 1983a: 47). The family ate most of the hares, but some he raised. Mountain village children also hunted hares with hounds in what was known as 'hare-chasing' (*usagioi*) (KHI 1979: 44–5). This form of child's play was seen as contributing to village livelihood by reducing the numbers of one of the main farm pests. Hongū men remember the summer activity of catching snakes using bamboo sticks, from which they earned pocket money by selling the snakes (for one yen each!) to the *hebiya* (snake collector) (who would in turn sell them to the *kanpōyakuya* (healer) or make snake alcohol extract), or to another village household where there was a sick person (cf. Matsutani 1994: 334–5).

Hunting is also a popular pastime among upland men. There are around a quarter of a million licensed hunters in Japan. In Hongū-chō in 1994 there were sixty-three registered gunholders and thirteen registered trappers. Many Hongū men spend winter weekends in the mountains hunting for wild boar, deer, rabbits, pheasants, turtledoves, and so on. Hunting (of boar and deer) involves groups of five or more men (with dogs), which feature a division of labour between, on the one hand, the *seko* (and his dog) who flushes out the wild boar from the mountains, and, on the other, the *machi* (shooters) who wait at concealed spots to fire on the fleeing animal. Hunting is a passion for most of those involved in it. Hounds are often an object of pride and of considerable debate and discussion among hunters. Many hunters breed their own hounds, and some spend large amounts of money in order to obtain superior hounds. They find nothing more exciting than the violent encounter between hound and wild boar. Peninsular hunters participate in annual boarhound trials at which local hounds compete to demonstrate their boar-stopping skills.

One word for hunter in Japanese is *sesshōnin* or 'lifetaker', for the most part a noun used by past generations of hunters. *Sesshōnin* has strong negative religious connotations because *sesshō* or lifetaking is expressly forbidden by Buddhism. The English term 'hunter' (*hantā*) is increasingly used among Japanese hunters, and conveys the sense that hunting is a modern recreational activity or 'sport' (*supōtsu*). Hunters sometimes draw analogies between hunting and other sports. One boarhunter, explaining to me the importance of hounds getting sufficient exercise between hunting seasons, said it was like baseball players having a good pre-season: one would not expect a top baseball player suddenly to start performing in the baseball season after having been denied exercise for the off-season.

The hunter pits his hunting skill against the 'natural wisdom' (*tennen no chie*) of the wild boar, often referred to by hunters as the 'opponent' (*aite*). The wild boar is recognized by hunters to be a 'smart animal' (*kashikoi dōbutsu*). It is not passively chased, but leads the hunting party into the most difficult, challenging terrain, as though it is testing the physical ability of the hunters and their dogs. The wild boar is said to tease hunters and hounds alike by taking them in one direction before suddenly reversing back. The wild boar is also an ill-willed (*ijiwarui*) animal which 'has confidence in its fighting ability' (Ue 1983a: 37). Hounds are often injured by the boar and sometimes killed. Many boarhunters have scars and injuries from past encounters. Some have been crippled, and a few have even been killed when charged by a wounded boar. Together, these two elements of difficulty and danger make boarhunting stand out from other forms of hunting.

Hunting also resembles a war game. In Japan, the general association between hunting and war is a long-established one, but applies especially to the wild boar. Boarhunting is often referred to as a 'war' or 'battle' (*tatakai*): the wild boar is said to have its own 'weapons' (*buki*) in the form of sharp tusks. Unlike the meek deer, the wild boar may well charge the hunter, and engage man and dog in a bloody battle. Moreover, even when it is trapped or shot, the boar offers brave resistance right to the end. A 1996 newspaper report, on the catching of an unusually large boar in Yoshino describes the bloody battle with the boar, in which three hunting dogs were gored, and how, when the boar was finally felled, the hunters spontaneously shouted '*banzai*', as though celebrating a great military victory (*Asahi Shinbun* 19/1/1996)!

Hunting groups also compete against each other. The more animals a group catches, the higher its 'marks' (*seizeki*). Hunting success always becomes public knowledge, for on return to the village neighbours will gather at the hunter's house, and may well be invited to eat together, while raw meat is also distributed among friends, relatives and neighbours. Hunting success becomes a topic of conversation for days afterwards, and the successful hunter receives praise for his achievements. Conversely, the lack of success of other groups comes to be noticed, and this too becomes the target of gossip and even ridicule. The rivalry between hunting groups (and to some extent within them) is further manifested in the many claims and counter-claims about the numbers of wild boar caught by the group in a season (or over the years), about the record size of an animal caught, and about the achievements of superlative boarhounds.

If hunting tends to be associated, first and foremost, with the excitement of the hunt, it can none the less be a source of relaxation for its practitioners. The forest is a refuge from the village. Hunting typically involves spending a whole day in the mountains, much of which is, for the *machi* shooter, spent alone in one spot waiting for an animal to appear. One Hongū *machi* told me that he enjoys the long hours of solitude in the forest, where he can think about things without being disturbed by family, by neighbours or by the telephone. He does not get bored because he has to remain alert to the sounds of the forest and to the occasional messages received from other hunters on the two-way radio.

Hunting is also ascribed a certain moral value. In Japan, as elsewhere, hunting is associated with manliness. Hunting wild boar in particular is a test of whether a man has 'courage' (*dokyō*) or not. Hunters themselves believe that through hunting they develop certain qualities, such as patience (in tracking) and calmness in the face of danger (when a wild boar is encountered). This idea – that hunting improves those who practise it – is expressed more formally in the term *ryōdō* or 'the way of hunting' (see Kitsu 1988: 96) in which hunting appears as a kind of spiritually enriching technical accomplishment similar to *jūdō*, *kendō* or *kyūdō*.

If hunting is principally a form of recreation, hunters believe it is also important in a number of other ways. First, some hunters make money from hunting – from the sale of meat, organs and hides of captured animals. The meat of wild boar and deer is sold to tourist inns, while the wild boar's gall bladder can also be sold, for medicinal purposes. Second, hunting helps to control the numbers of wild animals. Hunters point out that, at a time when local farming and forestry is subject to extensive wildlife damage (crop-raiding on farms, browsing of conifer saplings, and so on), hunting helps to keep down the numbers of wildlife pests such as the wild boar and the deer and therefore provides a public service to other villagers. Third, hunting is an expression of a local tradition which should be continued. After a kill, hunters still commonly offer one of the wild boar's organs (usually the heart) to the mountain spirit. The discovery of a Jōmon-era hunting camp in the Hongū area some years ago has further reinforced the status of hunting as local tradition.

Yet hunting is a form of forest play, which has its local critics. One Hongū forest landowner described an avid local hunter who spent most winter days in the mountains as a *himajin* or 'idler'. This particular critic of hunting felt strongly that many hunters might put their spare time to better use tending their family forest landholdings, finding extra waged work, or taking up an improving pastime. This view is well-known to hunters themselves. Indeed, the same point was later made by a hunter when explaining to me why some villagers in the area hunt and others do not. The non-hunting villagers were too busy earning money, he said. Hunters, by contrast, never become prosperous. The hunter recited the expression, 'little by little with the gun, all at once by gambling' (*jirijiri teppō ni dōsa bakuchi*). The saying succinctly states that, while the hunter loses gradually and the gambler loses in one go, in the end they both lose. Hunters, like gamblers, tend to end up poor and indebted.

Gathering

Mountain villagers in Japan have long gathered plants and mushrooms from the surrounding forests. The pine mushroom (*Tricholoma matsutake*, in Japanese *matsutake*) is one of the most popular of seasonal (late autumn) tastes in Japan (as well as in Korea and China). Pine mushrooms are cooked with rice to make *mattakegohan* or stewed with fish and vegetables, and are attributed medicinal qualities (even claimed to be a cure for cancer). Some people sell what they find – for those who know the mountains and the mushroom locations (foresters, for example), pine mushroom picking can be a handy source of extra income – but often the mushrooms are used to make a special family meal or are given away to relatives and friends.

For Hongū people, pine mushroom gathering is a favourite activity. One of the main village talking points in the early autumn is about the prospects for pine mushrooms in the coming season – given the amount of rainfall over the year, and so on. Some mountains are widely known to be 'pine mushroom mountains' (*mattakeyama*), but the problem remains of finding the exact spots on a large mountainside where the mushrooms cluster. Families go mushroom picking in the mountains together, taking lunch with them and making it a day out. The pleasure of mushroom picking is something that can be passed on down the family line. Ue points out that his old father, as a form of 'family inheritance', taught him his secret mushroom-picking locations (Ue 1983b: 114). In some cases, family pine mushroom picking occasions a weekend return visit by migrant children and their families.

Solo pine mushroom gathering is also common. People often leave for the mountains early in the morning while it is still dark – lest they be noticed or followed by other villagers. (It is said that if you meet other people on the way, they invariably notice which direction you are going in.) In earlier times when pine forests were plentiful, it was common for pickers to have their own secret spots. Nearby trees were discreetly marked (by scratching their stems) in order to recognize the spot in the future. When I went picking with a Hongū man in 1994, he stated that the precise spot in the forest we had found was 'one large cypress and three pines' (*hinoki ippon matsu sanpon no tokoro*), words he then repeated to himself, mantra like, many times under his breath in order to aid memorization. But solo pine mushroom picking, because it often entails travelling deep into the mountains, can be dangerous. From time to time pickers fail to return from the mountains, leading to the setting up of search parties to find them, and also to occasional deaths. The problem of finding lost mushroom pickers is greatly exacerbated by the secrecy with which the activity is undertaken.

In recent decades the decline of pine forests has greatly reduced the amount of pine mushrooms available in the Japanese mountains. In 1941, 12,000 tonnes of pine mushrooms were picked in Japan, but in the 1990s this had fallen to fewer than 1000 tonnes a year (Wang *et al.* 1997: 317). Because of this scarcity, some people claim that pine mushroom picking is no longer as enjoyable as it was. The diminishing number of spots tend to become widely known, and the prospect of somebody else locating one's spot is enough to make the onset of pine mushroom season a time of sleepless nights (Ue 1983b: 109). The effect of this intensified rivalry is that inferior mushrooms get picked as pickers take their mushrooms while they are still small rather than wait and risk having someone else find them first. But the new scarcity also makes the achievement of actually finding any pine mushrooms that much greater. In the 1990s, even a handful of small mushrooms count as success. On the other hand, successful pickers may well keep quiet about their feat. For to boast openly may well raise the suspicions of those whose annual mushroom spot has been discovered and raided by somebody else.

Wild plants are also gathered in the forest. This may be collecting firewood and plants for domestic consumption, but also collecting plants to sell. In the 1960s and 1970s, urban demand for a range of forest plants increased, including *shikibi* (star anise) and *sakaki* (*Cleyera japonica*) (which are offered to ancestors and *kami* spirits respectively), plants for *bonsai* (azaleas), and orchids. Collecting in the forest has tended to be a woman's occupation. While men were working in the timber forests, mountain village women earned seasonal income from gathering these various plants.

Because of the seasonal character of this income-earning gathering, it is often said to have been enjoyable, a kind of *asobi*. Drawing on their knowledge of the forest, women compete eagerly with each other to pick flowering fern (*zenmaitsumi*), for example. 'Herb-picking is largely the job of women. When the season of new grass comes, they get excited and cannot stop themselves from examining the ground they pass. But apart from material gain, it is also recreation [English word used]. They compete against each other in the mountains' (Ue 1980: 222).

An indication of the competitive character of herb picking is that women gatherers try to deter rivals from picking in certain spots – for example, by saying that a bear has been spotted in this or that mountain valley (Ue 1980: 222). Although this was a deception, in fact because of the felling of much of the remote forest, bears are known to stray to those areas of the *yama* where mixed forest remains, including the pine mushroom mountains, *shiitake* mountains and mountains where wild herbs grow profusely. A Hongū man also suggested to me that one reason why there are so many tales of wolves, venomous snakes, demons and monsters in this or that mountain valley is because in the past people sought to protect their favourite picking spot or hunting locale by scaring off rivals. Sometimes, forest gathering descends into disputes. In Hongū, for example, in the past gatherers from neighbouring villages argued and even fought over the right to collect the nuts of horse chestnut trees located on the boundary between the two villages (KMG 1985: 22).

Villagers also compete with wild animals in their forest gathering. Collectors of bamboo shoots or *yamaimo* yams, for example, often find that wild boar have beaten them to it. Chestnut or loquat collectors are likewise wary of monkeys, for a troop of monkeys can, in a single visit, strip clean a whole chestnut or loquat tree! With the increase in monkey numbers in recent years, chestnut gathering in the forest is a pastime that some people, after repeated disappointments, have given up altogether. Forest animals, as game for the hunters (in the case of wild boar), may be a source of 'forest play' or *yamaasobi* for village men, but they can spoil the nut gathering *yamaasobi* of village women. Older women still go out collecting in the forest: star anise for the ancestral altar and graves, *sakaki* for the *kamidana*, (in some cases still) firewood for the bath, and seasonal herbs and mushrooms for the kitchen. Sometimes they go alone, but they may also team up with one or two friends, taking a *bentō* (box lunch) with them. Flower-viewing (and picking) in the mountains is another popular activity in the spring – especially at the time of cherry blossoms.

Whether it is the gathering of mushrooms, wild herbs or orchids, or indeed hunting, in each activity there is an element of rivalry. Those engaged in these activities emphasize the difficulty of the undertaking, often invoking the change in the mountains in recent decades whereby the pine mushrooms, herbs, orchids or wild boar have become scarcer than before. On the one hand, this is expressed in regular complaints about there being no pine mushrooms or wild boar this year. On the other hand, it heightens the satisfaction felt at times of success, for one is aware that most other hunters or gatherers that day have not had such success.

Forest tourism

If forest recreation among mountain villagers is in decline, forest recreation among the national population is on the increase. Since the passing of the Resort Law in 1987, an enormous area of rural Japan has been transformed into golf-courses, ski-slopes, theme parks, conference centres, marinas, tennis courts, swimming pools, funfairs, as well as hotels, inns, bungalows, second homes and condominium blocks. In 1990 there were fifteen million golfers in Japan – for whom there existed 1706 golf-courses, with another 325 being built, while a further 983 were being planned (Shirafuji 1993: 93).

There has also been an increase in recreational activities in the forest itself, especially among younger Japanese. Hiking is particularly popular. According to a 1993 survey, 70 per cent of respondents in their 20s and 30s had visited 'the mountains, a forest, valley or other natural area for a non-work purpose during the past year' (Fujitake 1993). In a 1994 survey of urban workers in Tokyo, three-quarters of those surveyed stated that they would like to visit village areas, two-thirds of whom expressed a preference for forest hiking and rambling and one-third for fishing and forest gathering activities (Inoue 1996: 39). National park areas, which include much primary forest, from Shiretoko in the north to Yakushima in the south, have become major tourist destinations (Mitsuda and Geisler 1992: 33–4).

Hikers also gather wild herbs and mushrooms, pick flowers, birdwatch, or observe forest animals. Forest gathering is economically exploited by rural municipalities, with mushroom, herb and nut gathering becoming organized tourist activities with entry fees charged to forest picking spots.[2] In Hongū, a campsite called 'Acorn Village' (*Donguri mura*) was recently established in a mountain valley, with the idea that campers could, among other things, gather nuts in the mountains. The suggestion has been made that local people could be employed as herb-picking or mushroom-gathering tourist guides (Kamata and Nebuka 1992: 415).

Although hiking is often undertaken individually or in small groups, larger group hiking is also popular. A kind of organized group hiking, known as 'forest showering' or *shinrinyoku*, has grown in recent years (see Kamiyama 1993; Mishima 1994), and is promoted as a health-giving pastime by municipalities on the Kii Peninsula and elsewhere. Also known as the 'forest remedy' (*shinrin ryōhō*), it is claimed benignly to stimulate the workings of the main internal body organs.

Wildlife tourism is also on the increase. Wildlife parks – monkey parks, bear parks, deer parks, and so on – are found across the country. The main wildlife attraction on the Kii Peninsula is the 'Adventure World' resort complex in Shirahama, containing within it, among other things, a safari park known as 'Safari World' which, with its lions, zebras and flamingos, offers the visitor the chance to experience 'the great plains of Africa'. The Shirahama resort also contains 'Marine World' where one can observe dolphin and killer whale shows in a purpose-built stadium. Adventure World, with its 'safari' and 'marine' experiences, is an example of a 'nature theme park' based on the successful North American formula, but has little connection with local or indigenous wildlife.

But there are also indigenous wildlife attractions on the peninsula, including a serow park (*kamoshika bokujō*) and a wild monkey park (*nozaru kōen*). The serow park, while located in a remote mountainous setting, is a confined zoo-like facility where one observes the shy antelope-like animals through a fence. However, the monkey park consists of free roaming animals which continue to live much of their lives in the forest but congregate for periodic feeding at fixed observation points where they can be viewed out in the open. In addition to this formal human provisioning of wildlife for touristic observation, informal feeding occurs as tourists and passers-by offer food to wild animals they come across in the forest or on the roadside. This informal feeding usually involves monkeys and deer. In areas such as Odaigahara on the Kii Peninsula, deer have become tame through such tourist feeding, and can be readily photographed by visitors.

Frictions

These different forms of what might be called forest play are marked by certain frictions. First, there are frictions among upland dwellers pursuing different recreations. Hunting is an activity that can endanger other local people out gathering in the winter forest. In January 1999, in an interview with a boar trapper in Hongū, I recorded the following account of a close encounter the man had had with a plant collector:

> It was about seven or eight years ago. I was in the mountains, passing through the forest. There was something there but it was not [as I had thought] a young wild boar. You could tell from the footprints and sound [of the movement]. I stood there and thought it through, for about ten or even twenty minutes. It was strange. This wasn't an animal. I decided it must be a human being [over there]. Then, I blew on my whistle . . . There was no response. If it was a wild boar, what with my scent and the [noise of the] whistle, it would have run away there and then. Then I shouted out, '*oi*', but there was no response, nor any sound of movement . . . I started to get angry. 'You should answer me! Don't you know that hunters come around here? If you hide in that sort of place and you don't give an answer and you stay silent, that is what causes accidents!' . . . Then I realized what it must be – somebody collecting *sakaki*. That *sakaki*-gatherer had probably not got official permission to gather and was stealing it . . . It was somebody from the neighbourhood.

This incident ended safely, but the trapper was furious. He could easily have mistaken the gatherer for a wild boar with fatal consequences, although thankfully on that day he did not have a gun with him. There are many examples of hunting accidents, including fatal ones, involving village gatherers who wandered into hunting grounds (e.g. *Asahi shinbun* 6/12/1993). In the above incident the gatherer was a local person and should have known better. But there have been many similar incidents involving hikers and other people seeking recreation unwittingly entering hunting grounds in the forest.

Another danger to tourists arises from hunters chasing their quarry beyond the hunting grounds. A recent and much-publicized example of this was when a party of deerhunters chased a wounded deer into a tourist village; the animal jumped through the plate glass window of a guesthouse restaurant, pursued by the hunters, who then cornered it and administered the *coup de grace* in front of the shocked tourists (*Asahi shinbun* 21/1/1992). The danger posed by hunting extends to hunting dogs and wounded wild boar which occasionally attack hikers and other tourists.

As forestry gives way to tourism as the main industry in many upland areas, the preoccupation with public safety increases. Hunters on the Kii Peninsula see themselves as becoming subject to ever greater restriction. The hunting season has become shorter, hunting grounds smaller, licence acquisition and renewal stricter, dog control tighter, and the range of game animals narrower. Some hunters even foresee the eventual banning of hunting altogether.

Friction between locals and tourists extends to forest gathering. Locals and tourists often set out to pick the same mushrooms, herbs or flowers. The depletion of such a limited good by one side is the cause of complaint or anger by the other. Locals may dispute the outsiders' right to such forest goods. The situation can become particularly intense where wild herb gathering is both an important source of local income and a popular tourist activity. It is not uncommon for mountain villagers to go to their regular picking spots only to find that somebody (probably a tourist) has already been there. Apart from their sense that they have an informal right to the herb spot in question, as they have always hitherto picked herbs there, what angers local people is that, as farmers, they themselves were too busy to get there before the urban tourists (Katsuki 1995: 257)!

Tourists are also said to pick herbs in a reckless, irresponsible way which depletes herb growth in future years and to deplete the forest of its spring flowers too (Nomoto 1994: 231–2; NSSKS 1990: 95). In some areas local representatives have even raised the issue of gathering rights and outsider forest intrusion in municipal and prefectural assemblies, demanding action to protect local communities from the hordes of herb and mushroom pickers from the city (Nozoe 1994: 70–3).

In Hongū and elsewhere, 'no entry' noticeboards have been put up and forests declared off-limits – *tomeyama* or 'closed mountains' – by irate forest landowners in an effort to stop the gathering of valuable plants or mushrooms by outsiders. The problem for the landowner, however, is that to put up such a 'closed mountain' sign virtually amounts to a public declaration that there are pine mushrooms up there, risking the possibility that some pickers will take their chance. One way around this is to put up a further 'danger' sign stating that 'chemicals' have been used there! Not everybody observes such restrictions; one forest landowner showed me a 'closed mountain' sign that was dented, as though it had been kicked or battered by somebody. The problem, he explained, is that tourists think that when they come to the countryside, they can freely enter the mountains. Another problem with declaring forests off-limits is that it nominally refers to local people too, and can become a cause of anger among villagers who have customarily collected in the forest hitherto (see Ue 1990: 71–2).

Forest as *furusato*

Modern urban-industrial Japan is often said to be marked by a sense of loss or 'homelessness' (Robertson 1995: 101). The key word in this national sensibility is *furusato* – the 'old village' or village of origin. For urban Japan, the *furusato* consists in large part of a distinctive imagery – such as the green paddy fields against a mountainous backdrop. But the *furusato* also inheres in certain forms of behaviour. Forest foraging is one kind of prototypical *furusato* activity, as is indicated in the opening lines of the well-known song *Furusato*.

> I used to chase the rabbits over the hills.
> Oh, the brook where I caught rainbow trout.
> Even now my dreams wander there
> My unforgettable *furusato*.

In addition to hunting rabbits and fishing trout, herb gathering is another activity which occupies an important place in the *furusato* imagery. Herb (and mushroom) gathering in the forest is one of the things that urban migrants from Hongū tend to recall vividly from their childhood. Tōjō Yuriki begins her book 'The Natural Healing Method of Herbs' (*Yakusō no shizen chihō*) (1995) by recalling the forests of her home village in remote Iwate Prefecture and the herbs gathered there in her childhood – dandelion (*tanpopo*), mugwort (*yomogi*) and shepherd's purse (*nazuna*) – which also helped to cure her from a serious illness. She now lives in Tokyo, but when she returns to her home village she goes to the forest and greets the herbs and grasses on the mountainsides as 'old friends'.

  Along with this urban romanticization of the activities in the *furusato* forest, there is a widespread perception that they are in serious decline. Tanaka Senichi has recently expressed this concern.

> Among the youth and children who live there [in the villages], according to various statistics, outdoor play has decreased, and instead they cling to the television or are dispatched to the *juku* [cram school]. The everyday life of children in farming, mountain and fishing villages has changed greatly from forty years ago. They have come to pass their time in the same way as city children. Those who played in the river or in the fields have ceased to play in those places. In places once rich in nature, parks and pools have been built where children play on swings and practice swimming, and no longer play in the mountains or rivers. Schools teach children that rivers are dirty to play in, and the effect of this is that children's play has ceased to be very different from that in the city. As a result, among the people in farming, mountain and fishing villages, that which is wild and joined with nature has drastically decreased. This is also a serious problem for urban people, for in pre-war urban Japan it was often the case that people used this wildness to revitalize themselves . . . [This loss of the wild] is a matter not just for the farming, mountain and fishing villages themselves, but an extremely serious problem for Japanese culture as a whole.

> (Tanaka 1996: 7)

There is a recent widespread negative view of the *yama* whereby it is characterized as a 'dirty' and 'dangerous' place, with mothers warning their children of the danger of the *yama* or of catching insects there (Ogawa 1993: 78). As a result, there is no longer the routine familiarity with the *yama* among young people that there was among their parents and, even more so, their grandparents.

This is a concern voiced by mountain villagers themselves. There is a belief that the forest play of children helps to bind them to the locality – to 'love' their *furusato*. At a time when most high school graduates leave the area for the city, the issue of maintaining migrant ties to the *furusato* is a matter of great local concern. Some older people in Hongū predict grimly that the present generation of children, who have spent their free time in front of the television, or playing computer games rather than playing in the nearby forest, will not have the same nostalgia for the village – the nostalgia which, in many cases, induced their fathers to return-migrate from the city. The decline of forest play among the upland population appears consistent with the view that rural Japan has been culturally absorbed by the metropolitan centre as an urbanized periphery (Takada 1995: 112–3), and that there is no longer really such a thing as a distinctive, separate rural society.

The rise of forest tourism might appear to be a kind of antidote to this trend. If upland dwellers are more and more estranged from the forests around them, urbanites seem to be increasingly drawn to the forests. The growth of rural tourism in Japan is often cited as an expression of the recovery – or at least attempted recovery – of the *furusato*. After all, many tourist areas are self-styled '*furusato*' which invoke the language of intimacy and warmth to encourage visitors to feel at home. Some even take the *furusato* theme one stage further and allow tourists to affiliate with them in certain semi-formal ways – for example, by joining a *furusatokai* or 'hometown association' and becoming a 'member' or 'special villager' (see Knight 1998a). The language of *furusato* can also be invoked by new resorts. Golf courses and other resort developments sometimes strategically present themselves as *furusato*-like – for example, as consistent with 'making a *furusato*' (*furusatozukuri*), a place where people from the city can feel at home (Suzuki 1994: 160, 163). Tourism – even large-scale resort tourism – can provide a medium through which the modern sense of 'homelessness' is mitigated and a sense of inclusion among visitors created. Through the tourist industry, urban Japanese can enjoy the experience of the *furusato* play of their ancestors. In other words, the rural recreation industry in Japan does not simply *divert* its visitors, but culturally *connects with* them.

Yet this trend can destroy the very *furusato* towards which re-connection is sought. Resort construction often involves transforming or destroying the forest through the establishment of golf courses, ski slopes and theme parks. In some cases, local communities have opposed plans for golf course and other forms of forest clearing development on the grounds that the forest is the 'children's playground' (*kodomo no asobiba*) (Ogawa 1993: 74–5; Maruyama 1995). On a visit to his home town, the journalist Honda Katsuichi discovered that 'the mountains have become bald from all the ski-slopes' (Honda 1993: 178). Resort development threatened to destroy his home town: '[m]y hometown is being invaded' (1993: 179). '[T]he invading economy leads to the destruction of the regional economy and the collapse of human relations. Villagers are tantamount to slaves of the invading urban developers and become the modern "primitives"' (Honda 1993: 179). Resort development represents not just 'nature destruction' (*shizen hakai*) but also '*furusato* destruction' (*furusato hakai*) (Kurahashi 1994: 106; Funaki 1994: 46).

Conclusion

One major obstacle to forest recreation in Japan is the legacy of upland forestry. As a consequence of the postwar reforestation movement, conifer plantations now cover most of the visible Japanese mountain side, much to the aesthetic displeasure of many tourists (see Knight 1999). But in this chapter we have seen that it is not just upland occupations such as forestry, which pose problems for forest tourism. Upland recreations, especially hunting given the dangers associated with it, are another obstacle to the conversion of the Japanese forest into a recreational space for the national population.

One practical answer to the frictions between hunters and hikers would be an enhanced form of zoning within the forest to ensure a clearer separation of hunting grounds and hiking trails. But in the longer term, as the Japanese *yama* increasingly becomes a national playground, there is likely to be far less tolerance of the presence of hunters. Upland hunting, as the 'forest play' of local men, may well be subject to tighter restrictions. Recalling the outburst of the angry hunter mentioned at the beginning of this chapter, it is likely that his reprimand to the hiker will eventually be turned on its head – that is, that it will be hunters who find that their 'permission to hunt' open to challenge, while hikers see their 'permission to hike' extended.

Yet the dream of a forest free of hunting is unlikely to be realized. For the more the Japanese forest is customized for tourism – through forest thinning to create light, airy woodland with herbaceous undergrowth and flower growth, as well as lush grasslands – the more necessary will management become, including some form of predatory activity. This is because the new woodland and grassland tends to lead to a growth of wild herbivore populations which, if left unchecked, could lead to the destruction of the newly created tourist forests. In some areas of Japan, proliferating deer numbers have caused great damage to precisely the native forest vegetation so valued by recreational visitors.

Since the extinction of the wolf at the beginning of the twentieth century, forest herbivores in Japan have no major natural predator. In this context, predatory responsibilities are left to humankind. In fact, in the area of wildlife management, measures have been proposed, such as wolf re-introduction (see Knight 1998b), that might at least reduce the need for human predation in the Japanese forest. But even if such a controversial proposal were ever to be realized, it would represent not the replacement of predation but its naturalization, and might well lead to a new kind of predation anxiety of its own (i.e. fear of wolf attacks).

In postwar Japan hunting has been credited with helping to contain the numbers of forest wildlife. The forestry industry has looked to hunting – *qua* culling – to remove herbivorous pests and manage the forest for timber growing. It seems probable that the tourist industry will also come to rely, to some extent, on hunting as a means of managing the forest for the new set of recreational land uses discussed in this chapter. For this reason, hunting is unlikely to disappear from the Japanese forest in the foreseeable future. Hunters and hikers, despite recurrent frictions and disputes between them, will continue to share the Japanese forest in the twenty-first century.

Notes

1   Under the heading 'forest play' or *yama no asobi*, a 1979 local publication on Nakahechichō (the neighbouring municipality to the west of Hongūchō) describes no fewer than 115 separate child play activities, including various forms of hunting, insect collecting and plant and berry collecting (KHI 1979: 10–52).
2   See, for example, Miki (1994: 93) and Sakanaga (1994); see also Nakazawa (1992: 213) and Kitsu (1994: 171).

Bibliography

Arima, T. (1991) *Mura okoshi machizukuri seikō no kimete* (Tips for success in village revival and townmaking), Tokyo: Kō Shobō.

Asahi shinbun (29/1/1988) 'Gurume bumu bōsō – Hokkaido de ezoshika tairō mitsuryō' (Runaway gourmet boom – large scale deer poaching in Hokkaido).

Asahi shinbun (10/3/1988) 'Ezoshika no mitsuryō de bōryokudan kanbu ra taiho' (Arrests at gang headquarters over deer poaching).

Asahi shinbun (21/1/1992) 'Hantā, hoterunai de shika shasatsu' (Hunter shoots deer in a hotel).

Asahi shinbun (6/12/1993) 'Shika to machigai happō, Hyōgo de sasatori no shufushibō' (Mistaken for a deer and shot, the death of a Hyogo housewife out collecting bamboo grass).

Asahi shinbun (7/12/1993) 'Shuryōka e' (To hunters).

Asahi shinbun (23/7/1995) 'Ōdaigahara, Hakkotsu jurin, Naraken Kamikitayama mura, midori o taberu shika' (Odaigahara, Hakkotsu forest, Kamikitayama village, Nara prefecture – Deer eating greenery).

Asahi shinbun (19/1/1996) 'Nara Yoshino de taijū 148 kiro no oinoshishi shitomeru' (Catching a giant boar of 148 kg in Yoshino, Nara), Osaka Edition.

Fujitake, A. (1993) 'The green of health', *Japan Update* no. 22.

Funaki, T. (1994) 'Ikimono no mirai ni me o muketa tachiki torasuto' (The standing tree trust facing the future), in Yamada Kunihiro (ed.) *Satoyama torasuto: ippon no tachiki ga chiiki to toshi o musubu* (The Satoyama trust: one tree can join region and city), Hokuto Shuppan, pp. 34–46.

Honda, K. (1993) 'Why resorts?' in John Lie (ed.) *The Impoverished Spirit in Contemporary Japan: Selected Essays of Honda Katsuichi*, New York: Monthly Review Press, pp. 178–9.

Inoue, K. (1996) 'Toshi seikatsusha to gurīn tsūrizumu' (Urban dwellers and green tourism), in K. Inoue, O. Nakamura and M. Yamazaki (eds) *Nihongata gurīn tsūrizumu* (Japanese-style green tourism), Tokyo: Toshi Bunkasha, pp. 25–40.

KHI (Kumanoji hensan iinkai) (1979) *Kodomo fūdoki* (Record of local customs for children), Tanabe: Kumano Nakahechi Kankokai.

KMG (Kinki minzoku gakkai) (1985) *Kumano No Minzoku: Wakayamaken Hongūchō* (The folklore of Kumano: Hongūchō, Wakayama prefecture), Adogawa, Shiga: Kinki Minzoku Gakkai.

Kamata, K., and Nebuka, M. (1992) 'Shirakami sanchi ni nokosareta mono to sono mirai' (Things left in the Shirakami Mountains and their future), in M. Nebuka (ed.) *Mori o kangaeru* (Thinking about the forest), Tokyo: Rippū shobō, pp. 411–20.

Kamiyama, K. (1993) *Mori no Fushigi* (The mystery of the forest), Tokyo: Iwanami Shinsho.

Katō, A. (1993) '*Chiiki no midori to yamazato rizōto*' (The green of the regions and mountain village resorts), in K. Masao (ed.) *Mori, hito, machizukuri* (The forest, man and town-making), Tokyo: Gakugei shuppansha, pp. 195–216.

Katsuki, Y. (1995) *Yama ni sumu* (Inhabiting the mountains), Tokyo: Miraisha.

Kitsu, H. (1988) '*Yasashisa o motomeru hantā o kokorogaketai mono*' (Wishing for hunters with gentleness), *Shuryōkai* 32(7): 96.

Kitsu, K. (1994) '*Sanson no toshika ni tsuite*' (On the urbanization of mountain villages), in Sanson keizai kenkyūsho (ed.) *Sanson ga kowareru sono mae ni* (Before mountain villages are destroyed), Tokyo: Nihon Keizai Hyōronsha, pp. 170–80.

Knight, J. (1998a) 'Selling mother's love: mail order village food in Japan', *Journal of Material Culture* 3(2): 153–73.

Knight, J. (1998b) 'Wolves in Japan? an examination of the reintroduction proposal', *Japan Forum* 10(1): 47–65.

Knight, J. (1999) 'From timber to tourism? Recommoditizing the Japanese forest', *Development and Change* 30(3): 341–59.

Kurahashi, N. (1994) '*Toshi jūmin ni totte no torasuto*' (The trust from the perspective of urban residents), in Y. Kunihiro (ed.) *Satoyama Torasuto: Ippon No Tachiki Ga Chiiki to Toshi o Musubu* (The Satoyama Trust: one tree can join region and city), Hokuto shuppan, pp. 103–6.

Maruyama, H. (1995) '*Asobi wa kodomo no shigoto*' (Play is the job of children), in *Mori Ga Suki Desuka?* (Do you like the forest?), Sapporo: Hoppō Ringyōkai, pp. 74–9.

Matsutani, M. (1994) *Mokurei, heibi* (Tree spirits and snakes). Tokyo: Rippū Shobō.

Miki, M. (1994) '*Satoyama no aru seikatsu – kagawa no zokibayashi kara*' (Life in the nearby forest: from a Kagawa mixed forest), in Yamada Kunihiro (ed.) *Satoyama Torasuto: Ippon No Tachiki Ga Chiiki to Toshi o Musubu* (The Satoyama Trust: one tree can join region and city), Hokuto Shuppan, pp. 87–94.

Mishima, A. (1994) *Jōmon sugi no keishō* (Alarm bells for Jomon Cryptomeria), Tokyo: Meisō Shuppan.

Mitsuda, H. and Geisler, C. (1992) 'Imperilled parks and Imperilled people: lessons from Japan's Shiretoko National Park', *Environmental History Review* 16(2): 23–39.

NSSKS (Nōson seikatsu sōgo kenkyū sentā) (1990) *Sanchison shūraku no seikatsu kōzō* (The livelihood structure of mountain villages), Tokyo: NSSKS, Seikatsu Kenkyū, Report no. 31.

Nakazawa, K. (1992) *Nihon no mori o sasaeru hitotachi* (The people who maintain Japan's forests), Tokyo: Shobunsha.

Nomoto, K. (1994) *Kyōsei no fōkuroa* (The folklore of co-existence), Tokyo: Seidōsha.

Nozoe, K. (1994) *Furusato no saizei no michi* (The road to the rebirth of the Furusato), Tokyo: Ochanomizu Shobō.

Ogawa, K. (1993) '*Shizen to kodomo*' (Nature and children), in Daigokai Nihon no mori to shizen o mamoru zenkoku shūkai no kinen kankōkai (ed.) *Genseirin, Satoyama, Suiden O Mamoru!* (Defend primeval forest, village forest and ricefields!), Akita: Mumeisha Shuppan, pp. 70–81.

Robertson, J. (1995) 'Hegemonic nostalgia, tourism, and nation-making in Japan', in T. Umesao, H. Befu and S. Ishimori (eds) *Japanese Civilization in the Modern World IX: Tourism*, Osaka: National Museum of Ethnology, Senri Ethnological Series, 38, 89–103.

Sakanaga, Y. (1994) '*Shizentai de ayumu nabarando – posuto gorufujō o shiitake'en de*' (Mushroom land in accord with nature: a mushroom park in place of a golf-course), in Y. Kunihiro (ed.) *Satoyama torasuto: ippon no tachiki ga chiiki to toshi o musubu* (The Satoyama Trust: one tree can join region and city), Hokuto shuppan, pp. 82–6.

Shirafuji, C. (1993) '*Rizōtohō haishi ni mukete*' (Looking towards the abolition of the resort law), in Daigokai Nihon no mori to shizen o mamoru zenkoku shūkai no kinen kankkai (ed.) *Genseirin, satoyama, suiden o mamoru!* (Defend primeval forest, village forest and ricefields!), Akita: Mumeisha Shuppan, pp. 82–95.

Suzuki, A. (1994) '*Shinokiyama kara mietekita nōgyō to toshi no kadai*' (Farming and the city problem viewed from pasania forest), in Y. Kunihiro (ed.) *Satoyama torasuto: ippon no tachiki ga chiiki to toshi o musubu* (The Satoyama Trust: one tree can join region and city), Hokuto Shuppan, pp. 153–64.

Takada, M. (1995) 'The city and its model: a civilization's mechanism for self-expression as the object of tourism', in T. Umesao, H. Befu and S. Ishimori (eds) *Japanese Civilization in the Modern World IX: Tourism*, Senri, Osaka: National Museum of Ethnology, Senri Ethnological Series no. 38, pp. 105–24.

Tanaka, S. (1996) '*Furusato oyobi furusatokan no henyō*' (The transformation of furusato and furusato consciousness), *Nihon minzokugaku* 206: 2–12.

Tōjō Y. (1995) *Yakusō no shizen chihō* (The natural healing method of herbs), Tokyo: Ikeda Shobō.

Ue, T. (1980) *Yamabito no ki* (Diary of a mountain person), Tokyo: Chūkō shinsho.

Ue, T. (1983a) *Yamabito no dōbutsushi* (A mountain villager's record of animals), Tokyo: Fukuinkan shoten.

Ue, T. (1983b) *Yama ni sumu nari* (Inhabiting the mountains), Tokyo: Shinjuku Shobō.

Ue, T. (1990) *Kumano soshi* (Kumano storybook), Tokyo: Sōshisha.

Ue, T. (1994) *Mori no megumi* (The blessing of the forest), Tokyo: Iwanami Shoten.

Wang, Y., Hall, I.R. and Evans, L.A. (1997) 'Ectomycorrhizal fungi with edible fruiting Bodies 1. Tricholoma matsutake and related fungi', *Economic Botany* 51(3): 311–27.

Yukawa, Y. (1991) *Henyō suru sanson: minzoku saikō* (Changing mountain villages: reconsidering folklore), Tokyo: Nihon Editāsukuru shuppanbu.

18 Japan at play in TDL (Tokyo Disneyland)

The dialectics of *asobi* and *rejā*

Aviad E. Raz

> The opening of Tokyo Disneyland was, in retrospect, the greatest cultural event in Japan during the 80's.
>
> (Notoji Masako, *The Holy Land Called Disneyland*)

This chapter discusses local Japanese responses to play and the ideology of contemporary leisure (*rejā*). My case study is Tokyo Disneyland (TDL), an extremely successful transplant of the original theme park from the US which was re-made in Japan. TDL is a unique amusement park, a 'total environment' of imagineered attractions.[1] In this chapter I focus on the 'off-stage' reception of TDL rather than on its modified layout (onstage) or backstage.[2] For this selective 'audience research' I focus here on one particular group of respondents-cum-anthropologists. These are IPA Japan members (IPA stands for International Play Association). The chapter will hence consist of a reflexive re-interpretation of TDL as a controlled play environment, seen through the eyes of local 'play ideologues' (IPA Japan members) and compared to other local play environments.[3]

Tokyo Disneyland (TDL) is a Japanese-owned theme park licensed by the Walt Disney company. Opened in April 1983 on reclaimed land in the Tokyo bay area, it is now a big organization and a big success. In 1996 it had 12,390 employees, about 2000 regulars and 10,000 part-timers. This makes TDL the biggest workplace among Japan's diversionary outings. In the same year, TDL was visited by slightly more than 16 million people (about 17 million in 1997). This makes it the most successful theme park in the world (Leisure Industry Data 1994). TDL is owned and operated by a Japanese company, Oriental Land Company (OLC), which is a partnership between Mitsui Real Estate Development (*Mitsui fudōsan*) and Keizei Electric Railway (*Keizei dentetsu*). OLC was licenced by Disney in return for 10 per cent of the admissions and 5 per cent of food and souvenir sales.

Disneyland and the control of play

Is Disneyland an amusement park or a playground? For some observers, this distinction is critical. I begin by discussing the literature on the original Disneylands – Disneyland (DL) and Walt Disney World (WDW) – and then move to their Japanese transplant. Both DL and WDW are controlled environments designed by an extremely rational organization. The managed onstage goes hand-in-hand with the managed backstage and the 'managed heart' of cast members. While appealing to most visitors, the Disney fixation with control bothers others, in Japan as well as in the US.[4]

A major element of the Disney parks is control: control over the immediate, 'imagineered' environment, control of visitors' movements and imagination, control over the appearance and behaviour of employees. Control is used to achieve predictability and efficiency, the two pillars of 'scientific management'.[5] There is a well-known anecdote, according to Bright (1987; cited in Bryman 1995: 118), in which

> Walt went on a Jungle Cruise at Disneyland and timed it at four-and-a-half minutes. He discovered that the ride should have been seven minutes, which prompted him to fulminate about the deficiency to Dick Nunis, who at the time managed Adventureland. Walt complained that the ride was too fast . . . For three weeks Nunis retrained the boat operators until the rides were timed to perfection.

Efficiency, predictability, division of management and labour, and specification of job responsibilities are all instilled to the smallest detail in the Disney manuals. TDL is no exception; as part of its licensing, it had to import and implement the original Disney Way. Every job in the Disney parks is specifically defined and broken down to a previously memorized checklist: 'Did you smile?', 'Was it an honest smile?', 'Did you say thank you?' Shift changes are punctually defined. The park is obsessed with time standards based on the most efficient way of doing the job. Attractions are timed in seconds and half-seconds. Lines are timed, and re-timed, in minutes. There is also an obsession with standardizing the requirements for materials, machines, tools, working conditions, and the people to fill the job. Wage charts for various hours and shifts are meticulously defined and standardized. Finally, a comprehensive system of inspection and control to assure adherence to standards is daily at work in the park, in the form of visible and invisible supervisors, Leads (managers) and 'shoppers' (a Disney term for supervisors disguised as customers).

Perhaps the Disney version of amusement could be better illuminated by comparing it with Disneyland's most successful forerunner at the turn of this century: Coney Island. Located on the southwestern end of Long Island (New York), this amusement centre flourished from 1895 until the years before the First World War, its success coinciding with America's coming of age as an urban-industrial society. Coney Island was a true carnival city, with three enclosed amusement parks (Steeplechase, Luna Park, and Dreamland) as well as various sideshows along its main promenade, where the grotesque was prominently represented: midgets, giants, fat ladies, ape men, and other freak shows (my description is based on Kasson's excellent book, published in 1978). Walt Disney knew, of course, about Coney Island. He made explicit that he wanted Disneyland to be different from those amusement parks which were, in his words, 'dirty, phony places run by tough-looking people' (Schickel 1968; cited in Spinelli 1992: 350). Besides his fixation with cleanliness, Walt Disney also wanted controlled family entertainment. This was intended as a complete contrast to Coney Island's various freak shows and libertarian sea shores, which emphasized the grotesque and the sexual, and its many attractions that encouraged visitors to break away from social control. Steeplechase, for example, installed a number of devices designed to catch patrons off guard in a way that would never be thought of in a Disneyland. Visitors entering Steeplechase from the ocean side had to:

> pass through the 'Barrel of Fun', a huge, slowly revolving cylinder which frequently rolled patrons off their feet and brought strangers into sudden, intimate contact. The main lobby led customers inescapably to the Blowhole Theater, where concealed compressed-air jets sent hats flying and skirts shooting upward.
>
> (Kasson 1978:61)

This carnivalesque spirit of release was cloaked, in Disneyland, by cutting-edge technology. Steeplechase, very much like the carnival, provided a release from social control; Disneyland, in contrast, provides the illusion of control. At Steeplechase – as in the traditional Japanese ghost house (*obakeyashiki*) – patrons were encouraged to play the fool; in Disneyland, guests are never an active part of the show. The popularity of mirror attractions (such as the Laughing Gallery) at Steeplechase, and their absence from Disneyland, is not a coincidence. Mirrors encourage reflexivity, as does playing the fool; together, they may very well destroy the performative illusion of Disneyland (see also Little 1993).

TDL as a cultural icon: the view from IPA Japan

This section explores the critical reactions to TDL among some of its consumers. My exposition begins in the IPA Japan (International Play Association) annual meeting, held in Osaka in December 1995, where I was invited to give a paper on 'the structure of play in Tokyo Disneyland'. IPA is an international non-governmental organization, recognized by UNESCO and UNICEF with consultative status. Founded in Denmark in 1961, it currently has 'national action groups' in nearly fifty countries. It is interdisciplinary and embraces members of all professions. IPA Japan is comprised of about several hundred members, while the 'hard core' of activists contains about thirty to forty people. Members include academics, school teachers, labour union activists and artizans, with a majority of white-collar, middle-aged professionals.

The IPA Japan 1995 Osaka meeting centred around the Osaka municipality's plans for a new *kodomo no shiro* (literally, 'children's castle'), a modern three-storied activity centre and a children's museum. It was the first time that a municipality sent its official representatives to an IPA Japan meeting and was willing to listen to their opinions. According to IPA member Sonoda Takaaki (associate professor of chemistry at Kyushu University), this willingness was 'mainly *tatemae* (face); the municipality promoted this new project under the slogan of "residential participation", and they merely wanted us to endorse their slogan'. The standpoint of IPA members was that the museum was too much hardware (in the *katakana* version, *hādo*) and too little software (*sofuto*). In other words, its technological environment did not promote enough creative activity and free play. It provided *rejā*, but not *asobi*.

This opposition later transpired as a major ideological premise of the IPA Japan world view. It was not incidental that they chose *rejā*, a *katakana* loanword denoting 'leisure', to stand for activities which are designated as play but do not foster it in reality, or that are merely 'fun' but do not have the added value of 'play'. The opposite word, *asobi*, was made to stand for the Japanese tradition of children engaging in creative, free play. The word *asobi*, however, also carried with it a wide semantic array of 'traditional' concepts, from outings, freedom and indulgence, to ritual worship (*kamiasobi*). It was a distinctly 'Japanese' word, like *kokoro* (see Moriya 1989). Members explained that *rejā* is executed indoors and hinges on technology, for example the *famicon* (family computer, same as Nintendo).[6] *Asobi*, in contrast, is usually conducted outdoors, in natural settings and open spaces (*harappa*). While *rejā* consists of prescribed activities, *asobi* promotes the imagination. IPA members spoke of *asobi* as a creative, unexpected activity in which a stick, for example, can turn into a pirates' sword and a cardboard box into the pirates' ship.

While opposing the American-imported *rejā*, IPA members also fought what they considered as a growing control in Japan over children's lives and leisure time. In her article entitled 'Children's spirit of play and creativity being withered by adults' management', IPA member Okuda Rikuku (1995: 30) typically laments how

> Japanese children have lost their ability to play of their own free will. They lack creativity. A child asks a volunteer mother who works at an after-school playroom, 'What *origami* will you teach me today? Would you hurry because I have a piano lesson right after this'.

IPA members argued that children's life in Japan is increasingly managed by parents who send them to *juku* (cram schools) and teachers who do nothing but follow the rigid curriculum provided by the Ministry of Education (a stance not uncommon among contemporary Japanese intellectuals). IPA Japan members' paradigmatic opposition of *rejā* versus *asobi* therefore entailed further dichotomies, such as control versus freedom, technology versus nature, and Americanization versus 'traditional' Japan.

The big Nintendo

The IPA Japan meeting provided ample opportunities to discuss the meaning of TDL. At first, IPA members were cautious about saying what they thought was good about TDL. Sonoda told me that 'from the point of the design, it is the best theme park in Japan. It looks like real. Other parks don't have this. I think this is the reason for its success'. Tanpo, another IPA member and a furniture maker by profession, said that 'the quality of the hardware is much higher compared to the regular Japanese park'. According to Ogasawara Hirokata, an anthropologist, 'it is the closest thing to virtual reality. It's animated'. This praise, however, had in it the seeds of criticism, which was quickly to follow. TDL was *rejā*. It was built on 'manualized play' (*manyuaruka sareta asobi*) and on a totally controlled artificial environment which is the complete opposite of *harappa* (open space). According to Sonoda,

> 20 years ago Japanese children played completely different games. Free play, in the street, with friends . . . Today this is all changed. We sponsor here an exhibit of photographs (Haginoya 1995) that traces this change. Today, there's only mechanical leisure: Nintendo, Disneyland. Each of these is a technological environment, programmed and predictable, where the user does not have to show any creativity, only control of the machine.

The complaint regarding over control was also brought up by American WDW visitors. Willis (1995: 1) cites academics who said that they were 'bored during their entire Disney stay . . . The trip was pleasant, but everything was so contrived'. A similar criticism was also typical of Tokyo white-collar media professionals with whom I spoke. Meguro Keiki, an NHK (Japanese broadcasting corporation) manager who was interviewed by me on a different occasion in Tokyo, said that when 'I go to TDL, I feel like I'm stupid, simple-minded, *onoborisan*. Like those people who love *Torasan* movies. But this is mass culture, after all'. Klugman (1995: 106,109) cites an American architectural engineer who confessed that his visit to WDW

> was interesting, but once was enough . . . I like my vacations to be more active. Like going to museums in Washington. They supply ten percent, we have to supply ninety. At Disney, it's ninety/ten the other way. Disney does the ninety . . . I don't like to go somewhere where they chew the food for you.

The theme of control and predictability, however, was also suggested by many observers as the key to the success of the Disney parks (Bryman 1995: 99) as well as to TDL's success (Yoshimi 1996; Awata and Takanarita 1984: 140–222). For some of the Japanese writers this line of analysis carried with it shades of criticism, reflecting a frustration that comes with the realization of 'fakeness' and how in fact the TDL magic works. According to Yoshimi (1996: 56,63), TDL has 'sold off the spirit of *matsuri*'[7] replaced the carnivalesque with the predictable: 'people are never "enjoying like crazy" in TDL; you merely take your part in the show, becoming two-dimensional like in a cartoon'. Awata and Takanarita (1984: 140) similarly realize with disappointment that 'TDL may look like *matsuri*, but actually it is not. TDL is too clean, rich, pure and without anxieties'. The authors conclude with an apocalyptic tone: 'now Japan is light (*karui*) culture, everything is light, trendy, playful, nothing ideological, nothing personal, light like Disney. But maybe, sooner or later, we will get tired of this lightness, and look for another simulation' (1984: 228).

More than fifteen years later, the Japanese have not grown tired of the same TDL, which according to Yoshimi (1996: 62) is still a synthetic, sanitary setting, similar to the 'edited fairy tales in the Disney films' (cf. Zipes 1994). This criticism (like its object, perhaps) is probably beyond time and place. More than twenty-five years ago, Schickel (1968: 327) called it 'the Disney version':

> (In the park), as in the Disney movies, the whole world and all man's striving for dominion over self and nature, have been reduced to a sickening blend of cheap formulas packaged to sell. Romance, Adventure, Fantasy, Science are ballyhooed and marketed: life is bright colored, clean, cute, safe, mediocre, and somehow poignantly inhuman.

The behavior of Disney's 'guests' should ideally also be 'disnified.' Spinelli (1992: 283) cites a specific term used by cast members to describe patrons' behavior in the park: 'checking their minds into the lockers in front'. As one WDW cast member described it,

> After a couple of rides, Guests almost seem as if they are in a cattle round up or something, or they are like sheep and they would simply mindlessly do things . . . See, people are in a different environment and they sort of expect that they are going to be taken care of.
>
> (Spinelli 1992: 283)

The theme of audience infantilization is the flip side of over control. However, the critical remarks of IPA Japan members also had, in this context, an additional nationalist overtone. According to one of them,

> Americans exported Disney as a fantasy for the Japanese generation which distanced itself from the post-war ideal of 'America'. Disneyland is also a subtle mechanism of authority, you know. Read Dorfman about what Disney did in Chile.[8] Disneyland works to keep us as children, to infantilize us.

The ideological discourse of IPA Japan members inevitably constructed TDL as an *a priori* American 'black ship'[9] of leisure. TDL was ideologically cast as the ambassador of American capitalism, spreading around Japan a smokescreen of infantile happiness and false consciousness. As another member suggested:

> TDL pretends to add new attractions, while in fact it remains the same. They have to make an impression of new attractions, so that visitors will keep flowing in. But this is only a make-belief intended to make more money. They are just after the money. It's a capitalist machine.

The image of the infantile consumer is obviously partial and biased. TDL has many types of consumers and gets worked into various forms of consumption – from the *aficionado* to the critical, from anti-establishment to traditional. TDL as a black ship of infantile leisure was an ideological facade created by IPA members. In addition, members ignored the fact that TDL was owned by a Japanese company, that some of its attractions are original and some were changed, that its success is connected with the intrinsic changes that led the Japanese economy into its postindustrial stage in the 1980s, and that the spreading of 'foreign lands' around Japan also reflects a kind of Japanese cultural imperialism.[10]

Toon Town and Dragon Dunes

Certain IPA Japan members, who were also play experts, had an additional criticism of TDL, which extended beyond ideological facades. This was substantial criticism regarding the structure of play in TDL. Concisely put, the argument criticized TDL for offering only 'functional' play and no 'social' play. These two developmental categories of play are defined, for example, by Senda (1992: 12–13). The first, 'functional' stage of play involves experiencing the play structure, for example, sliding down a slide. The final, 'social' stage of play involves using the play structure as a medium, for example playing tag on a slide. From the point of view of IPA members (as well as many developmental psychologists), it was the 'social' stage which was the most important, since it promoted interpersonal communication and other forms of social competence. The rides in TDL simply did not allow for 'social' play. As Ogasawara said, 'you can slide down or swing on them, but that's it. They leave you socially incompetent'.

Obviously, TDL is not supposed to foster 'social' play. It is not the child's everyday playground but a special place to be visited once or twice a year. While agreeing with that observation, IPA members nevertheless claimed that a 'good park' should also provide a setting for social play. Some of them mentioned their favourite example: *Shōwa kinen kōen* (Showa Memorial Park), located west of Tokyo near Nishi Tachikawa station. Operated by the Parks and Recreation Foundation, this park comprises about 120 hectares and is advertised as the most up-to-date leisure spot in the Tokyo metropolitan area. In addition to the conventional type water play land, woodland hobby house and lakes, its special 'social play' attractions included Foggy Woods (a life-size maze filled with fog every 30 minutes), Rainbow Hammocks (a huge construction of inter-linked hammocks for climbing and jumping), and Dragon Dunes (huge air-filled polyethylene dunes for the same purpose). In addition, there are no queues (because all the children do the attraction at the same time) and the park entrance fee is 400 yen per adult and 80 yen per child, which is about 10 per cent of TDL's adult entrance fee and less than 3 per cent of the children's fee.

The Disney imagineers, it should be noted, are aware of and attentive to this line of criticism. One of TDL's imagineers noted in a personal interview with me that

> interactive play is a big thing now. We recently introduced it in Toon Town, the bouncing house for example, though you would probably regard it as too small and too clockwork as well. OLC always asks us for more 'interactive' things, but when they see the designs, they say it's too dangerous, too unpredictable. They say that Guests will get dirty or might hurt themselves.

Conclusion: play as ideology

While this chapter focused on play and its definitions, my intention was not to study the 'real,' objective meaning of play in TDL. The argument that Disneyland's attractions are geared more towards 'functional' than 'social' play is quite reasonable.[11] Notwithstanding, my focus here was on the subjective, connotative and ultimately ideological views of play in TDL. I am not interested in finding out which view of play is more correct. Rather, my purpose was to show that all definitions are 'correct' from the point of view of their ideology. I therefore attempted to highlight the social and ideological contexts from which IPA Japan members looked at TDL.

The ideological criticism of IPA Japan members against the control of play in TDL was in itself biased and contrived. Members used TDL as a scapegoat in a manner that re-affirmed and legitimized their own knowledge claims as play experts. This criticism was expressed in a political context where distinctions of 'play' were used to advance a particular agenda. The dichotomy of 'leisure/play' or '*rejā/asobi*' was a self-serving ideological construction, implying further ideological contradictions such as modern/traditional, fake/authentic, functional/social, and ultimately 'America'/'Japan'.

Ideologies of play are not, of course, unique to Japan. Looking at ideologies of play through the window of TDL, one can gain a better view of the interplay between the global and the local that underpins the articulation of such ideologies. The dialectics of the global and the local is arguably behind the dialectics of 'leisure' and 'play,' *rejā* and *asobi*. IPA Japan members, it should be borne in mind, were themselves local representatives of a global organization.

Ideologies of play had an important role, for example, in the discourse of progressive reformers in the US during the first decades of the twentieth century. I am using this particular example because one of the major scapegoats attacked by these progressive reformers was no other than Coney Island. For progressive reformers such as Simon Patten, Walter Rauschenbusch and Jane Addams, popular leisure attractions such as Coney Island, dance halls, music halls, penny arcades, picture houses, brothels and saloons were all *perversions of play*. In these places, 'the play instinct was exploited for gain', and the carnival spirit 'was worked up for maximal financial profit' (Kasson 1978: 101). This charge, it should be recalled, was raised against Coney Island – the symbol of free play, the 'true carnival city' with the freak shows and libertarian sea shores. It was in Coney Island that many attractions encouraged visitors to break away from social control, catching patrons off guard in a way that would never be thought of in Disneyland.

To restore the 'purity of play', progressive reformers advocated a characteristic progressive solution: government regulation and expert supervision. In their vision, public parks would replace city streets as the playgrounds of the poor. Luther H. Gulick – a leading figure of the 'play movement', as it was called – suggested that the approved progression of play was from imitative play through competitive play to co-operative play. While emanating from a completely different ideology, this progression is nevertheless compatible with the progression from functional play to social play advocated by IPA members.

Coney Island could be accused of 'perverting play' in a political context of progressive reformation. Conversely, TDL could be charged with the over control of play in the context of nationalistic purism combined with professional expertise. Both, however, were accused of being money-making machines that exploited the 'spirit of play' of innocent crowds. The fact that similar criticism was directed to such different establishments demonstrates the ideological context of this criticism. It is in the interest of those who claim to be experts to perform distinctions between 'true' and 'false', 'fake' and 'authentic', thus reassuring their expertise.

From their own local context and in their unique voice, IPA Japan members expressed what was also a conservative 'culture industry' criticism. Various critics have looked at Disney as a contaminating power where 'laughter is betrayed' (Kracauer 1950). In a similar manner to IPA Japan members, European social critics before the Second World War such as Benjamin and Adorno have looked at Disney as the site for American cultural imperialism and a prototype of the American 'culture industry'. Walter Benjamin's reflections on film and mass culture were haunted by Disney, whose films were described as 'pioneer ways of disarming the destructive effects of technology through technologically-mediated laughter' (Hansen 1993: 32). Recently, Benjamin's and Adorno's critiques of Disney were echoed in Fjellman's (1992: 3) assertion that WDW embodies the logic of Huxley's Brave New World, which 'predicted that we might be tamed by desire and pleasure'. Disney critique also erupted in Latin America with Dorfman and Mattelart (1975) and most recently re-surged in France with the opening, in 1991, of EuroDisney (Disneyland Paris), which suffered losses as well as a negative reception. Marguerite Duras likened it to a 'cultural Chernobyl' (*International Herald*, 6 December 1991) and many French intellectuals expressed the view that it was another form of 'creeping Americanism' (Van Maanen 1992).

In the context of TDL, nationalistic criticism loses its sting since the park is owned and operated by the Japanese, and was actually modified to cater for their consumerist predilections. The critical discourse of IPA members therefore stressed the more 'professional' issue of the control of play in TDL. Play, like everything else in the worlds of Disney, has become a commodity: controlled, predictable, functional, sanitized, computerized, a 'big Nintendo.'

Such a view is over demanding. The Disney magic apparently works for most people, while others will remain immune, or even become antagonized. As Willis (1995: 1) asks, 'Why are you so critical? Wasn't anything fun?' This is a question worth asking. If there is a 'problem with pleasure', as Disney's critics suggest, this problem is not altogether Disney's, but is rather ideologically read into Disney – a tendency which I have tried to avoid here. Disney is made to stand for societal processes such as late capitalism, Americanization, commodification, commercial-ization, globalization, and so on. In other words, Disney is reified.

My suggestion is that if there is ideology in Disney's worlds, it is too often in the form of meta-messages read by observers. Conventional 'culture industry' is modified in Disneyland from two directions: first, Disney's own amazing ideological flexibility; and second, the different ways by which Disney is consumed and worked into everyday life. Conventional ideological readings of Disney as a culture industry therefore centre on the text while neglecting its audiences. The 'culture industry' view tends to be de-populated. But the ideological vacuum of Disney does not remain empty; it is filled with various cultural and consumerist interpretations made by intellectuals, casual visitors and committed anthropologists, in Japan and elsewhere.

Notes

1 'Imagineering' is a Disney term that combines 'image' and 'engineering.' The Disney Imagineering Department is responsible for conceiving and designing parks and attractions.

2 This language is derived from DisneyTalk and reflects a basic Disney distinction: onstage, backstage, and offstage. Onstage refers to the park as a spectacle, what the 'guest' experiences as s/he enters the kingdom of dreams and magic. Backstage refers to the underground passages as well as to the organization proper; it involves work procedures, the division of labour, hiring, training, and organizational culture in general. Offstage is wherever the cast member (a Disney employee) is found while neither onstage nor backstage. In this chapter I focus on the offstage, extending its meaning to represent the local interpretation of TDL by its audience. This interpretation comes from the surrounding Japanese culture which is located 'offstage' to TDL. This chapter is part of a larger study of TDL (Raz 1999) where the onstage, backstage and offstage are all discussed in detail.

3 This study is the result of participant observation at TDL which was conducted between May 1995 and May 1996. Observations were also conducted on various TDL tours such as guided tours, hospitality tours and school excursions to TDL. The study also included interviews with managers and workers from OLC's four major divisions (Attractions, Merchandizing, Foods, and Personnel), as well as extensive analysis of TDL and OLC manuals, both local and imported. Additional interviews were conducted with Japanese scholars and journalists, as well as with Disneyland 'repeaters' and self-acclaimed 'Disney fans' (see Raz 1999). Funding for my research in Japan was provided by a Japan Foundation Doctoral Fellowship. The research has also benefited from funding generously provided by the Ben-Gurion Scholarship, Ministry of the Sciences, State of Israel; and by The Curiel Center for International Studies as well as the Horowitz Institute, both at Tel-Aviv University.

4 While my focus here is on the control of play in Disneyland, there are many studies about control in DL and WDW from additional perspectives. One of the first books to deal with Disney as an example of a highly effective American corporate organization was Schickel (1968). Another early book by Haden-Guest (1972) contained a section on the Disney training given at Anaheim. It was, however, John Van Maanen who, in a series of four innovative papers, made Disneyland into a case study of organizational culture and normative control (Van Maanen 1989; Van Maanen and Kunda 1989; Van Maanen 1991; Van Maanen 1992). Among business journalists, Disney is considered as the Sistine Chapel of service culture. The characteristics of its 'strong organizational culture' are praised and revered by business-minded authors who write 'in search of excellence,' like Peters and Waterman (1982) and Deal and Kennedy (1982). The Disney approach to training is especially admired (see Blocklyn 1988; Eisman 1993). The tremendous success of TDL has similarly spawned a thriving genre of 'how does it really work' books in Japanese (for example, Tsuromoki 1984; Awata and Takanarita 1984; Kano 1986; and most recently, Lipp 1994). These books examine TDL in terms of its human resource management and service manuals for

part-timers, hailed by many Japanese commentators as 'the secret of TDL's success' (Komuya 1989; Tadokoro 1990). Disney and control are also connected in the context of the park's contrived onstage. Neologisms such as 'disneyfication' and 'distory' (Disney history) are commonly used by scholars to denote the process by which Disney adapts, commodifies and controls its films, characters, landscapes and merchandises (see Fjellman 1992; Smoodin 1994; 'The Project on Disney' 1995; Marin 1977; Gottdiener 1982; and Rojek 1993).

5 Scientific management was a system for the rationalization of work advanced in the US around the turn of the twentieth century. One of its major proponents was Frederick Winslow Taylor (1856–1915), and the system was later also known as Taylorism (see Merkle 1980). Taylorite thought was introduced to Japan around 1913 with the publication of several Japanese renditions of Taylor's (1911) *The Principles of Scientific Management*. It can be later traced in the Japanese 'efficiency movement' of the 1920s, Depression era 'industrial rationalization,' the postwar drive for 'productivity' and later, total quality management (Tsutsui 1995; Warner 1994).

6 IPA Japan members were not the only ones to criticize the social influence of the *famicon*/Nintendo. For a general discussion of how computer and video games are radically re-defining patterns of interpersonal communication and social abilities, see Provenzano (1991). For a discussion of computer games in the Japanese context, see Okuno 1995; Takayama 1987.

7 TDL can be seen as a reversal of the social order: a place where adults are given social licence to be children again and the work ethic changes into a playful leisure time (not so, alas, for TDL's workers). TDL can therefore be seen to play a similar role to that traditionally found in Japanese festivals (*matsuri*). According to the famous Japanese ethnographer Yanagita Kunio (1964: 201–2), the *matsuri* is a utopian form of culture in which all social division dissolves in the ecstasy of communal celebration.

8 Dorfman and Mattelart (1975) have written the classic critique of Disney as an imperialist text in Latin America (more recently, see Cartwright and Goldfarb 1994 for a cultural critique of Disney's Health Education films for Latin America).

9 The 'black ship' is the central metaphor I use to refer to TDL (see Raz 1999). An ideological view might imagine TDL as a 'black ship', an exported, hegemonic model of American leisure and pop culture, which 'conquered' Japan. This 'black ship', however, is an illusive metaphor with multiple meanings. To begin with, the denotation is to the black ships of Commodore Perry, which have become an image of forced Americanization and the coerced opening of Japan to foreign influence. TDL was actually nicknamed '*kurofune*' (black ship) by its Japanese competitors in the amusement business, who cast it as the ambassador of American capitalism. TDL was also the 'black ship of leisure' that opened up in the 1980s the Japanese market of theme parks and local foreign lands. Yet it also was the Japanese who imported Disneyland for their leisure, translating and editing it to project a Japanese national identity, and consuming it in unique ways. The historical black ships of Commodore Perry actually feature in a TDL show called 'Meet The World,' an optimistic historical narrative of Japan, apparently made by and for the Japanese. The 'black ship' of TDL thus also becomes a symbol of Japan's appropriation of the other. The 'black ship' is a historical symbol, an ideological facade, a ride and a hyperbole.

10 From the 1980s to the 1990s, the leisure market in Japan experienced an exponential growth (The Economic Planning Agency 1995). Sports, hobbies, pastimes and tourism have all increased in range and volume (Harada 1994; Linhart 1988). This decade was also characterized by the thriving of municipal gala expositions (or simply 'Expos'). These Expos combined a worldly theme, an international ambience of consumerism and amusement facilities (large Ferris wheels, for example), and proved to be huge successes. One of the first Expos, The Osaka International Exposition – better known as 'Expo '70' – attracted some 64,220,000 visitors (over 60 per cent of the Japanese population) to the pavilions of the seventy-seven participating countries (Umesao 1985:

296 Aviad E. Raz

302). The same companies which organized these Expos (such as Senyo Kogyō, Togo, and Sansei Yusoki) later financed and propelled the theme park boom (Matsuura 1989,1990). Roller coasters were another popular form of amusement which thrived in the 1980s and continued to 'ride out the recession' (Matsuura 1994). In 1983, two of Japan's first theme parks were opened: TDL and *Orandamura* (Holland Village) in Sasebo, Nagasaki prefecture, later to become part of the larger *Huis Ten Bosch*. Following TDL's enormous success, little countries have been sprouting all over Japan. These include, in a chronological order, Glücks Kingdom in Obihiro City, Hokkaido; Space World in Kyushu; Canadian World in Ashibetsu City, Hokkaido; Tobu World Square near Nikko; Shima Spanish Village; Sea Paradise in Yokohama; and a Universal Studio Tour in Osaka. The term 'theme park' (*tēma pāku*) has recently become a central cultural idiom in Japan, featuring in advertisements, trendy magazines, scholarly books and even high school textbooks. In his book titled *The Theming of America*, Gottdiener (1997) argues that from Las Vegas to Disney World to local shopping malls, Americans are obsessed with 'themed environments.' The similar 'theming of Japan' is therefore, at least superficially, part of a global consumer culture. See Hendry 2000 for further analysis of the Japanese version of the phenomenon.

11 This argument is particularly true in relation to 'screamer-type' attractions. A classic 'screamer' such as Splash Mountain, TDL's most popular ride, is basically a wonderfully designed water sled. You climb into the 'people mover,' go to the top and slide down. This is 'functional play.' Other attractions, more quiet and thematic, such as 'It's a small world,' represent the 'dreamer' type. Even though there are many differences between 'screamers' and 'dreamers,' neither seem to foster any 'social play' as both depend solely on the control of the human-technology interface.

Bibliography

Ashkenazi, M. (1993) *Matsuri: Festivals of a Japanese Town*, Honolulu: Hawaii University Press.

Awata, F. (1988) 'Disneyland's dreamlike success', *Japan Quarterly* 35: 58–62.

Awata, F. and Takanarita, T. (1984) *Dizuniirando no keizai gaku* (An economic study of Disneyland), Tokyo: Asahi Shinbunsha.

Blocklyn, P.L. (1988) 'Making magic: the Disney approach to people management', *Personnel* 65: 28–35.

Bryman, A. (1995) *Disney and his Worlds*, London: Routledge.

Carey, R. (1995) '5 Top corporate training programs', *Successful Meetings*, February, pp. 56–61.

Cartwright, L. and Goldfarb, B. (1994) 'Cultural contagion: on Disney's health education films for Latin America', in E. Smoodin (ed.) *Disney Discourse: Producing the Magic Kingdom*, London: Routledge, pp. 169–81.

Deal, T.E. and Kennedy, A.A. (1982) *Corporate Cultures*, Reading, MA: Addison-Wesley.

Dorfman, A. and Mattelart, A. (1975) *How to Read Donald Duck: Imperialist Ideology in the Disney Comic*, New York: International General Additions.

The Economic Planning Agency (1995) *White Paper on the National Lifestyle*, Tokyo: Printing Bureau, Ministry of Finance, Government of Japan.

Eisman, R. (1993) 'Disney magic', *Incentive*, September, pp. 45–56.

Fjellman, S.M. (1992) *Vinyl Leaves: Walt Disney World and America*, Boulder, CO: Westview Press.

Gottdiener, M. (1982) 'Disneyland: a utopian urban space', *Urban Life* 11: 139–62.

—— (1997) *The Theming of America: Dreams, Visions, and Commerical Spaces*, Boulder, CO: Westview Press.

Haden-Guest, A. (1972) *Down the Programmed Rabbit Hole: Travels Through Muzak, Hilton, Coca-Cola, Walt Disney and Other World Empires*, London: Hart-Davis, MacGibbon.

Hansen, M. (1993) 'Of mice and ducks: Benjamin and Adorno on Disney', in S. Willis (ed.) *The World According to Disney*, special issue of *The South Atlantic Quarterly* 92(1): 27–63, Durham, NC: Duke University Press.

Harada, M. (1994) 'Towards a renaissance of leisure in Japan', *Leisure Studies*, 13, 277–87.

Hendry, J. (2000) *The Orient Strikes Back: A Global View of Cultural Display*, Oxford: Berg.

Heise, S. (1994) 'Disney approach to managing', *Executive Excellence*,18, October, pp. 18–19.

Henkoff, R. (1994) 'Finding, training and keeping the best service workers', *Fortune*, 2, October, pp.110–15.

Ito, M. (1995) *Tēma pāku sangyō: Kyōshū to sōzōryoku* (Theme park industry: nostalgia and creativity), Tokyo: Nihon keizai shinbun.

Kano, Y. (1986) *Tōkyōdizuniirando no shinso* (The true story of Tokyo Disneyland), Tokyo: Kindaiban geisha.

Kasson, J.F. (1978) *Amusing the Million: Coney Island at the Turn of the Century*, New York: Hill and Wang.

Keiki, H. (1995) *Machi kara kieta kodomo no asobi* (Children's lost street playing), Tokyo: Taishukan.

Kelly, J. (1982) *Scientific Management, Job Design, and Work Performance*, London: Academic Press.

Klugman, Karen (1995) 'Under the influence', in *The Project on Disney, Inside the Mouse: Work and Play at Disneyworld*, Durham: Duke University Press, pp. 98–110.

Komuya, K. (1989) *Tōkyōdizuniirando no keiei majikku* (Tokyo Disneyland's amazing management), Tokyo: Kōdansha.

Kracauer, S. (1950) 'Sturges or laughter betrayed', *Films in Review*, I, I, February, pp. 11–13, 43–7.

Kuenz, J. (1995) 'Working at the rat', in *The Project on Disney, Inside the Mouse: Work and Play at Disney World*, Durham, NC: Duke University Press, pp. 110–63.

Leisure Industry Data (*rejāsangyō shiryō*), (1994) 'Amusement business' (*amyúzumento bijinesu*) vol. 333, June, pp. 65–92, Tokyo: Unicom.

Linhart, S. (1986) 'Sakariba: zone of evaporation beween work and home', in J. Hendry and J. Webber (eds) *Interpreting Japanese Society*, Oxford: JASO, pp. 198–211.

—— (1988) 'From industrial to postindustrial society: changes in Japanese leisure-related values and behavior', *Journal of Japanese Studies*14(2): 271–307.

Lipp, D. (1994) *Tōkyōdizuniirando daiseikō no shinsō* (The truth about Tokyo Disneyland's great success), translated by K. Kimundo, Tokyo: NTT Shuppan.

Little, K. (1993) 'Masochism, spectacle, and the "Broken Mirror" entrée: a note on the anthropology of performance in postmodern culture', *Cultural Anthropology* 8(1): 117–29.

Marin, L. (1977) 'Disneyland: a degenerate utopia', *Glyph* 1: 50–66.

Matsuura, T. (1989) 'Amusement park business zooms, zips and soars', *Business Japan*, July, pp.113–16.

—— (1990) 'Leisure facilities to expand in the next decade', *Business Japan*, July, pp. 53–6.

—— (1993) 'Current trends and developments in the amusement business', *Japan 21st*, July, pp. 47–50.

—— (1994) 'Roller coasters ride out recession', *Japan 21st*, July, pp. 20–3.

Merkle, J. (1980) *Management and Ideology: The Legacy of the International Scientific Management Movement*, Berkeley, CA: University of California Press.

Moore, A. (1980) 'Walt Disney's world: bounded ritual and the playful pilgrimage center', *Anthropological Quarterly* 53: 207–18.

Moriya, T. (1989) *Nihonjin to asobi* (The Japanese and play), Tokyo: Domesu shuppan.

Notoji, M. (1988) 'Cultural boundaries and magic kingdom: a comparative symbolic analysis of Disneyland and Tokyo Disneyland', paper presented at the American Studies Association Annual Meetings, Miami Beach, October 27–30.

—— (1993) *Dizuniirando to iu seichi* (The holy land called Disneyland), Tokyo: Iwanami shoten.

Okuda, R. (1995) 'Children's spirit of play and creativity being withered by adults' management', *PlayRights*, XVII, 3, September, pp. 29–31.

Okuno, T. (1995) 'Technology and recreation: a look at the famicon and personal computer communication', in T. Umesao, B. Powell and I. Kumakura (eds) *Japanese Civilization in the Modern World, XI: Amusement*, Senri Ethnological Studies no. 40: 137–47, Osaka: National Museum of Ethnology.

Peters, T. and Waterman, R. (1982) *In Search of Excellence: Lessons from America's Best-Run Companies*, New York: Harper and Row.

The Project on Disney (1995) *Inside the Mouse: Work and Play at Disney World*, Durham, NC: Duke University Press.

Provenzano, E.F. (1991) *Video Kids: Making Sense of Nintendo*, Cambridge, MA: Harvard University Press.

Raz, A. (1999) *Riding the Black Ship: Tokyo Disneyland and Japan*, Cambridge, MA, Asia Center: Harvard University Press.

Rojek, C. (1993) 'Disney culture', *Leisure Studies* 12: 121–35.

Schickel, R. (1968) *The Disney Version*, New York: Simon and Schuster.

Senda, M. (1992) *Design of Children's Play Environments*, New York: McGraw-Hill.

Smoodin, E. (ed.) (1994) *Disney Discourse: Producing the Magic Kingdom*, London: Routledge.

Spinelli, M.L. (1992) *Fun and Power: Experience and Ideology at the Magic Kingdom*, unpublished PhD. dissertation, University of Massachusetts.

Tadokoro, M. (1990) *Tōkyōdizuniirando no majikku shōhō* (The magic business of Tokyo Disneyland), Tokyo: Yell Books.

Takayama, H. (1987) 'What modern japanese games reflect: children, TV games and comics', *The Wheel Extended* 18: 19–27, Tokyo: Toyota Publications.

TDL (1995) 'TDL dimensions and fact sheet', OLC Publicity Division, Maihama: Chiba.

Tsuromoki, Y. (1984) *Tōkyōdizuniirando o hadaka ni suru* (Stripping Tokyo Disneyland), Tokyo: Tsushinsha shuppanbu.

Tsutsui, W.M. (1995) 'From taylorism to quality control: scientific management in 20th century Japan', unpublished PhD Dissertation, Department of History, Princeton University.

Umesao, T. (ed.) (1985) *Seventy-Seven Keys to the Civilization of Japan*, Union City, CA: Heian International.

Van Maanen, J. (1989) 'Whistle while you work: on seeing Disneyland as the workers do', paper presented at the panel on The Magic Kingdom, American Anthropological Association Annual Meeting, Washington DC, 16 November.

—— (1991) 'The smile factory: work at Disneyland', in P.J. Frost, L.F. Moore, M.R. Louis, C.C. Lundberg and J. Martin (eds) *Reframing Organizational Culture*, Newbury Park, CA: Sage.

—— (1992) 'Displacing Disney: some notes on the flow of culture', *Qualitative Sociology*, 15(1): 5–35.

Van Maanen, J. and Kunda, G. (1989) '"Real feelings": emotional expression and organizational culture', *Research in Organizational Behavior*, 11: 43–103.

Wallace, M. (1985) 'Mickey mouse history: portraying the past at Disney World', *Radical History Review* 32: 33–57.

Warner, M. (1994) 'Japanese culture, Western management: Taylorism and human resource in Japan', *Organization Studies* 15 4: 509–33.

Warren, R. (1993) 'Theme parks flourish in Japan', *Japan 21st,* July, pp. 35–41.

Willis, S. (ed.) (1993) 'The world according to Disney', special issue of *The South Atlantic Quarterly* 92(1): Durham, NC: Duke University Press.

—— (1995) 'The problem with pleasure', in *The Project on Disney, Inside the Mouse: Work and Play at Disney World*, Durham, NC: Duke University Press, pp. 1–12.

Yanagita, K. (1964) '*Tanoshii seikatsu*' (Fun life), in *Teihon Yanagita Kunio shû* (Collected works of Yanagita Kunio), vol. 30, Tokyo: Chikuma shobō.

Yoshimi, S. (1996) '*Yūenchi no yutopiā*' (The utopia of amusement parks) and '*Dizuniirandoka suru toshi*' (Disneyfication), in *Riariti toransitō: jōhōshoni shakai no genza* (Realities in transit: the contemporary trend of infoconsumer society), Tokyo: Kinokuniya, pp. 45–87.

Yoshimoto, M. (1994) 'Images of empire: Tokyo Disneyland and Japanese cultural imperialism', in E. Smoodin (ed.) *Disney Discourse: Producing the Magic Kingdom*, London: Routledge, pp. 181–203.

Zipes, J. (1994) *Fairy Tale as Myth, Myth as Fairy Tale*, Kentucky: The University Press.

Index

Lightning Source UK Ltd.
Milton Keynes UK
UKOW06f0739030915

257942UK00003B/64/P